United Nations

**United Nations
Development
Programme**

ASIAN FOREIGN DIRECT INVESTMENT IN AFRICA

Towards a New Era of Cooperation among Developing Countries

UNITED NATIONS
New York and Geneva, 2007

NOTE

As the focal point in the United Nations system for investment and technology, and building on 30 years of experience in these areas, UNCTAD, through its Division on Investment, Technology and Enterprise Development (DITE), promotes understanding of, and helps build consensus on matters related to foreign direct investment (FDI), transfer of technology and development. DITE also assists developing countries to attract and benefit from FDI and to build their productive capacities and international competitiveness. The emphasis is on an integrated policy approach to investment, technological capacity building and enterprise development.

The term "country" as used in this study also refers, as appropriate, to territories or areas; the designations employed and the presentation of the material do not imply the expression of any opinion whatsoever on the part of the Secretariat of the United Nations concerning the legal status of any country, territory, city or area or of its authorities, or concerning the delimitation of its frontiers or boundaries. In addition, the designations of country groups are intended solely for statistical or analytical convenience and do not necessarily express a judgement about the stage of development reached by a particular country or area in the development process. The reference to a company and its activities should not be construed as an endorsement by UNCTAD of the company or its activities.

The boundaries and names shown and designations used on the maps presented in this publication do not imply official endorsement or acceptance by the United Nations.

The following symbols have been used in the tables:

Two dots (..) indicate that data are not available or are not separately reported. Rows in tables have been omitted in those cases where no data are available for any of the elements in the row.

A dash (-) indicates that the item is equal to zero or its value is negligible.

A blank in a table indicates that the item is not applicable, unless otherwise indicated.

A slash (/) between dates representing years, e.g., 1994/95, indicates a financial year.

Use of a hyphen (-) between dates representing years, e.g., 1994-1995, signifies the full period involved, including the beginning and end years.

Reference to "dollars" ($) means United States dollars, unless otherwise indicated.

Annual rates of growth or change, unless otherwise stated, refer to annual compound rates.

Details and percentages in tables do not necessarily add to totals because of rounding.

The material contained in this study may be freely quoted with appropriate acknowledgement.

UNCTAD/ITE/IIA/2007/1
UNITED NATIONS PUBLICATION
Sales No. E.07.II.D.1
ISBN-13: 978-92-1-112712-6

APR 2 4 2007

PREFACE

This publication marks the completion of the project on "Needs Assessment to Attract Asian FDI into Africa", undertaken with the financial support of the UNDP/Japan Human Resources Development Fund dedicated to South-South cooperation. This Report examines the various aspects of Asian foreign direct investment (FDI) in African economies with a view to improving understanding of the opportunities, constraints and steps needed to enhance Asian FDI in Africa.

Why focus on Asian FDI in Africa?

First, it is now generally recognized that FDI has become a significant source of external finance in developing countries. It has also become a useful means of integrating into the global marketplace. But Africa has largely been left out of this process for many reasons, including small market size, poor infrastructure, weak regulatory frameworks, debt problems and, in some cases, political instability. However, over the past decade, there has been considerable progress with reforms in several African economies. The region's debt problems are also being tackled, although international initiatives for debt relief need to be faster and bolder.

As we look to the future, the challenge is to find ways and means of harnessing more investment which contributes to reducing poverty and accelerating economic growth and development in Africa. This is a major concern of the United Nations, as reflected in the internationally agreed Millennium Development Goals which includes the overarching aim of halving extreme poverty by 2015, and the Monterrey Consensus on financing for development. This volume on Asian FDI in Africa should be seen as part of the United Nation's overall efforts in this regard. The objective is very specific: how to make the economic interests of Asian investors and African countries converge more closely. There is an untapped potential for Asian investors to invest in profitable projects in Africa and for African countries to derive benefits from Asian FDI, which offers great potential for furthering cooperation between the two developing regions.

This timely report looks at both the opportunities and possible obstacles for increasing Asian investment in Africa. Asian FDI is assuming greater importance, accounting for 10 per cent of the stock of FDI in the world. Some Asian firms have grown to rank among the top transnational corporations (TNCs) in the world. This trend is likely to be reinforced in the future. The rapid economic growth and industrial upgrading currently taking place in Asia provide ample opportunities for Africa to attract Asian FDI into both natural resources and manufacturing. Indeed, such FDI in Africa is becoming an important and promising facet of South-South economic cooperation.

Against this background, this book examines the opportunities and constraints for Asian investment in African countries. This publication is based on papers prepared for the project, "Needs Assessment to Attract Asian FDI into Africa", updated wherever possible. It begins with an overview of Asian FDI in Africa and a review of major Asian economies as FDI recipients as well as sources of FDI in Africa. This is followed by studies of five African countries that help to identify common features as well as conditions specific to each as hosts to FDI in general and Asian FDI in particular. It is hoped that this book will contribute to the formulation and implementation of concrete measures to bring greater Asian investment to African countries, and strengthen development cooperation between the two regions.

The book was prepared by a team at UNCTAD led by Masataka Fujita and comprising Guoyong Liang and Padma Mallampally under the direction of Anne Miroux, in cooperation with the Center for International Development at Harvard University. Principal research assistance was provided by Mohamed Chiraz Baly, Bradley Boicourt, Masayo Ishikawa, Lizanne Martinez, Barbara Myloni and Katja Weigl.

It was produced by Chistopher Corbet, Séverine Excoffier and Katia Vieu, edited by Praveen Bhalla and desktop-published by Teresita Ventura. It has benefited from the collaboration of various national institutes, and national and international experts from the public and private sector, both in Africa (Botswana, Ghana, Madagascar, Mozambique and the United Republic of Tanzania) and Asia (China and ASEAN countries). Inputs were received from Chia Siow Yue, Adrian Frey, Bryan Graham, K.S. Jomo, Daniel Kwagbenu, Lorah Madete, Hafiz Mirza, Li Qian and Sara Sievers. Helpful comments were received from Diana Barrowclough, Sérgio Chitarà, Horacio Dombo, Kumi Endo, K. Filson, Torbjörn Fredriksson, Joachim Karl, Ashok Mohinani, Brian Mosenene, Ulrick Mumburi, Salvador Namburete, Adiel Nyiti, Emmanuel D. Ole Naiko, Karl P. Sauvant and R. Yofi Grant, as well as the Chinese Academy of International Trade and Economic Cooperation.

Kemal Dervis
Administrator of UNDP

Supachai Panitchpakdi
Secretary-General of UNCTAD
January 2007

ABBREVIATIONS

ACP	African, Caribbean and Pacific (group of States)
AFTA	ASEAN Free Trade Area
AGOA	African Growth and Opportunity Act (United States)
AIA	ASEAN Investment Area
APEC	Asia Pacific Economic Cooperation
ASEAN	Association of Southeast Asian Nations
BIT	bilateral investment treaty
BOI	board of investment
CDC	Commonwealth Development Corporation
CFA	Communauté Financière Africaine, a grouping of most west and central African Francophone states (plus Guinea Bissau)
CPI	the Mozambique investment promotion centre
COMESA	Common Market for Eastern and Southern Africa
DTT	double taxation treaty
EAC	East African Community
ECOWAS	Economic Community of West African States
EDB	Economic Development Board
EIU	Economist Intelligence Unit
EPZ	export processing zone
EU	European Union
FDI	foreign direct investment
FIAS	Foreign Investment Advisory Service
GDP	gross domestic product
GIPC	Ghana Investment Promotion Centre
GNP	gross national product
GSP	Generalized System of Preferences
ICSID	International Centre for the Settlement of Investment Disputes
ICT	information and communications technology
IFC	International Finance Corporation
IPA	investment promotion agency
LDC	least developed country
M&As	mergers and acquisitions
MOFCOM	Ministry of Commerce
NAFTA	North American Free Trade Agreement/Area
NEPAD	New Partnership for Africa's Development
NIE	newly industrializing economy
ODA	official development assistance
OECD	Organisation for Economic Co-operation and Development
SACU	Southern African Customs Union
SADC	Southern African Development Community
SME	small and medium-sized enterprise
SOE	State-owned enterprise
TIC	Tanzania Investment Centre
TNC	transnational corporation
TRIMs	trade-related investment measures (Also Uruguay Round Agreement on Trade-Related Investment Measures)
TRIPS	trade-related aspects of intellectual property rights (Also Uruguay Round Agreement on Trade-related Aspects of Intellectual Property Rights)
UNCTAD	United Nations Conference on Trade and Development
UNIDO	United Nations Industrial Development Organization
WEF	World Economic Forum
WTO	World Trade Organization
USAID	United States Agency for International Development

TABLE OF CONTENTS

Page

PART TWO: SELECTED AFRICAN CASE STUDIES

Page

Page

Boxes

Figures

Page

Tables

Page

Box figures

Box tables

Annex tables

EXECUTIVE SUMMARY

With the growing recognition of the successful experience of East and South-East Asia, it is useful for African countries to examine the lessons that could be drawn from the development paths followed in that region, and to consider ways and means of strengthening economic cooperation with Asian economies. One important area of interest in this connection relates to foreign direct investment (FDI), which has played an increasingly important role in developing Asian economies. Understanding Asian experience and policies with respect to inward FDI could contribute to African countries' capabilities to attract and benefit from FDI. Furthermore, since the late 1980s, outward FDI from the economies of developing Asia has become significant, and even though these cross-border flows have so far remained largely limited to the Asian region they arouse interest as potential sources of investment in Africa. This interest, which declined somewhat as a result of the Asian financial crisis of 1997-1998, was renewed following the recovery of the crisis-hit countries and the continuing steady growth of the Chinese and Indian economies. The fast-growing Asian economies have come to be viewed not only as successful cases that could provide examples of development paths for African economies, but, increasingly, also as economic partners, particularly for trade and investment. This volume focuses on the investment aspects of such South-South cooperation. While still small, FDI flows from Asia to Africa reached $1.2 billion annually during the period 2002-2004, and they are set to increase further in the coming years.

This volume is organized into two main parts. In the first part, an introductory chapter on Asian FDI in Africa is followed by two chapters that review South-East Asia and China both as sources of FDI flows to Africa and as hosts of FDI inflows. The second part of this volume assesses the experiences of selected African economies as FDI recipients, mainly with a view to considering how best they could attract FDI in general and that from Asia in particular. Specific attention is given to the potential for FDI by small and medium-sized enterprises (SMEs) – an area that is often neglected, but is of particular importance for equitable and sustainable development in African countries.

Chapter I on Asian FDI in Africa focuses on Africa's potential for attracting FDI from developing Asia, with special attention given to FDI by Asian SMEs. It begins by reviewing recent trends in FDI flows to Africa from the developing economies of South, East and South-East Asia. The latter comprise mainly the high-growth economies of China, Hong Kong (China), the Republic of Korea, Malaysia, Singapore and Taiwan Province of China. Attention is also given to India, which historically has been an important source of immigration and investment especially in East and Southern Africa, but also in West Africa. The chapter examines why, despite the rapid growth of outward FDI from developing Asia, which has risen from 3 per cent of world FDI stock in 1990 to 8 per cent in 2005, little of that investment has gone to Africa. It argues that Africa can attract more Asian FDI, and proposes various policies to enhance such investment.

The chapter suggests some reasons why such a low share of Asian FDI goes to Africa: investing abroad is still a relatively recent phenomenon for many Asian firms, their transaction and information costs are higher when investing in Africa than in other Asian economies, and both host- and home-country regulatory frameworks often impose constraints. They thus tend to focus on intra-regional FDI. Asian economies had only just begun to build up their outward investment stock when they were struck by financial crisis in 1997. Their FDI in Africa declined following the crisis but has recently begun increasing again. Asian newly industrializing economies have recently become relatively large investors abroad. Asian developing economies invest almost as much in manufacturing as services. Services FDI is mainly in trade-related activities and financial services. Asian investments have been growing in all major regions, but still remain concentrated mainly in Asia. Singapore, India and Malaysia are the top Asian sources of FDI in Africa, with investment stocks estimated at about $3.5 billion (cumulative approved flows from 1996 to 2004), $1.9 billion and $1.9 billion respectively by 2004, followed by China, the Republic of Korea and Taiwan Province of China.

Asian SMEs have also become an important source of this new outward FDI, as more of them need to invest abroad to maintain and improve their competitiveness. Africa could benefit from a rapid expansion of a dynamic, internationally competitive SME sector.

Outward FDI from South-East Asia or ASEAN member states has been led mainly by Malaysia and Singapore. Chapter II highlights in particular Malaysia as its FDI in Africa is the most geographically and industrially dispersed. The Malaysian Government's support for outward FDI has been closely linked to South-South cooperation and promoting mutual benefits. The chapter also discusses the policies and experiences of FDI in South-East Asia that are of particular relevance for Africa. It reviews the region's experience both with attracting FDI and investing abroad, especially in Africa. It examines the role and pattern of FDI in the original five ASEAN member countries (Indonesia, Malaysia, the Philippines, Singapore and Thailand), and the trends in their FDI inflows with an emphasis on locational determinants and competitiveness.

Chapter II briefly describes FDI policy regimes in these ASEAN-5 economies, notably with regard to FDI promotion and facilitation, approval processes and entry restrictions, performance requirements and local supplier relations, as well as investment incentives and guarantees. It highlights various regional initiatives and the so-called "growth triangles" (i.e. areas of cross-border economic cooperation among three or more neighbouring countries in the region). It offers some lessons from the Asian financial crisis and concludes with a discussion of the prospects for East and South-East Asian investments in Africa.

Chapter III on Chinese FDI in Africa reviews China's experience, albeit with rather different emphasis. China's FDI outflows have been growing rapidly, from an average of less than $100 million per annum in the 1980s to $12 billion in 2005. A large proportion of these outflows has gone to East and South-East Asia as well as Latin America and the Caribbean. Africa accounted for only 3 per cent of China's total FDI outflows in 2005, and for about $1.6 billion of Chinese FDI stock, which has a presence in almost 48 African countries.

China's investments in Africa have mainly gone into manufacturing, resource extraction, construction and other services. Chinese companies now operating in Africa are mostly SMEs. By 2000, some 500 Chinese FDI projects were known in Africa, and only 30 of them having investments of over $10 million. While about one third of China's FDI projects abroad generated profits and another one-third were at break-even point, in Africa the returns were comparatively low. Still, more than half of Chinese foreign affiliates at least broke even.

Since the early 1980s, China's policies on outward FDI have evolved, moving towards a more transparent and proactive policy framework. In the late 1990s the central Government began encouraging outward FDI and launched the "going global" strategy. A series of incentive measures accompanied the strategy, such as easy access to bank loans, simplified border procedures, and preferential policies for taxation, imports and exports. Bilateral investment treaties have been another facilitation measure adopted not only to attract FDI but also promote better protection to Chinese companies investing abroad. The country signed 117 bilateral investment treaties, including 28 in Africa, by 2005. Most of the investments by Chinese firms are in the form of equity joint ventures with African enterprises, though not in the case of recent resource-seeking FDI.

The main lessons drawn from experiences of Chinese FDI in Africa point to the importance of finding a suitable African partner, host-government support, local market-oriented activity and technology transfer. Problems faced by Chinese enterprises operating in Africa are partly due to the economic environment of the host countries, a shortage of skilled workers, restrictions on foreign exchange, and inadequate or inappropriate incentives offered. Progress made by Sino-African joint ventures can partly be attributed to high-level visits by government and business leaders, the China-Africa Cooperation Forum, bilateral agreements, joint intergovernmental committees and cooperation between Chinese and African enterprises. The chapter also briefly reviews China's inward FDI policies and concludes that other developing countries, including those in Africa, may be able to draw lessons from China's success in attracting and effectively using FDI inflows over the past two decades.

Part Two of this volume focuses on five African countries, principally assessing their potential and need to attract FDI from developing Asia, along with proposals for policy reforms and initiatives that could help attract more FDI from Asian economies. Most FDI promotion measures tend to target large transnational corporations (TNCs), thus missing out on the various strengths and advantages that SMEs may be able to offer to African developing countries. Therefore each of the five chapters gives special attention to SMEs. Case studies provide illustrative examples or elaborate on issues that otherwise often do not receive adequate attention.

Chapter IV begins with a review of FDI in Botswana, in minerals – which constitute the key sector of its economy – as well as non-mining activities including manufacturing. The potential role of SMEs in the economy is considered, especially as recipients of FDI and in the context of the need to boost investment in sectors other than mining to promote economic diversification. FDI in Botswana my be attracted to the domestic market, demand for inputs by local businesses, the regional market and broader export markets. Factor costs and availability are also important, such as labour markets and costs, managerial skills and costs, local financial facilities, transport links and costs, investment zones, economic agglomerations and local SMEs that could benefit from FDI.

FDI in Botswana has been limited to date partly because of lack of knowledge among investors about investment opportunities, partly due to bureaucratic impediments. In response, policy reforms for attracting FDI from Asia should be considered. These may include expediting visa granting procedures, provision of serviced land and/or factory shells, strengthening investment promotion activities abroad, introducing wage policy reforms and seeking solutions to problems associated with being landlocked. Possible regional initiatives to promote FDI are suggested; they include reducing non-tariff barriers, improving regional infrastructure and avoidance of a regional race to the bottom. Finally, the chapter suggests what could be done in the area of national policies, regional and international cooperation and home country policies by the Government of Botswana, Asian investors and governments and bilateral and multilateral agencies.

Chapter V reviews FDI trends in Ghana with particular attention to investment from Asian sources. It makes a number of suggestions on ways to increase such flows. Many of the recommendations apply generally to inward FDI, but could also help to increase Asian FDI flows. There is also a focus on specific opportunities for Asian FDI in Ghana.

Ghana has taken a number of steps, going further than many other countries in Africa, to attract FDI, including improving its institutions and infrastructure to support investments. Nevertheless, additional steps are necessary to realize the country's full potential as an FDI location, including improving road and port facilities and introducing legislation to facilitate investment in infrastructure. Measures should be taken to support identified subsectors such as technology development, market and product development, links and networking. A more coherent and comprehensive SME policy would also be useful.

Potential Asian investors are often unaware of incentives offered and agencies concerned with investment in Ghana. Professional investment promotion and "matchmaking" services, along with concerted efforts to bridge cultural differences, can in this context make a difference. The chapter emphasizes the importance of macroeconomic stabilization and structural reforms. It concludes that, unlike other countries, much of Ghana's focus should be on following through on earlier initiatives rather than launching new ones, except those proposed as a response to inadequacies of earlier reforms.

Chapter VI focuses on Madagascar. Significant investment opportunities coexist with barriers to investment and international trade. Many initiatives have been undertaken since the late 1990s to enhance Madagascar's attractiveness to investors, including the creation of a commercial dispute resolution mechanism and export processing zones. The country also has the advantages of low labour costs and rich endowments of natural resources. However, poor infrastructure, weak institutions and a slow-moving bureaucracy have undermined the ability to attract and benefit from FDI. Although trade policy has been liberalized, investment opportunities could be improved by further liberalization of trade and capital flows. Several recommendations are made for consideration by the Government of Madagascar, foreign donors and the private sector, while acknowledging progress made thus far. It also identifies fiscal and customs management as areas in need of technical cooperation.

In Mozambique (chapter VII), large FDI projects related to the Mozal project – a major aluminium smelter involving several foreign investors – were prominent in the late 1990s. The country's strengths and weaknesses in attracting FDI are reviewed, as are policy reforms to attract FDI into Mozambique, especially from Asia. Specific sectors offering opportunities for investors in general and SMEs in particular are considered before concluding with additional policy proposals.

Asian investment in Mozambique has historically come from India and Pakistan, but recent investments have also come from China (including Hong Kong, China), Malaysia, the Republic of Korea and Singapore. A high proportion of FDI has involved small projects, suggesting that there is good potential for SMEs. However, the Government of Mozambique will need to take several steps to increase SME investment, improve matchmaking services, create a more welcoming domestic business environment, and introduce more attractive and transparent business regulations. The chapter acknowledges problems such as poor infrastructure, lack of skilled labour and other labour-related issues, and onerous investment-related administrative procedures, but notes considerable improvements over the past decade. It calls for Asian countries to help expand Asian FDI in SMEs in Mozambique by providing technical assistance, information, training, financial incentives and oversight of Asian firms already in Mozambique. It also urges a role for international and multilateral agencies to expand or publicize programmes for these purposes.

Chapter VIII on the United Republic of Tanzania suggests that the country could be a promising destination for Asian FDI once it becomes a more fully-fledged market economy. It examines the level and type of Asian FDI already in the country as well as issues to be addressed to attract greater FDI from Asia, including the opportunities and problems for Asian FDI and the sectors in which it would be the most beneficial. Regional trade groupings and international partnerships could also help promote investment in the region. There were large increases in FDI from the mid-1990s, with the most successful sector being mining. The Government has instituted fiscal incentives for foreign firms. Many new investors are ethnic Indians, a number of whom are related to families whose properties were expropriated in the early 1970s.

It is pointed out that SME investments are especially desirable for the United Republic of Tanzania because they are more innovative. SMEs should be promoted, for example by meeting their need for credit, market information and operating facilities. They should be encouraged to meet international quality standards without incurring high costs. SME policy should include policies to promote subcontracting to SMEs by larger firms. Such linkages could also facilitate technology transfer.

The chapter recommends measures to be taken by the Government to create more favourable conditions for FDI in the United Republic of Tanzania. It should have a long-term plan concerning sectors to be promoted, which could include textiles, manufacturing, fisheries and agro-processing. The Government also needs to streamline its regulations, eliminate undue red tape and simplify its tax system.

* * *

Asian FDI to Africa is likely to continue to grow, in view of the complementary nature of economic development between Asian and African countries. In particular, the rapid economic growth in Asia can be expected to lead to increased Asian investments in Africa, in natural resources, manufacturing as well as services. Moreover, the rapid industrial upgrading taking place in Asia provides ample opportunities for Africa to attract efficiency-seeking and export-oriented FDI from Asian economies. For export-oriented manufacturing, African economies, in particular African LDCs, enjoy the advantages of preferential market access to the large markets of the China, the EU, Japan and the United States. Asian SMEs have also become an important source of FDI in Africa. Appropriate policies at both national and international levels are crucial for addressing various challenges and turning the potential into reality. African countries will also need to make substantial efforts to enhance their productive capacity in particular industrial areas and related competitive advantages, thereby addressing one of the basic economic determinants of FDI. This requires investment promotion agencies to develop greater expertise and flexibility, rather than a sector-neutral and passive policy stance. Given such efforts and appropriate policies, Africa can attract increasing amounts of Asian FDI and benefit from the dynamism of the Asian corporate sector.

INTRODUCTION

Africa's poor growth performance after decolonization has been called "the worst economic tragedy of the 20th century" (Artadi and Sala-i-Martin, 2004, p.1). Between 1960 and 1980, the per capita GDP of the continent increased slightly, but has since then stagnated at a very low level. The 1980s was a lost decade for most of sub-Saharan Africa, and the 1990s were only marginally better. In comparison, many Asian economies have experienced rapid economic growth in recent decades. Economies in East and South-East Asia have grown particularly fast, embarking on accelerated industrialization.

In terms of attracting foreign direct investment (FDI), Africa has also remained far behind Asia. The failure of African countries to attract foreign investors is highlighted by the declining share of Africa in global FDI flows: from 4.6 per cent in the 1970s to 1.6 per cent in the 1990s, though they recovered somewhat in the first half of the 2000s (table 1). By contrast, the share of Asia jumped from 8.1 per cent to 17.2 per cent during the same period (table 1). According to the United Nations Economic Commission for Africa (ECA), $350 billion of private investment is required for Africa to meet the Millennium Development Goals (MDGs) by the target year of 2015. FDI could contribute substantially to this. In 2005, for instance, FDI inflows to African countries amounted to $31 billion.

Moreover, from the late 1980s, outward FDI from the economies of developing Asia has become significant, and, although these cross-border flows have remained largely limited to the Asian region, interest has also aroused in Asian economies as possible sources of FDI in Africa. While the amount of such FDI flows to Africa has been small ($1.2 billion during the period 2002-

2004) it comprises a major part of inter-regional FDI within the developing world (UNCTAD, 2006). There are also signs of rising interest among Asian companies in Africa as an investment location. Following the recovery and continued steady growth of South-East Asia after the 1997-1998 crisis as well as the rapid rise of the Chinese and Indian economies, there has been a renewed interest in some Asian countries, not only as examples of possible development paths, but, increasingly, also as economic partners, particularly for trade and investment.

Table 1. Shares of developing regions in global FDI inflows, 1970-2005
(Per cent)

Region	1970-1979	1980-1989	1990-1999	2000-2005
Africa	4.6	2.3	1.6	2.2
Asia and Oceania	8.1	12.6	17.2	16.3
Latin America and the Caribbean	13.3	7.9	11.2	10.0
Developing economies total	26.0	22.9	30.1	28.5
World FDI inflows ($ billion)	244	939	4 040	5 044

Source: UNCTAD, FDI/TNC database (www.unctad.org/fdistatistics).

Against this background, the objective of this research is to help African countries attract and benefit more from FDI inflows, in particular those from developing Asia. It also aims to help African economies in harnessing FDI to achieve long-term, sustained development based on lessons from the Asian experience.

It is worth nothing in that respect that subregions in Africa differ significantly socially, culturally and in their levels of economic development. Their performance in attracting FDI also varies significantly (table 2): North Africa has performed relatively better than other subregions, and West Africa has seen the sharpest decline in FDI inflows since the early 1970s. The share of Sub-Saharan Africa – where 33 of the world's least developed countries (LDCs) are located – in global FDI flows declined from 3.8 per cent in the 1970s to 1.1 per cent in the 1990s. This study focuses on this part of the African continent. Indeed, all five African countries selected for this study are sub-Saharan (figure 1). Three of them are LDCs: Madagascar (an island economy), Mozambique and the United Republic of Tanzania (both coastal countries); the other two are Ghana (a low-income developing economy) and Botswana (a landlocked country with one of the highest per capita incomes in Africa).

Table 2. Shares of African subregions in global FDI inflows, 1970-2005
(Per cent)

Subregion	1970-1979	1980-1989	1990-1999	2000-2005
Central Africa	0.7	0.4	0.2	0.5
East Africa	0.5	0.2	0.2	0.2
North Africa	0.8	1.0	0.5	0.7
Southern Africa	0.5	0.1	0.3	0.4
West Africa	2.1	0.8	0.5	0.4
Total African share in global FDI inflows	4.6	2.3	1.6	2.2
Total FDI inflows to Africa ($ billion)	11	22	66	109

Source: UNCTAD, FDI/TNC database (www.unctad.org/fdistatistics).

In each case, the following specific questions have been addressed: What are the main determinants of FDI performance? What are the strengths and weaknesses in terms of attracting FDI? What role can government policies play in improving the institutional environment and investment climate?

Figure 1. Five African countries selected for this study

Source: UNCTAD.

One major advantage of many African countries for attracting FDI is their abundance of natural resources. Indeed, a large and increasing share of inward FDI in Africa has been in the extractive industries, in particular in petroleum, which has benefited from increasingly large shares of FDI in recent years. The concentration of FDI in natural resources highlights the importance of diversification of TNC activities in Africa, which is crucial for the continent's long-term sustainable economic development. How can African countries enter into higher value-added manufacturing activities? How can Africa learn from some Asian countries, which successfully transformed their economies from primarily natural resource exporters into those with rapidly growing manufacturing industries in the 1980s and 1990s? These are also some important questions addressed by this study. It is in this context that the discussion below on the Asian experiences as regards FDI and their applicability to Africa should be considered.

PART ONE

ASIAN FDI IN AFRICA

CHAPTER I

ASIAN FDI IN AFRICA: AN OVERVIEW

Except during the financial crisis in the late 1990s, East and South-East Asian economies – in particular most of the developing economies of East Asia and some in South-East Asia[1] – generally enjoyed robust and sustained economic growth, a success that the World Bank once dubbed the "East Asian Miracle" (World Bank, 1993). Table I.1 compares the developing economies of East Asia with those of Africa in terms of some key economic magnitudes. In terms of GDP, most African economies are small, and the largest economy is South Africa. In East and South-East Asia, the economies of several developing countries – China, the Republic of Korea, Indonesia and Taiwan Province of China – are larger than that of South Africa. In terms of GDP per capita in 2005, the richest African countries are Equatorial Guinea ($13,410), Seychelles ($8,605), Gabon ($6,444), Libyan Arab Jamahiriya ($6,617) and Botswana ($5,230), while half of the economies have per capita incomes of less than $500. Among East and South-East Asian developing economies, Hong Kong (China) and Singapore have a per capita GDP of over $20,000, while the majority have per capita incomes of over $1,500 and only Cambodia, the Lao People's Democratic Republic, Myanmar, and Timor-Leste have a per capita GDP of less than $500. The GDP growth rate of developing East and South-East Asia has been much higher than that of Africa.

The disparity in income growth and levels between the two regions is mirrored in their FDI performance. East and South-East Asia has emerged as the leading location for FDI in the world, and at the same time has evolved into an important outward investor-region (UNCTAD, 2006), while Africa has attracted a relatively small share of global inward FDI and has limited outward FDI. However, in recent years, African countries have begun seeking FDI actively as part of their renewed efforts to accelerate development. With its strong inward FDI experience, developing Asia may provide Africa with policy insights on how to attract and benefit from FDI. Moreover, a number of Asian economies could be sources of increased FDI for African economies.

This chapter focuses on Africa's potential for attracting FDI from developing Asia with special attention to FDI by small and medium-size enterprises (SMEs). The first section briefly reviews trends in global FDI flows, including, among others the performance of Africa and Asia in attracting FDI. Section B deals with recent trends and patterns of FDI in Africa. Section C discusses trends in FDI from developing Asia to Africa, noting that Asian FDI flows and stocks in Africa remain low, but also that the potential is high. In particular, SMEs have become an important source of new outward FDI from Asia, as an increasing number of these firms find it necessary to invest abroad in order to maintain and improve their competitiveness. Therefore, this section also examines FDI by Asian SMEs. Section D examines why Asian FDI in Africa has remained low by considering the problems and constraints Asian firms face when investing there. The last section discusses policies that might enhance investment in Africa by developing Asian firms, including Asian SMEs.

Table I.1. East and South-East Asia and Africa: some statistical comparisons

Economy	Population (millions) 2005	GDP ($ million) 2005	GDP per capita ($) 2005	Real GDP growth rate 1980-1989	Real GDP growth rate 1990-1999	Real GDP growth rate 2000-2005
Africa	905.6	937 796	1 036	2.4	2.6	4.4
Algeria	32.9	102 026	3 105	2.9	1.7	5.2
Angola	15.9	28 860	1 810	3.6	1.0	9.8
Benin	8.4	4 425	524	3.4	4.5	4.5
Botswana	1.8	9 231	5 230	11.4	4.6	5.7
Burkina Faso	13.2	5 749	435	3.8	5.9	5.8
Burundi	7.5	801	106	4.4	-2.9	2.4
Cameroon	16.3	16 991	1 041	2.6	1.1	4.1
Cape Verde	0.5	993	1 959	5.6	6.8	5.1
Central African Republic	4.0	1 381	342	1.5	1.7	-1.5
Chad	9.7	5 431	557	6.7	3.5	13.9
Comoros	0.8	370	464	3.0	1.2	2.1
Congo	4.0	5 865	1 467	4.0	0.9	4.1
Congo, Democratic Republic of	57.5	7 169	125	2.1	-5.0	4.5
Côte d' Ivoire	18.2	16 204	893	3.4	3.5	-0.9
Djibouti	0.8	702	885	1.7	1.4	2.8
Egypt	74.0	93 045	1 257	6.4	4.1	3.7
Equatorial Guinea	0.5	6 752	13 410	2.3	21.2	24.8
Eritrea	4.4	954	217	..	..	3.5
Ethiopia	77.4	11 174	144	1.7	3.5	4.8
Gabon	1.4	8 917	6 444	0.3	2.6	1.6
Gambia	1.5	459	303	3.5	2.9	3.7
Ghana	22.1	10 694	484	2.6	4.3	5.1
Guinea	9.4	3 296	351	2.0	4.4	2.9
Guinea-Bissau	1.6	288	182	4.3	1.3	-1.0
Kenya	34.3	19 184	560	4.3	2.2	3.1
Lesotho	1.8	1 270	708	3.8	4.2	2.4
Liberia	3.3	484	147	-2.7	0.1	-6.6
Libyan Arab Jamahiriya	5.9	38 735	6 617	-1.1	1.4	6.8
Madagascar	18.6	4 713	253	0.9	1.7	1.9
Malawi	12.9	2 072	161	2.0	7.6	2.2
Mali	13.5	5 255	389	2.5	3.9	5.8
Mauritania	3.1	1 938	632	1.5	4.7	4.9
Mauritius	1.2	6 233	5 008	6.2	5.0	4.2
Morocco	31.5	51 986	1 651	4.2	2.4	4.2
Mozambique	19.8	6 728	340	-1.5	5.5	8.1
Namibia	2.0	6 121	3 013	2.2	4.2	3.0
Niger	14.0	3 493	250	-0.2	2.4	4.1
Nigeria	131.5	99 147	754	1.4	2.8	5.3
Rwanda	9.0	2 133	236	2.1	-1.2	5.5
São Tomé and Principe	0.2	70	447	-1.2	1.7	4.8
Senegal	11.7	8 332	715	3.2	3.3	4.9
Seychelles	0.1	694	8 605	3.7	4.7	-2.5
Sierra Leone	5.5	1 193	216	1.4	-5.4	13.7
Somalia	8.2	2 130	259	1.2	-4.0	2.9
South Africa	47.4	239 144	5 042	1.4	2.0	3.7
Sudan	36.2	27 699	764	2.8	5.3	6.1
Swaziland	1.0	2 532	2 452	7.5	3.4	2.4
Togo	6.1	2 114	344	1.8	3.6	1.9
Tunisia	10.1	30 185	2 988	3.2	4.6	4.4
Uganda	28.8	8 710	302	3.1	7.5	5.7
United Republic of Tanzania	38.3	12 167	317	2.4	5.8	6.9
Zambia	11.7	7 066	606	1.4	-0.3	4.7
Zimbabwe	13.0	4 491	345	3.3	2.1	-5.7
East Asia	1 420.0	3 568 080	2 513	9.2	8.2	9.6
China	1 315.8	2 224 811	1 691	10.6	11.1	4.3
Hong Kong, China	7.0	177 723	25 242	7.1	4.0	1.7
Korea, Dem. People's Rep. of	22.5	13 973	621	7.9	-3.5	4.6
Korea, Republic of	47.8	793 070	16 586	8.5	5.9	12.9
Macao, China	0.5	10 482	22 798	7.5	2.5	5.9
Mongolia	2.6	1 881	711	6.2	0.7	3.5
Taiwan Province of China	23.7	346 141	14 596	8.5	6.5	7.3
South-East Asia	555.8	868 077	1 562	4.8	5.5	5.0
Indonesia	222.8	276 004	1 239	5.7	4.8	4.7
Malaysia	25.3	130 796	5 160	4.9	7.4	4.8
Philippines	83.1	97 653	1 176	0.5	3.2	4.6
Singapore	4.3	117 882	27 253	6.3	8.0	4.2
Thailand	64.2	168 774	2 628	7.0	4.7	5.4
Brunei Darussalam	0.4	6 399	17 118	-1.0	1.2	2.9
Cambodia	14.1	5 419	385	-1.3	6.2	6.4
Lao People's Democratic Republic	5.9	2 735	462	4.5	6.6	6.2
Myanmar	50.5	11 160	221	0.9	6.6	11.1
Timor-Leste	0.9	355	375	..	-1.0	-0.5
Viet Nam	84.2	50 900	604	5.7	8.1	7.4
Memorandum:						
ASEAN-10	554.9	867 722	1 564	4.8	5.5	5.0
ASEAN-5 [a]	399.7	791 109	1 979	5.0	5.4	4.8
East and South-East Asia	1 975.8	4 436 157	2 245	7.9	7.6	6.8

Source: UNCTAD, based on data from United Nations, Department of Economics and Social Affairs, Statistics Division and World Bank, World Development Indicators online.

[a] Indonesia, Malaysia, Philippines, Singapore and Thailand.

A. GLOBAL TRENDS IN FDI AND THE DIVERGENT PERFORMANCE OF AFRICA AND ASIA

During the 1990s, global FDI flows grew at an average rate of 22 per cent annually, much higher than the growth of GDP (4 per cent) and exports (6 per cent). Global inflows reached a record high of $1.4 trillion in 2000, followed by a three-year decline to a low $558 billion in 2003. Thereafter, FDI flows rebounded, reaching $711 billion in 2004 and $916 billion in 2005 (UNCTAD, 2006). The surge of FDI since the early 1990s – interrupted by the FDI downturn in the early 2000s due largely to cyclical fluctuations in economic growth – reflects mainly the response of transnational corporations (TNCs) to competitive pressures and new opportunities from globalization. An increasing number of companies from both developed and developing countries are actively seeking foreign markets, resources and created assets through equity investments or non-equity arrangements. There are currently at least 77,000 TNCs in the world that own over 770,000 foreign affiliates (UNCTAD, 2006).

Developing countries received more than a third of world FDI inflows in 2005, or about $334 billion. South, East and South-East Asia continues to be the largest developing host region, as it has been for some time (UNCTAD, 2006). It has also seen its *outward* FDI grow rapidly, from a mere 3 per cent of world FDI stock in 1990 to 8 per cent in 2005 (figure I.1). The region's dynamic outward FDI growth since the early 1990s is more evident in FDI outflows than in FDI stock, as the phenomenon is relatively recent. About 13 per cent of world FDI outflows originated in the region in the mid-1990s, though this share declined to about 7 per cent following the 1997-1998 Asian financial crisis (figure I.1).[2] Since then, its share has increased again to around 9 per cent in recent years. Despite its declining share of outward FDI, compared with the mid-1990s, developing Asia remains, nevertheless, a significant investor in other developing countries, particularly those in the same region.

Figure I.1. Outward FDI from South, East and South-East Asia and the share of developing countries and South, East and South-East Asia in world FDI, 1980-2005

(Billions of dollars and per cent)

(a) FDI outward stock

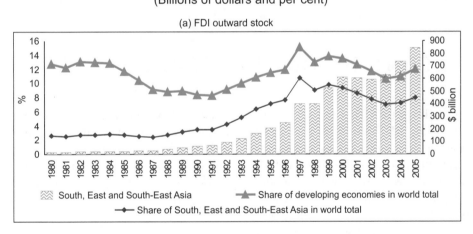

(b) FDI outward flows

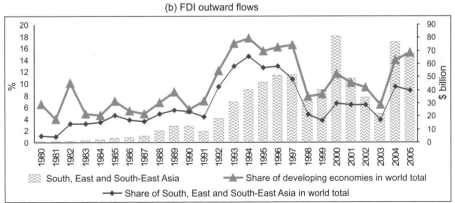

Source: UNCTAD, FDI/TNC database (www.unctad.org/fdistatistics).

FDI flows to Africa, unlike those to developing Asia, have remained small. Even though total FDI inflows to Africa rose to $31 billion in 2005, a historic high and almost three times as high as in the late 1990s, the region's share in global FDI was just over 3 per cent in 2005. Africa's share in developing-country inflows declined from 12 per cent during the second half of the 1980s to 5 per cent in the 1990s, and then rose somewhat

thereafter, reaching 9 per cent in 2005 (figure I.2). Political instability, a small market, poor infrastructure and policy changes that influence business assessment of expected returns and risk have all contributed to this poor performance. In this context, it may be said that Africa has probably missed some opportunities for growth and development through FDI.

Figure I.2.   Share of Africa and selected regions in developing economies' FDI inflows, 1980-2005

(Per cent)

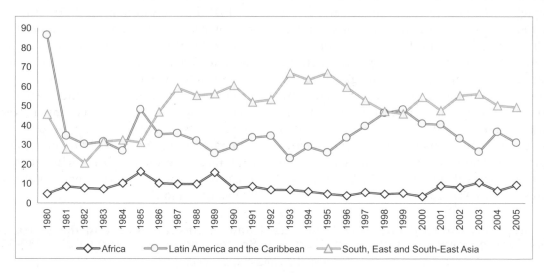

Source: UNCTAD, FDI/TNC database (www.unctad.org/fdistatistics).

B. RECENT TRENDS IN AFRICA'S INWARD FDI

The record flows to Africa in 2005 were largely driven by rising FDI in natural resources stimulated by soaring commodity prices and a one-off transaction in South Africa[3] (UNCTAD, 2006). The performance of various subregions in attracting FDI differs (figure I.3), with FDI largely concentrated in a few countries of the region (table I.2). Five recipients (Angola, Egypt, Morocco, Nigeria and South Africa) accounted for nearly two thirds of FDI inflows into Africa during the 1990s and more than half in the first half of the 2000s. On the other hand, the 33 least developed countries (LDCs) in Africa received very small amounts: in 2005, for instance, they received a total of around $8 billion, less than a fifth of the region's total FDI.

In recent years, FDI in natural resources in Africa has been particularly strong, reflecting the high prices of minerals and oil and the greater profitability of investment in the primary sector. High and rising prices of petroleum, metals and

minerals have induced TNCs to maintain relatively large levels of investment in new exploration projects or escalate existing production. Several large cross-border mergers and acquisitions (M&As) have been recently concluded in the mining industry.

Most FDI in Africa originates from Europe – led by investors from France, the Netherlands and the United Kingdom – and from South Africa and the United States; together these countries accounted for more than half of the region's inflows. Developing Asia has only recently become a significant source of FDI in Africa.

The low level of FDI in Africa and its small share in global inflows should however be seen in perspective (UNCTAD, 1999b):

•   The absolute level of FDI flows to Africa has been increasing. From a low level, they rose more than 10-fold between the latter half of

Figure I.3. FDI inflows to Africa, by subregion, 1980-2005
(Millions of dollars)

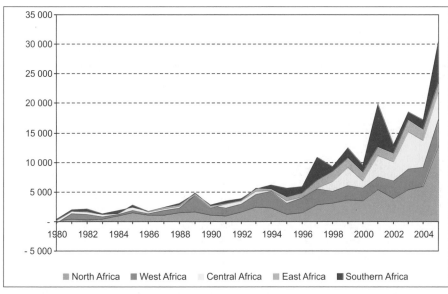

■ North Africa   ■ West Africa   ■ Central Africa   ■ East Africa   ■ Southern Africa

Source: UNCTAD, FDI/TNC database (www.unctad.org/fdistatistics).

the 1980s (1985-1989) and 2005. This growth, however, is lower than that of FDI flows to all developing countries, which registered more than a 14-fold increase.

• While FDI flows to Africa account for only a small share of inflows to developing countries, their importance for the host economies – as measured by the ratio of FDI to gross fixed capital formation – is not necessarily small. At 16 per cent during the period 2003-2005, their ratio for Africa as a whole was comparable to that of other regions.

• As a percentage of GDP, in 2005 Africa's FDI stock was 28 per cent, compared to 33 per cent for Europe, 26 per cent for South, East and South-East Asia, and 37 per cent for Latin America and the Caribbean. Since market size – an important determinant of FDI inflows – in African economies is relatively small and their level of development is generally low, the lower African ratio is not unexpected and, moreover, compares quite well with that in the other regions.

Notably, FDI flows to Africa are spreading into non-traditional sectors as well. While FDI in the primary sector remains more important in Africa than in other regions, the secondary and tertiary sectors are also becoming attractive to investors (table I.3).

C. RECENT TRENDS IN FDI FROM DEVELOPING ASIA

1. Asian FDI

As noted earlier, developing Asian economies have emerged as dynamic international investors since the early 1990s. Newly industrializing economies (NIEs) such as Hong Kong (China), the Republic of Korea and Taiwan Province of China are now relatively large overseas investors. China, India and several South-East Asian economies have also joined the ranks of countries with sizeable outward FDI, albeit at much lower levels than their inward FDI (see chapter II on ASEAN and chapter III on China).

Investment from Asian developing economies has been growing in all major regions. So far, however, it remains principally concentrated in Asia, which in 2002 was host to nearly half the outward FDI stock from Singapore (47 per cent), 40 per cent from Hong Kong (China), 38 per cent of that from Malaysia, 40 per cent of that from the Republic of Korea and 24 per cent from Taiwan Province of China. These investments are important for the host economies involved: for major Asian developing economies, FDI inflows from other Asian developing economies account for 25 per cent or more of total inflows, and are larger than

Table I.2. Ranking of host countries in Africa, by size of FDI inflows,[a] 1980-2005
(Millions of dollars)

Country/group of economies	Annual Average					2000	2001	2002	2003	2004	2005
	1980-1984	1985-1989	1990-1994	1995-1999	2000-2004						
South Africa	175	- 147	113	1 588	1 993	888	6 789	757	734	799	6 379
Egypt	563	1 157	757	852	957	1 235	510	647	237	2 157	5 376
Nigeria	158	710	1 490	1 498	1 785	1 310	1 277	2 040	2 171	2 127	3 403
Morocco	64	66	390	792	1 476	471	2 875	534	2 429	1 070	2 933
Sudan	12	1	13	170	908	392	574	713	1 349	1 511	2 305
Equatorial Guinea	1	2	20	182	894	108	945	323	1 431	1 664	1 860
Congo, Democratic Republic of	- 10	2	1	6	79	23	82	117	158	15	1 344
Algeria	62	7	22	286	826	438	1 113	1 065	634	882	1 081
Tunisia	259	99	414	426	662	779	486	821	584	639	782
Chad	2	22	12	33	538	115	460	924	713	478	705
United Republic of Tanzania	7	3	16	234	435	282	467	430	527	470	473
Congo	39	16	69	165	274	166	77	137	323	668	402
Namibia	..	5	84	92	222	188	365	182	149	226	349
Botswana	61	64	- 43	75	260	57	31	403	418	391	346
Gabon	68	63	- 14	- 250	85	- 43	- 89	30	206	323	300
Libyan Arab Jamahiriya	- 514	14	67	- 105	- 12	141	- 133	145	142	- 354	261
Zambia	21	82	127	156	137	122	72	82	172	239	259
Uganda	1	- 0	28	116	188	181	151	185	202	222	258
Ethiopia	1	- 0	8	131	350	135	349	255	465	545	205
Liberia	152	190	37	107	122	21	8	3	372	207	194
Côte d'Ivoire	47	52	86	320	234	235	273	213	165	283	192
Mali	4	0	1	47	136	82	122	244	132	101	159
Ghana	11	7	83	122	118	166	89	59	137	139	156
Mauritania	13	4	7	3	94	40	92	118	214	5	115
Mozambique	1	3	25	160	265	139	255	347	337	245	108
Zimbabwe	2	14	23	167	13	23	4	26	4	9	103
Guinea	- 0	10	16	25	44	10	2	30	83	98	102
Seychelles	10	18	19	46	47	24	65	48	58	37	82
Senegal	14	- 1	27	86	60	63	32	78	52	77	54
Togo	12	10	5	23	50	42	64	53	34	59	49
Madagascar	2	7	16	22	67	83	93	8	95	53	48
Lesotho	4	9	18	29	36	31	28	27	42	53	47
Sierra Leone	0	- 27	5	2	16	39	10	2	3	26	27
Somalia	- 5	- 4	2	1	4	0	0	0	- 1	21	24
Gambia	0	3	11	25	25	44	35	43	- 1	2	24
Mauritius	2	18	22	34	69	266	- 28	32	63	14	24
Djibouti	0	0	1	3	13	3	3	4	14	39	23
Kenya	28	33	18	24	54	111	5	28	82	46	21
Benin	1	13	55	21	45	60	44	14	45	64	21
Burkina Faso	2	2	5	10	18	23	6	15	29	14	19
Cape Verde	..	1	2	26	18	32	9	12	14	20	19
Cameroon	122	70	- 20	- 0	0	- 0	0	0	0	0	18
Niger	15	6	20	6	13	8	23	5	11	20	12
Eritrea	..	..	..	62	15	28	12	20	22	- 8	11
Guinea-Bissau	0	1	3	4	2	1	0	4	4	2	10
Rwanda	16	17	5	3	5	8	4	3	5	8	8
São Tomé and Principe	..	0	- 0	2	2	4	3	3	1	- 2	7
Central African Republic	6	4	- 4	6	0	1	5	6	3	- 13	6
Malawi	9	5	4	21	14	26	34	6	4	- 1	3
Comoros	0	3	0	0	1	0	1	0	1	- 0	1
Burundi	4	1	1	1	2	12	0	0	0	- 2	- 1
Swaziland	10	47	67	52	46	91	51	90	- 61	60	- 14
Angola	75	192	218	930	1 930	879	2 146	1 672	3 505	1 449	- 24
Memorandum											
Africa	1 527	2 876	4 359	8 837	15 636	9 577	19 894	12 999	18 513	17 199	30 672
North Africa	446	1 344	1 663	2 421	4 817	3 456	5 425	3 925	5 376	5 905	12 738
Other Africa	1 081	1 533	2 696	6 416	10 819	6 122	14 469	9 074	13 137	11 294	17 934

/...

Table I.2. Ranking of host countries in Africa, by size of FDI inflows,ᵃ 1980-2005 (concluded)
(Millions of dollars)

Country/group of economies	Annual Average					2000	2001	2002	2003	2004	2005
	1980-1984	1985-1989	1990-1994	1995-1999	2000-2004						
Least developed countries in Africa ᵇ	361	564	704	2 652	6 526	3 036	6 133	5 744	10 037	7 682	8 476
Heavily indebted poor countries in Africa	603	728	899	2 982	6 231	3 511	5 580	5 794	9 222	7 051	7 305
Major pertoleum exporters in Africa ᶜ	- 113	1 003	1 853	2 524	4 889	2 890	4 391	5 089	6 981	5 095	5 424
Major pertoleum exporters in North Africa	- 452	20	89	181	814	579	980	1 210	776	528	1 342
Major pertoleum exporters in Other Africa	339	982	1 764	2 343	4 075	2 311	3 411	3 879	6 205	4 567	4 081
Economic Community of the Great Lakes Countries - CEPGL	11	20	6	10	86	43	86	120	163	21	1 351
Common Market for Eastern and Southern Africa - COMESA	747	1 602	1 411	2 891	5 117	3 829	4 494	4 117	6 524	6 620	10 382
Arab Maghreb Union - UMA	- 116	190	899	1 402	3 046	1 868	4 434	2 683	4 003	2 241	5 173
Economic Community of West African States - ECOWAS	415	978	1 846	2 322	2 687	2 135	1 994	2 813	3 252	3 240	4 442
Southern African Development Community - SADAC	367	316	693	3 591	5 547	3 039	10 361	4 218	6 108	4 007	9 480
Economic Community of Central African States - ECCAS	322	390	286	1 077	3 811	1 272	3 633	3 215	6 344	4 589	4 625
Manu River Union - MRU	152	174	58	133	183	70	20	34	458	331	323
Economic and Monetary Community of Central Africa - CEMAC	237	178	62	135	1 792	347	1 398	1 420	2 676	3 121	3 291
West African Economic and Monetary Union - UEMOA	95	83	203	518	559	514	563	624	473	620	516
East African Countries - EAC	36	36	62	374	678	574	624	642	811	738	753
World	58 748	129 010	201 062	606 884	825 634	1 409 568	832 248	617 732	557 869	710 755	916 277
Developing countries	19 285	23 645	64 108	178 801	220 405	266 823	221 447	163 583	175 138	275 032	334 285
Developed countries	39 453	105 359	135 382	419 217	585 775	1 133 683	599 272	441 238	358 539	396 145	542 312
Least developed countries	406	607	1 356	3 692	7 479	4 067	7 125	6 595	10 868	8 740	9 680
Major pertoleum exporters	5 241	1 882	5 956	11 079	13 649	4 902	8 711	11 326	20 411	22 894	35 738
Heavily indebted poor countries	697	829	2 484	6 389	8 910	6 400	8 336	8 412	11 660	9 742	9 700

Source: UNCTAD, FDI/TNC database (www.unctad.org/fdistatistics).
ᵃ   Ranked on the basis of the magnitude of FDI inflows in 2005.
ᵇ   Least developed countries in Africa are Angola, Benin, Burkina Faso, Burundi, Cape Verde, Central African Republic, Chad, Comoros, Democratic Republic of the Congo, Djibouti, Equatorial Guinea, Eritrea, Ethiopia, Gambia, Guinea, Guinea-Bissau, Lesotho, Liberia, Madagascar, Malawi, Mali, Mauritania, Mozambique, Niger, Rwanda, Samoa, São Tomé and Principe, Senegal, Sierra Leone, Somalia, Sudan, Togo, Uganda, United Republic of Tanzania and Zambia.
ᶜ   Major Petroleum exporters in Africa are Algeria, Angola, Congo, Gabon, Libyan Arab Jamahiriya and Nigeria.

inflows from Europe, Japan or the United States. The other major destinations for FDI from developing Asia are Europe and North America.

Table I.4 suggests that manufacturing and services are of almost equal importance in outward FDI from the Republic of Korea and Thailand. For other Asian developing economies, the largest share of outward FDI is from the services sector, mostly of a trade-supporting nature (trade, finance and business service activities). Investment from the manufacturing sector is heavily biased towards the electronics industry, which accounts for 51 per cent of all outward FDI stock by manufacturing firms from Taiwan Province of China and 26 per cent of that from Thailand. Trade-related investment figures prominently, but FDI by financial services firms is equally important.

2. Asian FDI in Africa

TNCs based in developing Asia have begun to show interest in investing in Africa. Table I.5 shows FDI *stock* in Africa by selected Asian developing economies that are major investors in the continent. Table I.6 shows FDI *flows* to Africa from these economies. Total FDI outflows from developing Asia to Africa were estimated at an annual average of $1.2 billion during 2002-2004 (UNCTAD, 2006). Singapore, India and Malaysia are the top Asian sources of FDI in Africa, with investment stocks of $3.5 billion (accumulative approved flows from 1996 to 2004) and $1.9 billion each by 2004, respectively, followed by China, the Republic of Korea and Taiwan Province of China (table I.5). In the case of the Republic of Korea, since the late 1980s, *chaebols* have also set up

Table I.3. FDI stock in selected African countries, by industry, mid-1990s and latest year available
(Millions of dollars)

Sector/industry	Botswana 1997	Botswana 2003	Egypt 1995	Madagascar 2004	Morocco 2004	Namibia 1990	Namibia 1994	Nigeria 1996	Nigeria 2005	South Africa 1996	South Africa 2004	Swaziland 1988	Swaziland 1993	United Republic of Tanzania 1998	United Republic of Tanzania 2001	Zambia 2001
Total	1 280	1 720	13 355	940	19 883	2 047	1 712	10 910	27 270	12 538	63 071	348	456	3 386	3 777	1 085
Primary	956	1 176	541	86	1 096	1 626	1 312	5 848	20 384	695	19 957	53	58	1 347	1 309	367
Agriculture, hunting, forestry and fishing	-	-	541	26	162	-	-	-	-	76	128	47	52	211	252	127
Mining, quarrying and petroleum	956	1 176	-	60	935	-	-	5 848	20 384	619	19 829	6	6	1 136	1 057	241
Secondary	76	66	6 335	90	6 637	60	90	-	-	5 429	19 779	201	275	814	1 265	144
Food, beverages and tobacco	-	-	-	-	-	-	-	-	-	-	-	-	-	-	413	-
Textiles, clothing and leather	-	-	-	-	-	-	-	-	-	-	-	-	-	-	-	-
Coke, petroleum products and nuclear fuel	-	-	-	-	505	-	-	-	-	-	-	-	-	-	-	-
Chemicals and chemical products	-	-	-	-	-	-	-	-	-	-	-	-	-	-	163	-
Non-metallic mineral products	-	-	-	-	1 012	-	-	-	-	-	-	-	-	-	-	-
Machinery and equipment	-	-	-	-	-	-	-	-	-	-	-	-	-	-	4	-
Motor vehicles and other transport equipment	-	-	-	-	-	-	-	-	-	-	-	-	-	-	-	-
Other manufacturing	-	-	-	-	-	-	-	-	-	-	-	-	-	-	574	-
Tertiary	240	481	6 479	746	10 521	361	310	-	-	6 414	23 335	94	123	1 123	1 202	560
Electricity, gas and water	2	6	-	40	305	-	-	-	-	-	5	-	-	71	127	109
Construction	8	2	565	229	550	-	-	-	-	34	353	-	-	186	101	2
Trade	120	186	-	154	5 724	-	-	-	-	1 627	2 579	-	-	503	93	110
Hotels and restaurants	12	35	1 682	1	1 302	-	-	-	-	-	-	-	-	96	307	45
Transport, storage and communications	9	35	3 472	186	2 042	-	-	-	-	114	2 507	-	-	133	285	15
Finance	71	197	-	84	-	-	-	-	-	4 618	17 800	14	12	133	180	280
Business activities	17	21	-	53	-	-	-	-	-	-	-	-	-	-	45	-
Education	-	-	-	-	-	-	-	-	-	-	-	-	-	-	1	-
Health and social services	1	-	-	-	-	-	-	-	-	-	-	-	-	-	54	-
Community, social and personal service activities	-	-	-	-	-	-	-	-	-	21	92	-	-	3	8	-
Other services	-	-	759	-	600	-	-	-	-	-	-	80	111	-	-	-
Unspecified	8	- 3	-	18	1 628	-	-	5 062	6 885	-	-	-	-	102	1	14

Source: UNCTAD, FDI/TNC database (www.unctad.org/fdistatistics).

Table I.4. Outward FDI stock from selected developing Asian economies, by sector and industry, latest year available
(Millions of dollars)

Sector/industry	China 2005	Hong Kong, China 2004	India[a] 2004	Macao, China 2004	Republic of Korea 2002	Singapore 2002	Taiwan Province of China[b] 2002	Thailand 2004
Total	57 200	403 119	9 631	490	31 102	85 760	34 718	3 407
Primary	9 164	:	:	:	1 846	:	102	75
Agriculture, hunting, forestry and fishing	512	:	:	:	249	:	67	44
Mining, quarrying and petroleum	8 652	:	:	:	1 597	:	35	31
Secondary	5 770	20 392	5 281	14	16 346	17 904	12 457	1 210
Food, beverages and tobacco	:	:	:	:	:	:	491	218
Textiles, clothing and leather	:	:	:	:	:	:	1 066	54
Wood and wood products	:	:	:	:	:	:	480	-
Coke, petroleum products and nuclear fuel	:	:	:	:	:	:	-	3
Chemicals and chemical products	:	:	:	:	:	:	1 660	142
Rubber and plastic products	:	:	:	:	:	:	321	-
Non-metallic mineral products	:	:	:	:	:	:	426	62
Metal and metal products	:	:	:	:	:	:	895	185
Machinery and equipment	:	:	:	:	:	:	73	66
Electrical and electronic equipment	:	:	:	:	:	:	6 303	313
Precision instruments	:	:	:	:	:	:	166	-
Motor vehicles and other transport equipment	:	:	:	:	:	:	576	-
Tertiary	42 266	356 412	3 988	241	12 910	66 810	21 842	2 002
Electricity, gas and water	287	-	-	-	-	-	-	-
Construction	1 204	2 773	468	49	551	410	149	11
Trade	11 418	48 965	-	156	6 923	5 839	3 227	299
Hotels and restaurants	46	6 762	-	-	-	-	1	-
Transport, storage and communications	7 083	29 539	110	6	1 075	7 730	1 345	1 058
Finance	-	20 661	-	29	-	47 247	14 516	199
Business activities	16 554	247 713	-	-	-	5 584	-	-
Community, social and personal service activities	1 323	-	-	-	-	-	2 603	-
Other services	4 351	-	-	-	4 360	-	-	-
Unspecified	-	26 315	362	235	-	1 047	317	121

Source: UNCTAD, FDI/TNC database (www.unctad.org/fdistatistics).

a Based on data for approval flows, accumulated since 1999.
b Based on approved data.

marketing and production facilities abroad, though foreign investments in Africa have been mainly limited to market penetration efforts, largely associated with electrical and electronic products and automobiles. As for Chinese and Indian firms, it is likely that more Korean firms will soon be seeking to secure their own natural resources from Africa. India has long had economic relations with much of Africa, especially East Africa. With continued private-sector-led economic growth since the 1990s, Indian FDI in Africa will likely grow more rapidly in the near future. Much of Indian FDI in the past was linked to investors who had previously resided and invested in the continent (e.g. during the colonial or early post-colonial period). While this type of investment continues, large-scale investments in natural resources are in order. Pakistan is another source of FDI in Africa, although its FDI outflows are relatively small (table I.6). FDI from China and ASEAN will be dealt with in the following chapters.

Among African host economies, South Africa is a large recipient of Asian FDI, but Mauritius is the largest host country for FDI from India and Malaysia. However, Asian investments in Africa are dwarfed by those of the United Kingdom (with a total FDI stock of $30 billion in 2003), the United States ($19 billion in 2003), France ($11.5 billion in 2003) and Germany ($5.5 billion in 2003). Among the developed countries, Japan has relatively little FDI in Africa.

If Asian FDI in Africa is considered by mode of entry, there were 126 known greenfield FDI projects[4] and only 26 cross-border M&A deals during the period 2002-2005. TNCs use greenfield FDI more often than M&As as the mode of investment in developing countries, and especially in Africa (UNCTAD, 2000b). Among the 126 projects mentioned above, Indian companies accounted for the largest number (48 new investments), followed by Chinese companies (32). New investment projects by TNCs from developing Asia were spread over 27 countries (table I.7).

As regards cross-border M&As, a total of 77 deals between Asian TNCs and firms in Africa were recorded during 1987-2005 (table I.8). Malaysian companies have been the most active, accounting for more than 30 per cent of these deals. The largest acquisition of an African firm by an Asian firm was the $1.8 billion purchase of LNG (Egypt) by Petronas (Malaysia) in 2003 (annex table 2).[5]

A large share of FDI from Asia to Africa is located in South Africa (table I.5). However, there are numerous examples of Asian FDI in other African countries as well,[6] particularly in South Africa's neighbouring countries (e.g. Botswana; see chapter IV). Asian FDI in Africa declined soon after the 1997-1998 financial crisis, but it has been increasing again recently. There is no systematic data on Asian FDI in Africa by industry. Data on cross-border M&As and greenfield investments show that while recent investments are in the oil and gas industry, there are small investments in various industries such as foods and textiles in the manufacturing sector, and finance and business services in the services sector (annex tables 6-10). As these examples indicate, there is a growing interest of firms from Asian developing economies in investment opportunities in Africa.

3. FDI in Africa by Asian SMEs

FDI by SMEs has been dynamic, providing evidence of the role that it can play in development (Fujita, 1998). Small and medium-sized TNCs can supplement large TNCs in the international transfer and development of productive resources, capacity and capabilities. On the other hand, for SMEs with the necessary competitive advantages for investing abroad, FDI has become an integral part of corporate growth strategies. Developing countries should hence pay more attention to foreign SMEs as potential sources of investment.

Asian SMEs, like Asian firms in general, have traditionally taken several steps – such as exporting and licensing – towards internationalization before they invest abroad (UNCTAD, 1998). However, many high-technology SMEs based in developed countries produce abroad without necessarily first gaining international experience. Many such SMEs thus undertake FDI at an earlier stage of firm growth. Some have even developed international operations from the first year of their existence. This could mean that developing countries hosting their operations will be able to reap the benefits from pioneering technologies of such foreign SMEs within a relatively shorter time frame.

In Asia, only Japan and the Republic of Korea publish statistics on outward FDI by SMEs. Japanese small and medium-sized TNCs account for a significant share of that country's FDI, representing more than half the total number of

Table I.5. FDI stock in Africa from selected developing Asian economies
(Millions of dollars)

Region/country	China 1990[a]	China 2005	India[b] 1996	India[b] 2004	Malaysia 1991	Malaysia 2004	Pakistan 1990	Pakistan 2004	Republic of Korea 1995	Republic of Korea 2002	Singapore 1999	Singapore 2003	Taiwan Province of China[a] 1990	Taiwan Province of China[a] 2002
Africa	49.2	1 595.3	296.6	1 968.6	1.1	1 880.1	84.9	93.0	265.1	480.5	2 076.2	3 508.9	25.9	224.0
North Africa	3.4	618.4	32.5	974.5	-	416.9	18.1	58.5	248.3	349.0	..	..	..	..
Algeria	0.4	171.2	-	-	-	-	-	-	75.8	102.8	..	..	..	..
Egypt	1.8	39.8	-	-	-	93.8	-	-	50.5	102.3	..	..	..	..
Libyan Arab Jamahiriya	1.0	33.1	-	30.0	-	-	18.1	58.5	-	-	..	..	..	..
Morocco	0.2	20.6	32.5	32.5	-	2.3	-	-	2.1	39.3	..	..	..	..
Sudan	-	351.5	-	912.0	-	320.8	-	-	119.7	104.5	..	..	..	..
Tunisia	-	2.2	-	-	-	-	-	-	0.1	0.1	..	..	..	..
Other Africa	45.9	976.9	264.1	994.1	1.1	1 463.2	66.9	34.5	16.8	131.5	2 076.2	3 508.9	25.9	224.0
Angola	..	8.8	..	..	..	..	..	..	..	..	..	..	..	..
Botswana	..	18.1	..	..	..	..	..	..	..	..	..	..	..	..
Burkina Faso	0.0	..	..	..	..	..	..	..	..	..	..	..	..	..
Burundi	0.6	..	..	..	..	..	..	..	..	..	..	..	..	..
Cameroon	0.5	7.9	..	..	..	0.3	..	..	1.2	0.7	..	..	..	..
Cape Verde	..	0.6	..	..	..	..	..	..	..	..	..	..	..	..
Central African Republic	1.2	2.0	..	..	..	..	..	..	0.6	0.6	..	..	..	..
Chad	0.1	2.7	..	..	..	187.6	..	..	..	..	..	..	..	..
Congo	..	13.3	..	..	..	..	..	..	..	..	..	..	..	..
Congo, Democratic Rep. of	..	25.1	..	..	..	..	..	..	..	..	..	..	..	..
Côte d'Ivoire	0.6	29.1	..	..	..	..	..	..	0.4	36.3	..	..	..	..
Equatorial Guinea	..	16.6	..	..	..	..	..	..	..	..	..	..	..	..
Ethiopia	..	29.8	..	..	..	..	..	..	..	0.6	..	..	..	..
Gabon	2.9	35.4	..	..	..	19.7	..	..	..	..	..	..	..	..
Gambia	0.5	1.2	..	..	..	..	..	..	..	..	..	..	..	..
Ghana	..	7.3	..	..	..	55.3	..	..	0.1	1.9	..	..	..	..
Guinea	..	44.2	..	..	..	13.2	..	..	..	..	..	..	..	..
Guinea-Bissau	4.2	..	..	..	..	..	..	..	..	..	..	..	..	..
Kenya	0.5	58.3	..	..	..	0.3	..	..	1.5	2.0	..	..	..	..
Lesotho	0.6	..	..	..	..	..	..	..	..	..	..	..	..	..
Liberia	..	15.9	..	..	..	4.5	..	..	..	..	..	..	7.9	131.8
Madagascar	1.7	49.9	..	..	..	0.3	..	..	..	..	..	..	..	..
Malawi	..	0.7	..	..	..	3.3	..	..	..	..	..	..	..	..
Mali	0.0	13.3	..	..	..	..	..	..	..	..	..	..	..	..
Mauritania	..	2.4	..	..	..	..	..	..	..	..	..	..	..	..
Mauritius	6.3	26.8	221.6	948.9	1.1	618.7	..	..	..	..	2 076.2	3 508.9	..	..
Mozambique	0.1	14.7	..	..	..	9.1	..	..	..	..	..	..	..	..
Namibia	..	2.4	..	..	..	90.5	..	..	..	..	..	..	..	..
Niger	0.1	20.4	..	..	..	..	..	..	..	..	..	..	..	..
Nigeria	6.7	94.1	..	..	..	..	0.5	1.5	1.8	12.0	..	..	..	..
Rwanda	2.9	4.7	..	..	..	..	..	..	..	..	..	..	..	..
Senegal	0.2	2.4	22.2	22.2	..	..	..	..	0.4	0.5	..	..	..	..
Seychelles	..	4.2	..	..	..	0.3	..	..	..	..	..	..	..	..
Sierra Leone	1.1	18.4	..	..	..	..	..	..	..	..	..	..	..	..
South Africa	..	112.3	20.2	23.0	..	456.2	..	..	8.8	73.5	..	..	14.3	29.6
Swaziland	..	..	..	..	..	..	..	..	1.4	1.3	..	..	..	..
Togo	0.2	4.8	..	..	..	..	..	..	..	..	..	..	..	..
Uganda	..	5.0	..	..	..	..	..	..	..	..	..	..	..	..
United Republic of Tanzania	1.7	62.0	..	..	..	3.9	..	..	0.6	2.1	..	..	..	..
Zaire	7.6	..	..	..	..	..	..	..	..	..	..	..	..	..
Zambia	3.2	160.3	..	..	..	..	..	..	..	..	..	..	..	..
Zimbabwe	2.5	41.6	..	..	..	0.3	..	..	..	..	..	..	..	..
Total world	1 029	57 200	3 139	11 039	3 043	41 508	245	794	10 226	31 102	55 654	90 242	3 076	34 718

Source: UNCTAD, FDI/TNC database (www.unctad.org/fdistatistics).
[a] Based on approved data.
[b] Based on data for approval flows, accumulated since 1996.

Table I.6. FDI flows to Africa from selected Asian developing economies, 1990-2004
(Millions of dollars)

Year	China[a]	India[a]	Malaysia	Pakistan	Republic of Korea	Taiwan Province of China[a]	France	Germany	United Kingdom	United States
									Memorandum	
1990	..	..	..	5.0	24.1	13.0	5.5	- 284.5	348.0	- 450.0
1991	1.5	..	1.1	4.2	15.9	4.5	533.7	585.7	1 068.8	85.0
1992	7.7	..	12.6	8.2	27.7	16.9	143.4	529.8	523.0	305.0
1993	14.5	..	6.6	7.0	28.7	0.4	871.9	140.8	392.9	837.0
1994	28.0	..	36.2	5.5	111.1	18.7	327.6	97.6	500.4	762.0
1995	17.7	..	72.3	6.9	38.4	28.8	259.0	319.3	1 115.7	352.0
1996	..	..	496.0	5.8	8.1	20.9	740.1	314.5	875.2	1 678.0
1997	..	..	147.5	5.5	87.7	..	596.4	801.9	1 019.9	3 436.0
1998	..	..	77.5	4.4	81.2	36.2	..	1 362.7	- 41.4	3 075.0
1999	42.3	..	222.2	3.9	19.9	41.3	901.3	463.4	1 901.1	596.0
2000	85.0	243.3	77.7	4.3	23.8	7.0	1 300.9	651.4	2 119.7	716.0
2001	24.5	184.8	49.4	4.1	14.3	6.1	1 796.0	- 259.5	1 658.4	2 438.0
2002	30.1	883.4	340.1	2.1	- 6.5	17.4	855.4	- 328.4	3 291.3	- 578.0
2003	60.8	338.4	411.0	0.1	..	..	1 095.9	- 319.4	5 639.4	2 697.0
2004	..	22.1	175.6	- 0.1	..	..	1 028.1	181.3	10 588.1	1 325.0

Source: UNCTAD, FDI/TNC database (www.unctad.org/fdistatistics).
[a] Based on approval data.

Table I.7. Greenfield FDI projects in Africa by firms from selected Asian developing economies, 2002-2005
(Number)

Source economy	Number of projects	Destination country	Number of projects
India	48	Egypt	20
China	32	South Africa	19
Korea, Republic of	11	Nigeria	14
Malaysia	11	Mauritius	11
Singapore	5	Kenya	10
Indonesia	4	Sudan	7
Viet Nam	4	Morocco	6
Hong Kong, China	3	Algeria	5
Taiwan Province of China	3	Angola	4
Thailand	2	United Republic of Tanzania	4
Pakistan	1	Libyan Arab Jamahiriya	3
Philippines	1	Zambia	3
Sri Lanka	1	Ethiopia	2
Total Asia	**126**	Madagascar	2
		Seychelles	2
		Swaziland	2
		Uganda	2
		Gambia	1
		Ghana	1
		Mozambique	1
		Namibia	1
		Niger	1
		Rwanda	1
		Senegal	1
		Sierra Leone	1
		Tunisia	1
		Zimbabwe	1
		Total Africa	**126**

Source: UNCTAD, based on the data from LOCO Monitor, OCO Consulting (www.locomonitor.com).

overseas Japanese equity investments. During the period 1989-1998 (the latest year for which data are available), Japanese SMEs made 6,959 investments abroad, but only 12 were in Africa, mainly in non-manufacturing activities.[7] SME FDI from the Republic of Korea accounted for one third of the value of that country's outward FDI during 2000-2004, with an annual average value of $2.4 billion.

A number of industries in Asian countries are dominated by SMEs. A very high proportion of enterprises in economies such as the Republic of Korea, Singapore and Taiwan Province of China are SMEs, and they account for 40 to 60 per cent of output (UNCTAD, 1998). This implies an important reservoir of productive resources which could benefit other developing countries that are trying to promote local SMEs. In many developing countries, local SMEs play a less important role than they do in the leading East Asian NIEs. Thus FDI by Asian SMEs could play a dynamic complementary role in those countries, similar to their role in their home economies. However at present, FDI by SMEs, including Asian SMEs, in other developing countries remains limited.

Table I.8. Cross-border M&As in Africa by firms from selected developing Asian economies, 1987-2005
(Cumulative number of deals)

Host/home economy	Brunei Darussalam	China	Hong Kong, China	India	Indonesia	Malaysia	Pakistan	Philippines	Republic of Korea	Singapore	Thailand	Asia total
Cameroon	-	-	-	-	-	-	-	-	-	1	-	1
Egypt	-	-	-	3	-	2	-	-	2	1	-	8
Ghana	-	-	-	-	-	2	-	-	-	-	-	2
Guinea	-	-	-	-	-	1	-	-	-	-	-	1
Libyan Arab Jamahiriya	-	-	-	1	-	1	-	-	-	-	-	2
Madagascar	1	-	-	-	-	1	-	-	-	-	-	2
Mauritius	-	-	-	1	3	3	-	-	-	7	-	14
Mayotte	-	-	-	-	-	1	-	-	-	-	-	1
Morocco	-	-	-	-	-	-	-	-	2	-	-	2
Namibia	-	-	-	-	-	-	-	-	-	-	1	1
Seychelles	-	-	-	1	-	-	-	-	-	-	-	1
South Africa	-	-	5	3	1	12	1	1	1	3	-	27
Sudan	-	1	1	3	-	1	-	-	2	-	-	8
Uganda	-	1	-	-	-	1	-	-	-	-	-	2
United Republic of Tanzania	-	1	-	-	-	-	-	-	1	-	-	2
Zambia	-	-	-	3	-	-	-	-	-	-	-	3
Africa total	**1**	**3**	**6**	**15**	**4**	**25**	**1**	**1**	**8**	**12**	**1**	**77**

Source: UNCTAD, cross-border M&A database.

D.   WHY IS ASIAN FDI IN AFRICA LOW?

Firms from developing Asian economies face several constraints when investing abroad, and particularly in Africa:

- Outward FDI from developing Asia is still a relatively recent phenomenon, even if it increased at a fast pace. A number of firms from that region still face technological constraints in complex manufacturing activities and advanced services such as infrastructure development, communications, merchant banking or the media. However, some firms – especially from Hong Kong (China), Singapore, the Republic of Korea and Taiwan Province of China – that have built up the necessary competitive advantages to operate in foreign locations and have managed to become leading companies do invest abroad in manufacturing and more advanced services, as well as in trade-related activities (UNCTAD, 2006).

- For Asian investors, transaction and information costs, including those related to knowledge of local markets, cultures and conditions may appear to be higher when investing in Africa than in other places. Compared with European investors, who have relatively stronger linkages with African countries because of historical, geographic and language ties, Asian investors have to overcome higher barriers for investing in Africa.

- Most developing Asian country FDI is intra-regional. Firms tend to look for opportunities closer afield because of familiarity etc.; market seeking FDI is the most common and Africa does not generally have the types of markets most Asian firms are orientated to; much Asian FDI is also efficiency seeking which means that companies are looking for relatively skilled workers, good infrastructure (which Africa can improve) and there is a big difference between garments and electronics (so Asian FDI in the latter is very unlikely to go to Africa). However, (natural) resources motivated FDI is changing the picture a little. And the case of Malaysia shows that South-South FDI can be encouraged more widely, e.g. in infrastructure (chapter II).

- Both host- and home-country regulatory frameworks can constrain the expansion of FDI. African governments have greatly liberalized their inward FDI regimes, though some restrictions remain. Most Asian economies have begun to liberalize their outward FDI regimes only recently, although some have gone quite far in this respect and have even begun to promote outward FDI through various measures (UNCTAD, 2006).

Despite these constraints, there are certain pull and push factors that suggest a potential for more Asian FDI into Africa. The pull factors primarily need to be better recognized by Asian firms and governments. These include: access to an under-served market, which in the case of many goods and services may require a direct presence to be effective; location-specific advantages to access natural resources as well as cheap and abundant labour; investment opportunities in infrastructure and other government contracts; and the possibility to forge closer relations with African firms so as to exploit better the markets and resources that Africa offers. Indeed, profitability investment in Africa is not low compared to other regions (figure I.4; UNCTAD, 1999b).

The developing economies of Asia, with the exception of China, have not effectively reached most African markets through exports. While China is becoming an important exporter to Africa, total merchandise exports from developing Asia to Africa, worth $22 billion ($35 billion including China), were not much higher in 2004 than that of a single country, France ($24 billion) (IMF, 2005a). Successful exporting can lead to FDI in ways that complement trade, but developing Asia's FDI in Africa has hardly been driven by trade. Whether complementary to trade or not, FDI can result in the improved competitiveness of both investors and domestic firms through a more efficient allocation of resources, by providing technology and market feedback, and allowing the upgrading of domestic operations. But this virtuous circle has not so far developed with Asian FDI in Africa.

As regards SMEs, some of the major constraints to FDI faced by these firms are related to problems internal to the firms themselves such as management skills, host country conditions (e.g. market and infrastructure problems); or barriers created or allowed to persist by governments. In spite of liberalization policies in many African countries, regulatory impediments due to institutional or administrative factors or corruption remain serious problems in some of them. These problems are regarded as major deterrents particularly by SMEs, because such firms can less afford to be burdened by additional costs than large firms. Cultural differences are another major problem. SMEs often cannot afford the costs needed to address cultural and linguistic difficulties; moreover, their information requirements are relatively large because of their

limited international experience. Limited infrastructure is another constraint for SME investors in developing countries. Often, the most problematic are the telecommunications and transportation systems. Finally, finding suitable partners and access to reasonably priced finance are additional problems faced by SMEs.

Figure I.4. Profitability of Japanese and United States FDI, by region[a], 1983-2002

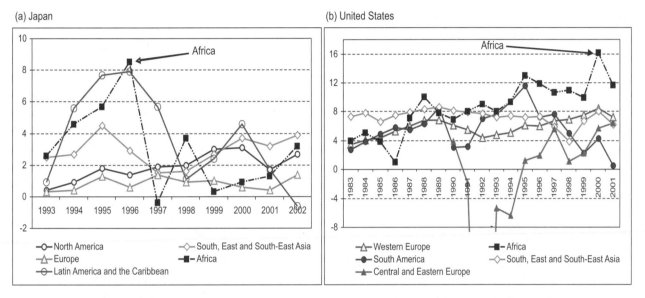

Source: UNCTAD, based on data from Japan, Ministry of Economy, Trade and Industry and United States, Department of Commerce.
[a] For Japan, ratio of current profit to sales of Japanese foreign affiliates and for the United States ratio of income to sales of United States foreign affiliates.

E. WHY AND HOW TO PROMOTE ASIAN FDI IN AFRICA

1. Why promote Asian FDI in Africa?

The recent increase in Asian FDI flows to Africa (table I.6) suggests a departure from earlier behaviour of Asian TNCs and implicitly confirms Africa's potential for Asian investors.

Increasing investment from Asia could bring benefits to both regions. Asian countries have shown a higher propensity to save than other regions, and prospects for continuing high rates of income growth are good. In 2005, 38 per cent of GDP was saved in developing Asia (IMF, 2006b: table 43). Furthermore, in many Asian countries savings exceed investments, implying abundant surplus savings available for investment, including abroad,[8] some of which could go to Africa. In exchange, Africa offers a wealth of natural resources, while its largely under-served markets provide investment opportunities for Asian firms. Increasing FDI flows also promote trade by

opening and expanding market opportunities. Governments in both Asia and Africa should therefore consider working to facilitate such investments.

2. Policies to enhance Asian FDI in Africa

What are the policy implications from a greater recognition of the benefits from Asian FDI in Africa and of the need to increase such FDI? Increasing Asian FDI in Africa requires, first and foremost, efforts by the enterprises themselves. Ultimately, the success of firms in establishing a stronger position in the region depends on the firms recognizing the opportunities that exist and on their elaborating strategies that allow them to tap these opportunities. Such strategies should also enable them to participate constructively in Africa's development. While action by governments cannot be a substitute for initiatives by Asian firms, public policies and institutional measures also have a very important role to play in creating a conducive legal and regulatory framework for capital flows between Asia and Africa.

In Africa, efforts need to focus on addressing fundamental economic and social problems as well as regulatory and other obstacles to investment. In Asia, the environment for investment abroad is becoming increasingly favourable as regulatory regimes become more liberalized, and governments take greater initiatives to promote outward FDI.

(a) Policies in Africa

African governments have taken a number of steps towards improving their image and offering increased incentives and institutional support to foreign firms investing in their countries. Investment promotion agencies (IPAs) in African countries provide information and initial contacts as well as other initial support. With the possible exception of large TNCs, firms, in particular SMEs, typically do not have sufficient information about investment opportunities in Africa, and contacts with domestic companies in the region are fairly limited. IPA programmes can thus be particularly valuable, as they help firms evaluate prospects for FDI.

The steady liberalization of investment regimes in Africa has contributed to increased FDI flows to African countries. Additional efforts are under way to further liberalize investment regimes, reduce market distortions, simplify procedures and disseminate information about progress made and investment opportunities available. National efforts to improve the investment climate of African economies could further benefit from regional arrangements, such as the Southern African Development Community (SADC), that increase the regional market size as well as the predictability, stability and transparency of the environment for investment in Africa. Efforts should also be considered to coordinate, and thus limit, excessive competition when providing incentives for FDI.

Failure to move rapidly on economic and social policies important for sustained development, and a weak emphasis on capacity building, have hampered the ability of many countries in the region to attract FDI, in particular in manufacturing. International market-access measures and initiatives targeting African countries

(such as the United States' African Growth and Opportunity Act) generally have not been very successful, thus far, in increasing FDI. In order to realize the potential for increased FDI and to derive greater benefits from it, African countries in general need to develop stronger industrial and technological capabilities. The need for international support to Africa's development has been stressed in several recent initiatives. For example, UNCTAD undertakes in-depth Investment Policy Reviews (IPRs) to help improve national FDI regimes.[9] The Commission for Africa (established by the United Kingdom) released a report in March 2005 recommending a substantial increase in aid to Africa. The report also supports an Investment Climate Facility for Africa under the New Economic Partnership for Africa's Development (NEPAD) initiative and the creation of a fund that would provide insurance to foreign investors in post-conflict countries in Africa.

(b) Policies in developing Asia

Asian FDI in Africa has been growing, but needs to be further nurtured, especially since most Asian firms have little or no experience in investing abroad. Again, governments have a role to play. Until the 1997-1998 financial crisis, there was a trend towards liberalization of outward FDI from developing Asian economies (as part of a broader, market-based, outward-oriented development strategy). More recently, as the economies have recovered from the effects of the crisis, this trend has accelerated. The process needs to take into account national development objectives, among various considerations and constraints. Where these constraints involve balance-of-payments effects of outward FDI, there are a number of ways to deal with them, including the application of approval procedures and various criteria.

Besides liberalization of capital outflows for FDI, a number of Asian governments have begun to assist their outward investors, but much more can be done in this respect. The principal areas of assistance are education, training and orientation programmes; provision of information services; providing contacts and promoting partnerships; and financial assistance. For example, Korean Trade Organization assists Korean firms in investing abroad, including Africa; Malaysian South-South Cooperation Berhad promotes bilateral trade and investment by serving as a platform and link between Malaysian firms and other developing country, including African, firms (chapter II for China; chapter III for ASEAN; UNCTAD, 2006; World Bank, 2004).

(c) Towards joint action

Asian and African governments could benefit from further cooperation or joint action in a number of areas. This applies for instance in the area of bilateral investment treaties agreements (BITs) or for the promotion and protection of FDI and double taxation treaties (DTTs), the most important elements in the international framework for FDI at present. As of 1 January 2006, all 53 African countries had concluded at least one BIT, and in total they had concluded 775 BITs. However, only 36 African countries had concluded with countries in South, East and South-East Asia totalling 90 (table I.9).

In the case of DTTs, 45 African countries had concluded 491 treaties by the beginning of 2006. However, only 19 countries had such treaties with developing South, East and South-East Asian economies totalling 50; 10 of which were between Mauritius alone and the Asian economies (table I.10).

At the national level, efforts to increase FDI flows from Asia to Africa could also benefit from active and practical cooperation between institutions in both these regions. Although limited in its regional coverage, the establishment of the Indian Ocean Rim Association for Regional Cooperation in 1995 points to growing interest in promoting trade and investment among participating countries in developing Asia and Africa. The declaration on a New Asian-African Strategic Partnership adopted in the Asian-African Summit in 2005 emphasizes the need to promote economic cooperation including investment. There are also several government initiatives to promote cooperation in China (chapter III), India (i.e. Focus Africa programme[10]) and other Asian countries (chapter II). At the firm level, actions to strengthen the relationship between Asian investors and domestic firms in Africa could contribute to increasing the benefits from FDI in host African economies (box I.1). Governments in both continents can help forge and strengthen such linkages.

In conclusion, over the next decade, increased globalization, made possible by rapid technological development and liberalization of investment and trade regimes, will further globalize economic activities and intensify competition. Developing Asia can be expected to remain the world's fastest growing region in terms of industrial production, investment flows and exports. Asian developing economies are not only major and growing markets, but also efficient producers, many of which have become global providers of a wide range of products, including products involving advanced technologies. For Africa, which remains a relatively untapped market with the potential to absorb more goods and services, this means additional sources of funds, technologies and competence to tap. Abundant natural resources could be used to develop capacity to industrialize. Greater investment by firms from Asia, in the context of increased economic cooperation, can only mutually enhance growth in both Asia and Africa.

Table I.9. Bilateral treaties for the promotion of FDI between South, East and South-East Asia and Africa, as of 1 January 2006

Partner / Region/economy[a]	South, East and South-east Asia	Brunei Darussalam	China	India	Indonesia	Korea, Democratic People's Rep. of	Korea, Republic of	Malaysia	Mongolia	Nepal	Pakistan	Singapore	Sri Lanka	Taiwan Province of China	Thailand	Viet Nam	Developing economies	Developed countries	Total world
Algeria	5		X		X		X	X								X	18	13	33
Angola	-																1	4	5
Benin	1		X														8	5	13
Botswana	2		X					X									6	2	8
Burkina Faso	2						X	X									9	4	13
Burundi	-																2	3	5
Cameroon	1		X														6	7	14
Cape Verde	1		X														3	6	9
Central African Republic	-																1	3	4
Chad	-																8	4	12
Comoros	-																5	1	6
Congo	1		X														3	6	9
Congo, Democratic Republic of	2		X					X									5	7	12
Côte d' Ivoire	1		X														3	7	10
Djibouti	3		X	X				X									4	1	5
Egypt	12		X	X	X	X	X	X	X			X	X	X		X	X	58	26	98
Equatorial Guinea	1		X														3	2	5
Eritrea	-																1	2	3
Ethiopia	2		X					X									11	9	21
Gabon	1		X														5	7	13
Gambia	-																1	3	4
Ghana	3		X	X				X									15	7	25
Guinea	2		X					X									14	3	18
Guinea-Bissau	-																-	1	1
Kenya	1		X														1	4	5
Lesotho	-																-	3	3
Liberia	-																-	4	4
Libyan Arab Jamahiriya	-																5	6	15
Madagascar	1		X														2	6	8
Malawi	2							X					X				4	2	6
Mali	1				X												10	3	13
Mauritania	1						X										11	4	16
Mauritius	6		X	X	X						X	X	X				26	8	35
Morocco	6		X	X	X		X	X			X						31	18	53
Mozambique	2		X		X												9	11	20
Namibia	2							X								X	3	8	11
Niger	-																3	2	5
Nigeria	3		X				X							X			7	9	19
Rwanda	-																1	3	4
Senegal	3						X	X						X			11	8	20
Seychelles	-																-	1	1
Sierra Leone	1		X														1	2	3
Somalia	-																1	1	2
South Africa	3	X	X				X										18	16	34
Sudan	4		X	X	X			X									17	6	25
Swaziland	1													X			3	2	5
São Tomé and Principe	-																-	1	1
Tanzania, United Republic of	1						X										4	8	12
Togo	-																1	2	3
Tunisia	4		X		X		X				X						27	19	49
Uganda	1		X														8	8	16
Zambia	1		X														4	7	12
Zimbabwe	6		X	X	X		X				X				X		16	11	29
Africa	90	1	28	7	8	2	11	14	1	1	4	3	1	4	2	3	414	316	775

Source: UNCTAD, database on BITS.

[a] Only those countries with which African countries have concluded a treaty have been listed.

Note: Some countries concluded twice with their partner country. Therefore the totals of individual countries do not necessarily add up.

Table I.10. Double taxation treaties between South, East and South-East Asia and Africa, as of 1 January 2006

Partner / Region/economy[a]	South, East and South-east Asia	China	India	Indonesia	Korea, Democratic People's Rep. of	Korea, Republic of	Malaysia	Mongolia	Nepal	Pakistan	Philippines	Singapore	Sri Lanka	Taiwan Province of China	Thailand	Viet Nam	Developing economies	Developed countries	Total world
Algeria	1															X	14	8	25
Benin	-																-	2	2
Botswana	-																3	3	6
Burkina Faso	-																1	1	2
Cameroon	-																1	3	4
Cape Verde	-																-	1	1
Central African Republic	-																-	1	1
Chad	-																1	-	1
Comoros	-																-	1	1
Congo	-																-	3	3
Congo, Democratic Republic of	-																1	1	2
Côte d' Ivoire	-																1	8	9
Egypt	7	X	X	X	X	X	X	X									17	23	48
Eritrea	-																1	-	1
Ethiopia	-																5	2	7
Gabon	-																2	2	4
Gambia	1													X			1	6	7
Ghana	-																1	7	8
Guinea	-																-	-	1
Kenya	1		X														2	9	11
Lesotho	-																3	2	5
Liberia	-																-	4	4
Libyan Arab Jamahiriya	2		X							X							4	1	5
Madagascar	-																1	1	2
Malawi	-																1	7	8
Mali	-																1	1	2
Mauritania	-																2	1	3
Mauritius	10	X	X	X			X		X	X		X	X		X		26	10	38
Morocco	2		X			X											14	23	40
Mozambique	-																2	1	3
Namibia	1						X										3	4	7
Niger	-																-	1	1
Nigeria	2									X	X						2	11	14
Senegal	1													X			9	4	13
Seychelles	4	X		X											X	X	7	3	10
Sierra Leone	1		X														1	3	4
South Africa	6	X				X								X	X		29	34	68
Sudan	3	X				X	X										10	1	11
Swaziland	-																3	2	5
Tanzania, United Republic of	1		X														4	6	10
Togo	-																1	1	2
Tunisia	4	X		X		X				X							22	23	46
Uganda	1		X														5	8	13
Zambia	1		X														5	14	19
Zimbabwe	1						X										3	9	14
Africa	50	7	9	5	1	5	5	1	1	4	1	1	1	4	3	2	209	256	491

Source: UNCTAD, database on DTTS.

[a] Only those countries with which African countries have concluded a treaty have been listed.

Note: Some countries concluded twice with their partner country. Therefore the totals of individual countries do not necessarily add up.

Box I.1. Promoting linkages between Asian investors and African SMEs

A programme to promote linkages between affiliates of Asian TNCs in Africa and African domestic firms could contribute significantly towards enhancing the benefits of Asian FDI for African host economies. The overall objective of the programme would be to promote mutually beneficial and sustainable Asian TNC-African SME linkages with a view to enhancing local productive capacity, efficiency and competitiveness of the domestic enterprise sector. SMEs have the potential to become the backbone of local economies in most African countries. Judging from experience in other regions, these enterprises can serve as vehicles for accelerating economic growth and for generating productive jobs, foreign exchange and tax revenues. The most likely benefits for SMEs from stronger linkages with TNCs are increases in output, revenue and employment. The effects on supplier capabilities through skill and technology upgrading are probably even more important. Linkages can be powerful channels for diffusing knowledge and skills between firms. To achieve these linkages, however, SMEs often need assistance to prepare them for partnerships.

Inter-firm cooperation nearly always entails an exchange of information, technical knowledge and skills. Strong linkages with affiliates of competitive Asian firms can promote production efficiency, productivity growth, technological and managerial capabilities and market diversification. The strengthening of suppliers can in turn have various indirect effects and spillovers for the rest of the host economy. Spillovers can take place through demonstration effects, mobility of trained labour, enterprise spin-offs and competition effects.

Another advantage of linkages between Asian foreign affiliates and domestic firms is that they increase the local integration and "rooting" of Asian TNCs and make them less footloose. Since backward linkages involve cost and effort by affiliates, stronger linkages make it more difficult for them to divest. Moreover, Asian TNCs' linkages with African SMEs can promote the formation and upgrading of industrial clusters in host economies, an important component of competitiveness.

However, experience shows that one of the major problems in forging backward linkages – and therefore in attracting quality FDI – is the absence of local enterprises which are considered ready to enter into partnerships with foreign affiliates. TNCs are normally in a strong position to choose their supplier counterparts. The decision to source locally in a host country depends on the cost, quality, reliability and flexibility of local suppliers relative to suppliers abroad. Local enterprises in host developing countries normally remain de-linked from foreign affiliates because they cannot meet international standards on crucial production issues, such as price, quality and delivery, and corporate requirements in terms of consistency/continuity and volumes of production. Another reason for weak linkages is that local enterprises do not know how to link with foreign affiliates even when able to meet the strict standards such as product quality required by foreign affiliates. As for foreign affiliates, they may not know of the existence of partnership-ready SMEs and could miss out on opportunities to create backward linkages with domestic enterprises.

Many TNCs, including Asian ones, have special supplier-development programmes to create and deepen linkages by actively finding suppliers and upgrading them through technology transfer, provision of training, sharing business information and contacts and facilitating access to finance. These programmes can be emulated by other TNCs. However, linkages do not necessarily happen automatically, and bridging the potentially complementary but still distant worlds of TNCs and SMEs may require special efforts. African and Asian governments, in partnership with TNCs, SMEs, and private business service providers, can intervene to encourage the creation and deepening of backward linkages by lowering the costs (e.g. subsidizing training costs) and increasing the rewards (e.g. reducing taxable income, lowering tax rates) of linkage formation for both TNCs and local SMEs.

Source: UNCTAD.

Notes

1 According to the UN classification, East Asia comprises China, Hong Kong (China), Democratic People's Republic of Korea, the Republic of Korea, Macao (China), Mongolia and Taiwan Province of China, and South-East Asia comprises 10 countries of the Association of Southeast Asia Nations (ASEAN) (Brunei Darussalam, Cambodia, Indonesia, Lao People's Democratic Republic, Malaysia, Myanmar, Philippines, Singapore, Thailand and Viet Nam).

2 The share of developing countries as a whole in world FDI outflows was 16 per cent and 11 per cent, respectively, in those two periods.

3 The acquisition of ABSA (South Africa) by an international bank group led by Barclays Bank (United Kingdom).

4 This relates to investment in new facilities and the establishment of new entities through entry as well as expansion as opposed to M&As, which refer to acquisitions of, or mergers with, existing local firms. The data on greenfield investment projects are available from the LOCOmonitor database (www.locomonitor.com).

5 This Malaysian company had already spent $725 million in 1996 and 1997 to purchase a controlling stake in Engen, a large South African oil refinery. Telekom Malaysia formed a consortium with United States-based SBC International to acquire a 30 per cent stake (for about $1.3 billion) in 1997 in the privatized South African Telekom.

6 Examples include the following: in 2005, Maxis Communications Bhd (Malaysia) purchased Global Commun Svcs Hldgs Ltd. in Mauritius for $75 million. In recent years there were several large acquisitions of oil and gas companies by ONGC (India) (annex table 1). There are slso examples in the 1990s, Hyundai (Republic of Korea) began building a new assembly plant in Botswana in 1996 to make vehicles for the African

market (which later failed). The JR Group (Hong Kong, China) is planning to expand into the Seychelles tourism industry and to set up an offshore bank there. Telekom Malaysia purchased a 30 per cent stake in Ghana Telecom (though it pulled out later). In addition, agreements were signed in 1996 between Malaysian firms and Ghana in activities as diverse as hotels, banking, television broadcasting, real estate and oil palm development, aimed at attracting FDI in joint ventures or in wholly foreign-owned projects in Ghana. Furthermore, in order to facilitate greater investments, Ghana and Malaysia accorded each other most-favoured-nation (MFN) status, and Ghana waived visa requirements for Malaysians. PRC Trading of Huang Gu (China) established a brewery in Accra in 1996, and another Chinese firm has expressed interest in processing cocoa in Ghana for export to Asia.

7 Information from Japan's Ministry of Economy, Trade and Industry, Small and Medium Enterprise Agency.

8 The surplus of (private) savings over (private) investments was 6.1 per cent of GDP in Asian NIEs (and 3.6 per cent in Japan) in 2005 (IMF, 2006b, table 43).

9 The IPRs assess a country's potential in attracting FDI and the effect of policies on the competitiveness of a country. They provide policy recommendations that are concise, practical and geared for implementation by decision makers. They also include proposals for coherent technical assistance and follow-up. To date, they have been completed in Algeria (2004), Benin (2005), Botswana (2003), Egypt (1999), Ethiopia (2002), Ghana (2003), Mauritius (2001), Lesotho (2003), Uganda (2000) and the United Republic of Tanzania (2002).

10 The Government of India in its Exim (Export-Import Bank) Policy of 2002-07 launched the "FOCUS AFRICA" to increase Indian export to the Sub-Saharan Africa region. This programme is specially designed and launched in order to tap the tremendous potential of export growth in this region. It covers seven African countries (Nigeria, South Africa, Mauritius, Kenya, Ethiopia, United Republic of Tanzania and Ghana).

CHAPTER II

FDI IN AND FROM SOUTH-EAST ASIA: POLICIES, EXPERIENCE AND RELEVANCE FOR AFRICA

As shown in chapter I, South-East Asia has been an important home subregion in Asia for FDI in Africa. This chapter first provides an overview of recent trends in FDI outflows from South-East Asia to Africa, covering some newly industrializing economies (NIEs), as well as countries of the Association of Southeast Asian Nations (ASEAN). Section A looks at Malaysia in more detail as policies of the Malaysian Government and private sector represent a useful case study of how an Asian country can become a significant investor in Africa and thereby potentially support the continent's development process. South-East Asia also provides an example par excellence of how FDI can be utilized to further a country's (and region's) development. Thus the following section discusses inward FDI in the original five members of ASEAN (ASEAN-5) – Indonesia, Malaysia, the Philippines, Singapore and Thailand – including their investment policy regimes. It offers valuable insights into the factors and policies that have attracted or limited such investment. Section C of this chapter focuses on relevance of the experience and policies of the ASEAN-5 with respect to inward FDI for Africa. It then addresses the relevance of their FDI policies and practices for African countries. The last section contains some concluding remarks on Africa as an investment destination and attempts to draw some lessons from South-East Asian experiences for FDI policy in African countries.

A. SOUTH-EAST ASIAN FDI IN AFRICA

Since the mid-1980s, outward FDI from East and South-East Asian developing economies has increased (chapter I, figure I.1). Sustained and rapid economic growth has led to growing land and labour shortages and rising operating costs, and, together with appreciating currencies, has pushed firms in the East Asian NIEs to relocate their labour-intensive industries and processes abroad to remain domestically and internationally competitive. The TNCs are mainly conglomerates in Hong Kong (China), the Republic of Korea, Singapore and Taiwan Province of China. Korean *chaebols* have done well abroad in heavy industry, construction and some consumer goods, while firms from Hong Kong (China) and Singapore have expanded abroad in real estate development, hotel development, air and sea transportation, and banking and finance. In addition, China and other ASEAN economies, particularly Malaysia, are emerging as significant FDI sources, both within the region and beyond (for China, see chapter III).

The Asian financial crisis affected the financial capacity of firms from Asian developing countries to engage in outward FDI. The Korean *chaebols* and the conglomerates in the ASEAN countries were severely affected by corporate debt and financial restructuring. Except for the surge of outward FDI in 2000, outflows from developing Asia after 1997 had been generally lower than their pre-crisis levels until 2003. In 2004 and 2005, however, outward FDI flows from East and South-East Asia grew to $74 billion and $66 billion, respectively, driven by stronger outflows from most major economies in the region.

FDI flows from East and South-East Asia to Africa have been mainly from NIEs. For example, investment from the Republic of Korea

averaged $44 million per annum during the 1990s, but they declined thereafter. The most important destinations for investment in Africa from the Republic of Korea have been Algeria, Sudan, Egypt and South Africa. The average annual investment from Taiwan Province of China in Africa was $18 million during the period 1990-2002, the highest level ($41 million) being in 1999.

Recently, a number of countries in South-East Asia have emerged as important sources of FDI (see figure II.1 for Malaysia, Singapore and

Figure II.1. FDI outflows from Malaysia, Singapore and Thailand, 1980-2005
(Billions of dollars)

(a) Malaysia

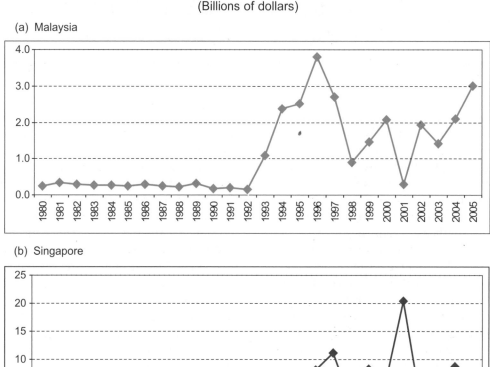

(b) Singapore

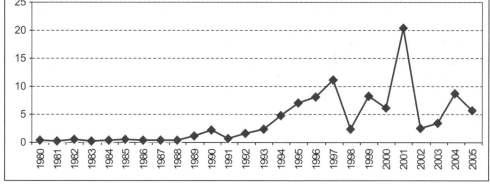

(c) Thailand

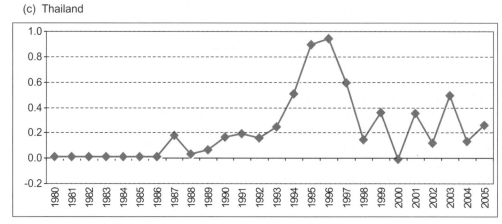

Source: UNCTAD, FDI/TNC database (www.unctad.org/fdistatistics).

Thailand), especially in developing countries. In 2005, the region accounted for 14 per cent of the total outward FDI stock from developing countries. Most of these investments originated in Singapore, Malaysia and Thailand, the first two of which are among the top sources of FDI from developing countries today (UNCTAD, 2006).

Among ASEAN countries, only Singapore and Malaysia have significant investments in Africa. As chapter I shows, Singapore's FDI stock in the region is about $3.5 billion or 4 per cent of the country's total outward FDI, while Malaysia's stock – at $ 1.9 billion – represents 5 per cent of its outward FDI. Though small in source country terms, these are significant amounts for African countries, especially LDCs. Singapore's FDI in Africa is highly concentrated and is preponderantly in Mauritius. In contrast, Malaysia's FDI is highly dispersed geographically throughout Africa, including in many LDCs such as Chad, Guinea, Malawi, Mozambique and the United Republic of Tanzania. This makes Malaysia an interesting case study of Asian FDI in Africa (box II.1).

Box. II.1. Malaysian FDI in Africa

Of the developing and transition economies, Malaysia has been among the 15 largest sources of FDI since 1980, and in 2005, it had the eighth largest stock of FDI after economies such as Hong Kong, China, the Russian Federation, Brazil and Taiwan Province of China (and ahead of the Republic of Korea and Mexico) (UNCTAD, 2006). Box table II.1.1 shows the country's relatively high level of outward FDI, with an outward FDI stock of about 34 per cent of GDP in 2005. Singapore also has a high ratio (94 per cent), while in contrast Thailand (another South-East Asian country with a lower, but similar level of development) has a ratio of only 2.3 per cent. In recent years 70 per cent or more of Malaysia's FDI has been targeted at other developing countries, with around 15 per cent of the total going to Africa (Zainal, 2005). The country's strong propensity to invest abroad, especially in other developing countries goes some way to explaining the size of its investments in Africa, as well as the dispersal of its investments. It is therefore worthwhile to examine its strategy in more detail.

Despite some concerns about over-liberal outward FDI policies, the Government of Malaysia has encouraged international investment by Malaysian TNCs, especially since the early 1990s (Malaysia, Ministry of International Trade and Industry, 1996). The main reason has been to ensure the development of world class Malaysian-owned companies, especially in the context of growing competition faced by Malaysian manufacturing exporters. This policy stance has remained broadly unchanged (Malaysia, Ministry of International Trade and Industry, 2006), with the Government providing considerable institutional support for outward FDI (Zainal, 2005).[a]

Box table II.1.1 Outward FDI from Malaysia: basic indicators, 2005

Indicator	Value
FDI outflows ($ billion)	3.0
Outward stock ($ billion)	44.5
Ratio of outward stock to GDP (%)	34.0
Share in global FDI outflows (%)	0.4
Share in global outward stock (%)	0.4

Source: UNCTAD FDI/TNC database.

The Malaysian Government's support for outward FDI has been closely linked to South-South cooperation and promoting mutual benefits, especially after the former Prime Minister Mahathir led an investment mission to a number of developing countries in the early 1990s. Most of this activity is undertaken under the aegis of the Malaysian South-South Association (MASSA) established in 1991.[b] This joint government and business support for South-South investment has helped to encourage FDI in Africa, as elsewhere, and offers Malaysian investors mutual support and confidence.

Malaysian TNCs have harnessed various sources of potential advantage in their South-South strategy. First, Malaysian companies originate from a successful economy and this gives them credibility and confidence overseas. From an African perspective, this gives impetus to improving their national policy and business structure. Second, this is bolstered by the Malaysian Government in a number of ways, for example within the framework of the Islamic Conference. Third, the country and its companies leverage their multiple identities – Malay, Chinese, Indian and other groups – very effectively: English is widely spoken in Africa,

/...

Box. II.1. Malaysian FDI in Africa (concluded)

there are Indian and Chinese diaspora in Africa and there are historic ties with Africa. Finally, many Malaysian TNCs that have a diverse economic base have a long history of doing business in far-flung places. While FDI outflows to Africa fluctuate, they show an upward trend (box figure II.1.1).

Box figure II.1.1. Malaysian FDI outflows to Africa, 1991-2004
(Millions of dollars)

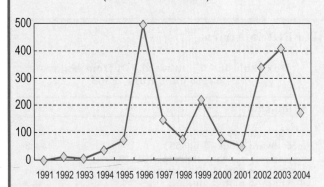

Source: UNCTAD, FDI/TNC database (www. unctad.org/fdistatistics).

Box table II.1.2 illustrates the diversity of Malaysia's TNCs, such as Sime Darby and Genting, which have significant investments in a number of African countries. Other companies have been investing in a variety of fields, such as hotels and leisure, shipping, broadcasting, financial services, oil and gas, palm oil refining and telecommunications, which shows the sectoral and industrial diversity of Malaysian investments.

Many of the Malaysian TNCs in box table II.1.2 gained experience through investments in ASEAN and China before venturing further afield to regions such as Africa and Latin America.

The Malaysian experience shows how a developing Asian Government can mobilize its TNCs to invest in developing countries such as those in Africa. What is essential is political will, a coherent institutional infrastructure and developing a close liaison or partnerships with the country's TNCs.

Box table II.1.2. Selected Malaysian TNCs with investments in Africa

Company	Industry or product	Location of investments
Genting	Conglomerate (including hotels and leisure, plantations, power generation)	Mauritius, South Africa
IOI Corp	Oil palm refining, property and trading	Mauritius
MISC	Shipping	Nigeria
MRCB	Broadcasting	Ghana
Opus International	Asset management	South Africa
Petronas	Oil and gas	Chad, Guinea, Mozambique, Niger, Somalia, Sudan, South Africa
Putera Capital	Financial services	Ghana, Mozambique, United Rep. of Tanzania
Ranhill Power	Power generation	Tanzania
Sime Darby	Palm oil refining	Egypt, United Rep. of Tanzania, Tunisia
Telekom Malaysia	Telecommunications	Guinea, Malawi

Source: UNCTAD, based on Zainal, 2006 and company websites.

Source: UNCTAD.

a   These include revisions of regulations (e.g. of the Central Bank of Malaysia Act 1958 in 1994 to expedite outward FDI); assistance from the Export Import Bank of Malaysia (e.g. information and advisory services); services of the Malaysian Export Credit Insurance, Berhad, especially for SMEs (including investment insurance schemes); encouragement, information, identification of partners, missions and other services from the Ministry of International Trade and Industry and the Malaysian Industrial Development Authority; market intelligence, training programmes and grants from the Malaysian Trade Development Corporation and the Small and Medium Industries Corporation; and incentives from the Inland Revenue Board, including double tax deduction for promotion of Malaysian Brands, incentives to acquire foreign companies, the non-taxation of repatriated profits from investments overseas, and agreements for the avoidance of double taxation.

b   MASSA is a non-profit consortium of about 180 member companies and associations, which promotes trade and investment between Malaysia and other developing countries. MASSA works closely with the Afrasia Business Council to promote business opportunities in Africa, most recently in Benin, Cameroon and Ghana. In addition to various levels of mutual support, MASSA set up the Malaysia South-South Corporation, Berhad (MASSCORP) in 1992, as an investment arm (e.g. it owns and operates the Malaysia Business Centre in Uganda which supports the country's TNC activities in East Africa).   Source: *MASSA News*, 2nd Quarter 2006 (on the association's website: www.massa.net.my).

B. TRENDS AND PATTERNS OF FDI IN THE ASEAN-5

In many respects, South-East Asia is the region where policies for an export-oriented, investment-led development strategy were first developed and tested, and, following their success, emulated in other parts of the world. Over time, this resulted in the region, especially the ASEAN-5, becoming an internationally competitive base for manufacturing and services. Their experience provides interesting lessons for African countries to pursue policies in which inward FDI plays a significant role.

The fist country to develop such a policy framework in the ASEAN region was Singapore (see below). Its success led the other ASEAN-5 to institute similar policies, beginning with Malaysia in the 1970s, followed by Indonesia, the Philippines and Thailand in the late 1970s and early 1980s (Mirza, 1986). Apart from Singapore, which is a small "city-state", the economies of the other four countries were largely resource-based before the 1970s, with some reliance on FDI in natural resources; they were major exporters of agricultural and mineral products such as rubber, copra, palm oil, timber, tin and oil and gas. From around the early 1970s, they began to industrialize rapidly, focusing on resource-based processing for export, and on import substitution and labour-intensive, export-oriented manufacturing. From the mid-1980s, economic conditions and reforms led to a renewed emphasis on export-oriented manufacturing and attracting FDI. This development strategy is of interest to many African countries, which are also rich in natural resources.

Prior to the outbreak of the Asian financial crisis from mid-1997, the ASEAN-5 combined were relatively large recipients of FDI inflows into Asia (table II.1). However, the dampening impact of the financial crisis led to a considerable decline in FDI inflows, and the ASEAN-5 faced a difficult task in restoring investor confidence (figure II.2). But, the downturn has been reversed in recent years. In 2004, their FDI inflows surged, recording the highest increase since the 1997 crisis and confirming that the impact of that crisis on FDI inflows is now in the past (UNCTAD, 2005). In 2005, inflows continued to surge, reaching $34 billion, a new record. This recovery was made possible by the large-scale diversification of the economic base, large segments of which are owned and operated by TNCs. Such an achievement is also of interest to African countries, many of which are still prone to the trade volatility that characterizes commodity-based economies.

Figure II.2. FDI inflows to the ASEAN-5, 1995-2005
(Billions of dollars)

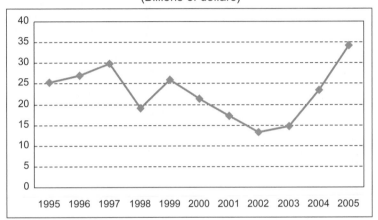

Source: UNCTAD, FDI/TNC database (www.unctad.org/fdistatistics).

1. The importance and changing structure of FDI inflows into the ASEAN-5

The importance of FDI for the economies of the ASEAN-5 is evident from their generally high inward FDI stock/GDP ratios and the high inward FDI inflow/gross fixed capital formation (GFCF) ratios. In 2005, the ratio of FDI stock to GDP was 41 per cent for the ASEAN-5 taken together, and ranged between 4 per cent and 62 per cent for the individual countries (table II.2). The ratio of FDI inflows to GFCF in 2003-2005 was 15 per cent for the ASEAN-5 as a whole.

FDI in the ASEAN-5 has contributed towards structural changes in the countries' economies over time, with a decline in the importance of the primary sector and a rise in that of manufacturing and services. In particular, FDI in banking and finance grew sharply in the 1990s, facilitated by liberalization of the financial sector and by M&As. Table II.3 shows the breakdown of FDI in approved manufacturing projects in the ASEAN countries during the period 1999-2004; the largest share went to radio, TV and communications equipment industries (19 per cent) and coke, refined petroleum products and nuclear

Table II.1. FDI inflows in East and South-East Asia, 1987-2005
(Millions of dollars)

Economy	Annual average			2002	2003	2004	2005
	1987-1992	1993-1997	1998-2001				
World	170 894	340 179	1013 442	617 732	557 869	710 755	916 277
Developing economies	36 892	129 102	230 428	163 583	175 138	275 032	334 285
Africa	3 396	6 807	12 802	12 999	18 513	17 199	30 672
East Asia	10 222	48 836	84 533	67 350	72 174	105 074	118 192
of which:							
China	4 627	37 157	43 343	52 743	53 505	60 630	72 406
Hong Kong, China	3 576	8 560	31 261	9 682	13 624	34 032	35 897
Korea, Republic of	774	1 448	6 804	3 043	3 892	7 727	7 198
Taiwan Province of China	1 127	1 593	3 046	1 445	453	1 898	1 625
South-East Asia	9 739	25 991	23 541	15 774	19 920	25 666	37 136
of which:							
Brunei Darussalam	5	390	599	1 035	3 375	212	275
Indonesia	998	3 866	-2 409	145	- 597	1 896	5 260
Malaysia	2 434	5 951	2 738	3 203	2 473	4 624	3 967
Philippines	644	1 411	1 359	1 542	491	688	1 132
Singapore	3 674	9 641	14 006	7 338	10 376	14 820	20 083
Thailand	1 679	2 293	5 205	947	1 952	1 414	3 687
Cambodia	6	147	193	145	84	131	381
Lao People's Democratic Rep.	4	80	39	25	19	17	28
Myanmar	111	401	347	191	291	251	300
Viet Nam	175	1 808	1 443	1 200	1 450	1 610	2 020
Memorandum:							
ASEAN-5	9 428	23 163	20 899	13 176	14 696	23 442	34 129
East and South-East Asia	19 961	74 827	108 074	83 124	92 094	130 740	155 328

Source: UNCTAD, FDI/TNC database (www.unctad.org/fdistatistics).

fuel industries (12 per cent).

In terms of source countries and regions, the bulk of FDI flowing into the ASEAN-5 until the early 1980s was from the United States and Western European countries. TNCs from these countries had ownership advantages stemming from their possession of abundant capital, technology, and managerial and marketing know-how, while the ASEAN-5 host countries offered location advantages in terms of markets, natural resources and low-priced labour (except Singapore), as well as excellent infrastructure and highly skilled human resources (Malaysia and Singapore). From the mid-1980s, large investments also flowed from Japan and the North-East Asian NIEs. Intra-ASEAN investment accounts for about one-fifth of the total FDI stock in the ASEAN subregion. Such flows increased from $0.8 billion in 2000 to $2.4 billion in 2004 (ASEAN Secretariat, 2005), and have become an integral part of intraregional investment in Asia (box II.2). Regional integration through such arrangements as the ASEAN Free Trade Area (AFTA), the ASEAN Industrial Cooperation scheme and the ASEAN Investment Area (AIA) has played a role. The increase in cross-border M&As by firms from within the subregion, as well as the relocation of certain activities within the region, have also

been major drivers of intra-ASEAN investment.

2. FDI determinants and location competitiveness

The major concern of investors, whether foreign or domestic, is to minimize risks and maximize returns and/or market share. The ASEAN-5 countries' attractiveness as host countries for FDI can be analysed in terms of the following competitiveness factors (equally valid in the African context):

Political stability and public governance. These reduce investment risks, uncertainty and business costs. For example, political instability in the Philippines in the 1980s and early 1990s slowed down economic growth and discouraged inward FDI, while a more stable regime during the period 1992-1997 contributed to increased FDI inflows. Likewise, the Asian

Table II.2. Share of inward FDI in gross fixed capital formation and in GDP in East and South-East Asia and Africa, 2003-2005
(Percentage)

Economy	Share of inward FDI flows in gross fixed capital formation Average 2003-2005	Share of inward FDI stock in GDP 2005
World	8.5	22.7
Developing economies	12.2	27.0
Africa	15.7	28.2
East Asia	9.6	27.0
of which:		
China	8.6	14.3
Hong Kong, China	78.9	299.9
Korea, Republic of	3.1	8.0
Taiwan Province of China	2.1	12.1
South-East Asia	14.7	43.2
of which:		
Brunei Darussalam	..	145.2
Cambodia	18.1	45.6
Indonesia	4.0	7.7
Lao People's Democratic Rep.	4.7	24.5
Malaysia	15.1	36.5
Myanmar	..	43.6
Philippines	5.4	14.4
Singapore	61.7	158.6
Thailand	5.5	33.5
Viet Nam	10.9	61.2
Memorandum:		
ASEAN-5	15.1	41.3
East and South-East Asia	10.3	30.2

Source: UNCTAD, FDI/TNC database (www.unctad.org/fdistatistics).

Box II.2. Drivers and impact of intraregional investment in Asia

As East Asian investors sought business opportunities abroad, locations elsewhere within developing Asia also became increasingly attractive to FDI owing to their abundant natural resources and labour, rapidly growing domestic markets, increasingly open trade and investment regimes, privatization programmes, and improved political and social stability. Geographical proximity reduced transaction costs for intraregional FDI and facilitated regional production networks and just-in-time manufacturing. Some common cultural and language elements between investing and recipient countries also helped.

The intraregional pattern of FDI – which assumed the "flying geese pattern" (UNCTAD, 1995, p. 260) – was facilitated by the diversity of resource endowments and levels of development among economies in the region. FDI led to relocation of labour-intensive production

and exports from source countries to lower-wage countries in a cascading pattern. Initially, the main source economies were the East Asian NIEs and the host economies were Indonesia, the Philippines, Malaysia, Thailand and China. The latter subsequently evolved into source economies as well, while the newer ASEAN members – Viet Nam, Lao People's Democratic Republic, Myanmar and Cambodia – joined the ranks of host countries. Intraregional foreign investments facilitated industrial restructuring of the more advanced economies and created new industrial capabilities in the lower-tier economies. At the same time, a horizontal division of labour began evolving in response to the rapid development of new technologies, shortened product life cycles and increasing globalization and regionalization of production. Increasingly, countries began to specialize in different parts of the value chain and developed advantages in different niches.

Source: UNCTAD.

---

financial crisis exposed weaknesses in public governance in the crisis-hit economies, which seriously undermined investor confidence; and the political turmoil in Indonesia in recent years had a negative impact on FDI inflows (negative investment during 1988-2001 and 2003).

Factor competitiveness. For investments driven by the quest for resources, favourable factor endowments – whether inherited or created – matter. The ASEAN-5 countries, excluding Singapore, are rich in natural resources, which have attracted considerable foreign and domestic investments. In particular, Indonesia and Malaysia have rich oil and gas deposits and other natural resources. Indonesia, the Philippines and Thailand also have sizeable populations, and therefore abundant labour resources. Increasingly, factors that determine FDI competitiveness extend beyond abundant natural resources or low-wage labour. As Singapore's continuing large FDI inflows demonstrate, foreign investors are also attracted by world-class physical, financial and business infrastructure and skilled human resources.

Business environment. This is essential for sales in the world market as well as in an open domestic market. Production and distribution costs are a function not only of low factor prices, but also of efficient institutions and factor productivity. For example, although Singapore has very high

wages in comparison with many developed and developing countries, it also has a highly efficient business environment.

Market competitiveness. A good deal of FDI is market-driven. For example, China's huge population and rapid growth of purchasing power act as a powerful magnet for FDI. Individual ASEAN countries do not have sizeable domestic markets, either because of small populations (Singapore, Malaysia) or low per capita incomes (Indonesia, Philippines), even though rapid economic growth has increased effective market size over the years. The creation of the ASEAN Free Trade Area (AFTA) is an effort to improve the attractiveness of the ASEAN subregion's market, even though it is small in effective market size when compared to China, the EU or the North American Free Trade Area (NAFTA).

Policy environment. Apart from sound economic fundamentals, a conducive policy environment attracts investors. This includes sound macro-economic management and FDI-friendly policies such as: liberal rules and regulations with regard to FDI entry and operations; open trade and payments regimes; policy reforms to deregulate and create market economies and privatize State-owned enterprises; and greater policy coherence in the use of investment incentives and performance requirements.

Table II.3. Foreign investment flows to manufacturing projects in ASEAN countries, by industry, 1999-2004
(Millions of dollars)

Industry	1999	2000	2001	2002	2003	2004	1999-2004	Percentage distribution 1999-2004
Food products and beverages	814	803	730	471	607	1 237	4 662	4.2
Tobacco products	8	15	31	36	2	8	100	0.1
Textiles	194	616	618	215	446	482	2 570	2.3
Wearing apparel; dressing and dyeing of fur	188	162	172	565	358	161	1 607	1.5
Tanning and dressing of leather; luggage, handbags, saddlery, harness and footwear	52	206	93	273	248	225	1 096	1.0
Wood and wood products and cork, except furniture; articles of straw and plaiting materials	158	151	113	164	1 022	386	1 994	1.8
Paper and paper products	1 005	55	1 475	77	156	662	3 431	3.1
Publishing, printing and reproduction of recorded media	24	53	21	55	10	22	185	0.2
Coke, refined petroleum products and nuclear fuel	3 027	2 803	1 399	2 963	2 957	231	13 379	12.1
Chemicals and chemical products	920	1 888	1 660	549	900	3 663	9 580	8.7
Rubber and plastics products	387	3 669	588	451	475	693	6 263	5.7
Other non-metallic mineral products	168	669	595	201	664	668	2 965	2.7
Basic metals	78	809	245	134	1 489	460	3 215	2.9
Fabricated metal products, except machinery and equipment	151	401	523	284	457	1 755	3 571	3.2
Machinery and equipment	324	434	426	503	629	929	3 245	2.9
Office, accounting and computing machinery	62	92	67	117	82	368	789	0.7
Electrical machinery and apparatus n.e.c.	160	335	337	534	211	287	1 865	1.7
Radio, television and communication equipment and apparatus	3 590	5 279	4 117	1 732	1 906	3 766	20 390	18.5
Medical, precision and optical instruments, watches and clocks	176	96	202	81	95	69	719	0.7
Motor vehicles, trailers and semi-trailers	35	311	375	348	965	897	2 931	2.7
Other transport equipment	78	144	195	143	1 080	82	1 721	1.6
Furniture; manufacturing n.e.c.	225	165	221	101	84	214	1 010	0.9
Recycling	2	25	3	21	2	3	55	0.1
Others	-	13	21	9	17	26	87	0.1
Natural gas	-	380	-	-	-	-	380	0.3
SUB-TOTAL[a]	11 825	19 574	14 228	10 028	14 863	17 293	87 811	79.6
Foreign investment commitments in the manufacturing sector in Singapore (foreign portion)	3 692	4 197	3 684	3 932	3 484	3 551	22 539	20.4
TOTAL	15 517	23 771	17 912	13 961	18 347	20 844	110 351	100.0

Source: ASEAN Secretariat - ASEAN FDI Database.

a   Not including Singapore

Notes: Data refer to the value of approved investment projects apportioned according to the equity interest of the investors from the different countries of origin. Singapore's figures are based on net fixed assets investment commitments as monitored by the Economic Development Board of Singapore. Viet Nam's apportionment figures are based on legal capital contribution ratio and commenced from 2000. The sub-total excludes Singapore, as disaggregated data by industry is not available. Figures for 1999 exclude Cambodia and Viet Nam. Figures for 2000 exclude Cambodia.

A positive image as an attractive investment destination plays an important role in attracting FDI. Prior to the outbreak of the East Asian financial crisis in July 1997, the ASEAN-5 enjoyed a positive image among international and regional investors. Widespread perceptions of regional and national political and social stability and economic dynamism suggested low investment risks and profitable investment opportunities. Some governments in the subregion were more authoritarian and less democratic than others, but this did not undermine investor confidence owing to overall political and social stability, law and order, as well as business and personal security. Governments were perceived to be development-oriented, with business-friendly policies that favoured FDI. Increasingly, policies were seen to be moving towards those of market economies, with progressive privatization, trade and investment liberalization. GDP growth rates were among the highest in the world. Each time economic growth and investment flows faltered, new policies were introduced which sought to improve competitiveness and achieve recovery. The positive image of the ASEAN-5 was, however, adversely affected by the financial crisis of 1997-1998 (box II.3).

Box II.3. Impact of the 1997-1998 financial crisis

The financial crisis had a significantly negative impact on inward FDI to the ASEAN-5: inflows declined from $30 billion in 1997 to $19 billion in 1998 (figure II.2).

The crisis highlighted a couple of lessons with respect to financial flows. First, FDI flows are much more stable than short-term portfolio capital flows and bank lending. While there were massive withdrawals of short-term funds from the East Asian region during 1997-1998, there was no parallel reversal of FDI. For governments in the region, this highlighted the benefits of such investment which, together with the shrinking of alternative sources of financing and conditionality imposed by the International Monetary Fund (IMF), led them to further liberalize their FDI regimes with a view to attracting not only greenfield investments, but also cross-border M&As. Interest in and opportunities for cross-border M&As grew as debt-ridden financial institutions and corporations required capital injections, and investors responded to acquisition opportunities and an improved policy environment.

Second, investor confidence had been undermined by perceptions of deteriorating public and corporate governance. Investors, both foreign and domestic, had become less tolerant of corrupt and other bad practices. While it was relatively easy for governments to liberalize their FDI policy regimes, it was an uphill task for countries in the region to rid themselves of corrupt practices in the public and private sectors.

The short-term effects of the crisis on FDI inflows were highly negative, although, as mentioned, FDI inflows were much less affected than foreign portfolio investments. The sharp economic downturn, shrinking domestic and regional markets, financial uncertainties (the instability of exchange rates and stock markets), the bursting of asset bubbles, financial and corporate sector weaknesses, and overcapacity in a range of manufacturing sectors (widely perceived to be the result of overinvestment during the boom years) deterred FDI. The financial capacities of most local enterprises were severely curtailed; foreign enterprises were also encumbered with corporate debt denominated in foreign currencies; and further investments in infrastructure projects on build-operate-transfer (BOT) bases were severely discouraged by financing, pricing and cash flow problems. However, the crisis helped improve the region's cost-competitiveness following the sharp currency devaluations and economic contractions of 1997-1998.

The negative impact of the crisis not only depressed both domestic and foreign investment but also eroded investor confidence. After the crisis, investment promotion agencies faced an uphill task to change the negative image of the region, such as perceptions of increased political and economic risks, and doubts about the sustainability of the economic recovery and the pace of institutional and structural reforms. There were concerns that economic recovery may not be sustainable due to perceptions of slow financial and corporate restructuring and rising public debt. There were also concerns over the continuing political and social turmoil in Indonesia, and threats to the stability of the political leaderships in Malaysia, the Philippines and Thailand. The economic downturns in the region in 2001, often attributed to the slowing down of the United States economy, also exacerbated such negative perceptions.

Source: UNCTAD.

Most of the crisis-affected economies rebounded rapidly after 1999. Accordingly, FDI to those economies from many important source countries resumed. However, inward FDI flows to the ASEAN-5 continued to decline for another three years (figure II.2), due partly to the downturn in global FDI flows as well as the above-mentioned concerns. In 2003, there was a slight rebound in FDI inflows to the ASEAN-5, signalling the end of the downturn. In recent years, the ASEAN-5 have witnessed a further rise in inflows – from $14 billion in 2003 to $34 billion in 2005 – the steepest increase since the financial crisis (figure II.2). This, as noted earlier, generally confirms that the impact of the crisis on FDI inflows to the region is now history.

C.   FDI POLICY REGIMES OF THE ASEAN-5

Given the success of the FDI policy regimes of a number of countries in South-East Asia, from the African perspective it is useful to look at these policies in detail. Singapore is examined first because, although it now has a per capita income far greater than that of any country in Africa, the fundamental policy framework it developed and incrementally improved as it moved into higher value-added industries is one which provides a valuable lesson to other economies worldwide. The Singapore model is also relevant because, examined over time, it provides a road map for the *types of* policy measures countries relying on inward FDI could adopt for developing their economies. However, it is clear that many African countries are not yet in a position to follow all of these policy measures

1. The Singapore model

At the time of political independence in 1965, many considered Singapore to be a small developing nation with bleak prospects. There was concern over the economic viability of such a small city State: it had no natural resources, its traditional twin economic pillars – as an entrepôt base and a British naval base – faced dim prospects as neighbouring countries increasingly pursued direct trade and the United Kingdom withdrew its military forces East of the Suez, and its lack of industrial skills and small domestic market were believed to be impediments to industrial development. Yet, in three decades Singapore progressed impressively to become one of the world's most competitive and affluent economies, as evident from its high per capita GDP and competitiveness ranking (World Economic Forum, 2006; see also table I.1).

Singapore overcame its initial handicaps by integrating into the regional and world economy, with inward FDI playing a crucial role. Key factors that contributed to its success in attracting FDI and in harnessing its resources for its economic development are discussed below.

Political and social stability in Singapore contribute to policy predictability, lower investment risks and low transaction costs, which are crucial for attracting FDI inflows. Despite ethnic, religious and linguistic diversity, social harmony has been carefully nurtured through various policy measures and institutions. It has been fostered through rapid economic growth with equity, and the building of a broad-based stakeholder society. Moreover rapid growth has contributed to a sharp decline in poverty. In addition, trade unions have been increasingly co-opted into the mainstream of policy-making and economic development. Finally, Singapore scores high in public governance, as evidenced in its competitiveness rankings (World Economic Forum, 2006).

Many small countries and island States are affected by the "tyranny of distance" from the economic centres of the world. Singapore, however, exploited the advantages of its geographic location with strategic investments in infrastructure. Comprehensive air and sea transport and telecommunications networks link Singapore with major cities and ports in the region and throughout the world. Industrial estates, business parks and science parks provide easy access to land and factory/office space, and to industrial, commercial and research facilities; for land-scarce countries such as Singapore this contributes to an optimal use of land, reduces the capital investment requirements of investors and allows quick start-ups. As a regional financial centre, Singapore provides well-developed and efficient financial services.

Since the mid-1960s, Singapore's educational system has been continually expanded to meet the need for technical, scientific, engineering, information technology, managerial and financial manpower. Training and skills development programmes supplement formal education, particularly for upgrading the skills of workers already in the workforce. Foreign TNCs are also encouraged to provide various types of vocational and professional training. The use of English as the language of government and business facilitates Singapore's linkages with the global economy as well as communications between the local workforce and foreign investors and management.

Given its small domestic market, Singapore opted for a strategy of export-oriented manufacturing after seceding from Malaysia in the mid-1960s. This went against the dominant policy thinking of the day, which favoured import substitution. To ensure the success of this strategy, in the absence of domestic industrial and marketing expertise, Singapore sought FDI from Western TNCs to provide not only capital resources, but also entrepreneurial experience, technological and managerial know-how, international marketing channels and well-established consumer brand names. As export-oriented FDI is much more mobile than FDI in natural resources and import-substituting manufacturing, Singapore adopted a liberal FDI policy regime with generous incentives and minimal restrictions. It should be emphasized that Singapore's highly successful FDI policy has rested on a holistic approach that provides a solid foundation of sound economic fundamentals as well as policy coherence and consistency.

With a free trade regime and the absence of foreign exchange controls, the policy emphasis for investment promotion in Singapore has been on moderating costs through adequate and efficient provision of factor supplies and services, besides keeping tax rates internationally competitive. Singapore has a single-tier government structure and moderate tax levels. The corporate income tax for both resident and non-resident companies has been progressively lowered, from a flat rate of 40 per cent in the early 1960s to 20 per cent currently. The effective tax rate has been lowered by various tax incentives.

There are no local content, export performance or technology transfer requirements imposed on FDI. Employment of foreign managers and professionals is subject to immigration regulations and employment passes, but these are liberally approved. Foreign enterprises in Singapore are free to make their own production, marketing, technology licensing and personnel recruitment

decisions, although they are encouraged to export, train manpower and engage in R&D. Policies are aimed not only at attracting new investments, but also at retaining existing investments and encouraging reinvestments. Singapore's FDI-friendly policy extends to appointing foreign investors and professionals to various official decision-making bodies and ad hoc committees. Investment protection is assured mainly through political social and economic stability (including policy and exchange rate stability), an established legal framework and the rule of law, bilateral investment guarantee agreements, and dispute settlement mechanisms.

While the Singapore FDI model demonstrates the effectiveness of a holistic approach to attracting FDI and overcoming the weaknesses inherent in being a city State, on the downside, Singapore's economy however is highly vulnerable to external developments and it has a relatively weak domestic entrepreneurial sector (Chia, 1999).

The country's Economic Development Board (EDB), one of the world's most effective investment promotion agencies, has functioned as a one-stop investment centre providing advice on investment opportunities and application procedures, and coordinating the various agencies and services that the foreign investor needs to deal with. The focus has been on both pre- and post-investment services and on keeping existing investors satisfied in order to encourage them to reinvest and expand. The EDB is not only an FDI promotion agency but also a development agency, closely involved in planning and implementing Singapore's development strategies and policies. It plays a key role in Singapore's industrial restructuring and in other efforts to maintain and enhance competitiveness.

One best practice that has been emulated elsewhere is the establishment by the EDB of training centres and institutes, undertaken since the early 1970s in partnership with TNCs, specialized manufacturers and foreign governments, to provide specialized training. Another one has been the Local Industries Upgrading Programme (LIUP) introduced in the mid-1980s, which aims at strengthening and expanding the base of local suppliers. The EDB has considerable authority as a development and investment promotion agency; it is able to function effectively as a one-stop investment centre and deliver on its promises. There is a high degree of cooperation among government ministries and agencies, and little public evidence of "turf battles" and inconsistencies in policy formulation and implementation.

2. FDI policy regimes of the other four ASEAN countries

Until the mid-1980s, FDI policy regimes in the other four ASEAN countries suggested varying degrees of ambivalence with respect to inward FDI, as reflected in the generous granting of fiscal and other investment incentives on the one hand, and widespread imposition of restrictions, regulations and performance requirements on the other. In some of the countries, constitutional provisions and economic nationalism prohibited, or severely restricted, foreign ownership of land, natural resources and corporate equity. The desire to nurture infant industries and protect domestic entrepreneurs led to import substitution and restrictions on foreign ownership in manufacturing, trade and financial services, among others. Moreover, abundant revenues from oil and/or other commodities and ready access to external financing encouraged these restrictive stances towards FDI. From the mid-1980s, all of these countries progressively liberalized their FDI policy regimes in response to several factors: (i) the adverse effects of falling oil and commodity prices; (ii) growing acknowledgement of the potential positive role of FDI, reinforced by the demonstration effect of Singapore; and (iii) fears of investment diversion to other regions, which put pressure on these governments to create a more competitive investment climate.

Two main features characterized the changes in the FDI regimes of these ASEAN countries. First, there were simpler, speedier investment approval procedures and better coordination among government agencies in policy formulation and implementation. This resulted in reduced administrative and other transaction costs and greater policy effectiveness. One-stop investment centres eased administrative hassles. Second, the FDI policy regime shifted away from the extensive use of restrictions and performance requirements towards recognition that it is net incentives that matter. Existing FDI legislation was amended and its restrictive elements were interpreted more liberally. Incentives were also more geared to promoting competitive industries and activities, with less reliance on protective measures such as tariffs and restrictive licensing, greater use of tax concessions, accelerated

depreciation allowances, import duty exemptions and concessions, and the provision of industrial infrastructure and facilities.

Not all international investors systematically scour the world for investment opportunities. Most are likely to consider only a small range of possible investment locations. As such, prospective host countries need to ensure that they get onto the investors' "radar screens". Smaller and/or poorer developing countries have to work harder at promotional campaigns to be noticed. They need to market themselves aggressively to provide information on investment opportunities, policies and procedures. The four ASEAN countries have all established national investment promotion agencies, which work actively to attract FDI inflows to the countries.

They are increasingly granting national treatment to FDI, including with respect to right of establishment, ownership and control of enterprises, equal taxation and protection under the law; and, like Singapore, they have adopted policies to foster domestic linkages to ensure transfer of the skills, know-how and technology that accompany FDI, and develop domestic enterprises. These policies take several forms: foreign equity ceilings and mandatory joint ventures with local enterprise; local content rules to foster domestic purchases; restrictions on employment of foreign personnel; and technology transfer requirements. As success in fostering domestic linkages also depends on local availability of skills, technical capabilities and supplier bases, these countries have developed programmes to support the upgrading of local supply industries as part of broader efforts to assist local SMEs.

In terms of investment incentives, the four ASEAN countries have made more extensive use of fiscal than financial incentives, as the former mainly entail foregone tax revenue, while the latter often entail actual financial outlays. Commonly used fiscal incentives are import tax exemptions on capital goods and intermediate and raw material production inputs, and tax holidays as well as tax allowances in various forms. Fiscal incentives have been used to encourage manufacturing activities, initially in import substitution, but increasingly also in export manufacturing. Selective and discretionary fiscal incentives give preference to certain industries, such as pioneer industries (industries where FDI is encouraged), export industries, heavy industries and high-tech industries. They are often linked to performance requirements such as use of local raw materials, local content, employment, training, industrial upgrading, technology transfer, R&D, international procurement, regional headquarters, and geographic decentralization. As competition for FDI has intensified, policies on FDI have increasingly emphasized the use of fiscal incentives and downplayed restrictions and performance requirements.

Industrial parks and export and investment zones have been established in the ASEAN-5 countries to provide enterprises in these zones with preferential treatment, because it was not feasible or desirable to extend such treatment throughout the economy. They also serve to decentralize investments into less developed areas, though questions have often been raised about the efficacy, equity and cost of government subsidies for the industrial infrastructure and facilities provided to these zones, leakage of duty-free imports, and the extent of linkages and spillover effects to the rest of the economy. In addition, all of these countries have entered into bilateral and multilateral investment protection agreements with other countries, as well as agreements for the protection of intellectual property rights and avoidance of double taxation.

3. Regional initiatives

Since the early 1990s, ASEAN has pursued a policy of strong intraregional cooperation, first for trade and later for investment:

ASEAN Free Trade Area. AFTA was announced in January 1992, with the scheduled lowering of tariffs for intra-ASEAN trade.[1] The six original ASEAN members (Brunei Darussalam, Indonesia, Malaysia, the Philippines, Singapore, Thailand) are set to eliminate all tariffs by 2015 and the newer members (Cambodia, Lao People's Democratic Republic, Myanmar, Viet Nam) by 2018. AFTA aims to make the ASEAN region more attractive to foreign and regional investors by attracting investments through greater regional rationalization and specialization.

In 2004, the ASEAN-10 had a combined market of over 548 million people and a GDP of $840 billion. However, despite the large population base, in economic terms the size of AFTA is only a small fraction of that of the EU or NAFTA and less than two-thirds that of China. Intra-ASEAN trade accounts for less than a quarter of the region's total trade. Given the relatively small size of the regional market, AFTA cannot afford to be inward

looking and is actively seeking interregional cooperation.

ASEAN Investment Area. The 1992 AFTA agreement contained no investment provision; it only required ASEAN countries to cooperate on investment facilitation and promotion. Agreement on the ASEAN Investment Area (AIA) was reached in 1998. The AIA aims to improve information on, and awareness of, the region's investment opportunities; enable a regional division of labour so as to improve efficiency and cost competitiveness; provide investors greater access to economic sectors within the region; and provide national treatment for ASEAN investors initially and for all investors eventually. The AIA's objectives are to be achieved through a three-pronged approach:

- A promotion and awareness programme to promote the ASEAN region as an investment destination with a stable image: this includes a series of high-level ASEAN joint investment promotion missions, creation of investment websites and databases, and publication of investment information.

- A cooperation and facilitation programme to enhance ASEAN's competitiveness and to provide investors with an efficient investment environment that offers low transaction costs: this includes human resource development, and upgrading the capabilities of ASEAN investment agencies.

- A liberalization programme involving measures to open up national investment regimes by eliminating investment barriers, liberalizing investment rules and policies, and granting national treatment: it includes opening up industries (manufacturing, manufacturing-related services, and manufacturing-related agriculture, mining, fisheries and forestry) to FDI, and providing national treatment to ASEAN investors by 2010 and to non-ASEAN investors by 2020, with exceptions specified in the Temporary Exclusion List (TEL), Sensitive List (SL) and General Exception List (GEL).[2]

ASEAN growth triangles. Another regional initiative pursued by ASEAN countries is the establishment of growth triangles. These are cross-border investment zones with minimal border restrictions within a zone that aim at taking advantage of economic complementarities and geographical proximity. Economic complementarities improve the locational advantages of the investment zone by allowing investors to pool resources and exploit differences in comparative advantage and cost structures of adjacent areas. Geographical proximity, supported by linguistic and cultural similarities and transport and telecommunications links, help minimize transaction and information costs, and achieve economies of agglomeration and scale. Three ASEAN growth triangles have been established with government support to facilitate private investment flows: the southern Indonesia-Malaysia-Singapore growth triangle, the northern Indonesia-Malaysia-Thailand growth triangle, and the eastern Brunei Darussalam-Indonesia-Malaysia-Philippines East ASEAN Growth Area. However, the Asian financial crisis greatly reduced investment activities in these growth triangles.

ASEAN Industrial Cooperation. The ASEAN Industrial Cooperation (AICO) scheme was launched in April 1996 to promote joint manufacturing activity by ASEAN-based (domestic) and extra-ASEAN (foreign) companies. An AICO arrangement is an approved strategic alliance between companies operating in at least two ASEAN countries. Participating firms benefit from lower production costs, economies of scale, and more efficient divisions of labour and industrial resource allocations. AICO final products, intermediate products and raw materials are entitled to immediate preferential tariff rates of 0 to 5 per cent under AFTA.

D. ASEAN FDI POLICIES AND PRACTICES: CAN THEY BE APPLIED TO AFRICA?

In the early 1970s, Africa absorbed more FDI per unit of GDP than Asia, and not much less than Latin America, but by the 1980s this had changed dramatically (UNCTAD, 1995, p.80). Although the situation improved during the 1990s and some African countries have succeeded in attracting sizeable FDI inflows, most countries in the region still attract very limited FDI. As a host for FDI, Africa suffers from a negative image, including perceptions of high investment risk, although data show that FDI in the region has been highly and consistently profitable, comparing favourably with rates of return to FDI in other regions (chapter I). How can African countries successfully attract FDI? The policies and practices of the ASEAN-5 countries can provide valuable lessons for investment promotion that may be useful for Africa.

The African continent is rich in natural resources and more than half of FDI inflows have gone into the natural resource sector. There is significant potential for diversification by attracting FDI into resource-based industries such as metal products, textiles, paper and wood products, rubber products and building materials. Other features that could attract FDI to African economies are: location advantages for manufactured exports including the availability of cheap labour; privileges arising from the Generalized System of Preferences (GSP); preferential market access to the EU under the

Cotonou Agreement, to the United States under AGOA, and to South Africa for those investing in the Southern African Development Community (SADC) regional bloc; possibilities of integration with the EU market for northern African countries; and prospects for catering to the protected domestic markets of host countries, given the weak competition from domestic producers. There is also potential for FDI in services, as domestic demand for many services has been growing rapidly while suppliers are limited. Africa also offers many tourist attractions that offer opportunities for FDI in tourism-related services.

Many African countries have been making substantial progress in improving their political and economic stability, recovering from civil war and unrest, reducing bureaucratic obstacles, adopting economic reforms, privatization and proactive investment measures, and improving their economic growth performance. It is imperative for Africa to improve its image as an investment location. While it is true that the rate of return on FDI in Africa is generally higher than in other regions, this also reflects the tendency for investors to invest only in projects that promise quick returns because of the perceived high risk of doing business there. Reality often differs from the images conveyed in the media (where only bad events tend to make the news); nevertheless Africa's negative image makes the task of investment promotion in the region's economies more challenging than for other developing regions.

1. Relevance of ASEAN-5 FDI policies and practices

ASEAN's experiences with FDI policy reforms point to the considerable complexities of integrating national economies into the world of TNCs and the international division of labour. Liberalization of FDI and related policies is only one element. Competition for FDI is increasingly related to factors such as costs and competitive advantage, political stability, investment security, predictability and transparency of laws and regulations, availability of good physical and commercial infrastructure, availability of skilled manpower, availability and proximity of quality suppliers, and availability of markets and profit opportunities.

Attracting FDI inflows into Africa requires considerable efforts to improve the economic fundamentals and other determinants of investment. However, many of these entail changes over the long term. More achievable in the short term are improvements in the design and, more importantly, implementation of government policies and practices affecting FDI. In this respect much can be learned from the best and worst practices of the ASEAN-5 and other countries.

(a) Investment promotion

The Singapore EDB for instance is able to function very effectively as a one-stop centre for investment promotion and implementation because it not only has adequate authority as well as financial and human resources, but is also marketing a success story. Governments should realistically assess national strengths and weaknesses, including location advantages, and design investment promotion strategies accordingly.

Investment promotion needs to incorporate investment facilitation – not just the marketing of locations – as well as providing investment-related services. Such services include "one-stop" facilitation of administrative approvals; provision of specialized physical, customs-related and technical infrastructure; support for labour procurement and skills development; matchmaking between investors and local suppliers; and

resolving administrative problems connected with various government bureaucracies.

Countries should examine whether elaborate FDI approval procedures are really necessary or whether a simple registration procedure would suffice. If a government still wishes to maintain an elaborate approval procedure, it should rely on simple and transparent rules to minimize abuse of discretionary powers by officials and to ensure the one-stop centre is effective.

The ASEAN-5 countries have different mixes of centralized and decentralized investment promotion, each with their pros and cons. Indonesia has a centralized agency, but owing to the sprawling archipelago there are delays in communications between the periphery and the centre (although physical distance should pose less of a problem in the IT age). There is also concern that concentration of power at the centre has led to the neglect of regional/local interests. Experiences in Malaysia and the Philippines suggest that decentralization can have advantages as well as disadvantages. Dynamic local authorities at the Subic and Clark military bases in the Philippines and in Penang in Malaysia have been much more successful in promoting FDI than the central agencies. However, it is important that local and central agencies avoid working at cross-purposes. Furthermore, competing investment incentives among local authorities within a country can reduce the potential benefits from FDI.

The ASEAN-5 governments frequently arrange high-profile overseas investment missions led by political leaders and government ministers. This helps generate international interest and media publicity. Increasingly, diplomacy and foreign policy is about trade and investment, rather than just politics and traditional security concerns. Of course, if a government has lost international credibility, the publicity may be more negative than positive. African countries could also consider mounting high profile overseas investment missions.

Cooperation among countries to establish a regional strategy to attract FDI may be more effective than going it alone. For example, African countries could consider collaborating in joint missions. Joint investment missions need to be carefully designed to provide useful information and potential partners for foreign investors.

(b) Policy consistency and coherence

The need for policy consistency and coherence bears stressing. Some ASEAN countries have gone through both policy liberalization and tightening, and others have made complicated investment laws and regulations. While changes in policy are to be expected in response to changing economic circumstances and industrial structures, when such changes are perceived as reflecting recurring economic nationalism, and policy changes are unexpected and adversely affect existing investments as well as new investors, they discourage long-term investments.

Policies should not only seek to woo new investors, but should also take care of "captive" investors already in the country. A favourable experience will encourage reinvestment, and these investors will serve as goodwill ambassadors for the country. For example, Singapore often includes representatives of TNCs already well-established there in its overseas investment missions and in efforts at further investment promotion.

The ASEAN countries have used investment incentives to woo investors, while imposing ownership restrictions and performance requirements on them to protect national sovereignty and maximize benefits from FDI. In fact, incentives and restrictions or requirements are often deliberately linked. However, it is net incentives – taking into account both the positive effects of the former and the often deterring effects of the latter – that matter for attracting FDI. Governments need to consider the overall package of incentives, restrictions and performance requirements to remove redundancy, improve coherence and maximize benefits.

In both investment approval and implementation, it is not uncommon for the investment promotion agency and other government agencies to work at cross purposes, causing damaging delays and uncertainties for investors.

(c) Fiscal and financial incentives

Fiscal and financial incentives are highly controversial investment policy tools (UNCTAD, 1996). In general, such incentives are provided to offset the negative effects of a high-tax regime and as part of a selective industrial policy. For the latter, experience in the ASEAN-5 suggests that the regional demonstration effect can be very strong. Incentives for specific investments and activities

introduced by one ASEAN country are soon followed by the other member countries, contributing to a zero-sum game where every host country offers the same incentive. What lessons can be drawn from the practices and experiences of the ASEAN-5 in this area?

Tax incentives cannot be substitutes for good economic fundamentals, sound macroeconomic management and a legal and regulatory framework that is perceived to be transparent and fair to foreign businesses. At best, incentives must be viewed as "icing on the cake". The icing is less important when location attractions are strong, as in location-specific investments in the natural resource sector and import-substituting manufacturing. It is more important in potentially footloose export-oriented manufacturing where investors have the choice of multiple locations.

Investment agencies need to examine carefully the effectiveness of various types of tax incentives in attracting FDI, and their effects on government fiscal revenue. A tax incentive to induce investments in a less developed peripheral area will not be very effective if it is not accompanied by measures to develop transportation links, and ensure power supply and other industrial support. Furthermore, the positive effects of tax incentives can be offset by the disincentive of performance requirements. Providing a tax incentive and then imposing local partnership or local content requirements will not be effective if the foreign investor faces serious difficulties in securing a suitable local business partner or in finding a suitable local parts and components supplier.

One issue facing host governments is whether to set effective tax rates at attractive but uniform levels for all investors, or to provide selective tax incentives for some investors. The uniform approach is attractive because it is non-distortionary, easier to administer and less prone to rent-seeking. The selective approach is attractive because it can minimize fiscal "loss", as some types of investment respond to tax incentives better than others, and it facilitates industrial targeting. For example, since footloose export industries are more responsive to low taxes, export processing zones can be created that provide exemptions and concessions from trade taxes and corporate taxes. In monopolies, such as extractive industries or transport and telecommunications, governments may wish to capture the high economic rents available through higher taxes. For example, Hong Kong (China) prefers a regime of low corporate and individual income tax rates, which reduces the need to offer tax holidays; Singapore minimizes the distortionary effects of the selective tax incentive strategy by targeting industries and activities with dynamic comparative advantage, ensuring transparency in the selection process, and severely punishing public sector corruption.

(d) Domestic linkages and spillover effects

All host governments seek to maximize the positive linkage and spillover effects of FDI, but policies and practices differ. Singapore has focused on the supply side through programmes to strengthen and expand local industries and foster supplier linkages with foreign affiliates in the country. Other ASEAN governments, until recently, preferred to focus on ownership restrictions and performance requirements by setting conditions relating to joint ventures, local content, use of local suppliers, employment of local managerial and professional personnel, technology transfer and R&D requirements.

Some ASEAN governments have imposed joint venture conditions to nurture domestic enterprise. Foreign investors will voluntarily look for local joint venture partners when such partners can add value to the investment by enabling privileged access to policy-makers, resulting in preferential treatment or special access to markets (including government contracts) that would otherwise be closed or difficult to penetrate, and because of their knowledge of local languages and customs and their ability to handle difficult labour and community relations. All ASEAN countries have exempted export-oriented FDI from the joint venture requirement. Malaysia imposes joint venture requirements as part of its *bumiputra* (pro-indigenous) policy. For joint venture requirements not to be a serious impediment to FDI, there should also be efforts to improve the supply of appropriately skilled local partners.

Among the ASEAN governments that attempted to increase domestic linkages through the local content requirement, Singapore was the first to promote a local supplier of electronic parts and components to serve TNC assembly plants without mandating local content. Its Local Industries Upgrading Programme has been much studied, and copied by some other countries in the region.

TNCs are often reluctant to employ local personnel in senior management and professional positions unless required to do so by host governments or unless abundant local expertise is available at lower wages. This is because they are usually wary of leakages of proprietary technology and difficulties arising from different management cultures and working languages. Nevertheless, an increasingly important factor in attracting FDI has been the availability of a technical and skills base, particularly when the host country aims to move beyond the low-skilled, labour-intensive stage of manufacturing. Some ASEAN countries impose restrictions on the employment of foreign personnel. However, for the requirement not to become a serious impediment to FDI or to efficient operations, there must be a corresponding development of qualified local personnel through rapid expansion and upgrading of appropriate technical education.

Finally, with the proliferation of multilateral investment rules (e.g. the WTO Agreement on Trade-related Investment Measures (TRIMs) and the General Agreement on Trade in Services (GATS)), and various regional agreements, such as those of the Asia-Pacific Economic Cooperation (APEC) forum and ASEAN, the scope for national governments to use restrictions and performance requirements – such as local content and market restrictions – is being increasingly constrained.

(e) Promoting regionalization

ASEAN is both a political and an economic grouping. Politically, the member States have agreed to work more closely together to resolve bilateral and regional problems through peaceful diplomatic means, thereby contributing to regional peace and stability. This has enabled individual member countries to concentrate their efforts and resources on national economic and social development agendas without having to worry about involvement in territorial disputes or military conflicts. It has also succeeded in putting individual ASEAN countries on the "radar screen" of the world's political leaders, policy-makers, news media and business leaders.

Economically, ASEAN as a regional bloc is more attractive and competitive as a production base, trading partner and investment location than its individual countries. African countries can similarly make more effective use of formal and institutionalized regional integration. For small economies in particular, forming regional groupings and alliances to improve trade and investment competitiveness can be crucial.

2. Lessons from the Asian financial crisis

The East Asian financial crisis undermined the image enjoyed by the ASEAN-5 countries as one of political and social stability and economic dynamism, where international and regional investors generally benefited from low investment risks and profitable investment opportunities. The fact that FDI inflows to the region lagged behind economic recovery following the crisis suggests that investors' perceptions of economic and political risks in the countries remained high for an extended period. ASEAN also faced a negative image problem as a regional grouping. Its image as a politically cohesive and economically dynamic grouping was affected by what was seen as a poor collective response to resolving the regional financial crisis, and it was also seen as being slow in implementing AFTA and AIA. Perceptions of political and economic weaknesses in individual countries also affected the region as a whole. The following observations contain some lessons from the 1997-1998 crisis for Africa:

The sullied image of the region adversely affected all the countries there. While Singapore continued to enjoy political and social stability, and law and order, and demonstrated considerable economic resilience throughout the crisis, it nonetheless suffered from the negative image of the region, and was forced to allow its currency to depreciate to remain competitive.

Perceived poor public and corporate governance in some countries in the region exacerbated investors' declining confidence. Investors increasingly demand government competence, transparency, responsibility and accountability, both because governance affects asset values and profitability, and because of pressures from civil society groups.

A favourable FDI policy regime is not a sufficient condition for attracting FDI. The post-crisis FDI policy regimes in ASEAN are much more liberal and FDI-friendly than before, but have failed to stimulate FDI inflows to several member countries because of poor economic, financial, political and social fundamentals.

While building a positive image for the region took decades, that image was lost very quickly when the region/countries sank into economic, political and social turmoil. National and regional efforts to restore investor confidence have not always been adequate and the negative image of the ASEAN-5 and East Asia generally since 1997 has not been easily reversed.

3. Lessons on development impact

The ASEAN-5 are among the few countries with sufficiently long experience to provide evidence of the benefits and costs of FDI-led development. The impact is seen at a number of levels, both direct and indirect (Mirza and Giroud, 2004). In ASEAN countries, the direct effects have been a significantly positive impact on employment, training and the development of local capital. There are three main indirect effects: consumption multiplier effects, value chain multiplier effects and spillover effects. The first effects relate to the impact on other sectors of the economy due to payment of taxes and payment of goods and services by foreign affiliates. The value chain multiplier effect occurs along the value chain (i.e. by increasing the output of suppliers through backward linkages, and of sales organizations through forward linkages). The multiplier will be affected by the degree to which the value chain linkages are within the host country or outside. In the case of ASEAN, the value chain multiplier is relatively low because inputs are imported from overseas due to a lack of local suppliers, or where local suppliers are used, these are often affiliates of TNCs, and because the output tends to be exported. However, this is partly the consequence of efficiency-oriented investments (at least until a local market has developed to a sufficient level). African countries need not worry much about this aspect, especially if the aim is to secure access to foreign markets.

The spillover effect is the result of both deliberate (e.g. training of workers, quality control enforcement among suppliers, or student scholarships) and non-deliberate actions (e.g. competitive pressures on local firms) (UNCTAD, 2001b). In the longer run, this is the most important benefit that can accrue to an economy from FDI because it enables indigenous firms to learn from foreign companies and thus contributes to the overall development effort. The greatest gain for the ASEAN-5 has come through the imparting of "world class" technology, knowledge and expertise to local suppliers, essentially because it is important for TNCs to maintain quality and efficiency in a global supply chain. This underscores the necessity for African countries to promote efficiency-seeking investment. One of the main reasons why there are often few spillovers is either because there is a dearth of local companies or because they lack the capabilities to absorb foreign knowledge. African countries therefore need to foster the capabilities of local firms to encourage foreign investment in them, and this could result in a virtuous circle as local firms improve further by working with foreign affiliates.

E. CONCLUSIONS

While the main attractions of many African economies have been their natural-resource endowments, it is crucial for them to go beyond this. The experience of South-East Asian countries demonstrates that rapid industrialization is imperative for long-term economic development, and both government policy and foreign investment can play important roles in promoting early industrialization.[3] Therefore, there is a need for governments of African countries to focus more on manufacturing and services activities. Currently, their focus could be on labour-intensive and resource-based processing, as well as export-oriented production in relatively low-technology manufacturing. The rapid industrial upgrading taking place in Asia provides ample opportunities for Africa to attract FDI in manufacturing from the Asian economies. Indeed, Asian FDI in Africa could become an important and promising facet of South-South economic cooperation in the future.

Because only a few African countries – Algeria, Egypt, Morocco, Nigeria and South Africa – have sizeable domestic markets, market-seeking FDI is constrained by market size. Economic development can increase the size of the markets, but that takes time. Market size can be enlarged through more effective regional economic integration arrangements, such as ASEAN which has been considerably strengthened over the past decade.

Efficiency-seeking and export-oriented manufacturing FDI has been very limited in Africa.

For export-oriented manufacturing, Africa enjoys the advantages of special and preferential market access under the GSP and through regional arrangements with the EU and the United States. However, preferential access will have to be complemented by cost competitiveness, which depends not only on abundant low-wage labour, but also on the availability of industrial skills and infrastructure, as well as stable industrial relations. In addition to offering profitable investment opportunities, the quality of the overall investment climate is an important factor for attracting investors. The Asian experience suggests that governments' strategic investments in education and infrastructure have been crucial for promoting economic development in general and attracting efficiency-seeking FDI in particular.

In conclusion, the experience of the ASEAN countries demonstrates that the following factors are crucial for attracting additional FDI: (i) improving political and social stability to reduce investment risks and uncertainties; (ii) developing human resources and infrastructure to improve cost competitiveness; (iii) promoting regional integration, market development and economic growth to improve market competitiveness; (iv) improving the institutional and policy framework to strengthen policy competitiveness; and (v) improving the investment climate and making investment promotion more effective through the provision of information, speedy investment approvals and a range of investment services to facilitate investments.

Notes

[1] The TEL contains industries and investment measures that are temporarily closed to investment and not granted national treatment, but it will be phased out within specified time frames; the SL covers industries and investment measures that are not subject to phasing out, and review by the AIA Council in 2003 and thereafter at subsequent intervals; and the GEL consists of industries and investment measures that cannot be opened up for investment or granted national treatment for reasons of national security, public morals, public health or environmental protection. Brunei Darussalam, Indonesia, Malaysia, Myanmar, the Philippines, Singapore and Thailand had until 1 January 2003 to phase out their TEL for the manufacturing sector. The newer members of ASEAN – Cambodia, Lao People's Democratic Republic and Viet Nam – have until 1 January 2010 (*Source*: ASEAN Secretariat, "ASEAN Investment Area: an update", http://www.aseansec.org/7664.htm). In 2006, the Ninth AIA Council endorsed the TEL and SL for services that are linked to manufacturing, agriculture, fishery, forestry, and mining and quarrying. (*Source*: ASEAN Secretariat, "Joint media statement of the Ninth ASEAN Investment Area Council Meeting, Kuala Lumpur, 21 August 2006", http://www.aseansec.org/18679.htm).

[2] 0-5 per cent and non-tariff barriers by 2003, except for products on an exclusion list.

[3] Several scholars have emphasized the central role played by governments in the economic development of the East Asian economies. Industrial policy is considered the main factor behind the rapid industrialization of those economies. Some important studies on the role of industrial policy in East Asian industrialization include those by Amsden (1989) on the Republic of Korea, Wade (1990) on Taiwan Province of China, and Johnson (1982) on Japan. In addition, Liang (2004) has examined the roles of both industrial policy and inward FDI in China's rapid process of industrial development.

CHAPTER III

CHINESE FDI IN AFRICA AND INWARD FDI IN CHINA: EXPERIENCE AND LESSONS

China started to open its economy to FDI in the late 1970s and has been the largest recipient of FDI among developing countries since the 1990s. Chinese firms have also started to invest in other countries and regions. Its major outflows go to other economies within Asia as well as Latin America and the Caribbean, but Africa is also emerging as an important destination. Experience with respect to China's FDI in Africa and China's own experience in using FDI to boost national economic development are both relevant for African countries seeking to attract and benefit from FDI.

This chapter is organized as follows. Section A briefly analyses trends in China's outward FDI, with a particular focus on its geographic distribution. Section B examines the framework of China's policies on outward FDI. Section C explores the trends and features of China's FDI outflows to Africa, while section D provides basic information on trends in China's inward FDI, its impact on the Chinese economy and a number of important policy issues. This section also addresses the relevance of the Chinese experience for African countries.

A. CHINA'S FDI OUTFLOWS

It has been more than 25 years since China began to open up and adopt market-oriented economic reforms. Its FDI outflows have grown significantly during the past two decades, from less than $100 million in the 1980s to $12 billion in 2005 (table III.1). With a large amount of "China dollars" and the rapid expansion of the Chinese economy, strong growth in the country's overseas investment, driven by various motives, will continue in the coming years. The country appears to become one of the world's largest FDI sources in the not too distant future, spurred by the Government's "going global" policy.

There are two official sources of data on FDI from China: the Ministry of Commerce (MOFCOM), which provides data on an approval basis before 2002 and on a balance-of-payments (BOP) basis afterwards, and the State Administration of Foreign Exchange (SAFE), which provides data on a BOP basis. Neither of

these agencies provide outward FDI data covering the financial sector.[1] Figure III.1 shows the trends in China's outward FDI since the early 1980s, using the SAFE data for 1982-2002 and the MOFCOM data for 2003-2005. China's outward FDI stock stood at $57 billion by the end of 2005 according to the MOFCOM data.

Table III.1. Outward FDI from China: basic indicators, 2005

Indicator	Value
FDI outflows ($ billion)	12.3
Outward stock ($ billion)	57.2
Ratio of outward stock to GDP (%)	2.6
Share in global FDI outflows (%)	1.6
Share in global outward stock (%)	0.5
Number of host countries of Chinese FDI	163

Source: UNCTAD, based on MOFCOM and UNCTAD FDI/TNC database (www.unctad.org/fdistatistics).

Figure III.1.   FDI outflows from China, 1982-2005
(Billions of dollars)

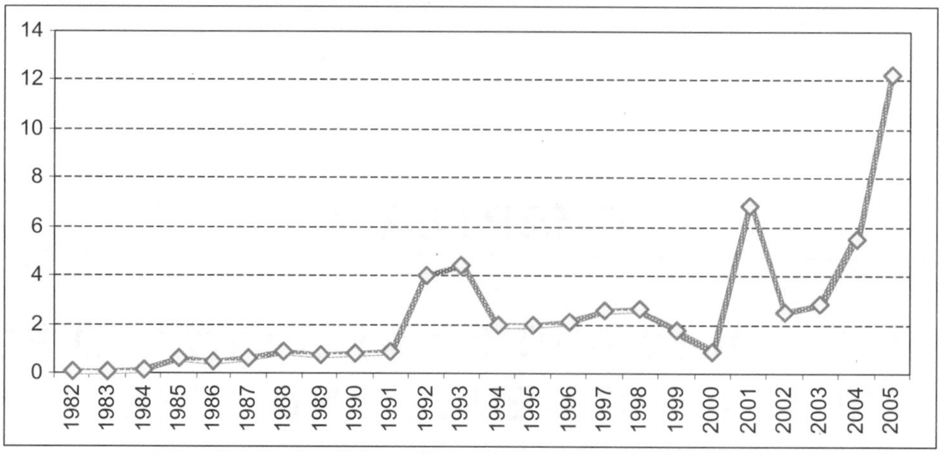

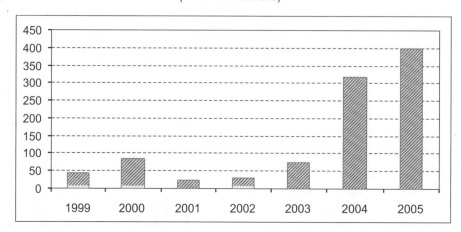

Source: UNCTAD, based on SAFE for 1982-2002 and MOFCOM for 2002-2005.

In the early years of China's economic transition to an open and market-based system, Chinese firms started with small investments abroad, mostly in neighbouring countries and regions, including Hong Kong (China) and Macao (China). This was due to the fact that, at that time, Chinese firms were new to the world economy and lacked the competitive advantages necessary for FDI as well as its related knowledge and experience.   In addition, China suffered heavily from a shortage of foreign exchange, and implemented very stringent monetary regulations and foreign exchange controls to limit capital outflows.

From the mid-1980s, outflows increased only slightly. Just a few Chinese FDI projects exceeded $5 million before 1990, and none of them were undertaken in Africa. After 1990, China's FDI outflows grew remarkably in both value of investment and the number of projects. By the end of 2000, Chinese companies had undertaken 6,296 FDI projects in 140 countries and regions.[2] Of China's total investment outflows in 2000 in terms of value, 25 per cent were to economies within Asia, including among others Hong Kong (China) and Macao (China), while North America and Oceania accounted for 37 per cent and Africa for 17 per cent. In terms of the absolute amount of flows, Africa has become an important FDI location for Chinese enterprises only in recent years. As of 2005, China's FDI stock in Africa had reached $1.6 billion, with increasing outflows to the continent in recent years (figure III.2). A number of African countries have received FDI flows from China (table III.2).

Figure III.2.   China's FDI outflows to Africa,[a] 1999-2005
(Millions of dollars)

Source: UNCTAD, based on MOFCOM.
[a]   Data of 1999-2002 are on an approval basis; data of 2003-2005 are on a BOP basis.

Table III.2 Approved outward FDI flows to African countries from China, 1999-2003
(Number of projects and value in millions of dollars)

Country	1999 Number	1999 Value	2000 Number	2000 Value	2001 Number	2001 Value	2002 Number	2002 Value	2003 Number	2003 Value
Zambia	4	6.7	3	11.6	3	4.3	1	0.3	..	-
South Africa	14	12.8	17	31.5	2	12.4	3	1.7	10	7.3
Mali	1	1.2	1	28.7	..	-	..	-	..	-
Egypt	5	3.8	3	9.7	2	1.4	3	16.3	5	7.8
Nigeria	2	1.6	1	2.6	8	6.4	9	11.4	13	11.8
Mauritius	..	-	..	-	..	-	..	-	1	20.7
United Rep. of Tanzania	3	16.3	1	1.0	..	-	2	0.4	2	0.4
Zimbabwe	..	-	..	-	..	-	..	-	..	2.0
TOTAL	**220**	**590.6**	**243**	**551.0**	**232**	**707.5**	**350**	**982.7**	**510**	**2 086.9**

Source: UNCTAD, based MOFCOM.

However, the share of Africa in total Chinese outward FDI remains marginal. In 2003, for instance, Africa accounted for only 3 per cent of FDI *outflows* from China, while Asia received more than half (53 per cent) of the total, followed by Latin America (37 per cent). In terms of share in the *stock* of China's outward FDI, the significance of Asia is even higher, with Hong Kong (China) playing a dominant role. As of 2005, Asia accounted for 71 per cent of the total, and Africa for only 3 per cent of China's outward stock. On a country basis, though, a few African countries are relatively important recipients of China's FDI: Sudan, Algeria and Zambia are the 9th, 18th and 19th largest recipients respectively of its outward FDI stock (table III.3).

FDI outflows play an increasingly important role in China's international economic cooperation, and have become a major means for Chinese enterprises to operate abroad and compete in the world market. A 2001 survey for MOFTEC (unpublished) showed that about one third of China's FDI projects abroad had positive rates of return while another one third broke even.

The internationalization of Chinese enterprises that has accelerated in recent years, driven by various motives (including market-, asset-, efficiency-, and resource-seeking) and encouraged by the "going global" strategy of the Chinese Government (see below), is expected to continue. The importance of China's foreign reserves (at $1 trillion at the end of 2006, the largest in the world) is also contributing to the expansion of Chinese outward FDI. Indeed, China is set to become a major foreign investor in the developing world (UNCTAD, 2005). Chinese investments in developed countries are also set to increase, as suggested by transactions such as the acquisition of IBM's Personal Computer business by Lenovo in late 2004.

Table III.3. China's outward FDI stock, top 20 host countries and territories, by 2005
(Millions of dollars)

Rank	Country/territory	Investment value
1	Hong Kong, China	36 510
2	Cayman Islands	8 936
3	British Virgin Islands	1 984
4	Korea, Rep. of	882
5	United States	823
6	Macau, China	599
7	Australia	587
8	Russian Federation	466
9	Sudan	352
10	Bermuda	337
11	Singapore	325
12	Germany	268
13	Kazakhstan	245
14	Viet Nam	229
15	Thailand	219
16	Pakistan	189
17	Malaysia	187
18	Algeria	171
19	Zambia	160
20	Japan	151
	Others	3 580
	TOTAL	**57 200**

Source: UNCTAD, based on MOFCOM.

B.   CHINA'S POLICY ON OUTWARD FDI

China's current policy framework on outward FDI covers a range of issues such as the approval process, the encouragement of specific types of projects, foreign currency management, State-owned assets management and statistics. The country has promulgated a series of regulations in these areas to promote and regulate foreign investment by Chinese firms (table III.4). According to the 2004 "Decision of the State Council on Reforming the Investment System", the

abroad. During this period, many Chinese firms invested abroad through the provision of production equipment, raw and processed materials and technology know-how since they were still short of foreign exchange. Their mode of investment was mostly in the form of joint ventures with local counterparts.

By the mid-1990s, China's national economy had developed at a rapid pace and improved its industrial structure. In the late 1990s

Table III.4. Regulations on China's outward FDI

Area	Regulation	Time of promulgation
Approval	Provisions on the Examination and Approval of Investment to Run Enterprises Abroad (MOFCOM)	1 October 2004
	The Interim Measures for the Administration of Examination and Approval of the Overseas Investment Projects (NDRC)	9 October 2004
	Detailed Rules for the Examination and Approval of Investments to Open and Operate Enterprises Abroad (MOFCOM)	17 October 2005
Encouragement	Circular on the Issues related to Granting Financing Support to Key Overseas Projects Encouraged by the State (NDRC)	9 May 2003
	Circular on the Supportive Credit Policy on Key Overseas Investment Projects Encouraged by the State (NDRC and the Export-Import Bank of China)	27 October 2004
	Circular on the Issues on Offering More Financing Support to Key Overseas Investment Projects (NDRC and the Export-Import Bank of China)	25 September 2005
State-owned asset management	The Interim Measures for the Administration of Overseas State-owned Assets (Ministry of Finance, SAFE, etc.)	27 September 1999
Foreign currency management	Circular of the State Administration of Foreign Exchange on Issues Concerning Deepening the Reform of Foreign Exchange Administration on Foreign Investment (SAFE)	15 October 2003
	Circular of the State Administration of Foreign Exchange on Issues on Broadening the Reform of Foreign Exchange Administration on Foreign Investment (SAFE)	19 May 2005
	Circular of the State Administration of Foreign Exchange on Adjusting Some Foreign Exchange Management Policies about Overseas Investments (SAFE)	6 June 2006
Statistics	Interim Measures for Joint Annual Inspection of Overseas Investment (MOFTEC and SAFE)	31 October 2002
	Statistic System of Overseas Investments (MOFTEC and National Bureau of Statistics)	4 December 2002
	System of Advance Reporting of Overseas M&As (MOFCOM)	31 March 2005

Source: MOFCOM.

authority for approval is vested in the central or provincial governments according to the category (resource or non-resource) and size of a project (table III.5).

Since the early 1980s, there has been an ongoing process of revision and adjustment to policies on China's FDI outflows, moving towards a more transparent and positive policy framework. In the early 1980s, the Chinese Government had a strict examination and approval system to evaluate outward FDI projects. This reflected the legacy of the central planning system; but it lasted for only a short period and from the late 1980s it gave way to a more flexible new arrangement that encouraged Chinese firms to expand

the central Government began encouraging outward FDI and announced the "going global" strategy. A series of incentives accompanied the strategy, such as easy access to bank loans, simplified border procedures, and preferential policies for taxation, imports and exports (box III.1). A selective support

Table III.5. China: authority-sharing in the approval of overseas FDI projects between central and provincial governments

Category of project	Central government	Provincial government
Resource exploration project	Investment > $30 million	Investment < $30 million
Non-resource project	Investment (in foreign exchange) > $10 million	Investment (in foreign exchange) < $10 million

Source: MOFCOM.
Note: Investment refers to that from the Chinese investor.

Box III.1. Incentives to Chinese firms investing abroad

In the wake of its rapid economic development, China has formulated a series of policies to encourage well-established Chinese enterprises to undertake FDI activities abroad to compete in the world marketplace. China's incentives to promote FDI outflows take four forms: special and general tax incentives, credit and loans, foreign exchange allowance, and a favourable import and export regime.

Tax incentives. In 1986 the Chinese Government introduced tax incentives for Chinese enterprises with overseas operations. All Chinese enterprises overseas are exempt from corporate income tax for five successive years after beginning operations. After five years of income tax exemption, Chinese enterprises operating in countries and regions that have concluded double taxation treaties with China are exempted from income tax. As of end-2005, six African countries (Egypt, Mauritius, Seychelles, South Africa, Sudan and Tunisia) had concluded such agreements with China (chapter I, table I.10). Chinese enterprises with assembly and processing businesses abroad may reinvest their earnings abroad as added capital funds for five years after they gain profits without taxes being levied.

In addition to the central Government's tax incentives, some local governments have additional policies at the provincial level to promote outward FDI, which entitle eligible enterprises or individuals to exemption from corporate and individual income tax for certain specified periods.

Loans and credit. Chinese enterprises with investments abroad are eligible for medium- and long-term commercial loans or soft loans from Chinese commercial banks. These banks have also been encouraged to grant export credit to Chinese enterprises that export to their foreign affiliates production equipment, technology know-how, parts and components, as well as raw and processed materials. Some recent regulations promulgated by the National Development and Reform Commission (NDRC) and the Export-Import Bank of China focus on granting financing support to key overseas projects encouraged by the Government (table III.4).

Foreign exchange. China's foreign exchange administration stipulates that Chinese enterprises are eligible for foreign exchange for foreign investment projects, subject to government approval. According to a 2005 survey of Chinese companies, existing restrictions on the use of foreign exchange were found to be too stringent (Yao and He, 2005). The decision in June 2006 by the State Administration of Foreign Exchange to abolish the quota control of foreign exchange purchase for overseas investment is an important step in the direction of addressing such concerns.

The import and export regime. Production equipment as well as raw and processed materials exported by Chinese enterprises for their overseas investment projects are treated the same as other exports and are entitled to exporters' refund of value-added tax. If there is a need for licensing or quotas for exports, the Government treats them as top priority. Products imported from overseas investments are also given preference when all other conditions – such as quality and price – are the same. For example, seafood imported from ocean fishing companies that have Chinese investments is exempt from customs tariffs.

Source: UNCTAD, based on MOFCOM.

policy has been adopted to encourage outward FDI. Emphasis has been given to 1) resource exploration projects, 2) projects that can promote the exports of domestic technologies, products, equipments and labours, 3) overseas research and development (R&D) centres, and 4) M&As that can enhance the international competitiveness of Chinese enterprises and accelerate their entry into foreign markets. The conclusion of bilateral investment treaties (BITs) has been another measure adopted for promoting outward FDI (box III.2).

In recent years, the pressure from the large amount of "China dollars" and their rapid expansion has made the promotion of outward FDI imperative for the Chinese Government. The policy framework encouraging Chinese enterprises to "go global" has become more explicit. In October 2004, for instance, the National Development and Reform Commission (NDRC) and the Export-Import Bank of China (EIBC) jointly promulgated a circular (table III.4) to encourage overseas investment projects in specific areas. A preferential credit

---

Box III.2. Bilateral investment treaties

By the end of 2005, China ranked second worldwide in terms of the number of BITs concluded with 117 agreements, including 28 BITs with African countries (Algeria, Benin, Botswana, Cameroon, Cape Verde, Congo, Côte d' Ivoire, Djibouti, Egypt, Equatorial Guinea, Ethiopia, Gabon, Ghana, Guinea, Kenya, Madagascar, Mali, Mauritius, Morocco, Mozambique, Nigeria, Sierra Leone, South Africa, Sudan, Tunisia, Uganda, Zambia and Zimbabwe) (chapter I, table I.9).

The BITs concluded by China have the following main features:

• They use a broad asset-based definition of investments covering, inter alia, movable and immovable property, real estate, corporate shares, stocks, copyright, intellectual property rights and royalties.

• They admit covered investments in accordance with domestic laws and regulations.
• As far as the treatment provisions are concerned, the BITs concluded by China grant fair and equitable treatment and most-favoured nation treatment for the foreign investor. The agreements also protect investors against expropriation and nationalization; guarantee the free transfer of funds related to investment; and contain a settlement mechanism for State-State disputes.

More recent BITs of China also include the principle of national treatment and rules on investor-State dispute settlement. To this purpose, China has recently renegotiated a number of its earlier BITs.

Source: UNCTAD.

---

policy has been granted to these key projects supported by the State. Under this scheme, the EIBC specifically earmarks a certain amount of loans, called "special loans for overseas investments", within its export credit plan in order to support the key overseas investment projects encouraged by the State. The interest rate of the special loans for overseas investment is the same as that for export credit. The EIBC also accelerates the process of project screening. The NDRC facilitates steps by other agencies to improve the risk management of overseas investment.

C. CHINESE FDI IN AFRICA

Africa is one of China's important partners for trade and economic cooperation. Trade between China and Africa increased from $11 billion in 2000 to almost $40 billion in 2005. China has become the third largest trading partner of Africa, following the United States and France. Chinese investment in Africa reached about $1.6 billion by 2005, with a presence in 48 African countries. The Chinese Government encourages outward FDI in certain industries in the industrial and agricultural sectors in Africa, and, currently, the main mode of entry is equity joint ventures.

1. Industrial priorities

China's investments in Africa have mainly gone into manufacturing, resource extraction, construction and other services (table III.6).

Table III.6. Sectoral distribution of China's FDI flows to Africa,[a] 1979-2000

Sector/industry	Number of projects	Investment value (Millions of dollars)
Agriculture	22	48
Resource extraction	44	188
Manufacturing	230	315
Machinery	20	16
Home appliances	36	25
Light industry	82	87
Textiles	58	102
Other manufacturing	34	86
Services	200	125
Others	3	6
Total	499	681

Souce: UNCTAD, based on information provided by the MOFCOM.
[a]   Data are on an approval basis.

Manufacturing (in particular textiles) and resource extraction were the two most important sectors during the period 1979-2000 (the most recent year for which data are available). A significant share of Chinese investment in the services sector in Africa has been in construction. In recent years, Chinese FDI increasingly targeted natural resources in Africa.

The Chinese Government has identified certain industries and types of projects in Africa in which it encourages Chinese enterprises to invest. These include:

- *Industrial processing*. China possesses comparatively advanced technology in the fields of electronics and machinery building, textiles and garments, and building materials.

- *Agriculture*. China and Africa have been working together to increase productivity and quality following China's experience in dealing with its own food supply problem.[3] In many African countries, agricultural exports are mostly unprocessed, exposing these countries to worsening terms of trade and the vagaries of commodity trading. Investment in African agriculture by China's well-established enterprises can help address the famine problem here and add value to Africa's exports.

- *Natural resources*. To support its economic growth China needs to secure access to natural resources. The African continent, rich in natural resources, particularly petroleum and high-value minerals can provide such resources.

- *Infrastructure and real estate development*. This is another area of significant potential for Chinese investment in Africa. Over 30 years ago, China already helped the United Republic of Tanzania and Zambia to build an important cross-border railway line (TAZARA). Chinese enterprises have also built roads, housing estates and hotels in Africa. In addition, they have set up oil-drilling companies in a number of drought-stricken countries, such as Mali and Mauritania. Infrastructure development projects are top priorities for many multilateral financial institutions, which provide long-term assistance and financial support not only for governmental projects, but also for private and commercial organizations in these sectors. There is a strong potential for cooperation in these projects between Chinese enterprises and their counterparts in Africa.

2. Experience of Chinese enterprises in Africa: selected projects

By 2000, Chinese investors had undertaken nearly 500 projects in Africa, 30 of them exceeding $10 million and spanning almost all African countries. These projects have been implemented in various host countries that differ in terms of their political systems, level of economic and social development, human resources and attractiveness as locations for China's investments.

In Africa alone, while the returns on investments from Chinese foreign affiliates were low compared to other regions according to a (unpublished) MOFTEC survey, more than half of the enterprises receiving Chinese FDI were operating at least broke even and only a small proportion recorded losses or were involved in disputes. Of those that were successful, many were not only able to meet local demand, but also exported to other African countries as well as to Europe and North America. Many of the Chinese firms operating in Africa are SMEs.

Three Chinese companies (COFCO, Sinochem Corporation, and China Minmetals Corporation), which ranked among the 50 largest TNCs from developing countries based on foreign assets in 2000 (UNCTAD, 2002c), have investments in Africa. In addition, China State Construction Engineering Corporation, Shougang Group and China Harbor Engineering Company also have significant investments in Africa. Boxes III.3 to III.5 describe some examples of FDI in African projects by relatively small Chinese firms, highlighting the potential for Sino-African cooperation. Large investments by Chinese firms include a $757 million investment project in oil by the China National Petroleum Corporation (CNPC) in Sudan.[4] CNOOC, another state-owned company paid $2.7 billion in 2006 to buy a minority interest in a Nigerian oilfield.

Box III.3. SVA Electronics (PTY) Ltd. in South Africa

Shanghai Audio and Video Electronics Co. Ltd. (SVA)[a] established SVA Electronics (PTY) Ltd. in South Africa in 1994. It took almost two years for the project to complete the various steps, from the pre-feasibility study to the start of production. With an investment of $1 million, including some idle equipment from the parent company worth $150,000, the South African affiliate was projected to produce 100,000 black and white television sets per year. It assembles and processes components and parts, which come mainly from China, for sale to the local market and to neighbouring countries. The production has been largely expanded and diversified, including via the acquisition of local companies.[b] In 2003, its profits reached $13 million.[c] Currently the affiliate has more than 200 employees, 90 per cent locally recruited.

Owing to an increase in demand for TVs in South Africa, in 1996 the company increased its output and also set up a production line for colour TVs. In 1998, demand for black and white TVs declined considerably and demand for colour TVs grew. This contributed to the company's increased profits. Also in 1996, the company, noting the large import volume of washing machines in South Africa, decided to establish a production line for these. Owing to the good market response, the initial output for the year of 10,000 units was soon increased, reaching 50,000 in 2000, all of which were sold locally. Now SVA's affiliate in South Africa has become one of the four major overseas production bases (the other three are in Argentina, Bulgaria and Pakistan).

The following are some of the reasons why a well-established company in Shanghai such as SVA set up its operations in South Africa:

• *Reduced transport costs.* The company had been receiving sizeable orders for TVs but claimed it did not make much profit from its exports to that country even though the export volume was large enough. It hoped that relocation might reduce costs and improve its profit margin. Thus, it chose to set up an affiliate to assemble and sell locally in South Africa with imported components from China.

• *Equipment exports.* The company had an idle production line for black and white TVs, as there was no longer domestic demand for them. Establishing an affiliate in South Africa would not only expand its share of that market, but also make use of idle equipment.

• *Overseas strategy.* In the mid-1990s, the company's share of the lower-end TV market and its profits had been considerable reduced due to excess supply in the domestic TV market. The management's strategy was hence to expand overseas and capture much of the growing market in Africa (and Latin America). After the investment in South Africa, the company has expanded its TV production to other developing countries, including Argentina, Pakistan and Bulgaria. Now overseas production bases, including that in South Africa, are significantly contributing to SVA's expansion in the global TV market.

The company encountered certain problems during its early years of operation in South Africa:

• *Foreign exchange.* Although South Africa had a good banking system with effective and efficient services, foreign investors were not allowed to have a foreign currency account and all transactions had to be done in the local currency. Taxes were imposed on expatriates and foreign enterprises for all foreign exchange remittances out of South Africa. There were no incentives for foreign investors in this regard.

• *High labour costs.* Despite high unemployment rates, labour costs are relatively high. Wages for unskilled workers are about $150-200 per month. Normally, such workers have not been technically trained and often fail to meet production requirements. The senior managerial personnel were brought from Shanghai, which increased costs.

• *Visas.* It is difficult to obtain a work permit from the South African consulate in Shanghai. The managerial personnel have to go to Beijing to apply for such visas and wait for as long as a year to obtain them. This, of course, adversely affects company operations in South Africa.

Source: UNCTAD, based on information provided by the Chinese Academy of International Trade and Economic Cooperation and information published by the company.

[a] The company is an affiliate of Shanghai Guangdian Electric Corporation, a public company listed in 1992.
[b] In August 2001, the company acquired UNIVA, a local firm producing ovens.
[c] According to http://www.btc.sh.cn/daynews/04news01.htm.

Box III.4. Friendship Textile Mill in the United Republic of Tanzania

Friendship Textile Factory in the United Republic of Tanzania was established in 1968 and expanded in 1975 with ODA from China. It was a large textile project at that time, with 40,000 spindles, 1,154 looms and two printing and dyeing lines. Its annual production capacity was 3,300 metres of grey cloth. From late 1980 to 1994, factory operations fell behind and production ground to a halt. In 1995, the factory was transformed into a Sino-Tanzanian joint venture. The China Jiangsu Changzhou Textile Corporation invested over $10 million to set up the joint venture with its Tanzanian counterpart and the factory resumed production in April 1994. By the end of 2000, revenue reached $33.5 million, with $6.96 million in taxes paid to the Tanzanian Government. The factory provided more than 1,800 jobs and paid $7.25 million in salaries and emoluments by 2000.

This Chinese enterprise in the United Republic of Tanzania also encountered some problems. First, the economic situation in the host country was weak and the local currency kept depreciating. Consumer purchasing power declined and the local market weakened further, which made marketing more difficult. Second, the environment for investment was worsening, and production costs were soaring. Utility prices have been two to three times higher than in neighbouring countries (chapter VIII), and local cotton prices have also been rising marginally. Third, because of insufficient training, it was not easy for workers to adapt quickly to new technology and operating requirements, and this resulted in low productivity and efficiency. Fourth, the tax structure was complicated, and some tax reductions and exemptions that Chinese investors were expecting never materialized. Last but not least, established welfare provisions added further costs to mill operations. For example, the factory had to cover the entire medical expenses of the workers and their families.

Nevertheless, the company has done well since the restructuring in the mid-1990s. For the period 1996-2005, it paid taxes of over 15 billion Tanzanian shillings to the Tanzanian Government and created 2000 jobs.

Source: UNCTAD, based on information provided by the Chinese Academy of International Trade and Economic Cooperation.

China's FDI flows into African countries are mainly in the form of equity joint ventures with local enterprises. Chinese investors have gained from their experience in partnering with their African counterparts. The motivations of Chinese enterprises investing directly in the continent vary as follows:

- *Direct access to the market*: Investors seek to disengage from their export agents and increase their market share in the world market, as in the case of SAV Electronics (Pty.) Ltd.

- *Increased market penetration*. This applies mainly to products for which supply largely exceeds demand in the domestic market.

- *Securing access to natural resources*. This motivation is becoming more and more important, reflecting a rise in demand from China. Large investments made or announced recently in Africa are related to this.

- *Reuse of idle equipment*. As in the case of SAV Electronics (Pty.) Ltd., some Chinese enterprises invest in Africa in order to maximize the marginal efficiency of used equipment, with benefits to both the parent company and the affiliate company.

- *Circumvent import quotas imposed on Chinese products*: Particularly important for textiles and light industrial projects.

The main lessons drawn from the experience of China's FDI in Africa include:

- *Finding suitable partners*. Chinese enterprises regard suitable partnership with a local company as the most important factor for project success. The partners' marketing channels, knowledge of local policies and business climate compensate for limited international experience on the part of the Chinese firms.

- *Local government support*. The legal framework and investment policies are crucial elements for creating a favourable climate to attract FDI. An enhanced government role in investment activities is likely to lead to better performance of the project.

Box III.5. Enitex Co. Ltd. in Nigeria

In 1997, Shanghai Huayuan Group Corporation, together with a Nigerian company, acquired a textile company previously owned by a French company. The Chinese firm invested $2.4 million for an 80 per cent stake. The newly acquired company (Enitex Co. Ltd) began production in August 1997, with an annual production capacity of 1,500 metres of printed and dyed cloth. Being of good quality and variety, the products sold well, and in 1999 the company made a profit of $0.4 million.

In 2000, the shareholders decided to carry out the second phase of the project by investing an additional $6 million and establishing a cotton-spinning mill with a capacity of 13,000 spindles. The project yielded results the same year: the company gained a net profit of $0.76 million and became one of the largest taxpayers in Nigeria, with total employees numbering nearly 1,000.

Enitex Co. Ltd. has set a fine example for Chinese firms carrying out investment activities in Africa. Its success can largely be attributed to the following factors:

- *Detailed and thorough research of the Nigerian textile market.* The parent company had exported textile products to Nigeria, and had good knowledge of the Nigerian textile market, while possessing marketing channels.

It conducted a study of the mill it was proposing to purchase, especially with regard to branding, equipment and the market share.

- *Ideal joint-venture partner.* The Nigerian partner, having studied in China, had good knowledge of China and Chinese culture, and showed a willingness to cooperate with Chinese companies. The partner emphasized the need for good governance and industrial relations, and kept a close watch on the local market. Good command of market information also contributed to the success of the project.

- *Parent company's financial strength and advanced expertise.* The parent company is a giant in China's textile industry. The company has both competitive financial strength as well as advanced textile technology and high quality management. Not only did the parent company invest financial resources into the project, it also contributed senior managerial staff with good command of technology and expertise.

- *Government support.* Both the Chinese and Nigerian Governments took considerable interest in the joint venture. The Chinese Government provided support of all kinds, including diplomatic and financial support, while the Nigerian Government showed commitment to the project with its incentives policy and rapid approval.

Source: UNCTAD, based on information provided by the Chinese Academy of International Trade and Economic Cooperation.

- *Market orientation.* Most African countries have liberalized and privatized their economies. This has helped structural adjustment and the establishment of market mechanisms. In identifying potential projects, a major consideration for Chinese enterprises when they target markets and formulate investment plans is market demand and business orientation.

- *Technology transfer.* Chinese firms do not necessarily possess the most advanced technology and expertise, but what they do possess may often be suitable for the needs of the African continent. With the advantages of relatively low-cost and ease of extension, Chinese technology has been adaptable to African countries at their present level of industrialization. As Enitex, SAV and many other companies have demonstrated,

technology improvement and advancement have played a key role in their business success.

Chinese enterprises have sometimes encountered problems and difficulties in their investment activities in Africa. These include a weak economic environment (limited market size), a shortage of skilled workers, foreign exchange controls and inadequate tax incentives.

- *Weak economic environment.* In general, the African region is the least developed in the world. Among the 50 LDCs categorized by the United Nations, 33 are in Africa. And of 63 low-income countries identified by the World Bank, 38 are in sub-Saharan Africa. A weak economic environment and an unstable foreign exchange system often exert negative pressure on investors.[5]

- *Shortage of skilled workers.* Low-cost labour is, of course, a major attraction for China's FDI in Africa, but the shortage of skilled workers reduces the continent's low-cost labour advantage, and adversely affects the quality of finished products and the efficiency of firms' operations;

- *Rigid foreign exchange regulations.* These are among the most sensitive issues for African countries and adversely affect the investment environment. Under rigid foreign exchange regimes, enterprises have to keep local currency accounts, which increases their foreign exchange risks. Even if they can remit foreign exchange out of the host countries, the fees are rather high, adding to enterprise costs.

- *Inadequate incentives.* Unfavourable tax treatment in some African countries has also been a factor affecting investment in Africa by Chinese enterprises.

3. Government efforts in investment promotion

The rapid growth of Chinese FDI in Africa is the result of common efforts by the Chinese and African governments. Such efforts include the following.

International cooperation. High-ranking official visits help consolidate mutual understanding and promote cooperation between China and the African countries. At several summit meetings, principles for Chinese-African economic and technical cooperation have been established and major economic and technical cooperation projects identified, including the establishment of the China-Africa Cooperation Forum in October 2000 (box III.6). During 2001-2003, 30 leaders of African countries visited China and former president Jiang Zemin and ex-premier Zhu Rongji have both visited Africa.[6] Chinese President Hu Jintao gave an important speech at the summit on the 60th anniversary of the establishment of the United Nations in September 2005, announcing a series of Chinese aid initiatives to help the world's poorest countries, African LDCs in particular, by providing, among other things, zero-tariff treatment, debt relief, $10 billion in concessional loans and job training.[7] Specific programmes will be implemented through such mechanisms as the China-Africa Cooperation Forum as well as bilateral channels. Most recently, at the Beijing

Summit of the China-Africa Cooperation in November 2006, the leaders of China endorsed a roadmap for cooperation in economies, politics, social development and international affairs (box III.6).

Intergovernmental joint committees. Joint committees for trade and economic cooperation between China and African countries convene regularly to discuss business issues in each side, review and examine ongoing economic cooperation projects, consult on investment activities and settle disputes. They also identify and promote new cooperation and investment projects.

Bilateral agreements. By 2005, China had concluded BITs with 25 African countries and DTTs with four African countries by 2005. The treaties aim to protect and promote FDI and to clarify the terms for FDI between partner countries. These legal agreements contribute to the creation of a more secure climate for Chinese investors in Africa. Under the Chinese legal system, such international treaties supersede domestic laws. In addition, China has reached economic and technical cooperation agreements with 38 African countries.

Investment promotion efforts by both public and private sectors. The strong and growing momentum of China's investment flows to Africa has been maintained by efforts on both sides. In recent years, as an increasing number of Chinese companies are exploring and planning investments in that continent, many Chinese business delegations have visited African countries to survey and negotiate investment projects.

A number of African companies have been set up to conduct investment promotion activities in China which aim to provide Chinese enterprises with consulting services for doing business in Africa. Such consulting companies are mainly from South Africa and Nigeria. To further promote investment to and trade with Africa by Chinese enterprises, 11 trade and investment promotion and service centres have been established in Africa with support from the Chinese Government.[8]

China's FDI to Africa is likely to continue to grow in view of the complementary nature of economic development between China and African countries, as well as the likely continued economic restructuring of China and its growing appetite for natural resources. Government efforts of the kind described above can contribute significantly to the process.

Box III.6. China-Africa Cooperation Forum

In October 2000, the China-Africa Cooperation Forum was convened in Beijing under the sponsorship of the Chinese Government. The Forum included four State presidents, nearly 80 African ministers and representatives from over 40 African countries, and about 20 international and regional organizations, as well as Chinese counterparts, to discuss the establishment of the new international political and economic order and cooperation between China and Africa.

The Forum adopted two documents – the China-Africa Cooperation Forum Beijing Declaration and the Programme for China-Africa Cooperation in Economic and Social Development – which mapped out the development course for long-term, stable and mutually beneficial Sino-African partnership in the 21st century. At the Forum, the Chinese Government pledged continued assistance to African countries, including:

- Pushing forward China-Africa cooperation in economic and social development;
- Reducing or exempting debts of African countries worth RMB 10 billion ($1.2 billion);
- Setting up a special fund to encourage and support well-established Chinese enterprises investing in Africa; and
- Establishing an African Human Resources Development Fund to train more professionals for African economic development.

Since the meeting, China and Africa have largely adhered the Forum's follow-up action plan. China established a committee consisting of 21 government departments. Ethiopia, Gabon, Sudan and Zambia also established follow-up action organizations. The China-Africa Cooperation Forum has become an important platform for dialogue and for strengthening solidarity and cooperation. According to the *Procedures on the Follow-up Mechanism*, China and Africa alternatively hold ministerial level forum meetings every three years, and hold high-level official meetings one year prior to ministerial meetings. The 2003 meeting reaffirmed the principles of the Forum and decided to make the new China-Africa partnership a highly dynamic and effective one by implementing some concrete measures.

The Beijing Summit of the China-Africa Cooperation Forum took place in November 2006. A total of 48 African countries including 41 heads of state and government participated in the meeting. The document endorsed by leaders of China and 48 African nations charted a roadmap of cooperation in politics, economy, international affairs and social development between China and Africa for the 2007-2009 period. President Hu Jintao announced that China would set up a China-Africa development fund totalling $5 billion to encourage Chinese companies to invest in Africa. A package of aid measures was also announced.

Source: UNCTAD.

D. FDI IN CHINA: LESSONS AND RELEVANCE FOR AFRICA

China is one of the top recipients of FDI in the world: in 2005, it received $72 billion in FDI inflows and its stock reached $318 billion. Some 280,000 foreign affiliates operate in China and play a crucial role in the Chinese economy.

FDI inflows to China are expected to remain high in the coming years due to the expansion of operations by TNCs and the further opening up of China's service industries. Rapid economic growth and an expanding market will all contribute to increased FDI inflows. The recent appreciation of the Chinese currency is likely to have a limited impact on such inflows. However, if the value of renminbi continues to rise, the attractiveness of China as a low-cost destination for efficiency-seeking, export-oriented FDI may decrease.

FDI has contributed significantly to the Chinese economy. Its share in fixed capital formation has been consistently over 10 per cent since 1993. About 95 per cent of *Fortune* magazine's Global 500 companies have operations in China, and some have moved their regional headquarters to Beijing, Shanghai and other Chinese cities. The 280,000 foreign affiliates employ in China 25 million people (more than 10 per cent of the total labour force), produce 29 per cent of the total industrial output and undertake 58 per cent of China's imports and exports (MOFCOM, 2006). FDI has also contributed to industrial upgrading and technological progress in China, helping improve the competitiveness of the Chinese corporate sector.

Actively attracting FDI has long been an integral part of China's development strategy, including through the use of preferential tax treatment. Although the Chinese economy has some unique characteristics, China's experience in attracting FDI and enhancing its benefits may offer some lessons for Africa (as well as other developing countries) engaged in formulating their own FDI strategies to promote national economic development.

With increasing globalization, every country and its enterprises need to optimize and deploy their resources on a larger market scale. Africa has the advantage of being endowed with rich natural and human resources. However, a major question for African countries is how to maximize these advantages. Globalization puts African countries in a vulnerable position, as most of their economies are still weak. China's experience shows that foreign TNCs with advanced technology, expertise and financial assistance can contribute to development in host countries. However, domestic efforts are crucial for reaping the benefits of FDI inflows. The following lessons can be learnt from the Chinese experience:

Regional strategy. China occupies a vast area of 96 million square kilometres with 23 provinces, five autonomous regions, four municipalities directly under the jurisdiction of the central Government and two special administrative regions (Hong Kong and Macao). Given the different economic situations and investment environments of its regions, the central Government adopted a series of strategies in line with its domestic economic and social development needs, in particular it developed a regional strategy.

China opened up to foreign investment gradually, beginning with the special economic zones and coastal provinces, followed by the inland regions along the Yangtze River, and then the interior border areas. From 1979 to the early 1990s,

the Chinese Government opened up the comparatively developed provinces and regions to FDI; these regions provided foreign investors with a more favourable environment and enhanced China's overall attractiveness for FDI. Since 1992, the Government has opened most of its domestic market to foreign investors, encouraging them to invest in any province.

To limit the risks involved in opening up to foreign investment, the Government adopted a gradualist strategy: first a pilot programme, and then extension after reviewing the experience. In the initial stages of the economic reforms, the central and local governments approved four special economic zones and 50 key economic and industrial development zones all over the country, mainly located in the coastal areas. Preferential policies for attracting FDI were applied mainly in special economic zones and economic and industrial development zones. Following the success of these policies, they were extended to other parts of the country. The practice of pilot projects and their extension reduced the risks of opening up.

Industrial strategy. Various industries were opened up at different stages to foreign investors, beginning with assembly and processing for export, real estate development, manufacturing, agriculture and natural resource extraction. At the initial stage of China's reforms and opening up in the late 1970s and early 1980s, FDI mainly flowed into industrial processing and real estate development. Starting from the mid-1980s, it began to flow also into manufacturing of a wide range of products, such as home appliances, textiles, foods, automobiles, electronics, metal products, chemicals, and oil exploitation and refining. After 1990, major TNCs increased their investments in China's industries, and expanded the scale of their investments. Since the mid-1990s, there has been increasing FDI in technology- and capital-intensive industries. Agricultural development and resource exploitation as well as mining and oil exploitation have also become priorities for FDI. From the mid-1990s, the Chinese Government decided to open up parts of China's services sector to foreign investors to catch up with the rapid development of world trade in services. In particular, with its entry into the World Trade Organization (WTO), China agreed to open up major services industries such as banking, insurance, transportation, distribution and telecommunications to foreign investment. In 2004, the services sector was further liberalized – for example, by liberalizing investment regulations relating to FDI in financial services, distribution services, media and education (UNCTAD, 2005). In particular, stringent qualifications, ownership restrictions and geographical limitations previously imposed on FDI in distribution services (such as wholesale, retail, franchising and commission agents' services) were removed. Today, almost all industries have been opened up to FDI after a gradual process of market entry and liberalization. Partly with the help of foreign capital, technology and managerial know-how introduced via FDI, Chinese industries are becoming internationally competitive.

Improving the investment climate. The Chinese Government has made many efforts to improve its investment climate to attract FDI. But, in most African countries infrastructure is relatively weak and does not meet foreign investors' expectations. This cannot be improved overnight. To better attract FDI inflows, it is also imperative for African countries to improve their investment environments (chapter II), for instance, inter alia, enabling foreign investors to repatriate profits across borders; encouraging foreign investors to use technology, equipment and raw and processing materials for capital investment; providing better tax incentives for capital goods; and providing more information about markets and relevant legal policies to familiarize foreign investors with African conditions so as to increase investment opportunities.

Improving labour skills and efficiency. FDI can contribute to improving the skills of the local workforce after foreign investors initially employ expatriate skilled labour, technical and management personnel, as necessary. Human resources are key to enabling African countries to become more attractive for FDI. In China, for quite a long period, foreign affiliates employed managerial personnel from abroad, particularly senior staff. Today, TNCs are mainly recruiting in China, and Chinese nationals are being hired in senior management positions.

For African countries, both foreign support and local efforts are crucial for strengthening the local educational infrastructure and providing educational opportunities to their citizens. The East Asian experience in general and the Chinese one in particular highlight the importance of education and human resource development in long-term economic development. Therefore, the nexus of education and investment policies is particularly important, and a long-term vision in terms of human resource development is imperative. African governments need to channel more domestic funding and ODA to the educational sector. At the current stage when the domestic education system, especially tertiary education, is weak, particular attention should be given to encouraging students to study abroad and come back after graduation or work experience in developed countries. The Chinese experience is particularly valuable in this regard.[9] Donors should initiate specific programmes to fund the overseas study of African students and provide incentives for attracting them back to their home countries.

Investment promotion. Attracting FDI requires strong promotion, including provision of up-to-date and accurate information, streamlining and simplifying approval procedures, and provision of various services to facilitate implementation of investment projects. China made significant efforts to this end. In Africa, there is still a lot to be done to enhance investment promotion, even though many African countries have established investment promotion agencies (IPA). China's experience in this area may provide useful lessons for investment promotion programmes in Africa.

Finally, the Chinese experience demonstrates the importance of the diaspora for attracting FDI in the early stage of economic openness. Although most African countries may not have large diaspora, their IPAs could pay particular attention to their citizens living and working abroad, particularly those in developed countries, as potential sources of FDI.

Notes

[1] In December 2002, MOFCOM established a new statistical system on outward FDI, also on a BOP basis. Before that, the MOFCOM data largely underestimated the scale of Chinese FDI outflows.

[2] Source: Ministry of Foreign Trade and Economic Cooperation (MOFTEC) (the predecessor of MOFCOM).

[3] See, for instance, the Forum on China-Africa Cooperation - Addis Ababa Action Plan (2004-2006), 26 December 2003 (http://www.fmprc.gov.cn/eng/topics/Second/t57032.htm).

[4] CNPC invested $757 million (not necessarily in the form of FDI) in the $1.7 billion project in the first phase (in the mid-1990s). Talisman Energy, a Canadian company, as well as Sudanese and Malaysian companies are also partners in the joint venture, the Greater Nile Petroleum Operating Company. The CNPC has a 40-per-cent share, while the Sudanese have 5 per cent (dry share), Malaysians 30 per cent and Canadians 25 per cent. The joint venture aims to construct an oil field, flow station and pipeline. The investors in this project get crude oil as their returns. The technology and equipment for oil exploitation by the company were imported from China and the construction was contracted to a Chinese petro-engineering construction company. In May 1999, an oil field with an annual production capacity of 10 million ton went into operation. One month later, crude oil began to be transported to a harbour through the 1,500-kilometer long-distance pipeline built by CNPC. In May 2000, the construction of a refinery with an annual oil refining volume of 2.5 million tons was finished. This and another project finished in early 2002 will be of key importance in the development of a complete oil industry in Sudan. In 2003, the construction of a 700-kilometer long-distance pipeline began. This project went into operation by the end of 2003. *Source*: information provided by the Chinese Academy of International Trade and Economic Cooperation and an article at www.China.org.cn (10 December 2003) (http://www.china.org.cn/english/features/China-Africa/81937.htm).

[5] For instance, devaluation of the Western African CFA franc in the early 1990s had serious effects on Chinese investors. For example, the value of their assets in the Economic Community of West African States (ECOWAS) countries shrank by half overnight. The weak macroeconomic climate and low rate of growth also constrain market growth and delays returns on investments.

[6] Source: http://www.china.org.cn/english/features/China-Africa/82189.htm.

[7] President Hu said that in order to increase assistance to other developing countries, China has decided to accord zero-tariff treatment to certain products from all the 39 LDCs having diplomatic relations with China, covering most of the China-bound exports from these countries. China will further expand its aid programmes to the heavily indebted poor countries (HIPCs) and LDCs and write off or forgive in other ways, within the next two years, the entire overdue portion as of the end of 2004 of the government loans owed by HIPCs. China will also provide $10 billion in concessional loans and preferential export credits to developing countries to improve their infrastructure and promote cooperation between enterprises on both sides. China will, in the next three years, increase its assistance to developing countries, African countries in particular, by providing them with anti-malaria drugs and other medicines, helping them set up and improve medical facilities and training medical staff. He also said China will help train 30,000 personnel of various professions for developing countries within the next three years (Source: "Chinese president announces more aid for other developing countries", September 15, 2005, People's Daily Online: http://english.people.com.cn/200509/15/eng20050915_208601.html).

[8] These centres are located in Cameroon, Côte d'Ivoire, Egypt, Gabon, Guinea, Kenya, Mali, Mozambique, Nigeria, the United Republic of Tanzania and Zambia. They were established by the former Ministry of Foreign Trade and Economic Cooperation (the predecessor of the Ministry of Commerce) and run by China National Service Corporation for Chinese Personnel Working Abroad, which is currently under the auspice of the State-owned Assets Supervision and Administration Commission. These centres provide information, consultation and other services to Chinese investors in Africa.

[9] According to the Ministry of Education of China, 933,400 Chinese students studied abroad during 1978-2005, and 232,900 of them returned back to China. Both returned students and those who work abroad have played important roles in China's economic and social development.

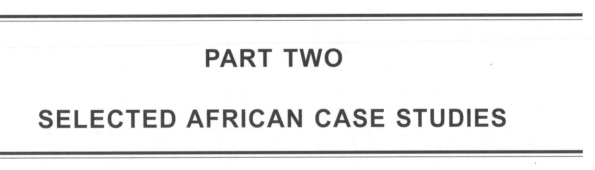

PART TWO

SELECTED AFRICAN CASE STUDIES

CHAPTER IV

BOTSWANA

Subregion	Southern Africa
Area ('000 km2)	566.7
Population (millions)	1.8
Currency	pula (BWP)
Exchange rate (pula per dollar), 2005 average	5.1104
GDP in current prices (millions of dollars), 2005	9 231
GDP per capita (dollars), 2005	5 230
Exports of goods and services (millions of dollars), 2004	3 380
Imports of goods and services (millions of dollars), 2004	2 740
Official development assistance (millions of dollars), 2004	38
FDI inflows (millions of dollars per annum) (2000-2005 period average)	274
FDI inward stock (millions of dollars), by 2005	1 084
FDI inward stock per capita ($), by 2005	614

INTRODUCTION

Within 30 years of its independence, Botswana progressed from being one of the world's poorest countries to an upper-middle-income economy.[1] So far it has been the only African country to upgrade from a least developed country (LDC) status. Diamond mining has fuelled much of its rapid economic expansion. While rich natural resource endowments certainly played a leading role in this process of economic upgrading, prudent financial management, political stability, continuous policy reform, investment in traditional economic sectors, and, most importantly, improved human resources all combined to achieve what is certainly sub-Saharan Africa's greatest economic success.

FDI was a driving force in the dramatic growth of Botswana's economy. However, increased FDI in the non-mining sector will be essential if Botswana is to achieve its goals of economic diversification and continued rapid growth – key components of its Vision 2016, the statement of long-term goals for the nation set forth by a Presidential Task Group in 1996.[2] This chapter assesses FDI and TNC activity in Botswana, discusses the types of FDI that the country needs, and outlines investment opportunities there. It also analyses the investment climate in the country and suggests key areas for policy reform. Where possible, it also examines the role of small and medium-sized enterprises (SMEs), especially as vehicles of FDI and particularly that played by Asian small investors. It concludes with a summary of recommended reforms and other courses of action needed for attracting investments.

A. FDI AND TNC ACTIVITY IN BOTSWANA

1. The background: Botswana's economy

During the 1980s, Botswana's GDP grew at an average annual rate of 11 per cent, placing the country among the world's leaders in economic growth. However, growth slowed down during the 1990s to 4.7 per cent per annum, largely due to a protracted recession in the first half of the decade. Recent data (figure IV.1) suggest that growth has returned to relatively higher levels, at an average 5.2 per cent during 2000-2005. The country's growth performance equals or exceeds that observed in the more widely discussed newly industrializing economies (NIEs) of East and South-East Asia over comparable time periods.

Botswana's rapid growth largely reflects the fortuitous discovery of rich diamond deposits in the centre of the country soon after it became independent in 1966. Figure VI.2 shows the growth rates of the mining and non-mining sectors, demonstrating that the unstable growth rates of the mining sector have contributed to the fluctuations in the growth of the economy.

Mining in 2004/05[3] accounted for 43.2 per cent of GDP (table IV.1), and this share may increase slightly with the completion of several new mining projects. However, Botswana's rapid growth cannot be attributed to its mineral wealth alone. Botswana owes much of its success to the fact that its record of macroeconomic management

Figure IV.1. GDP growth in Botswana, 1981-2005

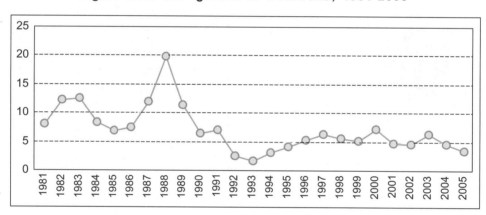

Source: International Monetary Fund, World Economic Outlook Database, April 2006.

Figure IV.2. Rates of growth in total GDP, and GDP in mining and non-mining sectors in Botswana, 1994/95-2004/05

(Per cent)

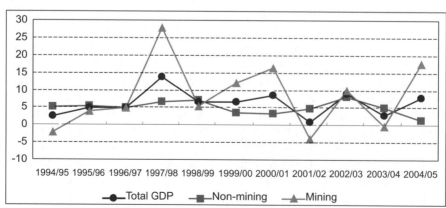

Source: Bank of Botswana, Annual Report 2005, based on data from the Central Statistical Office.
Note: The base year for constant prices has been changed from 1985/86 to 1993/94. The rebasing makes the series in some years 'non-additive', so that the estimate of total GDP does not equal the sum of its components. (The fiscal year is from July to June.)

Table IV.1. Value added by various types of economic activity in Botswana,[a] 1994/95, 1999/2000-2004/05[b]

(Per cent)

Economic activitiy	1994/95	1999/00[c]	2000/01[c]	2001/02[c]	2002/03[c]	2003/04[c]	2004/05[c]
	Per cent of total						
Agriculture	4.0	2.4	2.4	2.3	2.2	2.2	2.1
Mining	34.2	39.6	42.5	40.4	40.8	39.6	43.2
Manufacturing	4.7	4.1	3.7	3.7	3.5	3.4	3.0
Water and electricity	2.2	2.2	2.1	2.2	2.2	2.3	2.1
Construction	6.3	5.6	5.2	5.4	5.0	4.9	4.5
Trade, hotels and restaurants	9.5	9.5	9.3	9.9	9.8	10.6	9.1
Transport, post and telecommunication	3.8	3.6	3.3	3.4	3.1	2.9	2.8
Banks, insurance and business services	10.8	10.2	9.8	10.4	9.7	9.6	9.2
General government	15.5	14.8	14.5	15.4	16.1	16.4	15.6
Social and personal services	4.4	3.9	3.6	3.8	3.6	3.7	3.4
Total value added	**95.5**	**95.9**	**96.6**	**96.9**	**95.9**	**95.4**	**95.2**
GDP excluding mining	65.8	60.4	57.5	59.6	59.2	60.4	56.8
Memorandum:							
GDP at constant market prices (million pula)	**11 398**	**16 719**	**18 242**	**18 530**	**20 298**	**20 985**	**22 742**
GDP per capita (pula)	**7 844**	**10 164**	**10 822**	**10 725**	**11 474**	**11 583**	**12 259**
GDP per capita excluding mining (pula)	5 160	6 139	6 228	6 390	6 790	6 998	6 965
	Annual percentage change						
Agriculture	-1.7	-8.7	9.9	-2.6	1.8	2.8	3.3
Mining	-1.4	12.7	17.1	-3.4	10.6	0.3	18.2
Manufacturing	23.5	3.5	-0.4	0.2	3.1	0.8	-2.6
Water and electricity	6.7	11.3	5.5	3.7	9.5	6.4	3.3
Construction	1.7	2.4	1.6	4.7	0.6	2.1	0.7
Trade, hotels and restaurants	23.1	6.2	6.5	8.2	8.2	11.3	-6.6
Transport, post and telecommunication	7.2	2.9	1.7	3.3	0.9	-3.4	5.6
Banks, insurance and business services	7.6	4.3	5.1	7.1	2.6	2.4	4.1
General government	3.3	6.0	6.7	8.3	14.2	5.1	3.6
Social and personal services	7.2	4.4	2.8	6.2	2.8	7.0	-0.5
Total value added	**4.6**	**7.7**	**9.9**	**1.9**	**8.4**	**2.9**	**8.1**
GDP at constant market prices	**3.2**	**7.3**	**9.1**	**1.6**	**9.5**	**3.4**	**8.4**
GDP excluding mining	5.8	4.0	3.9	5.3	8.8	5.5	1.9
GDP per capita	**0.8**	**4.7**	**6.5**	**-0.9**	**7.0**	**1.0**	**5.8**
GDP per capita excluding mining	3.3	1.5	1.4	2.6	6.3	3.1	-0.5

Source: Bank of Botswana, *Annual Report 2005*, based on data from the Central Statistical Office.

[a]   The base year for constant prices has been changed from 1985/86 to 1993/94. The rebasing make the series in some years 'non-additive', such that the estimate of total GDP does not equal the sum of its components. Here the CSO has followed the guidelines in the 1993 System of National Accounts. Users who prefer to maintain additivity rather than the original aggregate growth estimate are able to do so using the information included here.

[b]   Financial year runs from July to June.

[c]   Provisional figures.

is among the best in the developing world. Its massive diamond revenues have been skilfully managed for long-term socio-economic development, characterized by rapid structural change and reallocation of workers into higher productivity sectors (box IV.1).

Historically, non-mining activities and, in particular, export-oriented manufacturing have not been major contributors to economic growth in Botswana. However, prudent macroeconomic management and extensive infrastructural investment by the Government has set the stage for these activities to become key engines of

growth in the future, notwithstanding the considerable untapped potential that remains in the mineral sector.

Despite its impressive record, the future of Botswana's economy is still uncertain. For a variety of reasons, its traditional sources of growth are unlikely to spur economic development in the future. Diversification and increased productivity are two main economic challenges for the country – challenges that could partly be met by increasing FDI inflows and the technical know-how accompanying such flows. Of course, this could be overshadowed by the economic and human

Box IV.1. Analysing Botswana's growth miracle: structural change and labour productivity

An examiniation of Botswana's changes in the structure of its economy and labour force sheds lights on the reasons for its rapid economic growth. From 1960 to 1995, growth in Botswana primarily reflected rapid structural change, as workers moved out of the low-productivity agricultural sector into mining, and subsequently into manufacturing and services – a process that to a certain extent reflected the expansion of the public sector that had been facilitated by high revenues from diamonds. Reduced labour market participation – reflecting, in part, lower female and child participation – was a modest drag on growth. However, the changing age structure – essentially a decline in the proportion of youth aged 15 and under in the population, driven by demographic transition – helped growth. Actual labour productivity growth accounted for about 1.9 percentage points, or slightly less than one third of total per capita GDP growth.Since growth gains from labour reallocation have largely been used up (agricultural employment is now less that 5 per cent of total employment), future growth in Botswana will depend on an improvement in labour productivity. While the growth rates of GDP per capita in Botswana have exceeded those

observed in other fast growers such as Malaysia, enhancement of labour productivity has been relatively modest. The relative rate of labour productivity growth in manufacturing during the period 1970-1995 was particularly disappointing. In sum, Botswana's growth miracle largely reflects one of the world's fastest rates of structural transformation (a fact underscored by the rapid rates of urbanization in the country) accompanied by modest productivity growth. A statistical procedure that attempts to decompose an observed rate of growth into its root causes (e.g. geography, economic policies, demography, health and political stability). While this procedure can be informative, its validity is subject to a number of restrictions that may be violated in practice, and it says more about the causes of growth, on average, across countries than for any specific country. A detailed description of growth can often be quite suggestive of its underlying causes. This approach simply decomposes growth into its contributory components such as a changing age structure, labour market participation, labour productivity growth at the sectoral level and structural change or a reallocation of labour across sectors.

Source: UNCTAD.

menace of the HIV/AIDS pandemic, which has hit Botswana hard, although its impact on the economy is difficult to forecast.[4]

2. FDI and TNC activity

TNCs have a long history of activity in Botswana, which has remained open to FDI since independence. An African front-runner in terms of attracting FDI, Botswana has received significant amounts of FDI in most of the years since the early 1980s. FDI inflows surged to record levels of $400 million in 2002 and 2003 (figure IV.3).

Traditionally, the main sources of FDI to Botswana have been South Africa, the United States and European countries, led by Luxembourg and the United Kingdom. FDI from Asia did not play a major role until recently; it increased considerably in 2001 and 2002 (table IV.2). FDI was critical in the first phase of diversification of Botswana's economy from agriculture to mining,

but its contribution to the second phase of diversification, "beyond diamonds", has been limited so far. It is largely confined to the mineral sector, although recently there have been significant investments outside this sector, particularly in the financial services, and increasingly in the manufacturing sector as well (table IV.3). In order to outline areas of opportunity for Asian TNCs, an analysis of existing TNC activity, focusing on mining, financial services and manufacturing activities is undertaken here.

TNCs and the mining sector. In 2003, over 68 per cent of FDI was in the mining sector, the bulk of it from Europe and South Africa (table IV.3). Significant TNC involvement in Botswana began with the opening of the Orapa diamond mine in 1971. This mine is owned and operated by Debswana Mining Company, a joint venture in which De Beers of South Africa and the Government of Botswana each have 50 per cent ownership. Several smaller diamond mines, also run by Debswana, operate in the country as well.

Figure IV.3. FDI flows to Botswana, 1975-2005
(Millions of dollars)

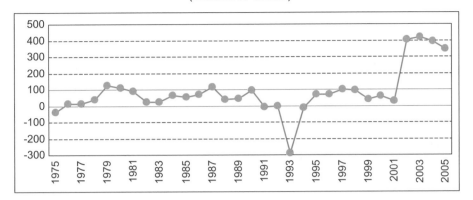

Source: UNCTAD, FDI/TNC database (www.unctad.org/fdistatistics).

Investment in new productive capacity continues, for example in the recent Orapa expansion project which has doubled the productive capacity of the mine, and in the planned new Capex mine that will be located near Orapa.

In addition to diamond mining, a copper-nickel mine is in operation near Selebi-Phikwe as a joint venture between the Government and Anglo-American of South Africa. Coal is also mined by Anglo-American, and proven reserves far exceed the current productive capacity. Ore quality, however, may not be sufficiently high to sustain large-scale commercial mining. Finally, soda ash is mined by Botash, which is jointly owned by the Government, De Beers, Anglo-American and AECI of South Africa.

The contribution of these TNC activities to the economy of Botswana has been, and continues to be, considerable. Indeed, mineral revenues provide over half of all government revenues. However, due to the capital-intensive nature of mining and the high economic rents involved, the contribution of the sector to employment is minimal. It employs less than 10 per cent of the workforce and its wage bill is only 6 per cent of total mining output. In addition, mining activities in general rarely have a significant impact through forward or backward linkages on other parts of the economy. This places the burden of channelling the substantial revenues generated by mining into the economy on the Government.

Generally speaking, the Government has proceeded in meeting this challenge; prudent management of mineral revenues lies at the centre of Botswana's success story. Indeed, as this chapter argues, it is precisely because of the prudent investment of mineral proceeds in the past that Botswana is an attractive location for non-mining FDI today. However, challenges persist: almost half the workforce is employed in the public sector,

Table IV.2. Inward FDI stock, by region, 1997-2003
(Millions of pula)

Home region/economy	1997	1998	1999	2000	2001	2002	2003
North and Central America	373	330	38	97	48	40	39
United States	356	325	37	97	45	32	18
Europe	1 519	2 278	3 517	3 628	3 665	4 051	4 380
Luxembourg	1 287	1 972	2 178	2 478	3 002	3 313	3 609
Netherlands	..	..	..	..	22	21	34
United Kingdom	105	74	1 227	970	591	613	537
Other Europe	..	..	88	121	48	95	94
Asia and the Pacific	30	7	1	..	103	107	..
Africa	2 932	3 453	3 709	599	6 303	3 588	3 135
South Africa	2 915	3 452	3 681	5 983	6 275	3 460	3 054
West Asia	..	92	83	102	109	22	87
Other Europe	23	..	..	..	208	68	3
Total	**4 877**	**6 160**	**7 348**	**9 826**	**10 435**	**7 876**	**7 643**

Source: Bank of Botswana, *Annual Report*, various issues.

Table IV.3. Inward FDI stock, by sector/industry, 1997-2003
(Millions of pula)

Sector/industry	1997	1998	1999	2000	2001	2002	2003
Mining	3 643	4 902	5 524	7 792	8 412	5 615	5 223
Manufacturing	291	333	273	343	274	280	295
Services	922	925	1 551	1 691	1 750	1 980	2 139
Electricity, gas and water	7	8	..	..	..	19	27
Construction	32	30	8	16	23	13	10
Wholesale and retail trade	457	392	670	773	651	756	826
Hotels and restaurants	46	60	83	17	135	129	154
Transport, storage and communication	33	47	43	105	96	155	154
Finance	270	226	523	619	729	803	873
Real estate and business services	65	112	144	161	115	104	94
Health and social work	4	..	..	..	..	..	..
Other	8	50	80	..	1	1	1
Total	**4 877**	**6 160**	**7 348**	**9 826**	**10 435**	**7 876**	**7 643**

Source: Bank of Botswana, *Annual Report*, various issues.

which illustrates the difficulty of using publicly channelled mineral proceeds to spur private-sector growth.

TNCs and the non-mining sector. Upstream and downstream investment related to the minerals sector has been minimal. Yet this is an area of opportunity for Asian investors, many of which have considerable experience in mining and related industries; they are generally well suited to operate in markets of Botswana's size and history. One notable exception to the otherwise rosy investment profile here is in mining equipment and heavy machinery. Both are currently imported from major manufacturers in the United States (Caterpillar captures about two-thirds of the market), although European (Dressner) and Japanese (Komatsu) firms are also important players. Given the large fixed costs involved in the production of this type of equipment, the scope for profitable import substitution here is highly unlikely, even if taken into account the wider regional Southern African market and its substantial mining component.

Obvious downstream activities for major diamond producers are cutting and polishing. Indeed, two plants were opened in 1992 and 1993, one run by Debswana and another by Lazare Kaplan International (United States), which was subsequently sold to Shacter and Namder (Israel) in 1998. However, both these operations have made significant retrenchments due to competition from Indian firms. For products of high value per unit of weight, such as diamonds, labour productivity and wages weigh more heavily than transport costs in locational decisions regarding processing. Despite Botswana's clear comparative advantage

in diamond mining, a comparative advantage in cutting and polishing does not automatically follow as they require different skills.

A major non-mining activity with significant foreign involvement is the provision of financial services. All five of the country's commercial banks are foreign: two of them, Barclays and Standard Chartered, are owned by United Kingdom investors, and the remaining three (Stanbic, First National, and Investec) are South African.[5] There is also foreign involvement in the insurance sector.[6] The financial sector accounts for about 11 per cent of FDI, and the manufacturing sector for only 4 per cent (table IV.3).

With little, if any, Asian presence in financial services, there might be an opportunity for market penetration by Asian firms in this sector. As has been observed in other African countries, there is often a high correlation between FDI by Asian banks and financing, on the one hand, and the presence of other Asian investment, in particular in smaller sized firms on the other. The former can facilitate Asian investment in general. An initial investment by a major Asian banking institution could easily trigger further economic activity and transfer of know-how and resources between the continents. In the retail and wholesale sector, FDI mainly goes to the South Asian and Chinese family-based immigrant sector in the country; these two ethnic groups have a strong, and occasionally controversial, presence in this sector.

Aside from downstream activities related to diamonds, TNC activity in the manufacturing sector of Botswana is sporadic and has traditionally generated mixed results. Asian firms in the sector have often faced costly plant closures for reasons discussed below. Clearly, there is need to examine the causes of recent investment failures and overcome these difficulties so that Botswana can attract the resources its economic profile merits, from Asia and elsewhere.

Examples of FDI in Botswana's manufacturing sector include investments by South African Breweries, which operates the highly successful Sechaba Brewery; Owens-Corning, which holds a 49 per cent stake in Flowtite Botswana, a company that produces plastic piping for water projects and exports regionally; China State Construction and Engineering Corporation, a Chinese State-owned enterprise; Fine Dec Botswana (box IV.2), which produces plastic flowers. Hyundai Motor Company, which began car assembly in Botswana in 1993, closed the plant in 2000 (box IV.3). There are also foreign investments in jewellery-making, brick-making and soap production.

Other investments include a cluster of textile and garment operations, mainly financed by the Government's Financial Assistance Policy (FAP) (box IV.4). Unfortunately, many of these operations, largely Asian run – not surprising, given Asian dominance in these industries worldwide – have failed to continue production. In part, this is due to changes in trade regulations in the markets of the developed countries. Nevertheless, the textile/garment sector continues to be an attractive sector for investment, particularly given

Botswana's preferential access to European and North American markets – the former through the re-negotiated Cotonou Agreement and the Everything-But-Arms initiative, and the latter through the African Growth and Opportunity Act (AGOA) passed in 2000 and extended in 2004.

Cross-border M&As are an important mode of entry of FDI into Botswana in both manufacturing and services. Most of the announced deals have been by South African companies (table IV.4). In 2004, for instance, Allied Technologies Ltd. (South Africa) acquired a 50 per cent stake in Econet Wireless Group in a deal worth $70 million.

Botswana is among the few countries in the developing world with no foreign exchange restrictions. The free movement of capital has facilitated both inward and outward portfolio investment in the country. Although the Botswana Stock Exchange has performed well and attracted some – mostly North American – interest, it has attracted insufficient funds to satisfy the country's needs for investment. Thus, as exchange controls have been progressively liberalized during the 1990s, there has generally been a net outflow of portfolio investment from the region. In contrast, FDI inflows have usually been well in excess of outflows (figure IV.4).

The net outflow of portfolio investment indicates that there are ample funds for investment and a dearth of local investment opportunities on the Botswana Stock Exchange. Initial public

---

Box IV.2. Fine Dec Botswana: the success story of a plastic-flower manufacturer

Fine Dec Botswana began operations in Botswana in mid-1994, moving from a production facility in South Africa due to rising labour costs in that country. The company produces a wide range of synthetic artificial flowers, using a labour-intensive production process. The move from South Africa proceeded smoothly and without undue cost, as Fine Dec was able to maintain its existing customer base in South Africa, where it dominates the market. Soon after moving to Botswana's capital city, Gaborone, the company was able to cut prices by 16 per cent and expand its market share. Owner-manager Frank H.T. Lai is an expatriate from Hong Kong

(China) and has been working in the plastic-flower industry for over 20 years. The Botswana production environment has proved to be fruitful for the company. With a 95-per-cent average attendance rate and a piece-rate-determined wage bonus, worker productivity and quality are high. Challenges, however, exist: expansion into European and North American markets has been inhibited by high transport costs, and securing land to expand operations has also proved hard. Notwithstanding these concerns, Fine Dec shows that a carefully formulated business plan – with a clearly identified market – can be highly successful in Botswana.

Source: UNCTAD, based on information provided by the Center for International Development at Harvard University.

Box IV.3. The rise and fall of Hyundai's car production in Botswana

Hyundai Motor Company began car assembly in Botswana on a modest scale in 1993. In 1998, it significantly upgraded its production facilities with a $51 million investment. The resulting state-of-the-art facility began attracting interest from other car manufacturers, with Volvo eventually deciding to use part of Hyundai's Gaborone plant to assemble its own vehicles. The economic rationale behind the investment was a reasonable one: the South African market is both sizeable and protected, and Botswana, by virtue of its membership of the Southern African Customs Union (SACU) and geographical location, provided an ideal site from which to penetrate this potentially lucrative market. Indeed, during the height of production activity at the facility, Botswana managed to capture a significant share of the South African market. The closure of the Hyundai vehicle assembly plant in 2000 was a serious blow for Botswana's manufacturing sector and for its non-mining exports. Before Hyundai withdrew from the country, vehicle exports amounted to $667 million ($144 million in 1995) in export earnings (table IV.7) and nearly half of total exports by the manufacturing sector. While the project was subsidized by the Government of Botswana, initial results were promising. However, in late 1999 it became evident that the operation was facing significant problems. Hyundai Motors Distributors – the dealership network in South Africa through which the production facility in Gaborone sold its cars – ran into problems with its creditors. After a series of creditor meetings, tax holidays and other bailout measures, all of which proved to be ineffective, the company's commercial creditors obtained a court order to seize the distribution company's assets as well as the assembled vehicles at the plant. In November 2000, Kim Car Co., a South African vehicle manufacturer, bought the already mentioned earlier Hyundai equipment, but has not been able to set up an assembly plant.[a] Hyundai Motors Distributors' case underscores the need for proper analysis prior to extending publicly financed investment incentives.

Source: UNCTAD.

[a]   Malema, P. "New Hyundai owners fine to pay up", Mmegil / *The Reporter*, 20 April 2001.

Box IV.4. Financial Assistance Policy (FAP) for manufacturing projects in Botswana

The Government's Financial Assistance Policy (FAP), introduced in 1982, was the centrepiece of Botswana's diversification drive for nearly 20 years. Essentially, it provided capital grants to manufacturing projects in proportion to projected employment. Wage subsidies were also provided for five years covering 80 per cent of wage costs – up to twice the relevant minimum wage – in the first year, with a lower contribution in subsequent years. Grants for approved training costs were also available. However, the programme became a political issue, mainly because of several high-profile cases of abuse and fraud among a cluster of Asian-owned firms located in Selebi-Phikwe, and was subsequently abolished in 2001. These cases are interesting as they highlighted the importance of designing incentive schemes that do not promote corruption. The fallout from these events has been considerable and has significantly cooled local attitudes towards aggressive recruitment of overseas investors (although this is not the case at the government level). One newspaper editorial observed, "Bitter experiences learnt from the influx of fly-by-night investors in Selebi-Phikwe textile projects are too painful to forget. Almost immediately after cashing in on the Financial Assistance Policy our foreign investors took flight, often without even the courtesy to bid anyone farewell." [a]The Botswana Institute of Development Policy Analysis, in its Government-commissioned review of the FAP, recommended its abolition in 2000 (BIDPA, 2000). The main lesson from the FAP for other African countries introducing such schemes is that cash incentives are likely to promote fraud. An alternative to grant-based assistance might be the provision of incentives in other forms (e.g. investment credits). While these can also create opportunities for cheating (as with any tax-incentive system), they do not result in the direct loss of government funds.

Source: UNCTAD, based on "Government to end FAP for foreign firms," *The Botswana Gazette*, 26 July 2000.

[a]   "Editorial," *The Midweek Sun*, 12 January 2000.

Table IV.4. Major cross-border M&As in Botswana
(Millions of dollars)

Year	Acquired company	Industry of the acquired company	Acquiring company	Home country	Value ($ million)	Shares acquired (per cent)
1993	Stockbrokers Botswana	Security brokers, dealers, and flotation companies	Fleming Martin (Fleming,Martin)	South Africa	..	25
1996	Tasman Botswana(Pty)Ltd	Textile goods, nec	Coastal Clothing Manufacturers	South Africa	10.7	77
1997	Algo Spinning & Weaving Mills	Textile goods, nec	Coastal Clothing Manufacturers	South Africa	3.9	39
2001	Flowtite	Fabricated pipe and pipe fittings	Amiantit Group	Saudi Arabia	..	100
2001	Penrich Employee Benefits	Pension, health and welfare funds	Unifer Holdings Ltd	South Africa	..	100
2004	Econet Wireless Group	Telephone communications, except radiotelephone	Allied Technologies Ltd	South Africa	70.0	50
2006	Dan Products(Pty) Ltd-Chewing	Chewing gum	Cadbury Schweppes PLC	United Kingdom	57.5	100

Source: UNCTAD, cross-border M&A database.

offerings (IPOs) of State-owned companies are expected to help increase the capitalization and liquidity of the stock market considerably and therefore reverse, or at least slow down, the tendency towards net outflows of portfolio investment.

3. Asian investment in Botswana: challenges and opportunities

Investment opportunities for Asian-based TNCs exist in all sectors of the economy, with the exception of mining, which is informally but tightly controlled by De Beers. However, it is in the manufacturing sector – where Asian success at home, both past and present, has been conspicuous – that the potential for an Asian contribution is

greatest. In 2004/2005, manufacturing accounted for only 3 per cent of value added in Botswana (table IV.1); but there is strong potential for growth in this sector, given the country's high level of infrastructure,[7] good record of macroeconomic and political stability, well-educated labour force, increasing potential managerial capacity (as evidenced by the rapid increase in the number of University of Botswana graduates), and tariff-free access to the South African market. Furthermore, the country offers an excellent platform from which to access the relatively large Southern African market.

Of course, significant obstacles persist. Instability in Botswana's neighbours to the north and south, poor regional infrastructure, non-tariff barriers to trade within SACU and high levels of

Figure IV.4. Structure of balance in investment flows[a] in Botswana, 1993-2005
(Millions of Pula)

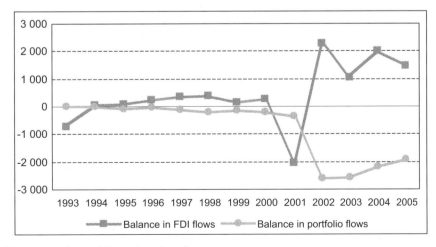

Source: Bank of Botswana, *Annual Report*, various issues.
a   Inflows less outflows.

income inequality in the subregion's countries, all raise the question as to whether the large Southern African market is more a mirage than a reality.

Furthermore, although Botswana is a peaceful multiracial democracy and its people are known for their tolerance and friendliness, a complex history has occasionally led to cultural misunderstandings towards Asians, which has emerged as a constant theme in explaining difficulties in achieving successful Asian investment in Botswana. Of course, problems of inter-cultural friction are not unique to Botswana, especially where cultural differences are closely aligned with socio-economic disparities, but they remain a significant barrier to successful Asian investment in the country. No cross-border M&A deal was concluded by developing Asian firms during 1987-2005, nor was any greenfield investment recorded during the period 2002-2004 (annex tables 1-10).

Notwithstanding the above concerns, Asians have a potentially large role to play in the development of Botswana. The country has shown considerable commitment in making its economy attractive to inward FDI by fully liberalizing the exchange rate regime, establishing financial benefits for serious investors, and instituting the lowest corporate and personal tax rates in the

region, all in an environment of political and policy stability and a growing economy. Today, Asian investors – as well as their counterparts worldwide – might show foresight by entering the country in larger numbers, with significant capital investments and legitimate and carefully formulated business plans, much as United States TNCs did in Asian countries a generation ago. And numerous profitable commercial opportunities exist in Botswana. Asian firms, with their extensive recent history of recording good returns in economies remarkably similar to Botswana's, are an obvious source of expertise, technology and capital, while Botswana is a country poised to offer good rates of return to experienced investors.

As of 2005, there were only 342 firms in Botswana with over 100 employees (table IV.5). Among these larger firms, there are few joint ventures with foreign firms outside the mining sector. Approximately two thirds of Botswana's 16,683 enterprises employed less than 30 workers in 2003, but few of them receive FDI. Yet, foreign firms may find joint ventures, especially with the larger SMEs, attractive, given that the latter have knowledge of local market conditions and might require relatively small injections of outside capital in order to upgrade technology. An estimated 30 to 45 per cent of GDP and about 50 per cent of formal employment in the country comes from

Table IV.5. Number of operating establishments in Botswana by economic activity and employment size, as at end September 2005

Economic Activity	Number of Employees								
	Nil	1-4	5-29	30-49	50-99	100+	Working proprietors[a]	Unknown	Total
Primary									
Agriculture and forestry	4	144	207	33	7	4	13	94	**506**
Fishing	-	-	1	-	-	-	-	-	**1**
Mining and quarrying	1	2	17	9	5	20	-	9	**63**
Manufacturing	-	254	640	126	66	78	23	115	**1 302**
Services									
Electricity, gas and water	3	9	18	3	1	9	71	6	**120**
Construction	6	132	462	66	32	53	22	323	**1 096**
Wholesale and retail trade	45	2 467	2 094	140	63	26	214	768	**5 817**
Hotels and restaurants	19	894	531	40	18	12	64	165	**1 743**
Transport, storage and communication	11	247	221	25	14	12	32	449	**1 011**
Financial Intermediaries	30	18	92	14	13	13	1	26	**207**
Real Estate, renting and business services	361	373	432	40	23	32	150	402	**1 813**
Public administration	1	2	102	53	36	56	-	10	**260**
Education	3	70	816	264	104	13	2	57	**1 329**
Health and social work	3	28	74	3	23	13	4	26	**174**
Other community and personal activities	701	167	172	11	5	1	31	125	**1 213**
Foreign missions	-	-	-	26	-	-	-	2	**28**
Total	**1 188**	**4 807**	**5 879**	**853**	**410**	**342**	**627**	**2 577**	**16 683**

Source: Central Statistics Office of Botswana.
[a] Owners and family members working in the business.

SMEs, which might also become important as industries for providing inputs and services to larger export-oriented firms (Botswana, Ministry of Commerce and Industry, 1998 and 1999). This could be particularly fruitful in the tourism sector, where larger operators require many support services (e.g. catering, game scouts and transport). As table IV.5 indicates, SMEs already dominate the hotel and restaurant sector. Asian firms are among the most experienced and savvy in investing in smaller sized firms abroad, and their experience in this respect could be useful for profitably expanding their FDI in SMEs in the manufacturing and services sectors in Botswana.

Asian firms have been particularly aggressive in taking advantage of privatization opportunities in Africa, for example, in telecommunications. As Botswana reinvigorates its privatization programme, Asian firms might show more interest in investing in Botswana, as they have done elsewhere in the region.

B. DETERMINANTS OF FDI IN BOTSWANA AND THEIR RELEVANCE FOR ASIAN INVESTORS

In order for a country to attract FDI, well-developed and accessible markets must exist for goods and services that TNCs can produce at a competitive cost in the country. Furthermore, the costs of doing business must be reasonable and at levels that make investment in the country more attractive than alternative locations. Botswana is regionally attractive on both counts. Moreover, it has a liberal policy with respect to FDI and a stable policy environment for the economy in general.

Botswana's stable policy environment is one of its most attractive features for potential foreign investors: its macroeconomic policy is of a high standard, open and predictable,[8] corporate taxes are low by regional and world standards (15 per cent for manufacturing firms and 25 per cent for all other establishments), corruption is low; and private assets are not subject to risk of confiscation or appropriation (as enshrined in law as well as a perfect track record of respect for property rights). Finally, there are no capital controls and access to foreign exchange is, for all intents and purposes, unlimited owing to the country's large foreign exchange reserves. Furthermore, the transport and communications infrastructure is excellent (e.g. the telephone network is fully digital). The general investment climate in Botswana is attractive in these respects, but sizable challenges remain for attracting FDI into non-mining sectors.

1. Local and export markets

Potential customers for goods and services produced in Botswana can be classified into four types: (i) local consumers; (ii) local businesses in need of inputs; (iii) regional (mainly South African) buyers of exports from Botswana; and (iv) broader, world export markets such as the Americas, Asia and Europe. All four of these markets are feasible areas of focus for foreign companies investing in Botswana, depending on the sector involved. However, investors should keep prospective target markets clearly in mind when formulating business plans.

Local consumers. Botswana's domestic market (with its population of only 1.8 million) is too small for investments that principally serve local consumers to be profitable (table IV.6). Therefore, TNCs in Botswana will need to be strongly export oriented, focusing in particular on exports to countries that are members of the SACU and SADC.

Since virtually all of Botswana's consumer needs are currently met by imports from South Africa, including products which South Africa imports from the rest of the world, direct import and marketing of certain consumer products (e.g.

Table IV.6. Market size in Botswana, SACU[a] and SADC[b], in terms of GDP, 1995, 2000 and 2005
(Millions of dollars)

Region	1995	2000	2005
Botswana	4 423	4 889	9 231
SACU	161 337	143 473	258 298
SADC	196 062	186 495	333 778

Source: UNCTAD database.
[a] SACU: Botswana, Lesotho, Namibia, South Africa and Swaziland.
[b] SADC: Angola, Botswana, Democratic Republic of the Congo, Lesotho, Malawi, Mauritius, Mozambique, Namibia, Seychelles, South Africa, Swaziland, United Republic of Tanzania, Zambia and Zimbabwe.

food, in which there is already some FDI activity) may be profitable, as would small-scale, import-substituting investments (table IV.7). Such opportunities may prove attractive for Asian investors and forge partnerships with local SMEs. A careful review of current import patterns may find a few areas where domestic production makes sense. Asian involvement – South Asian in particular – in the import/export sectors is widespread in various parts of Africa, but less so in Botswana, where there are good opportunities for investment and growth.

Local businesses. Botswana imports a considerable amount of heavy mining equipment annually. However, as mentioned above, due to the high fixed costs associated with production in this sector, as well as the need for a plethora of subsidiary businesses to support production, this sector may not be attractive for investment in Botswana. On the other hand, the production of lighter mining equipment, such as conveyor belts, welding rods and lubricants, offers potential for profit. This is an area in which Asian firms might consider gradual investment, given Asian expertise in the sector.

International tourism offers potential for high growth and large profits, with Botswana currently catering almost exclusively to the "luxury" end of the safari and ecotourism markets.

Currently, this sector has limited linkages with the rest of the economy. However, with the rapidly growing number of international arrivals and the consequent acute need for increased investment in services aimed at tourists, there will be greater scope for activity in this sector. Examples include hotel construction and operation, along with businesses that serve the hotel sector by providing goods and services such as customized soaps, napkins and the "linking" activities for SMEs. Finally, if Botswana's status as a regional banking centre materializes – following the recent development of the International Financial Services Centre (IFSC) (box IV.5) – there will be an increased need for the provision of services to the financial sector. An obvious example is information technology (IT) operations and installation; indeed, local Internet service providers have already started to emerge. Again, Singapore, Malaysia and other Asian countries might find that their strong expertise in bridging the digital divide gives them a competitive advantage over other investors.

Regional markets for exports. Botswana's membership in SACU provides for tariff-free access to the large South African market (table IV.6), although, as discussed in detail below, some non-tariff barriers can make it difficult to access this market. However, as regional integration proceeds within SADC, access to all Southern African

Table IV.7. Structure of merchandise trade of Botswana, 1995, 2000-2005
(Millions of Pula)

Commodity	1995	2000	2001	2002	2003	2004	2005 [a]
	Imports by principal comodity group (c.i.f)						
Food, beverages and tobacco	846	1 494	1 476	2 077	2 031	2 202	2 275
Fuel	271	523	712	768	824	1 783	2 202
Chemical and rubber products	491	1 033	1 090	1 366	1 428	1 792	1 972
Wood and paper products	402	817	928	921	1 050	1 463	1 358
Textile and footwear	400	617	494	585	580	732	775
Metal and metal products	461	769	814	1 015	921	1 257	1 255
Machinery and electrical goods	832	2 356	2 078	2 366	2 211	2 634	2 705
Vehicles and transport equipment	989	1 315	1 285	2 024	1 476	2 167	2 067
Other goods	617	1 688	1 680	1 715	1 598	1 756	1 982
Total	5 308	10 613	10 557	12 837	12 119	15 786	16 591
	Exports by principal merchandise						
Dimonds	3 994	11 398	11 260	12 479	11 707	13 133	16 980
Copper-Nickel	311	552	410	482	695	1 578	2 301
Beef	235	278	427	277	260	284	310
Soda Ash	70	208	225	268	230	251	332
Textiles	144	244	193	183	227	561	1 117
Vehicles	792	270	299	408	443	556	570
Gold	..	..	..	..	..	..	183
Total	5 941	14 260	14 658	16 109	13 910	16 490	22 459

Source: Bank of Botswana, *Annual Report 2004, 2005*, based on data from the Central Statistical Office.
[a] Provisional.

Box IV.5. The International Financial Services Centre (IFSC): a gateway for offshore financial services for Southern Africa

Botswana's high levels of human capital, excellent communications infrastructure, stable macroeconomic and foreign exchange environment and low taxes compared to the rest of the region, suggest that it could become a regional centre for international banking in Southern Africa. In 1995, a feasibility study for the creation of a financial services centre, commissioned by the Government of Botswana and the Botswana Development Corporation (BDC), concluded that Botswana had the potential to become a regional centre for offshore financial services. The IFSC was incorporated in 2003 and is owned by the Botswana Government through the Ministry of Finance and Development Planning. It is being developed as a location where active and substantive financial services business is undertaken. Fiscal incentives are provided to financial and non-financial institutions that provide such services under accreditation from the IFSC. Activities that qualify for IFSC support include funds management, banking services, insurance as well as financial intermediary services, as specified in the Income Tax (Amendment) Act 1999 (Part XVI). The following are some of the criteria for eligibility: services must be provided for clients outside Botswana; there must be a commitment to employment related in size to the scale of the proposed operations; and regulatory requirements of the Botswana authorities must be met. Applications for approval are administered by the BDC. Adjustments to the country's legal and regulatory framework have been made and an attractive incentives package prepared to encourage investment in qualified financial service activities in the IFSC. These incentives include a low corporate tax rate of 15 per cent and exemptions from withholding tax on interest and sales tax. The Government has also taken various steps to ensure that the new centre is a site of legitimate banking activities. The IFSC has already attracted several companies that have been approved for tax certification to carry out financial service activities in the IFSC. The African Banking Corporation was among the first projects approved. Shareholders include the Anglo-American Corporation, the International Finance Corporation and European funds. The African Banking Corporation carries out traditional banking services, and its holding company, ABC Holdings Ltd., undertakes group administration and financial services for its subsidiary non-banking businesses in the region. Another example is Seed Co. Ltd (Zimbabwe), which was established as a group holding company to carry out corporate treasury management for the group's operations in the region. Barclays has set up a central finance operation, previously performed in London, to manage some of the financial activities of the bank's affiliates in Africa. The bank thus benefits from lower tax rates and from operating in a lower cost location. Cyberplex Holding, an affiliate of Cyberplex Interactive Media (United States), acts as a regional holding company, providing consulting and technology services in electronic commerce for regional financial service providers. There are 33 companies registered in the IFSC which represent industries ranging from tourism to information technology, but still only a small number of regional banks and fund managers.[a] The IFSC is thus an important part of Botswana's efforts to develop a modern financial services sector that contributes to the diversification of the economy while maintaining the country's excellent reputation in the international financial community. Overall, the prospects for the IFSC appear bright, though there is concern about retaliatory measures from South Africa.

Source: UNCTAD, based on the International Financial Services Centre at www.botswanaifsc.com.

[a]   "FT Botswana", *Financial Times Special Report*, 20 June 2006.

---

markets will be facilitated. Proximity, familiarity with the region, and being "inside the tariff wall" give Botswana an edge in terms of production aimed at these markets, while recent infrastructural investments give it the capacity to serve them. Recent examples of regional market-oriented investment include the now-closed Hyundai assembly plant (see box IV.3), and the new IFSC, which aims to be a conduit for the flow of offshore funds into the region (see box IV.5). Asian investment in textile production is attempting to take advantage of Botswana's SACU membership as well as its high level of access to the markets of the United States and the EU. A significant success story in this industry is the result of a partnership between a Botswana investor and a firm from Taiwan Province of China (Salm *et al.* 2004).

Broader export markets. While SADC represents a market of over 200 million consumers, in terms of purchasing power it is relatively small (similar to the combined size of the relatively small states of New Hampshire, Vermont and Massachusetts in the United States). Although economic growth in the region will largely eliminate the problem of market size in the long run, in the near term some sectors will need to produce for world markets in order to be profitable. Furthermore, as transport costs and tariff barriers continue to fall worldwide, producers will need to be competitive on international markets, regardless of where they sell. Botswana's favourable access to European and United States textile and apparel markets make this industry a natural potential area for export-oriented investment.

Table IV.7 presents a snapshot of current patterns of Botswana's international trade. Of the country's exports of approximately $22 billion in 2005, diamonds and copper/nickel accounted for 86 per cent, textiles for 5 per cent and vehicles for 3 per cent. In the mid-1990s, vehicles surpassed copper/nickel to become the second largest export commodity after diamonds. However, this was reversed by the closure of Hyundai Motor's plant in 2000 (box IV.3). Botswana's import mix cuts across a wide variety of products, reflecting its dependence on imported goods and its narrow industrial base. Importantly, around 85 per cent of Botswana's imports represent intra-SACU trade, including imports from South Africa.

2. Costs and availability of factors of production

Setting up a profitable business requires a number of interrelated services: an affordable but high quality workforce, local managerial capacity, access to finance and credit on reasonable terms, and good transport infrastructure to get the produced goods to the market quickly and affordably. Other services, such as special investment zones for locating production facilities, can also help. In addition, existing firms in complementary sectors can make investment more attractive, as they might be potential suppliers or customers. This section outlines local conditions in Botswana of relevance to TNCs.

Local labour markets and labour costs. Broadly speaking, large-scale investments in Botswana outside the mineral sector (where economic rents dwarf factor payments) will not be

forthcoming unless available labour is affordable and sufficiently productive. Wages are lowest in the agricultural and manufacturing sectors, and highest in mining and those sectors with the greatest government involvement: utilities, finance and communications (table IV.8).

Table IV.8. Average monthly wages by economic activity in Botswana, 2003

Economic activity	Pula	US$
Primary		
Agriculture, hunting, forestry and fisheries[a]	599	95
Mining and quarrying	3 362	679
Manufacturing	944	191
Services		
Electricity, gas and water supply	5 569	1 125
Construction	1 050	212
Trade	1 380	279
Hotels and restaurants	854	173
Transport, storage and communications	3 597	727
Financial intermediation	5 321	1 075
Real estate, renting and business activities	2 117	428
Education	2 830	572
Health and social work	2 783	562
Other community, social and personal service activities	1 409	285
All industries	**1 719**	**347**

Source: ILO, 2005, table 5a.
[a]   Data refer to 2002.

From the perspective of a foreign investor, however, it is the wage-productivity mix relative to that available in alternative locations that matters. Table IV.9 compares Botswana's manufacturing wage costs to those observed in selected developing countries that attract significant amounts of manufacturing FDI. Highly labour-intensive products from Botswana are generally unlikely to be able to compete with production in a number of Asian countries, but the country's good access to developed-country markets may help in certain sectors.

Managers and professionals collectively account for a low share (only 8 per cent in 2001) of the workforce in Botswana (ILO, 2005). As in other countries, expatriate labour generally makes up for the shortage, although the granting of work

Table IV.9 Wages in Botswana and other selected countries, 2004
(Dollars)

Country	Average monthly wage in manufacturing
Botswana[a]	191
China	141
Malaysia[b]	403
Mauritius	265
Mexico	342

Source: UNCTAD, based on information from ILO, 2005, table 5b.
[a]   Data refer to 2003.
[b]   Data refer to 2001.

permits to expatriates is subject to a number of restrictions (e.g. the need to have a citizen as an assistant to be trained to eventually take over the expatriate's job), which, if enforced systematically, could create problems.

Local financing conditions. Table IV.10 summarizes the loan portfolio of the commercial banking sector in Botswana in December 2005. It shows that household borrowing dominates commercial bank loans, although loans for business services, trade, transport and parastatals are also important. Loans to the manufacturing sector account for only 4 per cent of all commercial bank loans – roughly equivalent to the sector's share of GDP.

The National Development Bank (NDB) and the BDC largely lend where commercial banks do not, although financing is conditional upon the economic viability of the proposed project. These institutions are also able to provide long-term loans not often provided by commercial banks. They both lend extensively to the manufacturing sector. They both banks send representatives on investment promotion trips organized by the Botswana Export Development and Investment Authority (BEDIA) in order to discuss project financing with potential investors. Generally, given sufficient equity and a sound business plan, the financing of

manufacturing and other projects is not a problem in Botswana. Commercial banks are willing to provide working capital to established firms with a good local track record, or to large firms with a solid international reputation, while the NDB, BDC and invested foreign funds provide start-up capital for new projects that show good long-term prospects.

Transport links and costs. As a landlocked country, Botswana faces significant challenges to achieving competitiveness in world export markets. However, in terms of regional markets Botswana's position is ideal. Gaborone is only a few hours by road or train from Johannesburg, the commercial heart of South Africa. Road and rail networks to the north are similarly well maintained and of high standard, as are connections to Mozambique and Namibia. Thus transport costs should be of little concern to regionally oriented exporters.

Transport costs, undesirably high as they are, do not in themselves preclude export to world markets, but they do require that these extra costs be made up elsewhere (e.g. through lower taxes or increased worker productivity). For example, for exports to the United Kingdom, the extra road transport necessitated by Botswana's landlocked situation increases freight costs by over 50 per cent (for more distant locations the premium is smaller in percentage terms). However, these high transport costs need not necessarily be high relative to the value of the exported product, as in the case of diamonds, which are, of course, a quintessential example of high-value exports.

Investment zones. Botswana has no export processing zones (EPZs) of the type pioneered elsewhere – notably in Malaysia, the Philippines and coastal China – although in the 1990s the Government's white paper on industrial policy identified such zones as worthy of consideration (Botswana, Ministry of Commerce and Industry, 1998). These zones may present advantages for Botswana in encouraging investment, as the current lack of available and serviced industrial plots is a constraint on starting new projects or in expanding existing establishments. Industrial zones might help alleviate this problem. Botswana has a duty drawback scheme, though it requires the payment of duty up front, inspection by custom officials on the export of the final goods, and then submission of paperwork and supporting documentation

Table IV.10. Commercial bank loans and advances outstanding in Botswana, by sector, December 2005

Category	Sector	Total loans and advances (Millions of Pula)	Total loans and advances (Millions of dollars)	As per cent of total
1	Central government	-	-	-
2	Local government	0.3	0.0	0.0
3	Parastatals	317.5	57.6	3.5
4	Households	5 320.4	965.1	58.7
5	Agriculture	129.1	23.4	1.4
6	Mining	18.7	3.4	0.2
7	Manufacturing	333.7	60.5	3.7
8	Electricity and water	71.8	13.0	0.8
9	Construction	191.6	34.8	2.1
10	Trade	516.7	93.7	5.7
11	Transport	297.3	53.9	3.3
12	Finance	52.8	9.6	0.6
13	Business services	1 508.6	273.7	16.7
14	Other[a]	298.8	54.2	3.3
	Total	9 057.1	1 643.0	100.0
1-3	Public sector	317.8	57.6	3.5
4	Households	5 320.4	965.1	58.7
5-14	Public sector	3 418.9	620.2	37.7

Source: Bank of Botswana, *Botswana Financial Statistics, May 2006.*

[a] Comprises real estate, community services and tourism and hotels sectors.

to the Director of Customs in order to get the duty refunded. This procedure is administratively cumbersome and slow. Investment zones, by creating an enclave outside Botswana's normal customs system, could eliminate this tedious process and provide a system familiar to Asian businesses accustomed to operating in environments with unusually liberal regulatory requirements.

Agglomerations of activity. Table IV.11 summarizes the spatial distribution of enterprises in Botswana by economic sector and location. Essentially, the bulk of establishments are located in Gaborone and Francistown. The hotels and restaurant sector has a more diverse spatial distribution, reflecting the location of different game parks in the country. Gaborone's proximity to the South African market, as well as to the ports from which exports to the rest of the world must pass, make it an obvious locational choice. However Francistown, Lobatse and Selebi-Phikwe are also sizeable centres of economic activity.

3. Why do the non-mining sectors attract little FDI?

Despite Botswana's strong economic performance over time and business-friendly environment, by developing-country standards, it attracts little FDI apart from that going to diamond mining. Indeed, many countries with far less attractive economic and/or business environments receive significant FDI in non-mining sectors. This raises questions concerning policy recommendations related to FDI for developing countries in general, as it challenges the conventional wisdom that conducive environments will eventually attract FDI. This section is intended to provide a comprehensive analysis of the various factors that affect FDI inflows to Botswana, particularly those of crucial importance to Asian firms.

Broadly speaking, there are three main categories of issues. First, there are those that reflect primarily fixed features of Botswana's economy, such as its geographical location or demographic characteristics. A second set of issues relates to regional integration, trade and infrastructure. Botswana cannot address these issues on its own; they need to be addressed at the regional level through such regional arrangements as SACU and SADC, perhaps with encouragement and assistance from donor institutions and countries. Third, there are issues that Botswana could address on its own, and, in principle, quite quickly and at little cost to the Government.

These three sets of issues have different effects on different types of investors. Large-scale investors might be deterred by the first two sets of issues, but smaller investors are likely to be

Table IV.11. Number of operating establishments in Botswana, by economic activity and location, as at end September 2005
(Number and per cent)

Economic activity	Gaborone	Francistown	Selebi-Phikwe	Lobatse	Other	Total	Per cent of total
Agriculture and forestry	87	55	16	38	310	506	3.0
Fishing	-	-	-	-	1	1	0.0
Mining and quarrying	10	8	3	-	42	63	0.4
Manufacturing	660	117	64	59	402	1 302	7.8
Electricity, gas and water	14	8	4	2	92	120	0.7
Construction	607	130	38	20	301	1 096	6.6
Wholesale and retail trade	1 738	537	250	210	3 082	5 817	34.9
Hotels and restaurants	258	151	50	33	1 251	1 743	10.4
Transport, storage and communication	560	92	68	61	230	1 011	6.1
Financial Intermediaries	125	19	9	10	44	207	1.2
Real estate, renting and business activities	1 234	199	69	71	240	1 813	10.9
Public administration	76	13	8	10	153	260	1.6
Education	142	47	33	26	1 081	1 329	8.0
Health and social work	71	22	5	10	66	174	1.0
Other community and personal activities	626	87	72	36	392	1 213	7.3
Foreign missions	28	-	-	-	-	28	0.2
Total	**6 236**	**1 485**	**689**	**586**	**7 687**	**16 683**	**100.0**

Source: Central Statistics Office of Botswana.

disproportionately affected by the third set, which is primarily procedural and administrative in scope. Since the high costs of establishing an enterprise are more likely to be prohibitive for smaller investors, efforts to speed up the procedural steps involved could help them considerably. Bigger investors are likely to have more resources for the maze of paperwork and for getting things done.

In recent years, the bulk of Asian investment abroad has been conducted by SMEs engaged in manufacturing and retail operations. For attracting more of this type of investment Botswana's future looks bright. Bigger corporations in some sectors are also likely to find Botswana attractive for reasons explained below. However, other large corporations may be willing to trade off security of market access against a less favourable policy environment.

(a) Geographical and demographic factors affecting FDI

Botswana is a small and landlocked country, and as such, it would not represent an interesting market for foreign firms; its relatively small population also constrains its attractiveness as a low-cost location for export-oriented manufacturing or services. The critical factor that has actually attracted FDI to the country is its natural-resource endowment in the form of diamonds. This natural resource has, until recently, driven the bulk of inward FDI to the country (UNCTAD, 2003), and today Botswana is the top diamond producer in the world.

(b) Regional factors affecting FDI

Although its own market is limited in size, Botswana is geographically well positioned to access its neighbours' markets. For example, Gaborone is only a few hours' drive from the greater Johannesburg area, which accounts for roughly a third of the South African market. Botswana has no exchange controls, and it offers low taxes, an enabling business environment, non-militant unions and little crime, which begs the question: Why are so few firms locating their regional operations in Gaborone?

Although SACU provides Botswana with tariff-free access to the South African market, many formal and informal non-tariff barriers significantly reduce market access opportunities. For instance,

South Africa unilaterally decided in early 1999 to start collecting a 14-per-cent value-added tax (VAT) at the border. The objective of the policy change, which was made without consultation with other SACU members, was to crack down on widespread VAT fraud.

Business legal frameworks between countries in the region can be quite different (for instance, different standards on intellectual property rights inhibit regional-market-oriented investment in certain R&D-intensive sectors such as pharmaceuticals). This can also be a serious impediment to FDI.

Botswana's main disadvantage as a location for FDI can be compensated for by access not only to the SACU market but also to the SADC regional market, which is in the making. Botswana has the most enabling environment in the region for the private sector (with the possible exception of Mauritius) and, if combined with liberalization of access to the SADC regional market, that could prove beneficial to Botswana as a host-country for FDI. Unfortunately, regional integration is a negotiated process; it took Europe 40 years to create a common market, and the social, political, economic and cultural differences between the United Kingdom and Greece are not nearly as large as those between Botswana and, for example, the Democratic Republic of the Congo.

(c) Factors affecting FDI that Botswana could address on its own

Investor ignorance about the country. Investors have difficulty discriminating between other countries in Africa and Botswana. This hypothesis is given credence by the comparatively larger amounts of FDI by South Africans, who are presumably more familiar with the region.

The process of starting a business is too slow. Several steps need to be taken to set up production. Consistently mentioned difficulties relate to: (i) obtaining visas to visit the country – highly relevant for Asian investors (e.g. India is one of the few Commonwealth countries whose nationals need a visa to enter Botswana); (ii) processing work and residence permits; (iii) finding serviced industrial land; and (iv) getting telephones and utilities connected. These interrelated bottlenecks could explain the lack of non-mining FDI in Botswana to a significant extent.

C.   POLICIES FOR PROMOTING FDI FLOWS TO BOTSWANA

As the preceding discussion suggests, efforts need to be made at both national and local levels to further remove impediments to investment and make Botswana more attractive to FDI in a diverse range of activities.

1. National policies

Various reforms that might help increase FDI inflows include the following:

Acquisition of visas and work and residence permits for non-citizens. Difficulties in obtaining visas deter many Asians from even visiting the country. Streamlining the process of visa acquisition may thus increase investor interest (UNCTAD, 2003). In addition, the issue of granting work permits for foreign employees is very complicated, mainly due to pressures for further localization of the workforce and of economic migration from neighbouring countries. It is recommended that the Government consider revising this policy by applying a flexible 5+5+5 scheme[9] as well as publishing processing statistics for benchmarking – similar schemes have been tried in Malaysia (box VI.7; UNCTAD, 2003).

Strengthening BEDIA. There is no foreign investment agency that screens foreign investors for approval to invest (UNCTAD, 2003, p. 25). The Botswana Export Development and Investment Authority (BEDIA) aims to be a "one-stop shop" for foreign investors (box IV.6). While it appears to be meeting its objectives in the provision of information and in promoting FDI, in terms of getting actual projects off the ground, problems remain. A possible solution to this problem is to have permanent representatives from all the relevant agencies and ministries (e.g. immigration, customs and land board) in BEDIA headquarters (UNCTAD, 2003). All applications could then be reviewed within BEDIA, and recommendations passed on to the relevant ministry for rubber stamping.

Provision of serviced land and/or factory shells. In principle, both BEDIA and the BDC are committed to facilitating access to serviced land and factory shells. In practice, adequate land is often not available, or slow to be provided. Possible measures that could improve this situation include re-zoning and more private investment in land development.

Introduction of a competition law. The introduction of a competition law as soon as possible is recommended in order to ensure protection against powerful foreign investors, preferably in cooperation with a South African or SADC-wide competition policy (UNCTAD, 2003).

Strengthening investment promotion activities in Botswana's missions abroad. Botswana's network of embassies worldwide provides a potential platform from which to conduct investment promotion activities in investor countries. BEDIA could provide relevant information to investment promotion officers in diplomatic missions abroad (and in Asia), and they could also be given the financial means for targeting and recruiting specific firms that are likely to reap a strategic advantage by locating in Botswana.

Maintain modest wage growth. Given the Government's large share of total employment, wage increases in the public sector risk causing demands for similar increases in the private sector. Wages in Botswana should remain attractive regionally, especially vis-à-vis South Africa (UNCTAD, 2003).

Enhancing education and skills development. Human capital development is slow in Botswana, resulting in low labour force trainability and productivity, as well as low entrepreneurship development. The Government seems to have realized this, and is making intensive efforts to accelerate education and skills development. The private sector should also be encouraged to participate actively in this effort, so as to support the Government's initiatives and ensure that the needs of business development are met (UNCTAD, 2003).

Establishing inland ports. Border crossings are a major problem for exporting companies. Addressing these problems will largely depend on cooperation and reform within SADC. However, establishing inland ports might alleviate the problem of inland transport for individual firms. Firms could simply drop off their goods at a local customs facility, with all remaining transport being

---

Box IV.6. The Botswana Export Development and Investment Authority (BEDIA): towards a "one-stop" investment promotion centre

The Botswana Export Development and Investment Authority (BEDIA) is an independent investment promotion authority established in 1999 to replace the former Trade and Investment Promotion Agency (TIPA) that was housed in the Ministry of Commerce and Industry. The main rationale behind the creation of BEDIA was to create a "one-stop shop" that would promote Botswana to potential investors by sponsoring visits from foreign missions and delegations, and help guide investors through the process of actually getting production under way in the country.So far, BEDIA has generated increased investor interest in the country by organizing meetings with potential investors from India, Mauritius and elsewhere. As a result, it has shown

the power of information: many investors approached had not even heard of Botswana before, but subsequently became interested in investing as they learned about the country's favourable economic climate.The true measure of BEDIA's success, however, will be the number of projects that actually commence operations in the coming months and years. Unfortunately, the organization's mandate to approve FDI is not nearly as powerful as that to promote it. Strengthening BEDIA may help transform "serious interest" into actual running projects. A number of policy recommendations in this direction are discussed in the main text of this chapter.

Source: BEDIA.

Box IV.7. Lessons from Malaysia's investment promotion programme: automatic work permits and industrial parks

Relatively large inflows of FDI are attributable to a considerable extent to a successful system of investment promotion and incentives in a country. The following incentives, pioneered in Malaysia, might be relevant to investment promotion in Botswana:

- *Automatic permanent work and residence permits for expatriates for projects requiring a specified amount of paid-up capital*. In Malaysia, five expatriate posts were automatically granted for projects with initial investments greater than $2 million. Given the skills shortage in Botswana, the

allowance of "no-strings-attached" expatriate posts might be attractive to foreign investors.
- *The establishment of industrial parks*. In the case of Malaysia, these also serve as export processing zones (i.e. enclaves that are administratively outside the country's customs system). However, for Botswana the main attraction of industrial parks might be the presence of serviced factory shells that are ready to rent. This would reduce the time gap between commitment to invest and the actual start-up of production.

Source: UNCTAD.

---

arranged by the relevant port authority. In practice, this may not be feasible without negotiation with Botswana's neighbours.

Strengthening the investment code. It is suggested that the recently proposed Foreign Investment Code be revised as it represents a tightening of the FDI regime in Botswana. The Government's concerns in proposing the new code have to do with attracting only "serious" and "bona fide" foreign investors, tackling the problem of economic refugees and protecting small local investors. However, such issues could be resolved without resorting to such a restrictive instrument.

Recommendations in that respect include a better-balanced FDI law, as well as a better conceptual separation of FDI and immigration (UNCTAD, 2003).

2. Regional actions and international cooperation

Making the SADC a true common market would help Botswana immensely by freeing it from the constraints imposed by its small domestic market. A Southern African regional market is increasingly becoming a reality, but while it will result in tariff reductions, several other barriers to trade remain:

Non-tariff barriers remain widespread and need to be tackled. Regional harmonization of standards, elimination of quota restrictions and removal of such impositions as VAT collection at the South African border are goals worth pursuing.

Regional border crossing needs to be streamlined. Enabling customs officials to become facilitators (as opposed to obstacles) of trade while still fulfilling their important and legitimate law enforcement role should be a regional priority. The United States Agency for International Development (USAID) is providing technical assistance in this regard from its Gaborone office – located there as Gaborone is home to the SADC secretariat.

Regional infrastructure needs improvement. Port facilities and regional road networks need improvement. Given the dependence of Botswana on ports outside its own country, it could participate in financing port upgrades in neighbouring countries in exchange for smooth access to the facilities.

Avoiding a regional race to the bottom. While tax holidays, investment credits and other incentive mechanisms can be powerful means to attract FDI, competition for FDI within SADC threatens to make the social costs of these incentives greater than the benefits they bring. A regional discussion on the limits of incentive mechanisms might therefore be beneficial. However, as FDI is sought largely for its employment creation potential, particularly given the high levels of urban underemployment and unemployment in the region, investment incentives remain a powerful means to attract FDI. This bias is even reflected in Botswana's own incentive mechanisms, which subsidize employment generation. This is therefore a complex issue. The pressure to deal with unemployment can be politically overwhelming as governments attempt to use FDI to address multiple social and economic goals.

Expanding the bilateral investment treaties (BIT) network. BITs had been concluded by Botswana with only eight countries (China, Egypt, Germany, Ghana, Malaysia, Mauritius, Switzerland and Zimbabwe) by 2005. Although this has not affected FDI, due to the country's good practices, an extension of the current BIT network would be desirable. Offering support for initiatives such as IFSC, as well as a prompt response to home-country requests are of particular importance. UNCTAD's forum for BIT negotiations could be used for this purpose (UNCTAD, 2003).

Botswana has the human capacity and financial resources to carry out the above-mentioned reforms. However, donor support at the regional level could be beneficial. Such support is already being provided in the form of technical assistance (e.g. training customs officials about the provisions of AGOA). Another form of support would be to ensure favourable access to developed-country markets (i.e. those of the United States, Europe and Japan).

3. What can Asian investors and governments do?

The prospect of significant FDI from Asia is particularly promising for helping Botswana realize the goals of economic diversification and continued rapid growth. The success of several Asian economies in attracting investment is well known, and Botswana can also learn from these success stories as it develops and refines its own FDI strategy (indeed it appears to have already done so in certain areas). Perhaps more important is the role that Asian investment could play in increasing FDI flows into the country to help promote diversification and raise productivity. For Botswana, to attract more FDI from Asia, important steps must be taken both at the national level and by existing and potential Asian investors.

First and foremost, Asian investors and governments should obtain information about commercial opportunities in Botswana. Supporting Botswana's investment promotion activities is one concrete way they can do this (e.g. by suggesting that companies interested in Southern Africa consider locating in Botswana or through delegations – as is already occurring on a small scale). Asian governments can also finance investment missions and other promotion activities. Finally, Asian aid missions to the region, besides their humanitarian work, could also focus on forging commercial links with Botswana.

4. Moving from vision to reality

Two key themes of the Government of Botswana's long-term investment and growth plan, Vision 2016, are economic diversification and an increase in inter-sectoral backward and forward linkages (Bank of Botswana, 2000, p. 99). In order to realize this vision, investment will be required in a broad range of industries. Although continued prospecting and expansion in the proven minerals sector remain important, a greater challenge will be that of increasing investment outside this sector. Initial ventures into non-traditional (for Botswana) areas of activity have generated mixed results. Fortunately, there is reason for optimism, as several areas of potentially profitable investment exist but remain underexploited.

FDI could play a significant role in facilitating diversification. Despite Botswana's small economy and geographical disadvantages, it is an attractive place to do business. It has the right policies in place, and recent trends in growth and productivity are also moving in the right direction. The main challenges are to improve public sector productivity and eliminate small bottlenecks in the business start-up process. Regional challenges include accelerating integration, and eliminating non-tariff barriers to trade. For their part, donor countries should help finance and support investment promotion activities as well as continue to ensure favourable access to their markets.

Many policy and institutional features required to attract FDI are already in place in Botswana; but it needs to continue to improve bureaucratic efficiency and undertake aggressive investment promotion. Investment promotion efforts in particular should be targeted rather than generalized. The Botswana investment promotion authorities should identify the types of investment needed, and which they have a reasonable chance of attracting (e.g. because the Botswana Government has undertaken complementary investments, or because Botswana has certain locational or other advantages over alternative host countries). A targeted investment promotion strategy also requires consideration of the full range of potential investors, including Asian investors as well as relatively small investors. Specific types of Asian investors, including SMEs, may then be identified based on a reasonable assessment of likely interest and investment feasibility. For instance, if a particular industrial cluster is to be promoted, the investors to be targeted may well be from different economies and of different sizes. For example, Japanese automobile assemblers in Thailand outsource parts from Malaysian suppliers who started off in joint ventures with Japanese suppliers, but can now offer more attractive prices. Thus, if Hyundai is to resume production in Botswana, it may be encouraged to outsource parts supplied by joint ventures with other Asian parts producers.

Notes

[1] Botswana had a per capita income of about pula 60 ($80) in 1966 when the country attained its independence (*Source*: http://www.gov.bw/economy/index.html). Its per capita income reached about $5,200 in 2005 (World Bank, 2006).

[2] See www.gov.bw/gem/vision_2016.html.

[3] The fiscal year is from July to June.

[4] While Botswana, compared to other African economies, might be in a relatively better position to weather the economic impact of HIV/AIDS, given that around two thirds of GDP is created through the mining sector and public sector, these sectors are not likely to be the major sources of future growth. Therefore, to maintain economic growth, further diversification of the economy will be needed, despite serious shortages of skilled labour and a potentially deteriorating investment climate. While basically all subgroups of the population are affected by HIV/AIDS, exacerbating the existing shortage of skilled labour, this can only partially be compensated by substituting capital for labour. It might therefore require more flexibility in terms of employing foreign labour, as well as maintaining foreign investor confidence in the economy.

[5] These banks are largely owned by their parent banks abroad, although the shares of three of them are also traded on the Botswana Stock Exchange (e.g. 70 per cent of First National Bank's shares are held by First Rand, with the remaining traded on the Exchange).

[6] For instance, St. Paul's Fire and Marine of the United States bought Botswana General Insurance.

[7] For example, Botswana's ranking in infrastructure was higher than most of the African countries in 2006: there are only 6 African countries which are ranked higher than Botswana and the rest (21 countries) are ranked below (World Economic Forum, 2006).

[8] This is reflected, for example, in the high country rating awarded by Moody's Investors Service's 2006 credit rating report on Botswana (see http://www.bankofbotswana.bw/article.php?articleid=1480) and the 2005 sovereign credit rating by Standard & Poor's (see http://www.bankofbotswana.bw/article.php?articleid=1237).

[9] All foreign investors exceeding a certain size will be automatically entitled to employ five non-citizens for key positions, as well as an additional five for managerial or technical posts. Work and residence permits will be issued for up to five years, depending on the duration of the employment contract.

CHAPTER V

GHANA

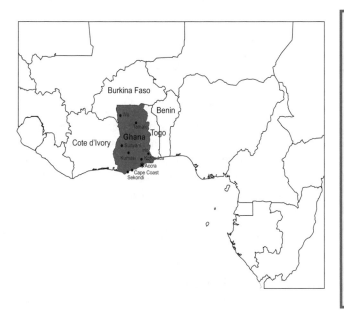

Subregion	West Africa
Area ('000 km2)	227.5
Population (millions)	22.1
Currency	cedi (GHC)
Exchange rate (cedi per dollar), 2005 average	9 072.5
GDP in current prices (millions of dollars), 2005	10 694
GDP per capita (dollars), 2005	484
Exports of goods and services (millions of dollars), 2004	3 487
Imports of goods and services (millions of dollars), 2004	5 356
Official development assistance (millions of dollars), 2004	1 357
FDI inflows (millions of dollars per annum) (2000-2005 period average)	124
FDI inward stock (millions of dollars), by 2005	2 073
FDI inward stock per capita (dollars), by 2005	94

INTRODUCTION

Ghana had a population of 22 million, a gross domestic product (GDP) of $10.7 billion and a per capita income of $484 in 2005. During the past 20 years, the annual economic growth rate in the country has averaged over 4 per cent. The economy slipped into a crisis in 1998, but has recovered in recent years. Reforms being carried out under Ghana's Vision 2020 plan, formulated in 1994, seek to transform the economy into a middle-income country by the year 2020. The plan envisages growth of the country's GDP at an accelerated rate of 8 per cent per annum. The Government further set up development goals to revitalize the private sector as specified in the National Medium Term Private Sector Development Strategy 2004-2008.

A politically stable country, Ghana has actively embraced the policy prescriptions of the World Bank and the International Monetary Fund (IMF). Since the early 1980s, it has been faithfully implementing market reforms and has promoted the private sector as the primary engine of growth for the economy. A structural adjustment programme was launched in 1983, and the free-market orientation of that programme continues to define Ghana's policy objectives. Progress with structural and macroeconomic reforms since 1984 has resulted in sustained output growth and increased private sector activity and investment over the past two decades.

The importance of FDI as a factor in development has been recognized by Ghana since the 1960s, and the climate for FDI improved considerably after it moved towards a market economy. However, Ghana's domestic market is relatively small – considerably smaller, for instance, than those of its two neighbours most likely to compete with it for FDI, Côte d'Ivoire and Nigeria. There is a strong feeling among business people and organizations that there is room for more foreign business activities in Ghana, but the country has not so far managed to attract significant levels of FDI, including that from Asia, commensurate with the investment opportunities it offers. This chapter investigates the reasons behind the relatively low levels of FDI and outlines policy options and measures that could enable Ghana to attract more FDI, particularly by Asian investors.

The chapter is organized as follows. Section A assesses Ghana's FDI performance. Section B analyses market opportunities for FDI in the country – which should facilitate a comparison of Ghana to other countries – and provides a brief review of possibilities for investment in different industries in Ghana, particularly by developing Asian firms. Conditions for FDI are examined in Section C, and the policy environment for FDI is explored in Section D. The last section discusses various measures needed to attract FDI inflows in general, and those from Asia in particular.

A. GHANA'S FDI PERFORMANCE

Ghana has had moderate success in attracting FDI in recent years. Annual FDI flows to the country declined from $244 million in 1999 to $59 million in 2002, but began to rise again in 2003, reaching $156 million in 2005. The Ghana Investment Promotion Centre (GIPC) recorded 152, 183 and 212 investment projects in 2003, 2004 and 2005, respectively, valued at $567 million over the three-year period.

On the basis of the magnitude of FDI stock by 2005, Ghana ranked only 20th among African countries. In terms of average annual FDI inflows during 2002-2005, the country ranked only 24th. However, in 2004, it ranked 16th in Africa according to UNCTAD's Inward FDI Potential Index, an index which measures a country's potential attractiveness for FDI inflows. (UNCTAD, 2006). This suggests that the level of FDI to Ghana has not been commensurate with its potential, even in comparison with other African countries.

Ghana has political stability and is free from social conflicts prevalent among its major neighbours: Nigeria, Liberia and Sierra Leone, and even Côte d'Ivoire and Burkina Faso. It has larger natural resources and agricultural potential than its Sahelian neighbours, and labour costs are much lower than in other parts of the developing world. In a continent where many countries are landlocked, Ghana has good ports that allow shipping directly to the United States and Europe. It is a member of the WTO, benefits from trade preferences accorded by the EU to African, Caribbean and Pacific (ACP) countries and is a beneficiary of the African Growth and Opportunity Act (AGOA) of the United States. It has a liberalized telecommunications sector and many Internet providers. It also has one of the few well-functioning stock exchanges in Africa, and provides a wide range of incentives for foreign investors.

1. FDI trends in Ghana

Figure V.1 shows trends in FDI inflows into Ghana over the period 1970-2005. There were relatively low levels of inflows until 1992. Thereafter, there was a more than tenfold increase: from an annual average of $11.1 million during 1980-1992, to $131.6 million during the period 1993-2005. The relatively higher levels of FDI inflows coincided with the period of economic and political reforms, albeit with a time lag. The post-1992 period marked the period of transition from a military regime (but stable government) to a constitutional democracy. As part of economic reforms, the Investment Code and Minerals Act was enacted and later revised by the GIPC Act 1994, which, as already mentioned, provides generous incentives for investment in Ghana. Though FDI inflows increased in the 1990s, they are still relatively low.

The sectoral distribution of registered FDI projects in Ghana during the period September 1994 to March 2006 shows that 26 per cent of investments went to the services sector (excluding trade, tourism and building and construction), 27 per cent to manufacturing, 16 per cent to trade and

Figure V.1. FDI inflows to Ghana, 1970-2005
(Millions of dollars)

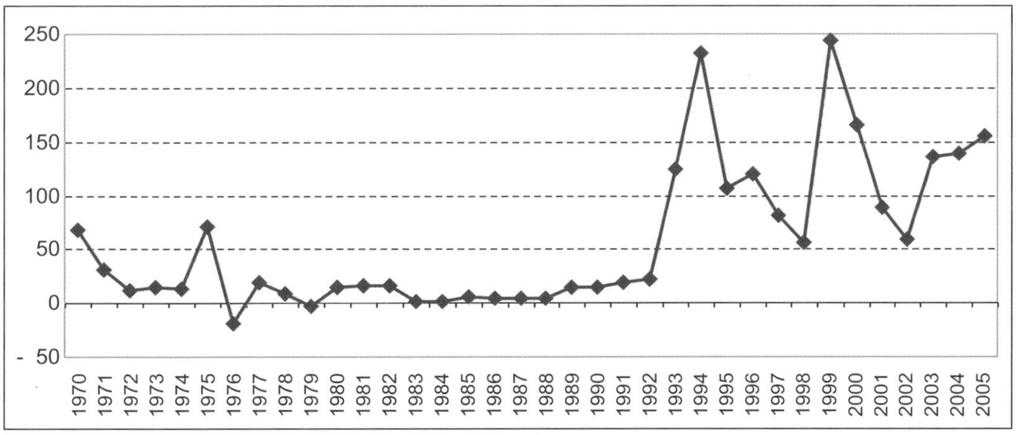

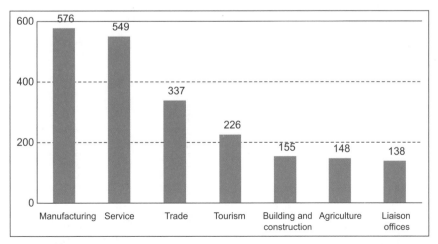

Source: UNCTAD, FDI/TNC database (www.unctad.org/fdistatistics).

11 per cent to tourism. The agriculture and construction sectors each attracted an average of 7 per cent of projects (figure V.2).

Of the leading investors during this period, a third (33 per cent) of the top 25 registered investors are from Asia, less than a third (29 per cent) from Europe, and under a tenth (8 per cent) from North America. Though FDI from Europe – particularly the United Kingdom, the former colonial power in Ghana – continues to dominate FDI stock in Ghana, there is comparable interest by investors from Asia; China and India have become the most important sources of FDI in Ghana in terms of the registered number of projects.

The distribution of FDI in Ghana by Asian investors is particularly skewed, with most investment coming from China, India and the Republic of Korea (and Lebanon from West Asia) (table V.1). None of the major outward-investor economies in Asia, such as Hong Kong (China), Japan and Singapore even feature among the top 20 investor countries in Ghana, reflecting the fact that the country has yet to catch the attention of large Asian investors. By far the largest investments from Asia (including, among others, Lebanon in West Asia) went to manufacturing (36 per cent), followed by trade (15 per cent), other services (15 per cent), tourism (12 per cent) and agriculture (6 per cent). Asian investments in Ghana serve mainly the domestic market.

**Figure V.2. Ghana: number of FDI projects registered by sector,
September 1994-March 2006**

Source: UNCTAD, based on Ghana Investment Promotion Centre.

Table V.1. Sectoral distribution and origin of FDI in Ghana: number of registered projects, September 1994-March 2006

Economy[a]	Agriculture	Manufacturing	Services							Total	Share in total (%)
			Total	Building/ construction	Exports	General Trade	Liaison	Tourism	Other services		
Europe	**50**	**143**	**433**	**58**	**37**	**34**	**50**	**61**	**193**	**626**	**29**
United Kingdom	4	39	155	17	9	16	25	16	72	198	9
Germany	13	28	74	9	4	2	5	12	42	115	5
Netherlands	10	8	55	4	9	2	3	9	28	73	3
Italy	2	32	32	14	4	2	1	8	3	66	3
Switzerland	6	11	36	5	4	3	6	3	15	53	2
France	4	12	30	2	1	2	3	9	13	46	2
Belgium	6	1	21	2	4	4	1	3	7	28	1
Denmark	2	6	19	1	1	1	6	..	10	27	1
Spain	3	6	11	4	1	2	..	1	3	20	1
North America	**17**	**32**	**124**	**14**	**5**	**5**	**6**	**24**	**70**	**173**	**8**
United States	14	24	95	9	4	1	6	20	55	133	6
Canada	3	8	29	5	1	4	..	4	15	40	2
Other developed economies	**3**	**10**	**26**	**1**	**1**	**1**	**2**	**3**	**18**	**39**	**2**
Australia	1	7	19	1	1	..	2	3	12	27	1
Israel	2	3	7	..	..	1	..	..	6	12	1
Asia	**41**	**255**	**412**	**38**	**36**	**108**	**37**	**87**	**106**	**708**	**33**
South, East and South-East Asia											
China	5	74	133	11	6	36	6	38	36	212	10
Hong Kong, China	..	2	9	..	..	3	5	1	..	11	1
India	19	86	112	7	22	32	19	13	19	217	10
Malaysia	..	1	11	..	..	..	3	..	8	12	1
Republic of Korea	13	19	39	3	1	4	3	10	18	71	3
Taiwan Province of China	1	9	5	..	1	1	..	1	2	15	1
West Asia											
Lebanon	3	64	103	17	6	32	1	24	23	170	8
Other developing economies	**3**	**19**	**101**	**8**	**4**	**11**	**12**	**4**	**62**	**123**	**6**
Nigeria	2	12	45	3	3	6	5	1	27	59	3
South Africa	..	2	33	2	..	4	4	1	22	35	2
British Virgin Islands	1	1	15	1	..	..	2	1	11	17	1
Côte D'Ivoire	..	4	8	2	1	1	1	1	2	12	1
Unspecified	34	117	309	36	31	64	31	47	100	460	22
Total	148	576	1 405	155	114	223	138	226	549	2 129	100

Source: UNCTAD, based on Ghana Investment Promotion Centre.
[a]   Ranked in descending order of the total number of projects.

FDI plays an important role in the Ghanaian economy. Since independence, many of the largest private sector firms have had foreign participation in one form or another. The vast majority of firms listed on the Ghana Stock Exchange are foreign owned. Indeed, it is striking how few sectors there are in the Ghanaian economy in which large foreign-controlled firms do not play a major role. The success of these firms – often over a very long period – demonstrates that Ghana is indeed a place where foreign firms can do business. Many of them are either European (many from the United Kingdom) or from the United States. With several notable exceptions described below, large Asian corporations have not established affiliates in Ghana, nor have they entered into joint ventures with the larger domestically owned enterprises. As ties between the regions increase, however, this trend is expected to shift.

Privatization of State-owned enterprises led to some large-scale cross-border M&As in Ghana in the 1990s (table V.2). The investors were from Canada, Libyan Arab Jamahiriya, Israel, Malaysia, the Netherlands and Norway, among others. For instance, an investor group from Malaysia (led by Telekom Malaysia) acquired a 30 per cent stake of Telecom Ghana in 1997 (though it pulled out later officially in 2005 – see box V.4). Heineken (the Netherlands) acquired Achimota Brewing Co. with investment of $13.5 million in the same year.

Non-privatization M&As have also been undertaken by investors from developed countries such as Belgium, Canada, France, the Netherlands, Norway and the United States (table V.3). In a deal in 1996, the Dutch brewer Heineken acquired another local player Kumasi Brewery Ltd. Companies from the United States and Canada are important investors in the natural resources sector, in particular in the extraction of gold ores (table V.3). In addition, large greenfield investments have also been made by United States companies in this sector as discussed later.

There is an important relationship between FDI in Ghana and other capital flows, particularly aid flows, to the country. In response to the high

Table V.2. Cross-border M&As in Ghana's privatization programme in the 1990s

Year	Acquired company	Industry of the acquired company	Acquiring company	Home country of the acquiring company	Value ($ million)	Shares acquired (per cent)
1994	Star Hotel(Ghana)	Hotels and motels	Rexol Group	Israel	1.1	100
1995	Ghana Natl Manganese(Ghana)	Nonferrous die-castings, except aluminum	Elkem AS	Norway	4.0	90
1995	Bibiani Project	Gold ores	Libyan Arab African Investment	Libyan Arab Jamahiriya	..	18
1997	Ghana Telecom(Ghana)	Radiotelephone communications	Investor Group	Malaysia	38.0	30
1997	Achimota Brewing Co	Malt beverages	Heineken NV(Heineken Holding)	Netherlands	13.5	90
1997	Tema Shipyard and Drydock Corp	Marine cargo handling	Business Focus Sdn Bhd	Malaysia	..	60
1998	Ghana Bauxite Co Ltd(Ghana)	Miscellaneous metal ores, nec	Alcan Aluminium Ltd	Canada	..	35
1999	Ghacem Ltd	Cement, hydraulic	Scancem International	Norway	17.0	35

Source: UNCTAD, cross-border M&A database.

Table V.3. Non-privatization cross-border M&As in Ghana, 1992-2005

Year	Acquired company	Industry of the acquired company	Acquiring company	Home country of the acquiring company	Value ($ million)	Shares acquired (per cent)
1992	Ghana Cement Works	Cement, hydraulic	Scancem Group Ltd	Norway	..	35
1996	Pramkese Gold-Diamond Concessi	Gold ores	Nora Exploration Inc	Canada	0.2	100
1996	EBI Gold Property(Amuany Co)	Gold ores	West Africa Mining Expl Corp	Canada	..	50
1996	Kumasi Brewery Ltd	Malt beverages	Heineken Holding NV	Netherlands	..	25
1996	Trust Bank Ltd	Banks	Banque Belgolaise(Generale Bk)	Belgium	..	35
1999	Bogoso Gold Ltd	Gold ores	Investor Group	United States	21.0	90
1999	Ashanti Goldfields Sporting	Professional sports clubs and promoters	AFC Ajax	Netherlands	..	51
2001	Bogoso Gold Ltd	Gold ores	Golden Star Resources Ltd	United States	0.9	20
2003	SSB Bank Ltd	Banks	Genefitec SA	France	23.0	50.7
2005	Afra Airlines Ltd	Air transportation, scheduled	Global Air Group Pty Ltd	Australia	..	100

Source: UNCTAD, cross-border M&A database.

cost of local capital, investors in Ghana frequently turn to aid agencies for long-term loans and grants. The earliest and largest investments, such as Kaiser's aluminium smelter, have relied heavily on funding from bilateral sources (in that case from the United States Government) and multilateral agencies (such as the International Finance Corporation or the World Bank). In Ghana, aid flows fund infrastructure development that promotes investment by private firms. Although driven by the private sector, much of the infrastructure for the free zones is also financed by aid grants or concessionary loans.

Ghana has relatively open capital markets and portfolio and direct investment are complementary.[1] The Ghana Stock Exchange, which has been functioning since 1990, had a capitalization of about $10 billion as of end 2004.[2] Much of the major upward movement in the Ghana Stock Exchange has been driven by the extensive privatization programme being undertaken in Ghana. The Government of Ghana has been committed to privatization since 1990 and there has been considerable progress: over 200 of the 300 State-owned enterprises have been privatized or slated for privatization,[3] in particular in manufacturing and tourism, as well as finance and energy-producing industries. Many of these companies have been sold to foreign investors who have since invested heavily in them.[4]

2. Types of FDI

(a) FDI aimed at the domestic market

Foreign firms have been successfully established in Ghana to provide goods and services for the domestic market. Nestlé is the largest producer of processed foods there, and British American Tobacco dominates the domestic cigarette market. Foreign firms prominent in the beverages industry are: Coca Cola, the largest soft drinks producer in Ghana and Guinness PLC. The largest textile firms in Ghana, GMC and GTMC, are affiliates of TNCs from the Netherlands and Hong Kong (China) respectively. Other large foreign firms in the manufacturing sector include, for instance, Ghacem[5] and Unilever (Ghana).[6] A number of foreign firms have also taken leading roles in the services sector. Standard Chartered, Barclays and the Ghana Commercial Bank dominate the banking sector. TNCs are also involved in the provision of infrastructure services

and utilities, as discussed separately below. The major telecommunications company, Ghana Telecommunications, was once controlled by the Malaysian State-controlled Telekom Malaysia (which pulled out in 2002). Another Malaysian group controls the television station TV3 and the film group GAMA. Finally, many Indian, Lebanese and Syrian businesses serve the domestic and tourist markets through general trading, import-export and the hospitality sector.[7] Indian businesses have also diversified into a range of manufactures, including plastics, packaging and jewellery.

(b) Export-oriented FDI

Natural resources for export. There has been a traditional concentration of activity by foreign firms in Ghana in export-oriented natural resource extraction, processing and services. The extent of this concentration is difficult to quantify, since data by industry on FDI stocks and flows for Ghana are problematic. However, the high proportion of greenfield FDI projects in the natural resource sector highlights the concentration (table V.4). The major traditional exports are gold, cocoa and timber. The mining sector is dominated by firms such as Ashanti Goldfields Company, with a large foreign participation,[8] Gold Fields Ghana Limited (a subsidiary of Gold Fields Limited of South Africa) and Teberebie (until recently 90 per cent owned by the Pioneer Group in Boston). Aluminium also constitutes a major export: Valco (Volta Aluminium Company Ltd), 90 per cent owned, till recently, by the Kaiser Corporation (United States), the largest United States investment in the country, has the largest aluminium smelter in Africa.[9] Almost all of the company's output of aluminium ingots has been exported to the United States.

Manufacturing for export. With the exception of FDI in the manufacture of wood products, investment in export-oriented manufacturing is a recent trend and one that the Ghanaian Government has long been keen to encourage. Pioneer Food Cannery is one of Ghana's largest companies, processing locally caught tuna for StarKist (a subsidiary of Heinz). Gafco (Germany) also processes tuna, sardines and wheat flour. West African Mills in Takoradi is a German-owned processor of cocoa butter, while the Swiss company Barry Callebaut (Gh) Ltd. processes cocoa. There are now also a series of firms involved in sectors such as plastics (e.g. the Indian-owned Top Industries Co. Ltd. and Letap Plastics), auto

Table V.4. Greenfield FDI projects in Ghana, 2002-2005

Year	Home country	Industry	Amount (Millions of dollars)	Name of investing company
2002	Australia	Metals/mining	..	Red Back Mining
2002	Sweden	Food and drink	..	Eurox
2003	Canada	Metals/mining	159	IAMGold
2003	Netherlands	Business services	..	Heineken
2003	South Africa	Metals/mining	159	Gold Fields
2003	United Kingdom	Food and drink	..	Diageo
2003	United Kingdom	Food and drink	19	Diageo
2003	United Kingdom	Financial services	..	Universe Group
2003	United States	Metals/mining	700	Newmont Mining
2003	United States	Energy	..	Haber
2003	United States	Metals/mining	..	Golden Star Resources
2003	United States	Metals/mining	..	Kaiser Aluminium
2003	United States	Financial services	..	Admedia Advertising Network Company
2003	United States	Business services	..	Cummings McClorey Davis & Acho
2004	Australia	Metals/mining	..	Red Back Mining
2004	Canada	Metals/mining	..	PMI Ventures
2004	Germany	Logistics and distribution	1	Deutsche Post
2004	United States	Metals/mining	30	Newmont Mining
2005	Canada	Metals/mining	..	AMT Resources
2005	Canada	Metals/mining	..	Keegan Resources
2005	Japan	Logistics and distribution	..	Mitsui OSK Lines (MOL)
2005	Nigeria	Financial services	..	Guaranty Trust Bank
2005	South Africa	Financial services	..	Metropolitan
2005	Spain	Food and drink	..	Angel Lopez Soto (ALFRIO)
2005	Sri Lanka	Textiles	3	Jinadasa Garments
2005	Switzerland	Food and drink	..	Barry Callebaut
2005	United States	Metals/mining	700	Alcoa
2005	United States	Energy	1 000	Alcoa
2005	United States	Metals/mining	2 000	Alcoa
2005	United States	Metals/mining	125	Golden Star Resources
2005	United States	Metals/mining	500	Newmont Mining
2005	United States	Metals/mining	..	Gold Coast Resources

Source: UNCTAD, based on information from OCO Consulting, Locomonitor website (www.locomonitor.com).

spare parts (e.g. the Indian-owned Automotive Springs or the Korean joint venture, Crystal Auto) and jewellery (e.g. the British-Indian La Mode de l'Afrique, or the Indian group Letap).

(c) Infrastructure and utilities

Foreign firms have had a long and successful history of working in construction and power supply in Ghana, playing a lead role in the country's construction industry. The premier construction company, Taysec, a branch of Britain's Taylor Woodrow, has been operating successfully in Ghana since 1947, well before independence. Other British and American firms have also been involved in construction, as have Chinese firms more recently.[10] It is noteworthy that, to date, all

major construction work on roads, public works or major buildings has been funded by some combination of aid money and government financing, with no major private funding.[11] A number of energy projects, some in response to the energy shortages of 1998, involve foreign firms. These include projects by the United States company, KMR, the Royal Dutch-Shell-Chevron West African Gas Pipeline from Nigeria, and the United Kingdom company, Dana Petroleum. Finally, as noted, with the purchase of a share in the major telecommunications company by a Malaysian firm, foreign investors have also entered the telecommunication services sector in Ghana. However, the foreign investor (Telekom Malaysia) pulled out after the Government of Ghana made a decision not to renew its technical and consultancy services agreement (see box V.4).

3. Experience of foreign firms

(a) General experiences

Some general points are worth highlighting. First, prior to the introduction of trade liberalizing reforms in the 1980s, many firms that serviced the domestic market were protected from import competition by high tariff barriers. However, since then, many of them, in order to survive, have had to adapt and become more competitive and innovative in terms of both pricing and product quality. These include foreign-owned firms, a typical example being Unilever Ghana Ltd. A large number of firms, most of which were SMEs owned mainly by Ghanaians, could not survive the competition and folded up.

Second, a number of companies have had a chequered history. Under the leadership of General Ignatius Kutu Kwasi Acheampong (1972-1978), 100 per cent foreign ownership of firms was not allowed and therefore such firms converted into joint ventures with State-owned or Ghanaian private-sector firms. Some of these continue today as joint ventures, while others have regained full foreign ownership. The Hong Kong-controlled group, GTMC, is an example of the former and Taysec (United Kingdom) of the latter.

Third, a variety of ownership structures appear to function well in Ghana. In particular, many firms have succeeded with a mixture of foreign and government participation: the Ghana Agro-Food Corporation is 25 per cent government-owned and 75 per cent Swiss-owned, while Barclays Bank of Ghana is 10 per cent government-owned. Most notably, the Government has a large stake in Ashanti Goldfields.

Fourth, historically, many firms that have been successful in Ghana have been large. These large firms are typically owned by TNCs from the United Kingdom, the United States or continental Europe. Asian firms (and Indian firms in particular), barring a few recent exceptions, have historically been involved in small-scale trading. But this is now changing. As mentioned earlier, in the mid-1990s, Malaysian companies bought into the major telecommunications company (Telecom Ghana) and the media (TV3 and GAMA Media Systems). They have also become involved in infrastructure investment through the Business Focus Group (Ghana), the key firm in the development of the free zones at Tema, and through a 40 per cent share in PSC Tema Shipyard Ltd. Groups from China and Hong Kong (China) are involved in construction, garments and textiles. Indian firms have become big players in plastics, but no Japanese firms are involved in manufacturing.[12]

(b) Investments from Asia

As noted, Asian investors accounted for about a third of FDI projects in Ghana during the past decade (table V.1). Discussions with business people, organizations and international groups in Ghana reveal a shared feeling that there are many unexploited opportunities for further investment in Ghana in a wide range of industries. A large number of these have requirements for the kinds of technical and managerial skills available in Asia.

Ghana has a cheap, underutilized labour force, which according to many employers is easily trained with education levels rising. Ghana is also a politically stable country and within easy distance of the large Nigerian market. There are clearly possibilities for Asian firms to engage in labour-intensive manufacturing for the regional market. There is little production of electronics in the region and only a limited assembly of computer hardware in Ghana, despite a constantly rising demand for electronic goods. Production of spare parts for automobiles and machinery is also very limited.[13] Besides these sectors, for which investment by Asian firms seems particularly well suited, there is a range of possibilities for processing Ghana's rich raw materials base through investments in SMEs for fish- and food-processing and the production of wood products, for instance.

Asian investors may regard some problems as opportunities. Despite embracing a market economy, Ghana does not have a long capitalist tradition. There are complaints about the lack of managerial skills among Ghanaian business people, while the Ghana Export Promotion Council (GEPC) complains of the lack of skills in preparing goods for export. These are skills that Asian investors might bring with them. Producers in Ghana also complain about the lack of easily available production inputs. An advantage that Indian traders and producers seem to have in Ghana is their access to established lines of supply of intermediate inputs from Asia, as illustrated by the successful experience of the Poly Group, established by an

Indian investor (box V.1). Other Asian producers can also make use of established supply lines. At the same time, taking advantage of the opportunities Ghana offers may not be easy, as the failure of some Asian investors shows (box V.2).

Box V.1. The Poly Group: nearly 40 years of successful investments

The Poly Group is one example of a successful Indian investment that has been in Ghana for an extended period of time. Established in the 1960s, the group now comprises five SMEs in Ghana: Poly Products, Poly Sacks, Poly Tanks, Poly Kraft and Somotex. They are involved in the production of a variety of plastic products such as plastic bags, plastic tanks, corrugated carton boxes and polythene sheeting; Somotex is also involved in trade. They export about 28 per cent of their output and sell 72 per cent on the domestic market. Somotex, Poly Products and Poly Kraft rank among the top 100 firms in the country.The company has found the Ghanaian labour force to be cheap and versatile, and has employed Ghanaians in management positions as well as in production. Its activities have contributed to the host economy both in terms of technology transfer and knowledge spillovers. The Poly Group not only trains Ghanaians locally, but has also sent them overseas for training. Its activities also have important forward linkages. Much of the reason for the Group's success lies in its ability to service larger firms in Ghana such as Nestlé (Ghana), Unilever (Ghana) and Heinz.As an indicator of its success, the Poly Group now also has factories in Nigeria (Montana Ltd.), Hong Kong (China) (Kiran's Impex), and India (Somotex Import and Export Pvt Ltd.), and a head office in London (Sara Ltd.).

Source: UNCTAD, based on company interview.

Box V.2. Examples of failed export-oriented FDI in Ghana

While some investments in Ghana may have been very successful, there have also been a string of failures. Some companies from Asia have been disappointed with production conditions or have found that markets were not as easy to access as they believed. In particular, some investors in the garment industries from China and Hong Kong (China) who came to Ghana for its cheap labour and access to United States markets have had to fold. These include Volta Garments and Ghana Apparel in the late 1990s, though details are sketchy.Volta Garments (Hong Kong, China) was one of the first companies to invest in Ghana's free zones. Soon after commencing production, it ran into severe labour problems. The management at Volta Garments tried to raise the productivity of its Ghanaian workers by introducing a piece-rate payments system, which the workers opposed as they felt this would have resulted in very low wages. The dispute was not resolved. Volta Garments failed to produce on schedule, a number of its contracts were cancelled by United States importers and it eventually closed in 1998.Ghana Apparel (Hong Kong, China) sent 70 experts from Hong Kong (China) to train Ghanaian workers on a one-on-one basis to produce for export to the United States market. However, the company found, that due to the absence of local suppliers, all raw materials had to be imported, from inputs to packing materials to tags and buttons, which was expensive. It had set up operations in Ghana to circumvent United States quotas on exports from Hong Kong (China). To be able to export more profitably to the United States, it was relying on AGOA, but its enactment was delayed. Consequently, the company's major client cancelled its orders and it subsequently quit Ghana. In both these cases, the main reasons for the failure of the companies remain uncertain. Representatives of the Ghana Free Zone Board (GFZB) claimed that the failure of these firms resulted from bad management, while acknowledging that its communications with the firms during the crucial periods were weak if not non-existent.

Source: UNCTAD, based on information from the Ghana Free Zone Board.

B. OPPORTUNITIES FOR ASIAN FDI IN GHANA

1. By market

(a) Domestic market

For several decades Ghana has attracted many successful TNCs to service the domestic market. However, there is an increasing demand for goods and services that has not been adequately satisfied, either due to high prices of goods or low quality. This represents profitable investment opportunities in the local market that FDI, including that from Asia, could help meet.

There is considerable potential, for instance, in investment in the provision of business inputs. Businesses in Ghana complain of difficulties in producing goods for market due to a lack of locally available inputs. While the inputs needed clearly depend on the nature of the business, there are some general requirements of numerous industries that are not being met. For example, firms involved in export complain about the poor supply of packaging materials. A range of support services – from labelling and marketing to trade-related intermediary services – is in high demand. The need for processing to add value to Ghana's primary products, and to get fresh produce to international markets, creates a number of downstream investment niches in, for example, transportation, warehousing, canning and refrigeration services. Finally, the manufacturing sector requires equipment, including basic tools for workers in the furniture sector, as well as for the production of spare parts for automobiles and electronics, as do the mining and the up-and-coming horticultural sectors.

(b) Export markets

Ghana is well placed to serve as a springboard to West African markets. Its location makes it an excellent anglophone base for penetrating the francophone markets of Burkina Faso, Côte d'Ivoire and Togo, with which it shares borders. Nonetheless, regional trade has been inhibited by administrative barriers, high transportation costs and exchange rate volatility. The Government of Ghana is aware of the problems facing regional exporters and is taking steps to address them.

The Ghana Free Zones Board (GFZB) claims a regional market for Ghana of some 250 million consumers. It is a market that is likely to grow rapidly, both in terms of population and GDP. The country lies within 150 miles of Nigeria, which has a population of 119 million and about half the GDP of the subregion, making it the largest market in sub-Saharan Africa after South Africa. In principle, Ghana's membership of the Economic Community of West African States (ECOWAS) should allow duty-free access to the regional market for goods produced by firms that are at least 25 per cent owned by citizens of ECOWAS countries, and should allow exemptions for goods that are at least 40 per cent produced within ECOWAS. However, implementation of these provisions remains very slow.

The establishment of the Ghana-Nigeria fast-track approach in 2001 towards subregional economic integration, which ensures the establishment of both a free trade area and a single monetary zone in anglophone West Africa, has speeded up the full implementation of trade liberalization protocols. The proposed monetary zone merged with the existing monetary zone of the francophone West African Economic and Monetary Union (UEMOA)[14] in 2004. These efforts are expected to be beneficial to Ghana, not only by enabling better access to the entire West African market, but also by reducing the foreign exchange constraints, eliminating exchange rate risks within the zone and reducing pressure on the balance of payments. To implement this fast-track initiative, institutions such as a technical committee, a task force and the West African Monetary Institute have already been established, with Ghana playing a dominant role; and in Ghana, a Ministry of Planning, Regional Economic Co-operation and Integration has been set up.

Another regional initiative that could serve to enhance Ghana's opportunities – not only as a gateway to the West African subregion, but also to the whole African region – is the anticipated African common market under the African Economic Community treaty signed in 1991. This is expected to be undertaken gradually in six phases over 34 years. In the current phase, the emphasis is still on liberalizing the trading regimes of the subregional groups. Eventually, all members States will have a common external tariff with monetary union plus other common socio-political institutions. The plan is fairly ambitious and difficulties could arise in implementation, as with the previous Lagos Plan of Action. Nevertheless, there appears to be widespread political support for it. The success of the common market will enable Ghana to access even larger markets, especially in Southern, Central and Eastern Africa, with which it currently has very little trade.

An examination of Ghana's trade performance shows about half of its exports going to European markets (figure V.3). Proximity, historical ties and a relatively well-developed air and sea transport network with Europe partly explain this pattern. But, perhaps, the most important factor for the dominant share of the EU in Ghana's exports is the preferential treatment Ghana receives under the Cotonou Agreement (successor to the Lomé Convention).[15] The preferential tariffs on different products exported to the European Union (EU) give Ghana a competitive advantage over non-Cotonou member states. This suggests further opportunities for FDI in Ghana, to produce goods such as palm oil, tuna, pineapple, cocoa butter, cocoa powder and cocoa paste for export to the EU market.

Another preferential trading arrangement that promises to promote market access further, to the large United States market, is AGOA.[16] The Act offers beneficiary sub-Saharan African countries duty-free and quota-free access to the United States market for virtually all products under the Generalized System of Preferences (GSP). It also provides additional security for investors and traders in African countries by ensuring GSP benefits for eight years. In addition, duty-free and quota-free access is extended beyond non-GSP items such as textiles and apparel (including footwear), luggage, handbags and watches from sub-Saharan Africa.

This preferential access to both the EU and United States markets is an advantage that should certainly help Ghana attract FDI. However, with increasing liberalization of the global economy, in the long run the country would have to develop a competitive base to sustain its attractiveness to foreign investors and become less reliant on such preferences.

2. By sector

(a) Agriculture

Ghana traditionally depended on cocoa as the mainstay of its economy, with about 80 per cent of cocoa output exported in its raw form (as beans). At present, apart from gold, cocoa is the leading foreign exchange earner, constituting about 15 per cent of agricultural GDP. There is considerable talk in Ghana about adding value to cocoa exports by increasing exports of processed cocoa, either in the form of powder or chocolate. This would reduce variations in cocoa earnings mainly arising from cyclical swings in international cocoa-bean prices. Processed cocoa has a vast market, both in the subregion and the EU, and would be a good area for Asian investments, given the current premium on Ghanaian cocoa. The liberalized cocoa industry and low labour costs are further attractions for Asian investments in this industry that aim at competing in the vast Asian market, which at present mainly depends on Europe for cocoa products.

Other cash crops produced on a small scale but with great potential are coffee and rubber. At present, Ghana concentrates on growing robusta coffee. Rubber plantations suffered in the early 1980s, but it has been the policy of the Government to revitalize the rubber industry with the development of new plantations.

There is also potential for increased production of a range of other food and horticultural products, many of them underdeveloped in Ghana. These include flowers, fruit and high quality, organically farmed products such as tomatoes. While there is undoubtedly scope for profitable investment in these areas, their growth may not bring concomitant benefits to the rest of the economy – in terms of knowledge and technology spillovers or forward and backward linkages –

Figure V.3. Direction of Ghana's exports, 2005

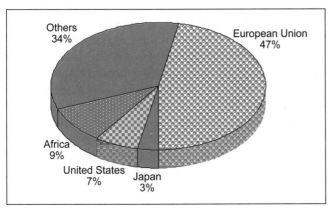

Others 34%

European Union 47%

Africa 9%

United States 7%

Japan 3%

Source: IMF, Direction of Trade Statistics, CD-ROM, July 2006.

as might be expected from investment in manufacturing.

(b) Manufacturing

Garments and textiles. Information on labour costs suggests that Ghanaian firms should be competitive in garment manufacturing for EU and United States markets. For example, labour in the Ghanaian garments sector costs less than one-tenth of the rate paid by firms in Mauritius, although the industries in the two countries use similar capital/labour mixes. However, garment manufacturers in Ghana have sometimes run into trouble mainly because of unreliable local supplies of inputs and expensive imported inputs due to high transportation costs. This sector could be attractive as a result of AGOA which covers, among others, garments and apparel.[17] Asian industries could therefore take advantage of this to penetrate the United States market and, by so doing, also promote downstream processing of cotton and its by-products in Ghana.

Wood products. Ghana's forestry policy is geared towards promoting the downstream processing of wood products. A tax on exports of timber logs is aimed at promoting greater domestic value added by encouraging such downstream processing.

There has been considerable growth in the export of non-traditional wood products, especially building materials, furniture and furniture parts. This suggests a growing market that stretches beyond Ghana to the subregion. This is a viable area of investment for Asian countries. However, the low technical efficiency of wood-processing industries in Ghana is a hindrance. Labour productivity is low due partly to the use of old equipment, poor saw maintenance and poor factory management. Most Asian countries have the essential technical expertise in this area; they could, therefore, take advantage of favourable government policies to improve the standard of wood products from Ghana and benefit from the potential subregional and international markets.

Processed foods. Ghana produces a range of foods that are in demand in export markets, but it presently fails to reach those markets due to their perishable nature and the poor infrastructure for refrigerated storage and shipping. Part of the solution is investment in the infrastructure for getting fresh produce to market. Another is investment in processing industries, including

seafood (notably tuna), sunflower oil, coconut milk, fruit juices (pineapple juice in particular) and, of course, cocoa. Heinz is already involved in tuna processing in Ghana and, more recently, other firms from the Republic of Korea and Singapore as well as the Ghana Agro-Food Company Ltd (GAFCO), which was formed in 1994 following the privatization of the Tema Food Complex Corporation, have also become involved in this sector. Indications are that there is room for considerable expansion in these industries.

However, Ghana's competitiveness in tuna exports currently depends heavily on EU trade preferences. Under the Cotonou Agreement, Ghanaian exports enter the EU duty-free, while Asian competitors pay GSP duties equal to 24 per cent. Even with this duty differential, Asian tuna is reported to cost slightly less than Ghana's tuna. The higher cost of the Ghanaian fish seems to be due to inefficient fishing technology, canning and energy costs. These are areas where Asians have a competitive advantage, which could be used by investing in the sector in Ghana so as to take advantage of EU duty exemption.[18]

Another area of importance is the oil palm industry, which was initially developed as a substitute for imported tallow. Many small producers are now producing palm oil for export. Malaysian firms, for example, have considerable expertise that could be used for developing the sector in Ghana.

There is also considerable scope for profitable investment in salt production in Ghana. The country has the potential to become a major salt exporter to the region, especially to Nigeria for the growing chemical industries there,[19] and to neighbouring landlocked Burkina Faso. However, development of this industry is presently limited by various problems, especially by poor transport infrastructure and costly shipping.

Agricultural by-products. There is much potential in Ghana for manufacturing that uses agricultural by-products. Two industries with promising potential are the production of starch from cassava and the production of materials from coconut husks, such as wood substitutes, composting material, cordage or doormats. The Government's objective is to export more processed cassava products, such as starch for industrial use and it is encouraging private-sector participation. There are a large number of growers that any investment project could rely on to supply the necessary inputs for processing.

Equipment and spare parts. Low-end electronic goods and spare parts is a viable area for private sector investment from Asia, especially from China and ASEAN countries.

Asian-made automobile parts and electronic appliances are imported on a large scale into Ghana. At present, there is a good domestic and subregional market for individual businesses to import spare parts for these automobiles and electronic appliances to serve both the growing Ghanaian market and neighbouring countries. The import markets for motor vehicle parts and telecom equipment were valued at $187 million in 2004 in Ghana,[20] and the market is even larger in Nigeria and the other West African countries. Furthermore, the telecoms industry is likely to grow rapidly in Ghana and throughout the region. These are areas where Asian producers have considerable expertise. It would be viable for them to assemble these products and import spare parts for this large and growing market. The largely untapped semi-skilled technical and vocational graduates from the secondary, technical and vocational institutions in Ghana[21] would be a source of cheap labour. Thus, Ghana would be a good location for producers looking for a West African base to produce these goods.

Equipment for furniture-making and horticulture is another area for potential investment from Asia, as steel, wood and labour which are central to its production are in ample supply in Ghana. Low-cost producers of tools in Taiwan Province of China, for example could produce in Ghana to service the regional market.

(c) Services

IT services. West Africa in general, and Ghana in particular, are catching up fast in information technology. Most institutions are embarking on computerization, which creates a demand for mid-level technical manpower. Ghana could be well placed to become a regional hub for e-commerce. Ghanaians are increasingly using the Internet, with an estimated 401,300 subscribers in 2006.[22] More importantly for exports, Ghana's web presence is attracting the interest of world markets. Given its low labour costs, even by African standards, the country is well placed to attract FDI by companies skilled in e-commerce to export services such as data processing and software development.

However, for this to be significant, as it is in India, various challenges to the further development of the IT sector would need to be addressed. The sector needs an efficient infrastructure base for low-cost broadband width Internet services, accessible and efficient telecommunications and uninterrupted electricity supply. Software development would also require building the appropriate skills.

Efforts by the Government to improve the IT infrastructure base include the SAT-3 project, which involves laying a new submarine fibre-optic cable from Portugal along the West African coastline to South Africa. Completion of this project is expected to reduce costs associated with carriage and transit charges, while facilitating efficient communications between Ghana and the rest of the world.

The Government has taken steps to woo investors into the IT sector. Besides using foreign missions, IT trade fairs are also being held in Ghana, such as Infotech 2002, to encourage networks of IT professionals, both within and outside Ghana. Finally, the Government is also supporting private-sector participation in the telecoms market by deregulating it, thus allowing the entry of new investors (for example, a third GSM operator entered Ghana's cellular market in 2002).

Recent start-ups in the private sector that appear promising involve mainly United States investors or United States-Ghanaian joint ventures outsourcing data from large United States companies and electronically processing them in Accra. Firms that export a significant proportion of their output can apply for stand-alone export processing zone status, enabling them to be eligible for all fiscal incentives such as tax breaks and duty exemptions. The attractiveness of Ghana as a place from which to export IT services, in spite of its weaknesses, is illustrated by Rising Data Solutions (United States), one of the new firms to start up in Accra in 2001, which attributes its location decision to:

"...there is an untapped wealth of talent in developing countries. Countries with educated, English speaking citizens, a strong work ethic, and stable governments. The challenge became finding the best location and people to build a company. In addition to our first-hand experience, the evaluation of countries was based on

information from a broad range of sources including: the World Bank, International Monetary Fund, the CIA, The Economist country reports, United Nations reports, United States Embassy Country Commercial guides and other sources. Our research brought us to the West African country of Ghana, where we have established our operations... "[23]

Another IT firm, the United States-based firm ACS-BPS has found its Ghana centre to be the most efficient among the six sites used globally by its parent company (box V.3). This has led to closure of part of its business in Mexico in favour of its Accra office. All these are signs of the potential of Ghana's IT sector. As many Asian countries, particularly India, have considerable expertise in this sector, their investors may also want to invest in Ghana's IT sector. Recognizing India's strength in IT, an investment mission, in August 2002 led by the President, resulted in a memorandum of understanding on IT services (and other sectors) between Ghana and India. India's

Ministry of Information Technology has allocated $2 million to set up a technology training centre in Ghana to provide training in programming.

Tourism. Tourism has been identified as one of the major sources of foreign exchange, and the Government has a policy to make Ghana a major international and regional tourist destination. Private-sector participation in tourism development has been a priority of Government policy. To further this objective, there is a company tax rebate of 25 to 35 per cent for rural investments. The Tourism Ministry also offers a special tax rebate to small standard hotels of at least 50 rooms, and they can defer payment of import duties until project completion and commencement of operations, thereby spreading out the initial costs of their investment.

In addition, the Government has a medium-term tourism policy (1992-2010), aimed at improving both the public and private sector institutional framework for investment. Included

---

Box V.3. FDI in data processing in Ghana: implications for Asian investors

A Dallas (United States)-based firm, Affiliated Computer Services – Business Process Solutions (ACS-BPS) has set up a data processing affiliate in Ghana which services large United States companies such as UPS, Aetna and American Express. It has become one of Ghana's largest private employers, with more than 1,800 employees in 2006. The key factors attracting these investors to locate in Ghana include the availability of a cheap and reasonably skilled pool of labour, a sufficiently flexible labour market allowing the use of a piece-rate system of payments, favourable investment incentives and the availability of basic telecommunications infrastructure.To overcome weaknesses in the telecommunications infrastructure, ACS-BPS installed its own satellite connection, thus bypassing the local phone system.[a] Another start-up difficulty faced by the firm was that the national communications authority had never before dealt with a private network outside the traditional telecoms environment, and therefore lacked the experience to arbitrate between the demands of the data processing firm and the

traditional players.[c]The sustained success of this company represents a great opportunity to enable Ghana to market itself as an attractive destination for data-processing-related FDI. Given the large size of the global market for data processing and the growing tendency for companies to engage in complex integrated production systems (i.e. locating different aspects of the production system in the most competitive countries), this could offer immense potential for Ghana to attract Asian FDI. It is particularly promising for attracting Asian investors from countries with high labour costs that are seeking to relocate aspects of their operations to low-cost, efficient developing countries. However, to be able to do so will require further improvements in Ghana's infrastructure, including telecommunications and an uninterrupted power supply. At present, the demand for labour for data processing is being satisfied. However, venturing into software development will require further upgrading of IT skills of the labour force, especially software programming.

Source: UNCTAD, based on World Bank, 2001.

a   An initial difficulty encountered by the firm in setting up was the high cost of satellite connections. While the connection fee from the United States to the satellite cost $8,000 per month, the Ghanaian agents (Westel and Ghana Telecom) wanted to charge $27,000 per month. This was however negotiated downwards to a more reasonable level through the intervention of Intelsat, a global communications leader (World Bank, 2001).

in this framework are adoption of tourism investment incentives to attract foreign investors, simplified investment procedures, establishment of a tourism credit-financing programme and creation of a tourism development fund to be financed from a 1 per cent tax on hotel and restaurant expenditure. These policies aim at reducing the initial costs of investment. Asian investors can take advantage of this by making a head start to share in Ghana's quest to become the gateway to the subregion.

Another area of potential investment is domestic tourism by Ghanaians. Foreign investors can participate by developing urban and rural tourism sites and promoting domestic interest in tourism and family vacation sites. Ghana is increasingly becoming an important destination for tourists and business people, as well as a major location in the subregion for meetings, seminars and conventions. This is promising for the hotel business in Ghana, but some improvements to services, such as room reservations, are needed so as to conform to international standards. Also needed are marketing services through franchises and correcting a negative "image" problem concerning security and reliability of services.

Transportation. Rural and urban transportation is one of the most underdeveloped sectors of Ghana and the subregion. Road transport operations are unreliable as they are scattered and lack uniform standards of operation. Problems in this sector are mainly due to private ownership of public transportation vehicles with some corporate involvement, with the exception of the State Transport Corporation (now Vanef STC Ltd.). First, vehicles are often very polluting and unsafe. Because profits are so low, operators often use tires until they explode. Second, while they are effective for low-volume feeder trips, they are not as efficient in main corridors, where they tend to cause congestion and conflict with other road users. Third, they follow no predictable schedule, stopping randomly and without notice.[24]

Well-organized corporate involvement, especially in urban transport, has considerable potential. It is the Government's policy to improve mass public transportation, especially in the cities, to reduce traffic congestion. This is an area where the expertise of Asian investors could be sought.

Under the project for making Accra the gateway to the subregion, the Government adopted a liberal "open skies" policy aimed at deregulating the air transport industry. At present, there are no restrictions on domestic air operations, except that carriers must be licensed by the Air Traffic Licensing Authority and satisfy regulations set by the Ghana Civil Aviation Authority. Currently, Ghana's domestic air routes are underdeveloped, with no scheduled domestic flights. Services of Golden Airways, FanAir and MukAir were suspended back in 1999 due to poor management that resulted in unreliable service, and thus a loss of public confidence.

C. LOCAL COSTS AND CONDITIONS FOR FDI

1. Labour markets and costs

The minimum wage in Ghana in 2004 was $1.5 a day,[25] which is not considered a constraint by foreign firms. Indeed, they tend to pay well above the minimum wage. Wages are commonly set in consultation with firms or industry unions. For construction workers, this process has resulted in wages of $1.5 to $2.0 a day. However, Ghana has not been able to translate this cheap-labour advantage into booming export-oriented manufacturing, for instance in the garment industry. One of the reasons could be the labour regulations (see the discussion of Volta Garments in box V.2). Poor work ethic and an inadequately educated workforce are identified as problematic factors for doing business in the country (World Economic Forum, 2005). Productivity in large firms in Ghana also appears to be relatively low, in comparison to Mauritius (Teal, 1999), for example.[26] Evidence suggests that although wages in Ghana are one sixth of those in Mauritius, on average, productivity is four times higher in Mauritius.[27] Wages vary considerably by sector and firm size. The average wage in firms with more than 100 employees is twice that in firms with fewer than 100 employees.[28]

A number of foreign-controlled firms have succeeded in finding excellent Ghanaian staff for senior management positions. They find that using local management, when available, is more cost-effective than using expatriate staff. But there are complaints that the educational system does not provide enough workers with sufficient skills and that the supply of local managerial staff is inadequate. Investment may be attracted by cheap, unskilled labour, but a minimum ratio of local skilled labour is required for successful operations.

2. Financing conditions

Generally, firms in Ghana complain of difficulties in accessing credit facilities. Access to financing is the most problematic factor for doing business in the country (World Economic Forum, 2005). High real interest rates substantially heighten the cost of credit. Furthermore, due to high collateral requirements, many SMEs are ineligible for loans from the main banks. The banks appear to be more interested in large and established companies.[29] Banks' lack of interest in supporting SMEs is partly due to the high-interest-yielding, risk-free government treasury bills that effectively deprive the private sector of much-needed finances. However, this situation is being addressed by the Government through moves to finance the government deficit by non-bank sources such as raising securities in secondary financial markets. Generally, however, large firms, including established exporters, can readily access working capital for finance.

About 50 credit facilities funded from external sources and available through local financial institutions exist in Ghana. These credit facilities amount to $300 to $500 million available for trade finance, investment (imports of capital goods) and venture capital.[30] Small, targeted concessionary finance for non-traditional exports has also been made available through trade and investment reform programmes sponsored by the United States Agency for International Development (USAID). This has been critical in the development of the non-traditional handicrafts sector.

3. Utilities

Table V.5 provides several indicators of the quality of infrastructure in Ghana. The country ranks relatively high in Africa in postal efficiency, port infrastructure quality and electricity supply. In 2004, main telephone lines, mobile telephone subscribers and Internet users per 1,000 inhabitants were merely 14.5, 78.2 and 17.0 respectively. The Ghanaian telecommunications market has opened up to competition,[31] but there are ongoing problems in the telecommunications sector. The Government has acknowledged the challenges facing this sector and intends to develop a comprehensive information, communication and technology (ICT) policy.

Ghana relies heavily on hydroelectricity for its power needs.[32] This has caused problems due to rain shortages, leading to severe power shortages in the late 1990s. In response to uncertainty in the power supply, large firms attempt to limit their dependence on local supplies by using their own power generators. Nevertheless, it seems that the energy situation is improving in Ghana as several projects have been completed or are being undertaken.[33]

4. Transportation

The Gateway Project[34] aims to strengthen Ghana's infrastructure and institutional capacity, to make international trade more efficient and less costly and promote Ghana as the gateway to West Africa.

- Shipping. Ghana has two major ports: one in the industrial town of Tema, close to Accra, and the other in Sekondi-Takoradi, some 130 miles from Accra. The quality of services at these ports is improving. The turnaround time for ships in Ghana's ports is estimated to be the fastest for West Africa.[35]

- Airways. There is considerable potential for increased air haulage from Ghana. The national airport is particularly active and has direct links with the United States, Europe and Southern Africa.[36] It also has regular links with China and India. In particular, Ghana has good links with other West African countries.

- Roads. Ghana has an estimated 24,000 miles of roads – 9,200 of which are trunk roads – that carry 98 per cent of freight. There has been a marked improvement in the quality of roads in Ghana.[37] However, if Ghana wishes to act as a gateway to West Africa, it will need an adequate road network linking it to neighbouring countries and a reduction in regulatory barriers that at present hinder trade by road. Another area requiring priority attention is the construction of feeder roads to rural communities.

Table V.5. Indicators of the quality of infrastructure in Ghana, 2004

Item	Rank out of 25 African countries	Rank out of 102 countries[a]
Overall infrastructure quality	12	71
Railroad infrastructure development	17	79
Postal efficiency	7	62
Quality of electricity supply	10	78
Air transport infrastructure quality	12	74
Port infrastructure quality	9	67
Telephone infrastructure quality	18	91

Source: World Economic Forum, 2004a.
[a] According to World Economic Forum, *Global Competitiveness Report 2003-2004*.

D. POLICY ENVIRONMENT FOR FDI

Ghana began courting FDI long before it moved towards a market economy. As far back as 1963 the importance of FDI was recognized, as demonstrated by the Capital Investment Act of 1963. However the wide range of fiscal and other concessions offered to potential foreign investors was accompanied by various conditions that served as deterrents to investment. Subsequent revisions to the investment code have substantially improved the climate for foreign investment. Attracting FDI remains a key objective of Ghana's economic recovery programme, which started in 1983 under the auspices of the World Bank and the IMF. The Ghana Investment Promotion Centre Act of 1994 set up the GIPC as a promotional agency providing a wide range of investment incentives. In addition to these incentives, ongoing privatization of State-owned enterprises provides profitable investment opportunities. A number of other policy developments, such as those relating to SMEs, international trade, the exchange rate and infrastructure linkages with other West African countries, have also favourably influenced the environment for FDI in the country.

1. FDI policies

Responsibility for investments in various sectors has been divided up among different agencies of the Government of Ghana. The five main agencies are the Minerals Commission and the Ghana National Petroleum Corporation for investments in the mining and petroleum sectors, respectively; the Divestiture Implementation Committee for investments in companies sold by the Government; the Ghana Free Zones Board (GFZB),[38] for investments exporting 70 per cent or more of their products, and the GIPC, which deals with all other investments. All these institutions offer generous incentives to prospective investors.

(a) The Ghana Investment Promotion Centre Act

Under the GIPC Act 1994 investors are entitled to tax holidays, accelerated depreciation allowances, exemptions from import duties on machinery and equipment, investment allowances and remittance of dividends. Tax holidays of up to five years are applicable for investments in general farming, fisheries, aquaculture, livestock and real estate, and up to 10 years for rural banking and cattle ranching. Firms exporting non-traditional exports are entitled to a reduced tax rate of 8 per cent, and licensed hotels to a reduced tax rate of 25 per cent. Besides the import-duty exemptions on machinery and equipment, the GIPC is empowered to grant additional incentives or special investments, with approval from the President.

The GIPC Act accords national treatment to foreign investors and reserves only a few activities for Ghanaians, such as petty trading, operation of taxi-fleet services of less than 10, pool betting, lotteries, beauty salons and barber shops. Furthermore, Ghana does not impose performance and local content requirements on foreign investors. Last, but not least, foreign investors with paid-up capital of $10,000 but less than $100,000 or its equivalent in cedis, shall be entitled to an initial automatic maximum immigrant quota of one person.[39]

With the creation of the GIPC, the Government of Ghana has greatly eased the administrative requirements for foreign investments and facilitated processes for investors. Registering with the GIPC takes a maximum of five days, is inexpensive, and offers companies registered with it exemption from an approval process. There is little doubt that the GIPC is a serious and dedicated promotion agency. Even though the Government has not spelt out specific policies in the Act for Asian FDI, encouraging these investors to take advantage of Ghana's investment incentives seems to be high on the agenda of its promotional activities.

(b) Incentives in the minerals sector

Similarly, generous incentives are offered to FDI in the minerals sector via the Minerals and Mining Law of 1986 and the Amendment of the 1994 Act 475. These seek to provide a more conducive environment for private investment in the mining sector. Ghana has abundant mineral resources, including gold, bauxite, manganese, diamonds and limestone, which are governed by the Mining and Minerals Act. Incentives provided under the revised Minerals Act include a reduction in the minimum royalties payable and in the corporate tax (from 55 per cent to 35 per cent), as well as tax exemptions for imported plant and equipment. Companies are allowed to capitalize all expenditures during the reconnaissance, prospecting and development stages. Since reforms, the mining sector has been rejuvenated, with gold exports currently overtaking cocoa as Ghana's leading export earner. The inflow of private investment through these improved incentives has undoubtedly played a role.

(c) Ghana Free Zones Programme

One of the key initiatives to attract FDI into non-traditional exports (i.e. excluding minerals, cocoa and timber) has been the promulgation of the Free Zones Act in September 1995. The Act offers even more generous incentives than the GIPC Act, 1994. The incentives package includes exemptions for free zone developers from revenue or profit tax for 10 years, income tax after the 10-year holiday is not to exceed 8 per cent, and there is an exemption from withholding tax on dividends.

Under the Free Zones Act, investors are spared various bureaucratic restrictions and other statutory requirements. There is an expedited investment approval process (not exceeding 28 days), unimpeded issue of expatriate work and residence permits, and accelerated on-site customs inspection. Furthermore, a policy of free ports and open skies is in place to further reduce bureaucratic impediments. The Gateway Project complements the Free Zones Programme as it seeks to improve upon Ghana's infrastructure facilities at the ports, with a view to making Ghana the trading hub for West Africa.

The Free Zones Programme adopts an innovative approach through the establishment of enclaves and single factory zones. This enables access to a vast array of resources around the country as well as providing focused enclaves, within which firms can benefit from agglomeration economies.

(d) Investment guarantees

Guarantees against expropriation and nationalization are enshrined in the provisions of Ghana's constitution and investment legislation. Ghana has also ratified the convention establishing the Multilateral Investment Guarantee Agency (MIGA) of the World Bank, which reduces non-commercial risks of FDI in developing countries. The State may only acquire an enterprise if it is

in the national interest for a public purpose, on payment of fair and adequate compensation. Disputes are to be resolved by reference to the rules of arbitration of the United Nations Commission on International Trade Law or, where relevant, to bilateral investment agreements. Asian countries with which Ghana currently has bilateral agreements are China, India and Malaysia.

2. Other related policies

(a) Privatization

An important component of Ghana's economic reforms has been the divestiture of State-owned enterprises, which commenced in 1988. The privatization programme has resulted in the sale of more than 300 of approximately 350 State-owned enterprises.[40] It has been carried out through sales of shares, joint ventures, leases, sales of assets and liquidations. Major divestitures have included selling government shares in the Ashanti Goldfields ($462 million), various State-owned banks ($65.2 million), and Ghana Telecom ($38 million) which was purchased by Malaysian investors (box V.4). The privatization timetable until 2003 included four wholly-owned large and strategic enterprises and several medium-sized enterprises. The divestiture process is open to foreign investors, and deferred payments for up to three years may be negotiated. The Divestiture Implementation Committee cites several success stories, including West African Mills and GAFCO, but there have also been some failures such as Ghana Telecom.

(b) Small and medium-sized enterprises

Currently, there is no comprehensive policy on SMEs in Ghana. However, over the years various Governments have initiated projects to support the SME sector, recognizing it as an important employer and producer in the domestic economy. There has thus been both financial support – via the recently terminated Businesses Assistance Fund – and through various training programmes organized by government and quasi-government institutions, such as the National Board for Small Scale Industries and EMPRETEC Ghana. The most recent initiative, implemented by the Export Development and Investment Fund, seeks to encourage the SME sector to venture into exports. Specifically, the Ghana Investment Fund was established to help finance small and medium-scale agro-processing and export-oriented companies in Ghana.[41] Since these initiatives are non-discriminatory, both indigenous and foreign SMEs can access these funds, including Asian SMEs investing in Ghana.

(c) Trade policy

Liberalization of the trade regime has been pursued through substitution of quantitative instruments with price instruments, increased transparency and a gradual reduction of import tariff rates. Thus by 1989, the import-quota system had been abolished, and by 2000, tariff levels had fallen to 0, 5, 10 and 20 per cent from their 1982 levels of 35, 60 and 100 per cent. The simple average tariff rate has been levied at 14.7 per cent since February 2000, reduced from over 30 per cent. It is noteworthy that companies in the free trade zones enjoy a ten-year tax holiday and a zero duty on imports (United States, Department of State, 2006). Ghana's liberalized trade regime thus affords opportunities for both existing and potential investors, including Asian investors, to access essential materials at competitive prices. These benefits are even greater for firms registered in the EPZs, since they are exempt from duty and enjoy various tax breaks.

Ghana is party to several multilateral and regional institutions and agreements on international trade. These include the WTO, the Cotonou Agreement and ECOWAS. Bilateral agreements also exist with the Czech Republic, Egypt, Malaysia, South Africa, Trinidad and Tobago, Turkey and the United States, among others. The current focus of trade policy is continued liberalization of the trade regime, and, more importantly, a higher degree of economic integration within the West African subregion. To this end, there is a Ghana/Nigeria fast-track approach to subregional economic integration, which offers market opportunities in both countries and in others in the subregion. By intensifying efforts towards subregional integration, Ghana hopes to become the gateway for Asian investors interested in accessing the West African market.

(d) Exchange rate policy

The ostensible objectives of exchange rate policy reforms in Ghana have been to increase the overall availability of foreign exchange and to improve foreign exchange allocation mechanisms. This has been pursued through gradual liberalization of the foreign exchange market, from a system of export bonuses financed by import surcharges and systematic quarterly devaluations in the early 1980s, to the current free-floating exchange rate regime with the operation of foreign exchange bureaus and the inter-bank market. These policies have enabled the Ghanaian currency, the cedi, to depreciate in value from 30 cedis per dollar in 1983 to 9,073 cedis per dollar in 2005.

While there are concerns about its rate of depreciation and the impact this has on macroeconomic stability, the current administration is committed to a floating exchange rate as well as preventing nominal depreciation that induces

---

Box V.4. Privatization of Ghana Telecom and its aftermath

Ghana Telecom (GT) was partially privatized in February 1997 through the sale of 30 per cent of its shares to G-Com, a consortium led by Telekom Malaysia (TM). After that, GT expanded its network and its subscribers, but not to the extent stipulated by the National Communication Authority (NCA). Due to the sluggish economic situation, GT also faced increasing complaints about inadequate supply of telephone service and high access charges. In November 2001, the new Government of Ghana made a decision not to renew the Technical and Consultancy Services Agreement between GT and TM after its expiry in February 2002. The company therefore sued the Government by filing an injunction at the High Court in The Hague to recover the value of its shares in GT. According to the International Finance Corporation's Summary of Project Information (25 August 2005) on the Ghana Telecom II Project, a settlement between the Government of Ghana and TM regarding TM's exit was finalized in May 2005 paving the way for the Government to pursue its plan to increase private sector ownership of GT through privatization of at least 51 per cent of the Company within a two year time frame to a strategic investor (http://www.ifc.org/ifcext/).

Source: UNCTAD.

macro-instability. These objectives are being pursued through continued adoption of a flexible exchange rate regime and a tight fiscal and monetary policy stance. Increased liberalization of the exchange rate regime within a stable macroeconomic environment offers Asian investors attractive possibilities to establish export-oriented units of production in Ghana. All the more so since Ghana's liberalized regime enables its exports to be more competitive on world markets, barring other domestic capacity and external market access constraints.

E. MEASURES NEEDED TO ATTRACT ASIAN FDI

Various measures are needed to attract more FDI inflows in general, and those from Asia in particular, including various proactive policy measures and the removal of obstacles identified as hindering FDI. Coherent policies are essential for attracting and benefiting from FDI.

1. Macroeconomic stabilization

High inflation is one of the most problematic factors for doing business in Ghana (World Economic Forum, 2005). Even though economic growth and development has been restored since economic reforms were launched in 1983, macroeconomic stability has proved elusive. High rates of currency depreciation largely increase the cost of imported inputs. This is made worse by the fact that many firms use a high proportion of imported raw materials and spare parts. They also increase the cost of servicing foreign loans, especially for FDI geared for the domestic market. Last, but not least, increased depreciation rates cause increased uncertainty as they reduce the predictability of both costs and revenue, which in turn deters new or increased investments. Though one could argue that high depreciation rates also increase the profitability of exports, this is limited to the extent that the increased input costs and risks arising from high depreciation limit investment in the exportable sectors.

Existing high interest rates (over 20 per cent) in Ghana are prohibitive, and deter local contributions to investments, thus inhibiting joint-venture investments.

Owing to the adverse effects of relatively unstable macroeconomic environment on the competitiveness of the country, Ghana would stand to benefit a great deal from improving that environment. Acutely aware of this, the administration is giving priority to attaining macroeconomic stability. Measures have been taken to reduce expenditures and increase revenue in recognition of the fact that fiscal indiscipline is the major cause of macroeconomic instability. Since future terms-of-trade shocks cannot be ruled out, the Government also needs to take steps to reduce their potential impact on the country's macroeconomic stability. In the long run, the solution lies in diversification of the export base; hence the need to continue to encourage investments in non-traditional exports.

2. Strengthening regional trade and investment integration

Facing intense competition for FDI, Ghana needs to develop its niche in the global market for FDI, including investment from Asia. The advantages it could highlight include first of all, its politically stable and peaceful environment, as many investors perceive Africa otherwise; and second, its series of reforms that have opened up the economy and created several investment opportunities. One of the major determinants of FDI is market size. Since Ghana's own market size is relatively small, it could attract market-seeking FDI by promoting itself as the gateway to the larger market of the West African subregion (UNCTAD, 2002b). As mentioned earlier, Ghana and Nigeria are on a fast-track programme to integrate their economies, but there is still a low level of integration in the subregion. With a few exceptions, countries in the West African subregion tend to trade more with the EU than among themselves. They would do well to learn from other regional blocs such as ASEAN, the North American Free Trade Area (NAFTA) and the EU where intraregional trade is a very important reason for high FDI.

One hindrance to subregional integration is the lack of implementation of some of the trade liberalization protocols under ECOWAS. Countries in the UEMOA do not accord MFN treatment to non-UEMOA countries within the subregion. For instance, firms registered under the ECOWAS trade liberalization scheme continue to express their frustration at not being able to realize the benefits of lower import tariffs in other West African countries. A second factor hindering integration in the subregion is the large number of checkpoints, leading to the loss of valuable time, and increased costs associated with bribery.

Third, the low level of intra-African trade is attributable in large part to the poor infrastructure facilities between African countries. In West Africa, for instance, charges for phone calls to neighbouring countries are exorbitant. Obviously, subregional problems cannot be solved by a single country. Cooperation is needed between the Ghanaian Government and other member Governments of ECOWAS, not only to improve infrastructure provision, but also compliance with the trade protocols of ECOWAS.

Member States of ECOWAS should also pursue an investment framework agreement at the subregional level, which could provide greater protection, transparency, stability and predictability, and encourage further liberalization. Ghana should renew its commitment to enforce the ECOWAS trade liberalization scheme and accelerate regional infrastructure development (UNCTAD, 2002a). This should prove to be beneficial in promoting a well-integrated West African market, thus enabling potential investors to gain access to the whole region through investments in one of its member countries. It could also be followed up with interregional pacts, for example, between ECOWAS and ASEAN to promote trade between the two regions. Increased trade between them might also increase FDI inflows from Asia to the West African subregion.

3. Improving infrastructure

One factor that could position Ghana as a favourable investment destination among developing countries competing for similar investments is the creation of an efficient infrastructure base. This is considered one of the strong attractions to investment in Singapore for instance. Current efforts by the Ghanaian authorities to improve the trade infrastructure via the Gateway Project and the creation of three export processing zones are commendable. However, given the Government's budget

constraints, its ability to improve the overall infrastructure is limited. To this end, the Government should take steps towards the introduction of an adequate regulatory framework for utilities and infrastructure development, possibly by promoting the creation of partnerships between the public and the private sectors. Appropriate regulatory authorities should develop a code of practice for the utilities and be responsible for monitoring the provision of public services (UNCTAD, 2002a).

Private investors could therefore be encouraged to participate in infrastructure development as investment, an opportunity in itself. This includes increasing the physical capacity of the ports to reduce congestion, providing refrigeration facilities at KIA airport, improving the roads linking major cities (e.g. the Accra-Takoradi road) as well as feeder roads linking fertile agricultural land to the road network, widening Internet access (currently limited) and providing reliable energy and water supplies to relevant businesses. The GIPC has already started advertising for investors in some build-operate-transfer (BOT) and manage-operate-transfer (MOT) infrastructure projects.[42]

All these improvements are important for attracting FDI to Ghana. However, to further encourage FDI from Asian sources, infrastructure links serving the interests of Asian investors will need to be improved. This would have more to do with improvements in the level of services such as banking, telecommunications and transport between Asian countries and Ghana.

4. Promoting labour skills

Ghana's relatively cheap labour costs, even by West African standards, are an obvious advantage, but should be complemented by higher productivity levels. The inefficiency of the science and technology system to transfer, use and adapt imported technology plays a major role in low productivity (UNCTAD, 2002a). Policies to improve labour productivity are particularly important for Ghana in its efforts to attract export-oriented investments. Labour productivity could be increased by training the labour force in required skills, as has been done in Malaysia and Singapore. The polytechnics, universities and other manpower development institutes could help by introducing appropriate courses and workshops. Moreover, the

Government should encourage the participation of the private sector in offering training programmes by providing appropriate incentives, such as fiscal incentives for training expenditures. Cooperation between the private and public sector could also lead to the establishment of an employment agency (UNCTAD, 2002a).

The improvement of labour competitiveness may require some policy adjustments. Current labour legislation, such as the high cost of severance pay or labour right provisions that often lead to strikes, could deter foreign investors. A new labour bill that provides for the creation of a National Labour Commission is a positive step towards the settlement of conflicts related to labour issues (UNCTAD, 2002a).

5. Overcoming cultural barriers and geographical distance

Cultural barriers also present obstacles to FDI. Compared with European and North American investors, Asian investors are more likely to face such barriers due to weak historical ties and limited interactions with Ghanaians through education or trade. There have been reports in the Ghanaian news media attesting to poor employer-employee work relations within sections of the Asian investor community. Such tensions and misunderstandings could be alleviated or even avoided if both Ghanaian workers and Asian investors are sensitized to each other's cultures. The GIPC could possibly look into this aspect and provide appropriate information to investors and Ghanaian missions in Asia. Joint ventures may also serve to reduce the learning cost of the two cultures as well as easing the initial difficulties involved in settling and operating in a new environment.

Geographical distance could serve as a barrier to trade and FDI. However, technological advances and lower transport costs are significantly reducing the distance between nations. Asian economies in general are not close to Ghana, nor is there much traffic between them. There is no direct flight connection to any Asian country; Ethiopian Airlines is the main carrier to Asia, with services to India and China. Shipping vessels going to Asia pass through several ports, hence delaying shipments to Asia. All this increases the time and costs of a particular transaction, making Asia appear even more distant in this modern age. However, this could be addressed by the Government through a further opening up of the airline and maritime industry to allow Asian airlines and shipping vessels access to the African market.

6. Strengthening the role of the GIPC

As the main investment promotion agency, the GIPC plays a vital role in attracting FDI. It could improve its capacity to deliver services to its users in the following ways (UNCTAD, 2002a):

Provision of efficient after-investment services. Given the importance of after-investment services, the GIPC needs to take steps not only to attract foreign investors, but also to support them once they have arrived.

Improved data collection. There is consensus on the need for good analysis and data to inform investors about the policies and actions of FDI promotion agencies in Ghana.

Professionalizing the GIPC. Ghana's investment promotion agencies need staff with more experience in successful private sector ventures.

More detailed sector profiling. The GIPC's present sectoral guides are not adequate; they need to be more detailed and should be prepared by people with successful business experience.

Greater prioritizing of sectors. Ghana should be able to set priorities according to which sectors are most in need of investments. The GIPC should then collect data to try to estimate the extent to which firms' activities are compatible with its policy objectives.

Studying failed investments. Ghana needs to look carefully at cases of failed investments (e.g. investment by Telekom Malaysia). Much can be learned from these cases. They may provide valuable lessons for government agencies as well as for prospective investors.

7. Proposals for specific measures

UNCTAD, in collaboration with the Japan Bank for International Corporation, has prepared and proposed 15 measures for implementation within a 12-month time frame to attract larger FDI flows to Ghana (box V.5). One of them is specifically related to Asian investment (measure 15) (UNCTAD and JBIC, 2006).

8. International cooperation

Ghana stands to gain from Asian FDI inflows, and significant reforms are being implemented to attract such investment. However, there remain areas for improvement, which require efforts, both domestic and external, to enable Ghana to attract more significant Asian FDI flows. Domestic reforms are needed at the macro and micro levels, while external reforms refer to those that can be unilaterally pursued by Ghana as well as those that require the assistance or cooperation of other countries.

Areas that require the cooperation of other countries, for example, are the regional integration schemes in West Africa in particular, and Africa in general, as noted above. Most importantly, regional cooperation is required to improve the image of Africa collectively vis-à-vis the global investor community. Last, but not least, is the need for bilateral and regional agreements with Asian countries or the ASEAN regional bloc to provide a more favourable framework for Asian FDI flows to Africa.

There are also measures that Asian countries, and, more generally, the international community, can undertake to encourage Asian FDI flows to Ghana. These include sponsoring trade missions to and from Ghana, providing training opportunities in Asian firms and universities, promoting market access for Asian investors in Ghana and providing insurance schemes, investment guarantees and credit for Asian investors in Africa. Asian investors also could:

- Re-evaluate Ghana as a place to do business, as there exists considerable potential for profitable investment opportunities;

- Be reminded of the many incentives offered by the Government of Ghana, and reforms introduced, including dispute resolution mechanisms; and

---

Box V.5. Measures for investment promotion

In 2006, UNCTAD and JBIC prepared the Blue Book on Best Practice in Investment Promotion and Facilitation for Ghana, which proposes 15 measures along with concrete action plans.

Measure 1.	Revise the Bilateral Investment Treaty Model to guide future negotiations and expand the double taxation treaty network.
Measure 2.	Improve the application of the new labour law.
Measure 3.	Develop a training programme to increase productivity among factory workers.
Measure 4.	Reform the duty drawback refund system and set deadlines and penalties in the administration of customs duty drawback.
Measure 5.	Attract investment into new power generation projects.
Measure 6.	Commercialize VoIP calling facilities.
Measure 7.	Develop a Land Bank Portal.
Measure 8.	Set up an online tax information service.
Measure 9.	Prepare a model stability agreement for mining.
Measure 10.	Develop a package of measures to facilitate investment in value-adding downstream processing of minerals.
Measure 11.	Enact the competition law.
Measure 12.	Establish a digital One-Stop Shop.
Measure 13.	Set up a promotion strategy in two key sectors and prepare and distribute investment promotion material.
Measure 14.	Design an investment promotion training programme for diplomats.
Measure 15.	Organise a matchmaking event with 10 large and medium size Asian TNC.

Source: UNCTAD and JBIC, 2006.

- Be encouraged to articulate their problems to the management of the GIPC, should they arise.

Ghana has rich potential, but lacks technical expertise and capital in many industries. While particular sectors may have some specific problems, they are generally not insurmountable. Asian consumer-goods firms may consider switching from exporting from Asia to establishing local production in Ghana and developing an African product, if not brand name.

Ghanaian institutions should become more proactive towards companies that run into difficulties. They should also improve communications with foreign companies after they have become established in Ghana. Failed projects mean more than a loss in investments and jobs – they send negative signals to other potential investors. Satisfied companies, on the other hand, increase their investments and are good advertisers of success.

Notes

1   Data on FDI are poor, but Ghanaian agencies are taking steps to improve their quality; for example, a survey of firms was undertaken at the end of 2000 to gather data on the size of investments by firms. Data on portfolio investment are also poor and inconsistent. For example, IMF data for Ghana record no portfolio investment.

2   Information from the Ghana Stock Exchange (www.gse.com.gh).

3   A list of companies to be wholly or partially divested may be found at: www.webstar.com.gh/dic/

4   Some of these privatizations have resulted in large increases in production; for example, the production of cocoa butter has tripled.

5   It is 94.5 per cent owned by Scancem International, which has head offices in Norway and is in turn owned by the German group Heidelberger Zement. The same group owns or has important shares in Cimbenin (Benin) (48.7 per cent), Ciments du Togo (Togo), Leocem (Sierra Leone) (50 per cent), Liberia Cement (Liberia) (63.7 per cent), Nova Cimangola (Angola) (24.5 per cent), Tanzania Portland Cement (Tanzania) (41 per cent) and Société Nigérienne de Cimenteries (Niger) (77 per cent).

6   It is 79 per cent owned by non-resident foreigners.

7   The Ghana Indian Association directory records the presence of about 1,000 Indian firms in Ghana.

8   Complete data on the foreign-owned share of Ashanti are not available. The major shareholders are the Government of Ghana and United Kingdom-based Lonrho (registered in South Africa). Depositary Nominee, Inc. (Global Depositary Receipts) has 40.74 per cent, Lonrho Plc (listed in London and Johannesburg, changed its name to Lonmin Plc in March 1999) has 31.89 per cent, and the Government of Ghana has 19.46 per cent.

9   In October 2004, Kaiser Aluminum & Chemical Corporation completed the sale of its interests in Valco to the Government of Ghana (*source*: Form 8-k for Kaiser Aluminum and Chemical Corp., at biz.yahoo.com/e/ 041104/ksacm8-k.html)".

10   Information on recent Chinese cooperation projects in Ghana is available from China's Ministry of Commerce and Ministry of Foreign Affairs; According to Ministry of Foreign Affairs, "China has helped Ghana build a number of complete projects such as the Ghana National Theatre, an agricultural cooperation project, a rice grinding mill, Afefi Irrigation Project and the grain depot, and the Ghana Vocational and Technical Training Centre. The two countries started cooperation in project contracting and labour services in 1983. By the end of 2000, Chinese companies in Ghana had signed over 200 contracts on project construction and labour services, the total value of which amounted to about $120 million. Chinese companies have successfully contracted and constructed the Bank of Ghana building, a woollen sweater mill, school hostel and water supply project, among others. At present there are more than 10 Chinese companies registered in Ghana such as the China State Construction and Engineering Corp., the China International Water and Electric Corp., the China Communications Construction Corp., the Guangzhou International Economic and Technical Cooperation Corp. and the Shaanxi Construction and Engineering Company" (*source*: http://www.fmprc.gov.cn/eng/4351.html).

11   A possible exception is the Labadi Beach Hotel. Many other large hotels have been financed by the Government or with foreign aid; the construction of Novotel, for example, was funded by French aid through the Agence Française de Développement (AFD - Caisse Centrale); the Dutch Golden Tulip Hotel was funded by the Libyan Arab Jamahiriya for the 1991 Non-Aligned Movement Conference. Both were built by Taysec.

12   Japanese activity in the Ghanaian economy is essentially limited to retailing Japanese products, such as Toyota vehicles, and construction and other projects arising from Japanese ODA. The GIPC attributes this to the distance of Japan from Ghana. This is unlikely to be the full explanation. The distance is certainly long – Tokyo is 8,500 miles from Accra – but investment has come to Ghana from other economies almost equally far: Hong Kong and Beijing are around 7,500 miles from Accra, Taipei and Seoul are 8,000 miles from Accra, and Canberra is 9,600 miles away.

13   There is no car assembly in Ghana either, but the market for new cars may be quite small. The United States Department of State (1999) noted that "used vehicles (5-10 years old) constitute about 70 per cent of vehicles imported into Ghana."

14   The monetary zone involves eight francophone countries in West Africa: Benin, Burkina Faso, Côte d'Ivoire, Guinea-Bissau, Mali, Niger, Senegal and Togo.

15   The Doha Development Round under the aegis of the WTO allows the EU to provide preferential tariff treatment for products originating in African, Caribbean and Pacific (ACP) States as required by the ACP-EC Partnership Agreement (the Cotonou Agreement). This Agreement replaced the Lomé Convention, which had provided the structure for trade and cooperation between the ACP and the Community since 1975. It entered into

force in 2000 and will last 20 years with revisions every five years.

16 For more information on AGOA and eligibility criteria for goods and countries, see the website: http//www.agoa.gov

17 AGOA extends duty-free access to a broader range of sub-Saharan African products, as well as duty- and quota-free access for apparel assembled (or cut and assembled) in Africa from the United States or African fabrics/yarns for up to 1.5 per cent of United States apparel imports in the first year, increasing gradually to 3.5 per cent. The main benefit to Ghana is quota-free access for apparel exports to the United States market without restrictions as to the origin of the yarns and fabrics. However, Ghana has to be certified annually on the basis of its economic and social policies in order to enjoy these preferences.

18 Canned tuna exporters are registered free zone companies, which exempts them from duties and VAT and should reduce import and export clearing times. This status is an additional incentive for investors.

19 At present, Nigeria imports a large quantity of salt. And other landlocked countries in the subregion would also constitute a ready market for salt from Ghana.

20 According to the United Nations Comtrade Database.

21 Ghana's educational reform focuses mainly on technical and vocational training, which is a good foundation for any investment in the areas of assembly and manufacturing of electronic and computer accessories. In addition, Ghana has a comparative advantage in terms of labour costs.

22 *Source*: Internet World Stats (http://www.internetworldstats.com).

23 Quote from the company's website (http://www.risingdata.com). Accessed in 2005.

24 See http://www.arch.columbia.edu/Studio/Spring2003/UP/Accra/PDF's%20to%20printer/12%20-%20transportation.pdf.

25 *Source*: Ghana Investment Promotion Centre (www.gipc.org.gh).

26 On the other hand, small firms in Ghana appear to be more productive.

27 This still makes Ghanaian labour cheaper per efficiency unit. However, wage/productivity ratios between Ghana and Mauritius vary with firm size in ways that may discriminate against Ghanaian exports in manufacturing.

28 Employees in these larger firms also have two years' more education on average. However, Teal (1999), using firm level data, finds no evidence that the average number of years of education of employees in a firm affects value added per employee.

29 As indicated by Vishnu Mohan, Managing Director of Standard Chartered, "Our strategy has been to associate ourselves with multinationals, large corporations and trade-related business." (http://specials.ft.com/ln/ftsurveys/country/sc9c62.htm).

30 According to a survey conducted in for the African Project Development Fund, established and managed by IFC and

cosponsored by the United Nations Development Programme (UNDP) and the African Development Bank.

31 In 1996 Ghana Telecoms (GT) was privatized (with a 30 per cent share bought by Telekom Malaysia), and a second operator, Westel, was granted a licence.

32 The bulk of Ghana's energy derives from hydroelectric power generation at the Akasombo dam.

33 For instance, the Volta River Authority is expanding or planning expansions of the power supply.

34 Established in 1998, the project's main ingredients include the development of three export processing zones by private operators with the Government providing off-site infrastructure; improving front-line public services related to trade and investment; and divestiture of ports and infrastructure to accommodate the growing traffic in goods and passengers. Ghana has other advantages over its subregional neighbours as a location for FDI: it is politically stable, and its labour costs are competitive – estimated to be 30 to 50 per cent lower than those of Côte d'Ivoire. It offers favourable fiscal incentives, reliable services such as electricity and water, lower transaction costs and generally pleasant conditions to live and work. Not surprisingly, Ghana's exports to the subregion have been growing faster than the regional average, and this is expected to further increase as the subregion becomes increasingly integrated.

35 *Source*: EIU, *Ghana Country Report* (various editions).

36 In March 2000, Ghana concluded an open skies agreement with the United States, which greatly reduces regulations on air services to and from the United States.

37 Although Ghana inherited an excellent road network at independence in 1957, by the 1970s most of the 9,000-mile road network had deteriorated (see e.g. Mwale, 1997).

38 The GFZB is described at http://www.ghanaclassifieds.com/gfzb/ as an integrated programme to promote processing and manufacturing of goods through the establishment of export processing zones and encourage the development of commercial and service activities at seaport and airport areas. In essence, the whole of Ghana is accessible to potential investors, who have the opportunity to use the free zones as focal points to produce goods and services for foreign markets. Completely private-sector-driven, the Government's role in the programme is limited to facilitate, regulate and monitor activities of zone developers/operators and enterprises.

39 If paid-up capital is between $100,000 and $500,000, or its equivalent in cedis, the quota is for two persons; if more than $500,000, the quota is for four persons.

40 According to "Ghana: 2004 Investment Climate Statement" (http://accra.usembassy.gov/wwwhecons.html).

41 See website http://www.ghanaweb.com (*Business News*, 1 August 2002).

42 See http://www.gipc.org.gh/IPA_Information.asp?hdnGroupID=8&hdnLevelID=6.

CHAPTER VI

MADAGASCAR

Subregion	East Africa
Area ('000 km2)	581.5
Population (millions)	18.6
Currency	Madagascar ariary (MGA)[a]
Exchange rate (MGA per dollar), 2005 average	2 003
GDP in current prices (millions of dollars), 2005	4 713
GDP per capita (dollars), 2005	253
Exports of goods and services (millions of dollars), 2004	1 326
Imports of goods and services (millions of dollars), 2004	2 107
Official development assistance (millions of dollars), 2004	1 236
FDI inflows (millions of dollars per annum) (average for 2000-2005)	63
FDI inward stock (millions of dollars), 2005	651
FDI inward stock per capita (dollars), 2005	35

[a] The Madagascar ariary (MGA) replaced the previous currency, the Malagasy franc (MGF), on January 2005. One Malagasy franc was valued at 0.2 ariaries. This chapter uses MGF, without converting it into MGA.

INTRODUCTION

Madagascar, one of the world's largest island countries, is also one of the poorest countries and is categorized as a least developed country (LDC), with a per capita income of about $250 per annum in 2005. Madagascar's socialist experiment and its aftermath from the mid-1970s to the early 1990s transformed a relatively buoyant and developing economy into a stagnant one. Average GDP growth for the 1980s was less than 1 per cent, and FDI came to a standstill (figure VI.1). With economic liberalization gaining pace after the mid-1990s, the economy has grown, except for the political crisis year of 2002, recording an average GDP growth rate of about 3 per cent during 1996 and 2005. Privatization, liberalization and FDI in special export processing zones (EPZs) around the

capital, Antananarivo, were at the core of the turnaround. Export earnings have doubled since 1996, spurred by the expansion of EPZ exports and high international vanilla prices. FDI inflows surged in 1999 and continued to rise in 2000 and 2001 before a sharp decline in 2002 due to the political crisis (figure VI.1). As investors regained confidence, FDI rebounded in 2003, reaching $96 million, higher than the record level of 2001, but it declined again in 2004-2005, and prospects for increased FDI are mixed.

This chapter is intended to shed light on available and growing opportunities for FDI in Madagascar, including that from Asia, and to evaluate the economy critically with a view to

Figure VI.1. FDI inflows to Madagascar, 1970-2005
(Millions of dollars)

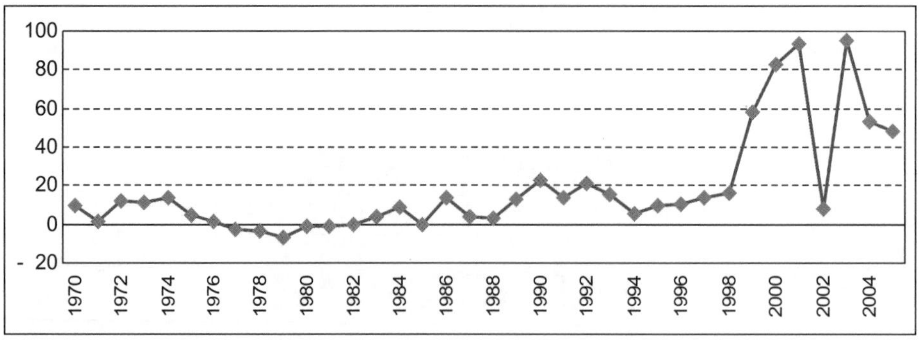

Source: UNCTAD, FDI/TNC database (www.unctad.org/fdistatistics).

considering how these opportunities might be sustained and exploited by Asian FDI. The chapter is organized as follows: following an examination of recent trends in FDI inflows, new opportunities and incentives for investment are considered, and constraints to exploiting these opportunities are discussed. Finally, policies and measures for realizing Madagascar's investment potential are proposed.

A. FDI INFLOWS TO MADAGASCAR

A number of attractive conditions exist for those interested in investing in Madagascar. Among them are relatively low labour costs and a large, trainable workforce; an international language (French) spoken by a significant proportion of the population; insignificant time differences with Europe; a one-stop shop (*guichet unique*) for new project proposals; and a recently liberalized trade regime. Since October 2000, the country has been a member of the Common Market for Eastern and Southern Africa (COMESA). More recently, it has become a main destination for FDI among the Indian Ocean destinations, particularly due to relatively low labour costs, fishing and mining opportunities, and the existence of EPZs that produce textiles and garments for the United States and European markets. Historically, most FDI to Madagascar has originated in France, now its largest trading partner, but other countries such as Japan have also had investments in the country for over 40 years.

FDI inflows to Madagascar increased substantially from 1999 to 2001, and after a steep decline in 2002, picked up again in 2003 (figure VI.1). The two largest sources of FDI are France and Mauritius, which together account for 70 per cent of the total inward FDI stock (table VI.1). Hong Kong (China) is the third largest source, accounting for 9 per cent of inward FDI stock,

Table VI.1. Sources of FDI to Madagascar, 2004
(Millions of dollars)

Region/economy	FDI inflows	FDI inward stock
Developed countries	24.0	117.8
Europe	23.8	111.6
European Union	23.8	103.3
Belgium / Luxembourg	0.4	13.3
Denmark	0.3	0.4
France	23.0	89.1
Netherlands	-	0.5
Other developed Europe	-	8.2
Switzerland	-	8.2
North America	0.2	6.2
Canada	-	5.2
United States	0.2	1.0
Developing economies	28.4	68.2
Africa	6.4	44.6
Mauritius	5.5	42.5
Reunion	0.7	1.9
South Africa	0.2	0.2
Latin America and the Caribbean	5.7	5.7
Bermuda	5.7	5.7
Asia	16.3	17.9
South, East and South-East Asia	16.3	17.9
China	0.4	0.6
Hong Kong, China	15.8	16.4
Sri Lanka	-	0.9
Unspecified	0.4	2.0
Total world	52.8	188.0

Source: UNCTAD, based on Banque Centrale de Madagascar 2005 and UNCTAD's FDI/TNC database (www.unctad.org/fdistatistics).

followed by Belgium/Luxembourg (7 per cent), Switzerland (4 per cent), Bermuda (3 per cent) and Canada (3 per cent). Among Asian countries, other than China, Sri Lanka also has some investments in Madagascar. Table VI.2 shows the sectoral breakdown of FDI: four fifths of the country's inward stock is in services, mainly construction, transport, storage and communications, and trade.

Table VI.2. Sectoral breakdown of inward FDI stock in Madagascar, 2004
(Millions of dollars)

Sector/industry	2004
Primary	17.2
Agriculture, hunting, forestry and fisheries	5.1
Forestry and fisheries	5.1
Fisheries, operation of fish hatcheries and fish farms	5.1
Mining, quarrying and petroleum	12.1
Secondary	18.0
Tertiary	149.2
Electricity, gas and water	7.9
Construction	45.8
Trade	30.8
Hotels and restaurants	0.1
Transport, storage and communications	37.1
Finance	16.8
Business activities	10.7
Unspecified	3.5
Total	188.0

Source: UNCTAD, based on Banque Centrale de Madagascar 2005 and UNCTAD's FDI/TNC database (www.unctad.org/fdistatistics).

As part of the Government's export promotion strategy in the early 1990s, EPZs were established to attract FDI inflows. This has contributed to the expansion of manufacturing activities and job creation in Madagascar. Table VI.3 indicates the main activities of manufacturing firms in the EPZs. The total number of employees reached 110,000 in 2001, but fell sharply to 67,200 in 2002 due to the crisis. Since then, industrial activities in the EPZs have been recovering steadily, the main focus of activities being in textiles and clothing. By the end of 2004, the EPZs employed 91,540 workers in that industry out of a total of 115,000 EPZ employees (IMF, 2005b).

The EPZs have attracted an increasing and significant proportion of FDI inflows.

Between 1990 and 2001, 42.5 per cent of FDI in the zones was in textiles, 7.8 per cent in agro-food processing, and 3 per cent in wood processing (table VI.4). In recent years, foreign investors have also been showing an increasing interest in the natural resources sector. In 2005, for instance, Rio Tinto Group (United Kingdom) announced its board approval to invest $775 million in a mineral mining project (titanium dioxide) in Madagascar. Other important mining projects in recent years include, for instance, Vanco Energy Company (United States)[1] and Pan African Mining Corp. (Canada).[2]

As of 2004, 289 foreign affiliates were operating in Madagascar, accounting for total sales of 6,569 billion Malagasy francs (MGF) ($703 million), MGF 1,379 billion ($148 million) in value added and 51,717 employees (Institut National de la Statistique, 2005). Joint venture is a common mode of greenfield investment. Malagasy partners are typically required to tackle the burdensome bureaucratic process and to acquire ownership of land, which, though legally sanctioned, is extremely difficult for foreigners to obtain. Among many recent joint ventures is one between the Malagasy firm Coroi and the French group Biolandes. With an investment of $9.4 million, this partnership intends to produce scented plants and essential oils in the Diego-Suares region. Another recently established joint venture is between the Malagasy Government and the German engineering and textile group Seditex.

Cross-border M&As are also an important mode of foreign entry. Several deals have been recorded since the mid-1990s (table IV.5). For instance, American Benefits (United States) merged with Stones & Wood Corp. SARL in a $4 million

Table VI.3. Enterprises operating in EPZs in Madagascar, 1999-2004

Item	1999	2000	2001	2002	2003	2004
Number of manufacturing enterprises operating in EPZs	267	283	307	355	377	419
Textiles and hides	135	149	164	183	204	231
Wood processing	22	22	22	25	25	25
Food, beverages and tobacco	31	32	33	34	39	41
Other (mainly jewelry and handicrafts)	79	80	88	113	109	122
Total number of employees	64 100	81 000	110 000	67 200	85 000	115 000
(Per cent of total manufacturing sector)	25.8	27.5	29.5	..	..	..
Wages paid (billions of ariary)	202.0	237.0	332.0	83.6	223.1	353.0
Value added (billions of ariary)	328.0	360.0	447.0	170.0	339.0	482.7
Exports (billions of ariary)	1 157.0	1 236.0	1 368.0	658.1	1 167.1	1 791.9
Imports (billions of ariary)	512.0	599.0	735.0	722.0	1 402.9	2 632.4

Source: IMF, 2005b.

Table VI.4. Economic activities of enterprises in Madagascar's EPZs, 1999–2001

Industry	EPZ charters granted			Cumulative EPZ charters granted			Total commitments, 1990-2001[a]	
							Employment (Number of employees)	Investment (Billions of Malagasy francs)
	1999	2000	2001	1999	2000	2001		
Agro-food processing	-	1	1	31	32	33	3 106	113.6
Textiles	5	14	15	129	143	158	68 649	615.7
Hides and skins	1	-	-	6	6	6	761	12.1
Wood processing	1	-	-	22	22	22	1 589	43.0
Data processing	2	-	-	28	28	28	2 213	20.9
Chemicals	1	-	2	9	9	11	673	31.4
Electrical and mechanical	-	-	-	4	4	4	129	5.0
Mineral processing	1	-	-	6	6	6	424	32.5
Handicrafts	1	-	1	16	16	17	2 960	13.7
Jewelry	1	-	-	12	12	12	519	11.8
Enterprises promoting EPZs	1	-	3	3	3	6	142	28.0
Enterprises managing EPZs	-	1	-	1	2	2	106	520.3
Total	12	16	22	267	283	305	81 271	1 448.0

Source: IMF, 2005b.

[a] Cumulative totals of investment and employment commitments indicated in proposals and business plans of EPZ charter applications.

deal in 1999. The same United States company also acquired Saowani Development SARL a year before.

Asian investment in Madagascar is small, originating mainly from Hong Kong (China), that, at $16.4 million, accounts for 90 per cent of the estimated FDI stock held by Asian firms in the country (table VI.1). These firms are mainly operating in the EPZs. Most recent investments from Asian economies are in textile manufacturing and international trade. Thailand and Indonesia are among the countries that have become interested in the recent discovery of important sapphire deposits in the north and south of the country (United States, Department of State, 2000). A Malaysian firm is among the four mobile telephone service providers with unrestricted access to the international network authorized to operate in Madagascar.

Table VI.5. Cross-border M&As in Madagascar, 1996-2005

Year	Acquired company	Industry of the acquired company	Acquiring company	Home country	Value ($ million)	Shares acquired (per cent)
1996	Cia Agricole et Industrielle[a]	Life insurance	Investor Group	Brunei Darussalam	58.4	100.0
1997	Loteri Nationale De Madagascar	Amusement and recreation svcs	Magnum(Dunlop Estates)	Malaysia	0.1	23.5
1998	Saowani Development SARL	Miscellaneous nonmetallic minerals, except fuels	American Benefits	United States	..	90.0
1999	Stones & Wood Corp SARL	Miscellaneous nonmetallic minerals, except fuels	American Benefits	United States	4.0	100.0
2001	JBA Production SA	Women's, misses', & children's underwear,nightwear	Tefron Ltd	Israel	..	50.0
2003	North Fork 17 Mining Project[b]	Miscellaneous nonmetallic minerals, except fuels	Platinum Works Inc.	United States	5.0	100.0
2004	Societe Siranna SARL	Miscellaneous nonmetallic minerals, except fuels	Savoy Capital Investments Inc	United States	..	97.0
2005	Ambatovy Nickel Project[c]	Ferroalloy ores, except vanadium	Dynatec Corp	Canada	15.9	47.0
2005	Ambatovy Nickel Project[c]	Ferroalloy ores, except vanadium	Impala Platinum Holdings Ltd	South Africa	..	50.0

Source: UNCTAD, cross-border M&A database.

[a] The ultimate acquired company, AXA-UAP, is based in France.
[b] The ultimate acquired company, International Mining Co. of America, is based in the United States.
[c] The ultimate acquired company, Dynatec Corp., is based in Canada.

B.   NEW INVESTMENT OPPORTUNITIES

Most industries in Madagascar are open to 100 per cent foreign ownership. Apart from FDI in the traditional industries of the EPZs and ongoing privatization, there is increasing potential for FDI in Madagascar's agro-industries (e.g. aquaculture, cotton, sugar, coffee etc.), natural resources (bauxite, gold, titanium and petroleum exploration), infrastructure (railways, telecommunication, air traffic) and tourism. Since the mid-1980s, the production of beverages and tobacco, wood products, textiles and clothing, energy and construction materials in Madagascar increased significantly. In recent years, there has also been a notable growth of production in industries such as mineral products, paper, petroleum products, housing amenities and energy (table VI.6), which may suggest investment opportunities for both domestic and foreign firms in these sectors as well.

Table VI.6. Index of industrial production by industry in Madagascar (excluding the EPZs), 2001-2004 (2000 = 100)

Sector	2001	2003	2004
Agro-industry and food industries	87.9	106.3	108.8
Consumer goods	80.4	96.4	100.3
Clothing and leather goods	72.8	93.9	89.8
Paper	97.6	113.8	119.9
Pharmaceuticals	73.0	84.7	98.0
Housing amenities	91.9	98.6	109.5
Equipment goods	83.3	95.6	98.4
Ships	86.9	98.3	101.5
Electrical appliances	72.8	87.8	89.4
Intermediary goods	74.1	94.0	98.1
Mineral products	80.9	112.3	123.1
Textile products	57.2	75.4	73.8
Wood and paper products	78.1	87.1	87.7
Chemicals and rubber products	94.9	101.9	100.1
Metallurgical products	61.7	73.0	77.7
Energy	69.1	107.0	109.2
Petroleum products	52.6	110.8	116.2
Water, gas and electricity	81.4	104.2	104.1

Source: IMF, 2005b.

1. Agriculture and food processing

Agriculture still accounts for about two thirds of Madagascar's economy and employs more than four fifths of Madagascar's economically active population. The main agricultural products are rice and cassava (for domestic consumption), coffee, cloves and vanilla (for export), sugar cane, groundnuts and cotton (industrial products) (IMF, 2005b). Especially, Coffee production, and cotton and sugar grown on large State-owned farms offer particularly interesting investment opportunities. The State-owned cotton company Hasnya is up for privatization and an upgrade of its production could make it more important as a supplier to the garment and textiles industries in the EPZs. The State-owned sugar company Sirama is for the time being managed by a private company.

2. Textiles

While the major export market remains the EU, firms in the EPZs have profited from the favourable impact of the United States' African Growth and Opportunity Act (AGOA). The AGOA has encouraged some American brands to place orders in Madagascar to benefit from this trade arrangement. Textile exports to the United States doubled in 2001, and have risen steadily since 2003 (IMF, 2005a). Madagascar has become eligible for benefits that could further increase exports to the EU under the Everything But Arms initiative, adopted by the European Commission in February 2001. This initiative grants duty-free access to imports of all products from LDCs without any quantitative restrictions, except for arms and munitions. Only imports of fresh bananas, rice and sugar have not been fully liberalized immediately.[3]

3. Mining

A new mining law aimed at reducing government involvement and promoting foreign investment was approved in 1999. Among the mining products under consideration are chromite, cobalt, emeralds, gold, graphite, ilmenite, nickel, and sapphires, and titanium ore. Recent production and export trends in major minerals are presented in table VI.7. Some mining investment depends on improved infrastructure, especially in the north of the country. To that effect it is promising that Madarail, a joint venture led by the South African Comzar Group, won a licence to operate Madagascar's northern railway system.

4. Tourism

The country's extraordinary biodiversity, including its lemurs, is the major tourist attraction in Madagascar, besides its beaches. The number of tourists, as well as hotel capacity, has increased steadily (table VI.8). Roughly 70 per cent of all

Table VI.7. Madagascar: production and export of major minerals, 1999-2003

Minerals	1999	2000	2001	2002	2003
Production (thousands of tons)					
Chromite	0.1	131.3	60.9	10.7	..
Graphite	16.1	40.3	12.6	7.5	..
Exports (thousands of tons)					
Chromite	81.5	70.0	50.5	66.1	68.2
Graphite	14.1	16.8	11.4	9.0	8.2
Export value (millions of SDRs)					
Chromite	3.2	4.2	1.8	2.3	3.4
Graphite	4.3	5.2	3.7	3.1	3.7
Unit value (SDRs per ton)					
Chromite	39.8	59.8	35.2	34.2	50.2
Graphite	305.3	311.1	329.4	338.7	452.8

Source: IMF, 2005b.
Note: SDRs - special drawing rights.

tourists (some 230,000 in 2004) come for ecotourism, which is service intensive. While most of the tourists arrive from France (50 per cent), an increasing number come from other countries of the European Union and from South Africa.

Significant growth in this sector can be attributed to government efforts to boost tourism and to reduce transportation costs. In 1991, a national tourism development committee and a tourism agency were established, and legislation to reform the industry was promulgated in 1995 and 1996. In 1997, it became possible to obtain tourist visas upon arrival, rather than only in advance. Extraordinarily high hotel room rates for foreigners were reduced, and measures to improve tourism support services, including infrastructure and staff training, were undertaken (EIU, 2000a). In addition, internal and regional airline routes were opened to competition in 1994, and four additional carriers began operating in Madagascar: Air Austral (from Réunion), Air Mauritius (Mauritius), Interair (South Africa) and Corsair (France).

5. Oil and gas

Liberalization of rules governing the oil and gas industry began with legislation in 1996, but it was not until June 2000 that the State-owned oil distributing company was privatized. Opportunities exist for investment in the entire range of activities in this sector, from exploration to distribution. Licensing agreements for blocks off the coast of Madagascar were signed with two North American firms in 1997 and with two more United States companies in 1999. Among them, Vanco Energy Company (the United States) signed a production-sharing contract with OMNIS, Madagascar's State-owned oil company in 2001. During 2003, Vanco and OMNIS jointly surveyed the coastal outcrop belt, and the expectation for good reservoirs led ExxonMobil and Norsk Hydro to join Vanco in the ongoing Majunga Basin exploration project in 2004.

Table VI.8. Madagascar's tourism industry, selected indicators, 1999-2004[a]

Indicator	1999	2000	2001	2002	2003	2004[a]
Number of tourists						
(thousands)	138.3	160.1	170.2	61.7	139.2	228.8
Annual growth (per cent)	14.1	15.8	6.3	- 63.8	125.8	64.3
Hotel capacity						
(number of rooms, thousands)	7.2	7.8	8.4	8.8	9.3	10.2
Number of tourist nights						
(thousands)	2 627	3 041	3 234	493	1 949	4 347
Annual growth (per cent)	14.1	15.8	6.3	- 84.7	295.1	123.0
Average length of stay (days)	20.0	20.0	20.0	9.0	15.0	20.0
Foreign exchange receipts						
(millions of SDRs)	72.9	91.9	90.2	27.8	54.0	104.3
Annual growth (per cent)	11.3	26.1	- 1.8	- 69.2	94.2	93.1

Source: IMF, 2005b.
[a]   Preliminary.

C. THE INVESTMENT REGIME

Under the socialist policies that were implemented in Madagascar from 1975 to the mid-1980s, FDI was officially discouraged and a number of large foreign firms were nationalized. It was only after 1995, when policies conducive to FDI, including a new investment code were

adopted, that FDI began to return to Madagascar. The features of the more open trade regime that have been cited as most attractive by investors are: insignificant non-tariff barriers, removal of most, though not all, import licences and the elimination of export controls (EIU, 2000a).

The following important reforms to attract foreign investors were undertaken in 1998-1999 (United States, Department of State, 2000): long-term leasing of land; relaxation of visas for foreign investors and tourists; abolition of prior approval for equity-capital contributions by foreign investors (above a threshold of 20 per cent of a company's authorized capital); simplification of procedures for registering corporations; adoption of a legal and institutional framework to mitigate anti-competitive practices (approval pending); signing of agreements eliminating double taxation with countries that are potential sources of private capital; adoption of modern arbitration legislation; and establishment of a new office within the Ministry of Industry to promote local and foreign investment.

EPZs have been critical for attracting investment and the Malagasy Government offers several incentives to firms located in these zones. Legislation governing the activities of EPZ operators, the Industrial Free Zone Regime Act, was passed in 1991. The fiscal, financial, employment and legal incentives, which constitute the bulk of incentives for EPZ firms, are briefly reviewed here.

The fiscal incentives offered by the Malagasy Government are fairly standard and favour manufacturing. Depending on the nature of a firm's activity, firms are totally exempt from corporate and other taxes for at least two years and up to 15 years in the EPZs. After the exemption period, up to 75 per cent of the firm's tax liabilities may be reduced according to the magnitude of its investment. In general, imported inputs and exports are not subject to tariffs. A tax rate of 10 per cent is immediately applicable to dividends, as is a payroll tax up to a maximum rate of 35 per cent.

Service companies, that are often important suppliers to manufacturing companies (e.g. telecommunications, data processing, software development), receive unfavourable tax treatment relative to other activities, like manufacturing. Yet there is substantial and growing empirical evidence to suggest that the most successfully integrated firms in international supply chains rely significantly on information and communication technology (ICT) services for contact with buyers and suppliers abroad. However, it is not clear which firms are exporting firms. Typically, tax authorities, concerned about distortions that might arise from the leakage of products earmarked for export into the domestic economy, define the proportion of output that must be exported by these firms in order to be considered for EPZ tax relief. Also, there appears to be no comparable treatment for firms that supply to exporting firms. Besides discriminating against domestic firms, there is often an opportunity missed in terms of introducing international competition to domestic firms, which could help raise standards. In a number of successful EPZs in other countries, domestic firms that supply exporting firms are treated as exporters so that these domestic suppliers are entitled to be treated in the same way as foreign suppliers.

While there is convertibility of the Malagasy franc (now the Madagascar ariary) for current-account purposes, financial restrictions still exist. All capital movements are subject to prior government approval. Residents and non-residents may open foreign exchange accounts but are subject to a number of restrictions.

Labour laws applicable to firms in the free zones are relatively liberal. Firms are allowed to employ foreign labour, although they are constrained by Malagasy social legislation that governs leave, vacation, employee compensation, and employer and employee contributions to social security and health insurance. Work permits and residence visas are to be delivered within 15 days of an employee's submission of applications to the Ministries of Labour and Internal Affairs respectively. However, there are restrictions on repatriation of foreigners' earnings.

Land leases in the free zones are granted for 20 to 50 years, but, in practice, foreign firms face restrictions on land ownership. The Malagasy authorities have recently attempted to address this constraint by lengthening lease periods, but it is unclear whether this action has had any effect. Arbitration proceedings are well specified and governed by three sets of regulations or agreements: i) Title IV of the Free Zone Law; ii) the Dispute Settlement Convention introduced by the World Bank and agreed by its members; and iii) supplementary regulations approved by the International Centre for the Settlement of Investment Disputes (ICSID).[4]

D.   INVESTMENT CONSTRAINTS

The investment climate in Madagascar, whether for local, Asian or other foreign investors, is mixed. There are both significant opportunities and obstacles to investment and international trade. On the one hand, various positive factors exist to attract FDI, including low labour costs, rich natural resources, the EPZ regime, a commercial dispute resolution mechanism, and a new business-minded government. On the other hand, the Malagasy potential to absorb and maximize FDI inflows is constrained by government policies and practices, lack of financing, poor infrastructure, low skills of the labour force and weak institutions.

The country is ranked 21st among the 25 African countries listed in the Growth Competitiveness Index compiled by the World Economic Forum (table IV.9). Although the country is considered "mostly free" according to the *2005 Index of Economic Freedom* of the Heritage Foundation, based on a number of indicators, significant barriers to FDI still exist (table IV.10).

According to a survey by the World Economic Forum, the most problematic factors for doing business in Madagascar are access to financing, inadequate supply of infrastructure, corruption and an inefficient government bureaucracy (figure VI.2). The Government needs to address these problems in order to spur investment and, therefore, economic development in Madagascar. Specific factors constraining investment are discussed below.

1. Finance

Access to financing is considered the most problematic factor for doing business in Madagascar. There are seven commercial banks, mostly owned by foreign investors from France and Mauritius. Although the country ranks high in the "soundness of banks" in Africa (table VI.9), given the difficult access to loans and large gaps between deposit and lending rates, this sector is still underdeveloped and offers limited long-term investment financing. This may deter the willingness to invest by both domestic and foreign enterprises.

Madagascar ranks the second lowest in terms of "ease of access to loans" in Africa, (table VI.9). Malagasy entrepreneurs have little confidence in the banking system's ability and willingness to fund private industry. Instead, personal relations are extremely important in determining the outcome of loan applications. However, progress has been made in the banking sector, particularly with respect to privatization.

2. Infrastructure

The overall quality of infrastructure in Madagascar is among the lowest in Africa (table VI.11). Transport services and infrastructure suffer from lack of investment and maintenance. Paved roads, railways and telephony are less developed compared with most other African countries.

Figure VI.2. Most problematic factors for doing business in Madagascar

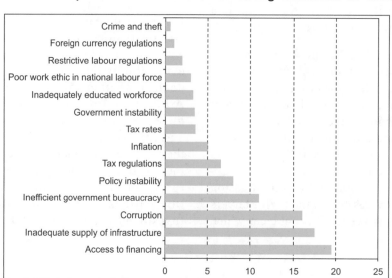

Source: World Economic Forum, Executive Option Survey 2003.

Table VI.9. National competitiveness balance sheet of Madagascar, 2004

Notable competitive advantages	Rank[a]	Notable competitive disadvantages	Rank[a]
Macroeconomic environment		**Macroeconomic environment**	
Recession expectations	7	National savings rate, 2002	22
Inflation, 2002	9	Access to credit	21
		Real exchange rate, 2002	23
		Interest rate spread, 2002	20
		Diversion of public funds	18
		Government surplus/deficit, 2002	16
		Public trust of politicians	20
		Extent of distortive government subsidies	15
Technology		**Technology**	
Utility patents, 2002	8	Telephone lines, 2002	23
Firm-level technology absorption	8	Internet access in schools	21
		Cellular telephones, 2002	20
		Laws relating to ICT	21
		Personal computers, 2002	20
		Tertiary enrolment	17
		Internet hosts, 2002	17
		Company spending on research and development	17
		University/industry research collaboration	18
		Technological sophistication	15
		Quality of competition in the ISP sector	15
		Prevalence of foreign technology licensing	22
		FDI and technology transfer	21
Other indicators		**Other indicators**	
Soundness of banks	5	Ease of access to loans	24
Private-sector employment of women	5	Railroad infrastructure development	25
Availability of scientists and engineers	8	Overall infrastructure quality	22
		Postal efficiency	21
		Nature of competitive advantage	20
		Quality of electricity supply	19
		Air transport infrastructure quality	21
		Informal sector	22
		Port infrastructure quality	18
		Telephone infrastructure quality	16
		Quality of public schools	21
		Extent of staff training	20
		Reliability of police services	20
		Reliance on professional management	18
		Government effectiveness in reducing poverty	16

Source: World Economic Forum, 2004a.

[a]   Rank out of 25 African countries.

Telephone and Internet users are few, even by African standards. In 2004, main telephone lines, mobile telephone subscribers and Internet users per 1,000 inhabitants were merely 3.4 (2003), 18.4 and 5.0 respectively. The State-owned telephone company Telecom Malagasy (Telma), privatized in 2000, was bought by Distacom (Hong Kong, China) in 2003.

3. Public institutions

Both the *Africa Competitiveness Report* and the *Index of Economic Freedom*, as well as other country assessment reviews such as the World Bank's Doing Business ranking,[6] suggest a picture of poorly performing institutions. Madagascar ranks among the highest in Africa in terms of government intervention (table VI.11). Despite relatively low levels of inflation and government expenditure, the Malagasy Government's deficit was the 16th largest among 25 African countries (table IV.9). Government regulations are both unclear and imprecise compared to other African countries. Malagasy entrepreneurs claim that government officials are not sufficiently helpful with industry-wide problems, and that obtaining licences and permits entails irregular payments being made (World Economic Forum, 2004a).

Table VI.10. Economic freedom indicators of Madagascar,[a] 2005

Criterion	Score	Explanation
Trade policy	2	Low level of protectionism: average tariff rate was 2.9 per cent in 2001, down from 5.3 per cent in 1995
Fiscal burden of government	3.3	Moderate income tax rates, high corporate tax rates and moderate decrease of government expenditure
Government intervention	1.5	Low level
Monetary policy	2	Low level of inflation
Capital flows and foreign investment	3	Moderate barriers
Banking and finance	3	Moderate level of restrictions
Wages and prices	2	Low level of intervention; price controls abolished on virtually all products
Property rights	3	Moderate level of protection
Regulation	3	Moderate level; lack of transparency and red tape persists
Informal market	4	High level of activity
Average score	2.68	Rank: 44 globally; Category: "Mostly Free"

Source: Heritage Foundation, 2005.

[a]   Scores for each indicator on a scale of 1 (most free/least restrictive) to 5 (least free/most restrictive). Previous scores: 1995: 3.74; 1996: 3.55; 1997: 3.44; 1998: 3.51; 1999: 3.45; 2000: 3.39; 2001:3.29; 2002: 3.29; 2003: 2.85; 2004: 3.14.

Irregular payments in tax collection, public utilities and exports and imports are high, and a significant proportion of the economy remains under State ownership and control. According to the World Bank (2006), the Government consumed 8.2 per cent of GDP in 2002.

In terms of the treatment accorded to foreign investors, the United States State Department (2004) reports that foreign investors have to deal with a thicket of bureaucratic obstacles as they seek the necessary permits and approvals; the process for establishing a new company is time consuming and requires considerable manoeuvring; investors in Madagascar face a legal environment in which contract enforcement is inadequate, and the security of private property is not well protected.

4. Human resources

According to the *Africa Competitiveness Report* (World Economic Forum, 2004a), Madagascar ranks high in terms of university education and the availability of scientists and engineers. A low level of intervention in labour markets is consistent with the findings of the *Index of Economic Freedom*. While labour is cheap and abundant and could help attract FDI, there are limits to the usefulness of such labour in terms of its ability to meet the needs and expectations of firms operating there.

Table VI.11. Indicators of the quality of infrastructure in Madagascar, 2004

Item	Rank out of 25 African countries	Rank out of 102 countries[a]
Overall infrastructure quality	22	96
Railroad infrastructure development	25	96
Postal efficiency	21	93
Quality of electricity supply	19	93
Air transport infrastructure quality	21	92
Port infrastructure quality	18	90
Telephone infrastructure quality	16	89

Source: World Economic Forum, 2004a.
[a]   According to World Economic Forum, 2004b.

E. MEASURES NEEDED TO ATTRACT FDI

While Madagascar's potential to attract FDI is high, conditions in the country need to be improved: poor infrastructure, weak institutions and a slow-moving bureaucracy are among the challenges to be addressed. Nonetheless, the Government, the donor community and the private sector have undertaken many initiatives since the late 1990s. The following are recommendations for their consideration in their efforts to promote additional FDI to Madagascar. At the present stage, efforts should be made to attract FDI in general; specific measures targeting Asian investors would be premature.

1. Greater openness

Since Madagascar's own market size is relatively small, it could attract market-seeking FDI by promoting itself as a gateway to larger export markets particularly to the United States and European markets (through their respective market). Madagascar has participated in the AGOA initiative, which promotes exports to the United States. Continued efforts to implement international agreements to increase international trade – such as through the Indian Ocean Commission (IOC), COMESA, SADC and AGOA – should be encouraged. The private sector in Madagascar is flexible and dynamic, and will likely respond to enhanced incentives to engage in international trade. Under AGOA, Malagasy firms could expand exports of apparel to the United States from $46 million (1999) before AGOA implementation to $178 million (2001) after implementation, reaching now over $300 million (2004).

2. Improved fiscal and regulatory arrangements

Madagascar's fiscal position is among the worst in sub-Saharan Africa and is mainly attributable to poor revenue collection and pervasive tax evasion. While the ratio of tax receipts to GDP increased from 8 per cent in the mid-1990s to an average of 11 per cent during 1999-2004, it still lagged behind the rest of sub-Saharan Africa. This performance was attributable to the continuing lack of well-organized customs services at secondary ports, as well as some exceptional exemptions granted in the run-up to the December 2001 presidential elections (IMF, 2003).

To reduce the government deficit, it is recommended that recent progress in collection be supplemented by more vigorous efforts on the part of the newly created Large Enterprise Tax Office and by broadening the VAT base. The donor community might offer technical assistance in this area, such as providing training and logistical support to the tax authorities. The private sector could open a dialogue with the Government concerning both the composition of government expenditure (e.g. raising the proportion of GDP spent on basic and university education) and the tax code, with a view to encouraging compliance.

Other government-related problems stem from the regulatory environment and bureaucratic red tape. Regulations are unclear, numerous and not properly enforced. This is probably what led firms responding to the survey on Madagascar by the World Economic Forum to report experiencing the longest delays for permits and the greatest need for irregular payments for permits and protection in Africa, as mentioned earlier (World Economic Forum, 2004a).

In 1999, the Government of Madagascar set up the Investment Promotion Space as a unit within the Ministry of Industry to aid foreign investors with administrative requirements, information and work permit procedures. In addition to offering technical and logistical assistance, donors might also consider supporting incentives to attract private-sector operators in enhancing the performance of these offices, and providing incentives to the employees of these agencies to mitigate these constraints.

3. Improved access to finance

The banking sector is still being developed in Madagascar, and firms are not yet confident of banks' ability to provide them with adequate financing. Domestic savings and investment rates are low, even by African standards. Raising domestic savings and using them in the most productive way should be a government priority. Efforts should also be made to encourage more investment in the financial sector through privatization or other means. One such privatization has been the creation of the Bank of Africa (BOA)/ Madagascar; the BOA network has experience in creating viable operations in low-income areas. The Bank's standing is strengthened by the involvement of French and Dutch private sector lending agencies, along with the IFC. Some 35 per cent of the shares are allocated to Malagasy private investors and the Government of Madagascar has 15 per cent of shares. Such donor and private sector initiatives can help develop the banking sector and assist entrepreneurs and investors to exploit existing or future opportunities presented by the Malagasy economy.

4. Infrastructure development

Firms often cite infrastructure as one of the principal factors determining where they invest in emerging markets. Government spending should be redirected to improve the number and quality of paved roads. Air transportation within Madagascar and with the rest of the world should be enhanced through better services, lower costs, and more routes for passengers and cargo. In mid-2002, the authorities decided to place Air Madagascar under a management contract with an internationally recognized foreign firm in order to improve its efficiency and pave the way for future privatization (IMF, 2003). At present, the private sector can do little, except inform and advise the Government and donors concerning infrastructure, since its involvement is constrained by the underdeveloped credit market and limited access to long-term finance. The World Bank has offered guarantees to encourage airport privatization, but more can be done through the IFC to support private participation in infrastructure development.

While steps have recently been taken to increase telephone coverage through the satellite, DOM SAT 2, and an increase in the number of mobile-phone operators to four, the ICT infrastructure in Madagascar is still poor. The privatization of Telma, increasing its customer base and lowering the cost of telephone use, is expected to improve the telecommunications infrastructure. The multi-million-dollar Telecommunications Restructuring Project could be key to achieving many of these objectives.

Only 90,000 people (0.5 per cent) in a population of 18.6 million were Internet users in Madagascar, compared to neighbouring Mauritius, where 15 per cent were Internet users in 2004. The Government could seek help from the international community for increasing its IT capacity and applications. The United States Leland Initiative, for example, is designed to provide African countries with computers and help authorities in writing and implementing anti-monopoly laws for the ICT sector. It appears that the private sector is already involved in developing this sector and its further involvement should be encouraged.

5. Skills improvement

To address Madagascar's needs with respect to secondary education and the education and skills of the local labour market, the education authorities should undertake measures to make secondary schooling more relevant for employment in the local economy. More vocational training, internships and school-to-work programmes for secondary schools are among measures that might improve the quality of the workforce in

Madagascar. Bilateral aid is being used to operate training centres for sewing, and more such aid for textile and other sectors would be valuable to current and potential investors. Private-public partnerships may also be formed to provide internships, apprenticeships and school-to-work programmes. Also needed are efforts to contain the spread of HIV/AIDS, although its prevalence in Madagascar is lower than in many other countries on the African continent.

6. Strengthening of institutions

The Malagasy Government needs to improve its public institutions and make the administrative system work effectively and fairly. Specifically, it must address inadequacies in the existing laws and bureaucratic processes, in particular those on permits and approvals of investment projects. In June 2000, a dispute resolution mechanism was established under a new arbitration law: the Centre d'Arbitrage et de Médiation de Madagascar (CAMM), a private sector initiative supported by USAID, which provides an alternative to litigation for commercial conflicts. Efforts to strengthen the bureaucracy should be undertaken to improve the investment environment for residents and foreigners alike.

Notes

[1] Vanco, joined by ExxonMobil and Norsk Hydro, is currently exploring offshore oil blocks.

[2] The operations of Pan African Mining Corp. in Madagascar are carried out through its operating subsidiary, PAM Madagascar SARL.

[3] Duties on those products will be gradually reduced until duty free access is granted for bananas in January 2006, for sugar in July 2009 and for rice in September 2009. (*Source*: European Commission, see http://europa.eu.int/comm/trade/issues/global/gsp/eba/index_en.htm).

[4] Madagascar adheres to the Convention on the Settlement of Investment Disputes Between States and Nationals of Other States and has done so since 1966 (Source: World Bank, see http://www.worldbank.org/icsid/constate/c-states-en.htm).

[5] See http://www.doingbusiness.org/EconomyRankings.

[6] Some private sector operators have also advocated adding another international language, such as English, to the secondary school curriculum to enhance students' marketability upon graduation and to make Malagasy students and workers competitive with their Mauritian counterparts.

CHAPTER VII

MOZAMBIQUE

Subregion	East Africa
Area ('000 km2)	784.1
Population (million)	19.8
Currency	Metical (MZM)
Exchange rate (MZM per dollar), 2005 average	23,061
GDP in current prices (millions of dollars), 2005	6,728
GDP per capita (dollars), 2005	340
Exports of goods and services (millions of dollars), 2004	1,759
Imports of goods and services (millions of dollars), 2004	2,381
Official development assistance (millions of dollars), 2004	1,232
FDI inflows (millions of dollars per annum) (average for 2000-2005)	239
FDI inward stock (millions of dollars), by 2005	2,386
FDI inward stock per capita (dollars), by 2005	121

INTRODUCTION

Mozambique has a population of about 20 million, a surface area of 784,100 square kilometres and considerable natural resources, including substantial mineral resources. Since the end of a devastating civil war in 1992, the country has successfully transformed into a multiparty democracy with a market economy. Comprehensive economic reforms since the early 1990s led to an average annual real GDP growth rate of 8 per cent over the period 1993-2005, reaching a high of 13 per cent in 2001 (figure VII.1). In addition, strong fiscal and monetary policies managed to reduce inflation from 48 per cent in 1996 to below 10 per cent in recent years.

The process of economic transformation and reforms launched in Mozambique in 1987 has been supported by World Bank and IMF loans. In 2004, a three-year loan was approved by the IMF through its Poverty Reduction and Growth Facility and the World Bank approved its first Poverty Reduction Support Credit for Mozambique; both credits support the Government's economic programme for 2004 to 2006.

Since the late 1980s, Mozambique has liberalized trade, lifted price controls and instituted privatization programmes that have resulted in the sale of more than 1,700 State-owned companies, including 50 large ones. Indeed, by the end of the 1990s, Mozambique was among the leading African countries in terms of privatisations, which earned the Government a total revenue of $144 million (UNCTAD, 2001a). Further reforms followed, with deregulation of the banking sector in 1992, and a restructuring of the public sector while expanding the role of the private sector in 1994. Privatization has continued, to such an extent that by the end of 1990s only about 12 service companies in activities such as airports, the

Figure VII.1. GDP growth of Mozambique, 1981-2005
(Per cent)

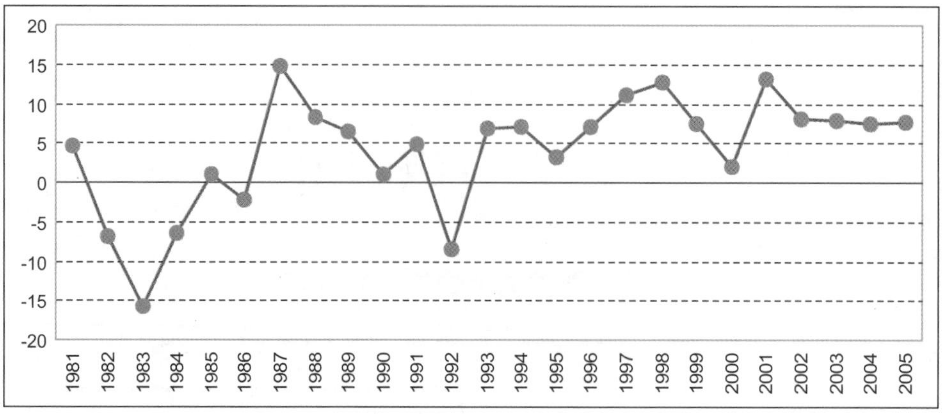

Source: IMF, 2006b.

national air carrier, utilities, petroleum and some areas of the ports and railways were still owned by the State. In these sectors, options for further privatization have been under consideration. The largest project was the privatization of the Maputo Corridor Railway in 2002 that generated $68 million in revenues.[1]

Mozambique's reform efforts, its size, rich natural resources, and its links with the southern African region, especially neighbouring South Africa, has led a number of TNCs to initiate major investment projects in the country. One of the main objectives of this chapter is to assess how FDI

inflows to Mozambique could be further increased, particularly those involving Asian investors. It is organized as follows. Section A presents recent investment trends in the country in the context of the benefits it could derive from different forms of FDI. Section B reviews Mozambique's strengths and weaknesses in terms of attracting FDI. Section C attempts to identify the factors behind these weaknesses and suggests policy reforms to attract more FDI. Specific sectors offering opportunities for investors in general, and SMEs in particular, are then considered in section D. The last section concludes with policy proposals to attract Asian FDI.

A. RECENT TRENDS IN FDI

The East and South-East Asian economies serve as outstanding examples of how to achieve rapid growth to escape poverty. Mozambique could draw lessons from their experiences, one of which is to give priority to increasing the involvement of foreign firms in its economy through FDI. This section surveys recent FDI trends, explores the types of investment that could help Mozambique's development, and explores some opportunities for potential investors. This is followed by a discussion concerning investment from Asia, especially in SMEs.

1. FDI trends and prospects

Figure VII.2 illustrates the trend of FDI flows to Mozambique from 1970 to 2005. These grew steadily each year from 1989 to 1998, but experienced fairly sharp fluctuations thereafter:

during 1997-1999 there was a steep rise followed by a rapid decline in 2000 and then another abrupt rise followed again by a sharp fall during the period 2003-2005 (figure VII.2). The 1998-1999 peak could be attributed to large projects, while the surge during the period 2001- 2004 was mainly due to large, natural-resources-relating projects (an aluminium smelter, gas extraction and transport, and titanium ore extraction).

Table VII.1 shows the number of approved investment projects (i.e. investments approved by the country's Investment Promotion Centre (CPI) before requesting incentives) since 1993, and their dollar values. They have followed roughly the same pattern as actual investments. They increased steadily from 1993 to 1999, but since then there has been a declining trend. The average value of approved investment projects has varied, from $0.7 million in 1993 to $10 million in 2001.

Figure VII.2. FDI inflows to Mozambique, 1970-2005
(Millions of dollars)

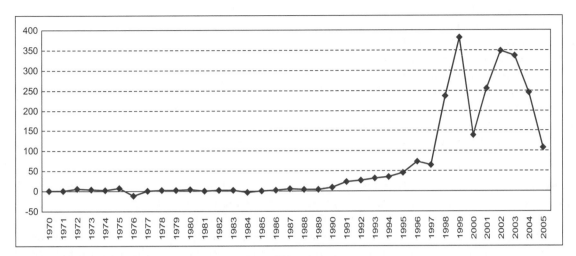

Source: UNCTAD, FDI/TNC database (www.unctad.org/fdistatistics).

Table VII.1. Approved investment projects in Mozambique, 1993-2004

| Year | Number of projects | | | Value (millions of dollars) | | | |
	FDI	NDI[a]	Total	FDI	NDI	Loans	Total
1993	27	27	54	18.0	7.6	45.6	71.2
1994	72	116	188	91.2	63.4	291.9	446.6
1995	55	150	205	50.4	52.6	176.0	279.0
1996	112	239	351	86.7	54.7	377.7	519.1
1997	91	152	243	695.3	60.5	998.6	1 754.3
1998	110	153	263	157.8	89.9	590.1	837.8
1999	125	183	308	122.0	105.7	539.7	767.4
2001	98	34	132	961.3	98.8	2956.6	4 016.7
2002	81	49	130	575.1	50.4	913.1	1 538.6
2003	90	32	122	122.0	34.5	711.5	868.0
2004[b]	77	26	103	54.5	28.0	133.8	216.3
Total	938	1161	2 099	2 934.3	646.1	7734.6	11 315.0

Source: Mozambique Investment Promotion Centre (CPI).
[a] NDI is national direct investment or domestic investment. Under the Bank of Mozambique definitions, FDI and NDI refer only to equity investments.
[b] Data for period 1 January to 30 September.

With regard to sectoral distribution of FDI, between 1997 and 2000 (latest year for which data are available), the bulk of FDI (in terms of value) went to manufacturing (table VII.2), driven largely by the $1.3 billion Mozal project (discussed below). Agriculture, forestry and fishery, and finance industries were distant second and third places respectively, although still well ahead of tourism.

Investment approvals have been much more skewed geographically. Almost three quarters of investment approvals were for projects in Maputo (province and city), even though it accounts for only 11 per cent of the country's population, but has a GDP per capita that is about six times higher than the national average. Maputo's proximity to South Africa and its port facilities for import and export explain its advantage in terms of location choice. The country's most populous provinces, Zambezia and Nampula, receive relatively little investment. For foreign trade purposes among others, being located in or near Maputo, the capital, offers the advantage of easier processing of approvals and other bureaucratic requirements involved in doing business.

It is extremely difficult to break down investment into export-oriented versus domestic-market-serving FDI. Certainly, in some industries, agriculture, fisheries and mineral investments are export-oriented, but Mozambique needs to give

Table VII.2. Cumulative FDI flows (on an approval basis) into Mozambique by sector, 1997-2000

Sector/industry	Number of projects	Value (millions of dollars)
Primary	**195**	**125**
Agriculture, forestry and fishing	193	125
Mining, quarrying and petroleum	2	0.1
Manufacturing	**225**	**622**
Services	**385**	**251**
Construction	67	17
Transport, storage and communications	151	67
Transport and communications	73	24
Tourism	78	43
Finance	21	102
Business services	146	65
TOTAL	**805**	**998**

Source: UNCTAD, 2001a.

high priority to attracting more of such investments, especially given the poor performance of its trade balance (table VII.3). Nevertheless, in recent years exports have been increasing more rapidly than imports, and GDP has also been growing, resulting in an improvement in the country's negative trade balance as a percentage of GDP, and this is expected to improve further with the revitalization of traditional industries through privatization and increased private domestic and foreign investments.

Mega projects involving foreign investments in large-scale industries, natural resource extraction or infrastructure have given a substantial boost to export performance (table VII.4). Among the mega projects, the Mozal Aluminium Smelter involves the construction and operation of 2 pot-line smelters to produce aluminium ingots for export.[2] Mozal has already helped improve the perception of Mozambique internationally and has attracted many other projects to the country, including investments from foreign SMEs (UNCTAD, 2001a). Other mega projects and infrastructure projects that will contribute to exports include the industrial park and free zone at Beluluane, the Maputo Corridor Development, the Maputo Iron and Steel Project and improvements to Maputo's port facilities.

Just as there is no clear breakdown of export-oriented FDI, there is none for market-seeking FDI either. However, a number of sectors would clearly fall in this category. One is banking and financial services. The banking system in Mozambique is open to FDI and has attracted a number of international banks, partly due to the privatization of State-owned banks since 1996 and partly to the opening up of the market. Today, the largest bank in Mozambique, Banco de Investimento de Moçambique is majority-owned by a private Portuguese Bank, BCP. The bank has its origin in the Banco Commercial de Mozambique, which was privatized in 1996. Mozambique's second largest bank, Banco Austral, the result of the 1997 privatization of Banco Popular de Desinvolvimento, was acquired in 2001 by a consortium led by Southern Bank Berhad of Malaysia, but after encountering difficulties it had to be rescued by the Government. In late 2001 this bank was acquired by the South African Bank ABSA.

Other banks in Mozambique with foreign investment include Banco Internacional de Comercio (ICB), Banco Standard Totta and Equator Bank. ICB is also Malaysian-owned, while Standard Totta is a joint venture between Banco Totta & Açores of Portugal and Standard Bank of South Africa. Equator Bank, which focuses primarily on trade finance, is now owned by the Hong Kong and Shanghai Bank and is diversifying its activities in the market. Finally, União Commercial de Bancos, with Mauritian interests, entered the market in 1999 by opening a branch in Maputo.

Besides the banking sector, manufacturing for the local market has attracted a number of transnational corporations (TNCs). They include Sociedade Internacional de Tabacos TIA-MA LDA (owned by investors from China, the United Kingdom and the United States, and partly by the Mozambican Government) for manufacturing and selling cigarettes; Coca-Cola (with some $20 million invested); South African Breweries; British Petroleum (BP) Mozambique Ltd for the distribution of petroleum products; and Alpha Industria e Comercio Limitada (owned by the Singapore company, Alpha Chem International

Table VII.3. Mozambique: pattern of trade, 1997-2004
(Millions of dollars and per cent)

Item		1997	1998	1999	2000	2001	2002	2003	2004
Imports	Value (million dollars)	739.0	790.0	1 139.0	1 158.0	1 063.0	1 263.0	1 753.0	1 970.0
	Growth rate (%)	- 2.6	6.9	44.2	1.7	- 8.2	18.8	38.8	12.4
Exports	Value (million dollars)	222.0	230.0	263.0	364.0	703.0	663.0	1 045.0	1 504.0
	Growth rate (%)	2.3	3.6	14.3	38.4	93.1	- 5.7	57.6	43.9
Trade balance	Value (million dollars)	-517.0	-560.0	-876.0	-794.0	-360.0	-600.0	-708.0	-466.0
	As % of GDP	15.2	14.5	22.0	21.0	9.7	14.7	14.8	7.7

Source: World Bank, 2006.
Note: Data refer to merchandise trade only.

Table VII.4. Mega FDI projects in Mozambique, 2006

Project	Owners	Location	Activity	Status	Value ($ million)
Mozal I and Mozal II	Billiton (South Africa), IDC (South Africa), Mitsubishi (Japan), Government of Mozambique	Beluluane, Maputo	Aluminium production	Implemented	2 000
Maputo Corridor Development (Johannesburg-Maputo Toll Road)	TRAC (Trans-Africa Concessions)	Johannesburg to Maputo	Toll road and development corridor leading into Maputo Port	Completed	90 for Mozambique portion (overall value of 300)
Gas pipeline	SASOL (South Africa), Government of Mozambique	Temane/Pande (off the coast of Inhambane) to Johannesburg	Gas extraction and transportation	Completed	1 000
Industrial Park of Beluluane	Chiefton (Australia), Government of Mozambique	Beluluane, Maputo	Industrial park and industrial free zone	ATAP	50
Maputo Iron and Steel Project (MISP)	Enron (United States), Duferco (Switzerland), Kobe Steel (Japan), Midrex (United States), VAI (Australia), Techint (Italy)	Maputo	Iron and steel production	ATAP; likely to be not realized due to bankruptcy of the main investor Enron	2 000
Ocean Terminal and Port, Porto Dobela	CFM, Porto Dobela Development Lda	Porto Dobela, Matutuine, Maputo	Port	NTAP	515
Beira Iron and Steel Project	JCI (South Africa), Leopardus (EU)	Beira	Iron and steel production	AAPP	500
Free Zone of Beira	JCI (South Africa), Leopardus (EU)	Beira	Development and operation of a free zone	AAPP	450
Petrochemical Complex of Beira	SASOL (South Africa)	Beira	Production of petrochemical products	NACP	1 700
Heavy Sands of Chibuto	Corridor Sands Ltd.	Chibuto	Development of heavy sands	NACP	1'000
Moma Titanium Mineral Project	Kenmare (Australia)	Moma, Nampula	Development of heavy sands	Viability study and financial arrangement have been concluded	400
Heavy Sands of Moebase	Billiton SA Limited (South Africa)	Moebase, Zambezia	Development of heavy sands	Pending	270 to 460

Sources: UNCTAD, based on Mozambique Investment Promotion (CPI), unpublished document and data on the CPI website, http://www.mozbusiness.gov.mz.

Notes:
ATAP   Approval of terms of authorization of the project.
NTAP   Negotiation of terms of authorization of the project.
AAPP   Approval of accord of principles of the project.
NACP   Negotiation of accord of principles of the project.

Limited) for manufacturing soap and detergent cream.

Finally, considerable foreign investment has begun in infrastructure, particularly Mozambique's port facilities. Investments are also needed for roads, railways, hotels, ports, reconstruction of social services such as schools and hospitals, and creation and expansion of networks of utilities such as water and electricity.

2. Investments from Asia

Table VII.5 provides a detailed list of proposed and ongoing projects with Asian investments as of 2005. It reveals a number of interesting patterns. First, several traditional investors are represented, specifically those from India and Pakistan. There are also some new investors as well, notably from Hong Kong

(China), China, the Republic of Korea, Malaysia and Singapore.

A noteworthy aspect of FDI in Mozambique is the size of the FDI projects: of the 28 projects listed in table VII.5 with dollar values, investments in more than half are valued at less than $1 million. A large number of these projects are undertaken by SMEs. This could have significant implications for the development of Mozambique, based on research findings on the importance of SMEs and of SME investors for economic growth (Fujita, 1998; UNCTAD, 1998).[3] SMEs from Asia might find locating in Mozambique especially attractive given its closeness to South Africa and to other locations of Asian investment like Mauritius, as well as to Asia itself in general. Moreover, Mozambique has a relatively large population of immigrants from various parts of Asia. Large-scale agriculture, agro-processing and light manufacturing would be the most likely areas for investment by Asian SMEs.

Table VII.5. Proposed and actual projects with Asian investment in Mozambique, 2005

Country	Project	Industry	Total value ($ thousands)
China	Mozambique – TV/VCD	..	3 000
China[a]	Agro Alfa Lda	Agriculture and agro-industry	1 727
Hong Kong (China)	Agricot	Agriculture and agro-industry	10 000
Hong Kong (China)	..	Cigarettes	2 920
Hong Kong (China)	..	Fisheries	8 666
India	Sharma Transportes Lda	Passenger and cargo transport	40
India	ACOREL- Agro Pecuaria e Representacoes	Trade (rural and urban stores)	190
India[b]	Cometal	Industry	9 546
India	Linkub Investiments Industria	Industry	240
India	Tata Exports, Lda	Vehicle assembly	1 101
Rep. of Korea	Sun Photos	..	158
Rep. of Korea	..	Photographic studio	177
Rep. of Korea	KMC-Sociedade Agro-Industrial do Caju	Agriculture and agro-industry	63
Rep. of Korea	Seoul Interprise	Photographic studio	134
Rep. of Korea	Sacos de Rafia	Industry	680
Rep. of Korea	Afrotex Mocambique	Industry	490
Malaysia	Banco (Southern Bank Berhad)	Banking and finance	6 000
Malaysia	ICB/Banco Internacional do Comercio	Banking and finance	1 385
Pakistan	Rainbow Plasticos	Industry	100
Pakistan	Avimar, Aviario Mohamed A. A. Rehman	Agriculture and agro-industry	87
Pakistan	Sunkis / Fabricq de Refrigerantes	Industry	..
Pakistan	Incopal	Industry (food)	1
Pakistan	Mercado Secundario de Cambios	Banking and finance	86
Pakistan	Canon ConfecHoes MoHambique	Industry (food)	398
Singapore	Mocambique Phill Photo	Film development and identity card manufacture	1 296
Singapore	Kodak Express	Photographic studio and instrument repair	277
Singapore	Alpha Industria e Comercio	..	1 186
Singapore	Wheatstone Mozambique	Fisheries	1 508
Memorandum			
Japan	Efripel/Maruha	Fisheries	7 263

Source: Mozambique Investment Promotion Centre (CPI).

[a] Also Cyprus.
[b] With CFM, the state ports and railway company.

B. MOZAMBIQUE'S ABILITY TO ATTRACT FDI

At present, while Mozambique has a good macroeconomic policy and certain favourable market conditions, shortcomings in other determinants adversely affect the costs of doing business there.

1. Potential markets

Four potential markets for TNCs can be distinguished: local consumers, local businesses in need of inputs, the regional market and broader export markets.

(a) Local consumer market

With a population of about 20 million, the Mozambique market is not negligible in size. At present, local manufacturing is unable to meet domestic demand. Many local firms adopt a high-price, high-margin strategy for domestic sales, which results in reduced sales volumes in favour of profits. They are able to do this with the help of import protection, and often sell imported goods that only they are able to import. This suggests that opportunities exist for locally manufactured goods and that domestic production of such goods will help reduce Mozambique's negative trade balance as well as benefiting local consumers.

(b) Inputs for local businesses

While it is not clear how deep the existing local business market is for domestically produced inputs, it is clear that several developing industries create demand for such goods. They include tourism, construction and manufacturing. The tourism industry, for example, is in need of supplies of goods and services (such as toiletries, agro-industrial products and processed foods) for hotels, lodges, game parks, restaurants and tour operators.

With new private infrastructure projects and the continuing reconstruction of the country, domestic and foreign construction firms will need all types of inputs to build hotels, roads, railways and ports. Mega projects will also need inputs. For example, Mozal has set up a facility with the Mozambique investment promotion centre (Centre pour la promotion des investissements (CPI)), for expediting foreign investment to meet Mozal's construction and operational needs. South Africa, through its Department of Trade and Industry, and Australia, through the Australian Trade Commission, have both signed agreements with the CPI, which enable firms from those countries to benefit from supplying inputs to meet Mozal's needs. In addition, given Mozambique's low ratio of telephones to population, many companies need more efficient telephone and Internet services.

(c) Regional markets for exports

As a member of the SADC regional trade bloc, Mozambique has preferential access to the SADC market. While this may not be meaningful yet, when the SADC Trade Protocol is fully implemented[4] Mozambique will have access to a market with a population of 224.6 million and an aggregate GDP of $333.8 billion (as of 2005).[5] This is one of the richest subregions in Africa in terms of natural resources, and one of the fastest growing, yet it remains largely unexploited. The ongoing rehabilitation of its ports and railways could eventually result in Mozambique becoming a gateway to most of the subregion. For example, the Maputo Corridor toll road provides the shortest and possibly most efficient road connection of any port city to Johannesburg.

(d) Broader export markets

By itself, the SADC market may not be enough to attract export-oriented industries to Mozambique. However, given the various trade preferences accorded to the country by developed-country markets, along with the ongoing port rehabilitation, there is potential for exports of products from Mozambique to broader export markets as well.

Under the Cotonou Agreement between the EU and the African, Caribbean and Pacific (ACP) group of States, primary products, such as aluminium, produced in Mozambique can enter the EU duty-free, while the EU's common external tariff imposes a 6-per-cent duty on such products from elsewhere. This agreement and the low electricity costs are among the key determinants of the choice of Mozambique for the Mozal project (Wells and Buehrer, 2000). In addition, Mozambique is eligible for quota-free access to the EU market under the Generalized System of Preferences (GSP) and for duty-free access to the United States market for a number of apparel products under the new African Growth and Opportunity Act (AGOA). Such favourable access to European and United States textile markets makes this sector a potential area for investment.

Finally, while shipping distances to Europe and North America are long, they are no longer than for other successful exporters. For example, Mozambique is less than 9,600 kilometres from France, and a little more than 12,000 kilometres from the United States – distances comparable to those between Mauritius and Viet Nam, for example.

2. Factor availability

(a) Local labour markets

Mozambique's skilled workforce is small. While data on skilled workers in each sector are not available, a number of indicators are revealing. Mozambique's illiteracy rates of 38 per cent for men and 69 per cent for women are much higher than the average illiteracy rates for the region, which are 18 and 24 per cent respectively. Table VII.6 shows illiteracy rates in SADC member countries in 2004. Mozambique's high rate can be explained by the country's unfortunate recent history. At independence in 1975, 93 per cent of the population was illiterate and during the civil war in the 1980s, many of the rural schools had to be closed.

At present, Mozambicans receive, on average, only 1.6 years of schooling – among the lowest in the world (SADC, 2000). Skills are lacking even for simple assembly work, resulting in low productivity of workers, which means that unit labour costs are likely to be high.

Apart from the poor quality of unskilled labour, there is also a lack of skilled managers. In fact, smaller firms have voiced concerns that mega projects will absorb all the skilled labour in the country once they begin operations, and this would increase the competition for the remaining managers and skilled workers. However, a number of employers speak highly of young Mozambican workers and their ability to learn. Thus there is considerable potential.

(b) Local financial conditions

Mozambique had a long civil war, and pursued socialist policies until 1990. It was only after this period that liberalization, including that of its financial services, began. Since then, the financial services sector has rapidly become dynamic with the entry of several international banks, mainly from Portugal and South Africa, but also from other countries (section A). These banks have diversified their activities into such areas as property development, trade finance and other loans. However, while bank services are diversifying, credit remains costly and difficult to access for many companies (World Bank *et al.*, 1998). Despite a sharp lowering of inflation since 2003 borrowing rates remain high. Real interest rates tend to be high, averaging about 20 per cent for the past three years.

(c) Infrastructure

Due to long periods of neglect and deterioration during the independence struggle of the 1970s and the civil war of the 1980s, as well as periodic floods, Mozambique's infrastructure is in urgent need of improvement. For instance, internal north-south transport is considered expensive, slow, monopolistic and bureaucratic. This has meant that suppliers of raw materials in the north have been unable to ship their goods to businesses that need them in the south. Despite these problems, there have been extensive improvements. The rehabilitation programme for ports and railways is one example, and is of considerable importance if Mozambique is to generate significant business for export. Until recently, all rail lines and ports were run by the Mozambique Ports and Railways (CFM), the country's largest public-sector enterprise. Over the past several years, it has created joint ventures with private enterprises for rehabilitation and management.

As with port and transport infrastructure, the telecommunications infrastructure is also somewhat lacking. Mozambique has one of the lowest ratios of telephones per 100 inhabitants (0.41 in 2003) among the SADC member countries, far below the regional average of 2.9/100 (World Bank, 2006). As with ports,

Table VII.6. Illiteracy rates of selected SADC-member countries, 2004 or latest year available

Country	Adult illiteracy rate		Youth illiteracy rate	
	Male[a]	Female[b]	Male[c]	Female[d]
Botswana	20	18	8	4
Lesotho	26	10	..	..
Malawi	25	46	18	29
Mauritius	12	19	6	5
Mozambique	*38*	*69*	*23*	*51*
Namibia	13	17	9	7
Seychelles	9	8	1	1
South Africa	16	19	7	6
Swaziland	19	22	13	10
United Republic of Tanzania	22	38	19	24
Zimbabwe	*1*	*4*	*6*	*14*
Average of countries shown above	18	24	11	15

Source: World Bank, 2006.
[a] Per cent of males ages 15 and above.
[b] Per cent of females ages 15 and above.
[c] Per cent of males ages 15-24.
[d] Per cent of females ages 15-24.

significant efforts have recently been made in the sector. However, improvements in telecommunications access are not uniform, with some cities well served, especially by cellular phone operators, while others, along with villages, are underserved. The existing telecommunications law has been changed and the new law abolishes the monopoly of the State-owned TDM of the fixed line network by 2008.

(d) Export processing zones

Under the guidance of a special joint committee, the Government Liaison Committee (GLC), Mozambique handed out its first Industrial Free Zone (IFZ) certificate to Mozal in 1997 (Wells and Buehrer, 2000). A second project, the Beira IFZ (Savane) in Sofala province has also been approved (UNCTAD, 2001a). It has a drawback mechanism that allows, on condition of appropriate justification, the refund of duty paid for inputs. Mozambique's free zone strategy could boost the infrastructure available to investors, and the country's ability to attract foreign firms. The strategy involves attracting mega projects to help

improve the infrastructure in and around the major ports. For Maputo, Mozal is the anchor, while a Sasol petrochemical project anchors Beira (see table VII.4). Infrastructure to be developed includes new road links to each harbour. The most advanced is the Industrial Park at Beluluane, which surrounds Mozal, and which will use Maputo Port and the Maputo Corridor road. This $50 million project is jointly owned by Chiefton Management of Australia and the Government of Mozambique.

The plan is to make these zones as efficient as possible, with world-class infrastructure, easier regulations for the hiring of expatriates, and Internet connections. Customs procedures are carried out in the zones, and the CPI hopes to employ expedited procedures with a 24-hour turnaround time. For example, all imports and exports destined for Beluluane, shipped through Maputo Port or any other point of entry, will go directly to the zone for customs inspection. Target firms include those involved in light assembly, such as textile and apparel companies, along with electronic assembly firms, for export mainly to EU and United States markets.

C. POLICY REFORMS NEEDED TO ATTRACT MORE FDI

Although Mozambique has maintained a good macroeconomic policy, is well endowed with minerals and other natural resources, and has a potential market for goods that could be produced by TNC affiliates, it has not attracted the amount or type of foreign investment, aside from that in the mega projects, needed for its development. Key problems facing foreign investors in Mozambique include poor infrastructure, lack of skilled labour and labour issues in general, onerous administrative procedures regarding investments, complex expatriate visa requirements, and difficulties in cross-border clearance of goods. The Government needs to listen and respond to the suggestions made by firms for improving the investment climate. An effective mechanism of public-private dialogue would help.

1. Labour issues

The Government's decision to allow private investment in education has already attracted a number of international schools and

the quality of local education has also been improved (UNCTAD, 2001a). Tax incentives for companies investing in training and providing benefits to private technical schools that could fill gaps in State-supported education are other measures that could be explored for strengthening the supply of skilled workers.

Mozambique's labour law of 1999 has made it difficult to hire foreign workers: the process can be long and the results are unpredictable. The Government recognized this in the case of Mozal, for example, by agreeing to an expedited procedure for expatriate labour. The Ministry of Labour agreed to accept a list of expatriate workers and review it as a whole, rather than case by case. The result was rapid processing and less paperwork (Wells and Buehrer, 2000). Furthermore, the Government plans to have more flexible rules for expatriate labour for firms in the Industrial Park in Beluluane. Recent labour reforms have somewhat eased the contracting of expatriate labour.

2. Administrative and legal framework

The establishment of a business is expensive due to the bureaucracy and regulations involved, especially for obtaining an operating licence and the right to employ skilled expatriate workers. These pose difficulties for FDI by SMEs in particular. Other problems relate to access to credit, land tenure, the general legal framework and business practices. As a result, Mozambique is ranked 20th out of 25 African countries in the Growth Competitiveness Index (World Economic Forum, 2004a). There is considerable optimism about Mozambique, but also much work ahead to attract further FDI.

Even though Mozambican officials have striven to reduce barriers and bureaucratic requirements, many administrative rules still deter investment, making it more costly to invest and resulting in lost opportunities. The first serious effort to evaluate administrative barriers was carried out a decade ago by the Foreign Investment Advisory Service (FIAS) of the International Finance Corporation (FIAS, 1996). The FIAS study categorized barriers under four groups: (i) general approval and registration; (ii) site development; (iii) major operating and trading licences; and (iv) operational requirements.[6]

There are frequent complaints about the need to obtain licences for specific types of business activity (rather than a general business licence), the procedural requirements for obtaining these licences and the timing. For example, in some cases, licences must be applied for after the business is completely set up. This means the business must pay rent and incur other expenses while still unable to operate, which can ruin a small enterprise if the delays are long. In addition, work permits for foreigners can only be applied for after the licence is received. Given the delays in granting licences, a business could expend a considerable amount of money without knowing whether it will be able to hire the expatriate workers it needs. Furthermore, foreign companies are reported to have more difficulties obtaining licences than domestic companies.

Mozal found the entry process so onerous for its subcontractors and suppliers that it worked with the Government of Mozambique to set up an alternative process – the Government Project Facilitation Centre – during its construction phase. This central office sought to ensure that permits

and registrations were obtained in a timely manner, including contractor registration, immigration permits, work permits, customs permits, professional engineer certifications and other requirements. In some ways, it helped turn the CPI from a reception organization to a delivery organization with a client-oriented approach (UNCTAD, 2001a). An extension of such a service to all foreign investment projects would significantly lower entry costs and risks.

There are other aspects of the legal and administrative framework that unnecessarily block investment. One problem seems to be an antiquated commercial code rooted in the late 19th century commercial code of Portugal. Another is the lack of implementation of regulations, procedures and mechanisms for about 25 to 30 new laws. Finally, there is apparently no formal bankruptcy procedure – a major problem common to many developing and transition economies. Thus legal reforms are among the necessary tasks for attracting FDI as well as for Mozambique's development in general.

A number of other problems exist, of which land tenure is a particular problem. Land cannot be owned by individuals or companies. The Government administers the land and its titling or concession for specific use. The process is administratively cumbersome and lacks transparency, leading to weak property rights enforcement. Firms have reported problems locating and securing sites for their operations. There have been some recent attempts by the Government to improve the land registration system, and it is now possible for foreign companies to lease land. However, the system for applying for land concession still lacks transparency (UNCTAD, 2001a). The absence of a clear land tenure system also harms finance for small businesses and agricultural companies, since small investors often lack any other collateral. Therefore, a more flexible land law and land administration would be beneficial for SME investors (UNCTAD, 2001a).

3. Trade barriers

While Mozambique does not have particularly high tariffs, bureaucratic requirements surrounding imports appear to be problematic. Once again, this can harm small businesses more than large ones because SMEs have no bargaining power to push the process along. Clearing imports through customs is reported to take three months in some cases. In addition, importers must pay duties and value added tax (VAT) for imports, even when their imports are tax-exempt. For example, capital goods are exempt from VAT. However, although refunds can be claimed, the process can take years, since VAT refunds are balanced against VAT collected on revenues, and capital goods might not generate revenue for some time. This can create difficult cash-flow problems for small firms.

Complex import procedures have two negative results. First, they encourage the creation of monopolies as firms or traders able to figure out a way to expedite imports of goods can exercise market power by raising prices and squeezing supply. This not only hurts consumers, but other businesses that need these goods as inputs. Second, this can result in illegal trade, and as firms go underground, both tax collection and the development of legitimately functioning markets are hampered.

Exporting has also been reported to face bureaucratic problems, though less so than importing. The main problem seems to be that certain administrative forms are easier to obtain in Maputo than elsewhere in the country, thus handicapping exporters elsewhere, especially in the north of the country.

To overcome these problems, the Government could consider re-evaluating its policies on tax collection for tax-exempt goods and ensure that tax-exempt goods are truly exempted from taxes. The customs experiment planned for the Beluluane Industrial Park should be closely followed – if a 24-hour expedited customs turnaround can be realized there, then Mozambique should strive to extend the same service to all ports. Privatization of the ports may also increase

efficiency, and Mozambique seems determined to address this problem.

4. Special measures for SMEs

Unlike many dynamic Asian economies that have special policies or agencies for SMEs (UNCTAD, 1998), Mozambique does not appear to have any form of direct support for SME investment even through its investment promotion centre, the CPI. However, there are no minimum investment requirements if no incentives are desired.

While the economy remains underdeveloped and local business partners are not necessarily widely available, there are efforts by international agencies to foster the development of SMEs, including Enterprise Mozambique, which was launched in October 1999 with the support of the United Nations Development Programme (UNDP). It involves selecting a number of enterprises with strong potential for succeeding, and giving them the technical support they need. These companies are likely to become an excellent group from which international investors could choose partners.

The Government itself will need to play a more proactive role, such as developing an explicit policy for SMEs and designating an agency responsible for their growth and development. While it is important to examine whether Mozambique's laws or policies discriminate unnecessarily against smaller firms, making an existing office responsible for overseeing SME policy – or creating a new office or an advocate for SME development within the Government – could help smaller firms reach key ministers and convey to policy-makers the problems they face in the Mozambican economy.

D. SPECIFIC SECTORS FOR ASIAN INVESTMENT IN MOZAMBIQUE

In the preceding sections, a number of sectors were cited that could prove profitable for investors and help Mozambique's development. This section focuses on those sectors, explains how investment could be increased in them, and discusses how Asian investors and SMEs could play a prominent role.

The most promising sectors for the future development of Mozambique are agriculture and agro-industry (including fisheries), simple assembly operations, tourism and infrastructure. The first three are ideal for SMEs, and also appropriate for Asian firms. Asian trading companies could bring their knowledge to bear on agriculture, fisheries, textiles, apparel, bicycles and other industries by and other industries by seeking out and developing opportunities in Mozambique. Asian tourism-oriented firms could also help transform Mozambique into a new adventure-tourism destination.

1. Agriculture and agro-industries

Agriculture accounted for about 22 per cent of Mozambique's GDP in 2004. It also accounts for 9 per cent of exports and 80 per cent of employment.[7] With most of the country's population earning a living in agriculture, advances in this sector could have an enormous positive impact on both growth and income distribution. Its agricultural potential is considered fairly high, with an estimated 36 million hectares of arable land, of which only 10 per cent is currently used productively (UNCTAD, 2001a). The land is particularly fertile, and can support all types of agriculture, including horticulture, forestry, livestock, fisheries, citrus fruit, sisal, tobacco, tea, tropical fruit, cotton and marine products, for export to Europe. To attract investments in this sector, Mozambique should continue to create and improve its internal transport systems, especially road transport in the four fertile northern regions, and rehabilitate its ports so that agricultural products may be efficiently exported.

2. Simple assembly operations

Simple assembly operations would work well in Mozambique for a number of reasons. Trade preferences with the EU and the United States present excellent short- and medium-term opportunities for exports of textiles and apparel. Furthermore, rising wage costs in Mauritius and other locations means that many firms are ready to move to cheaper, labour-efficient sites elsewhere. Though Mozambicans are generally under-skilled, many local business people and foreign investors have observed that they are trainable and willing to work. Other assembly operations intended to serve the growing SADC market also show promise. Less simple, but still needed, are the manufacture and assembly of such items as air conditioners. No export operation will survive with long and bureaucratic customs procedures. As the ports are rehabilitated and development corridors (such as the Maputo Corridor) opened, Mozambique will become a more inviting location for such industries. These operations present the best investment

opportunities for Asian SMEs and for investment in Mozambican SMEs. The expertise of Asian firms in running assembly operations and efficiently exporting their products to world markets is perhaps unparalleled. Mozambique can serve as an excellent platform for the African market and other, especially European, markets for such products.

3. Tourism

Tourism options include leisure travel to the country's many beaches, historical travel to Portuguese colonial sites and adventure travel to the interior. The country has 2,500 kilometres of coastline, a pleasant climate with sunshine all year round, and magnificent hotels inherited from the colonial period. Ten per cent of Mozambique's total land area is allocated to wildlife management, including national parks, game reserves and hunting areas. This means that there is opportunity for private-sector involvement in the wildlife sector, and for tourism development and marketing outside the core conservation areas. Some even argue that certain activities within the main conservation areas should be contracted out to the private sector.

Unfortunately, the tourism infrastructure is poorly developed. For the tourist industry to thrive investors will need to build hotels and other tourist facilities – most colonial hotels are in need of rehabilitation – and the Government will need to improve internal transportation.

4. Infrastructure

Another major sector with strong potential is infrastructure. This is considered one of the major barriers to investment. Through a variety of means, companies from around the world are building and rehabilitating ports, railway lines, roads and telecommunications networks. For example, using local labour, a Japanese general contractor, Konoike Construction of Osaka, has built 30 new bridges in Nampula, Manica, Sofala and Zambezia provinces. The Japan International Cooperation Agency undertook a project involving the reconstruction and restoration of 13 bridges that were selected as most urgently requiring attention in the international trunk road used for the transportation of materials to the Indian Ocean ports.[8]

5. Other sectors

Besides these sectors, a number of other sectors offer inviting prospects for investors, including technical schools, insurance and services for mega projects. Already, Asian firms have missed out on gaining first-mover advantages as suppliers of the many mega projects under implementation. They will also need to be made aware that Mozambique has advantages to offer for natural-resource-related services. The need for technical schools is illustrated by the constant mention of the unskilled nature of the workforce and by the demonstrated efforts of young Mozambicans to gain extra training. Furthermore, current investors lament the lack of qualified tradesmen as well as the lack of business knowledge.

As noted above, foreign banks have entered the market and are gradually opening up the banking sector. In contrast, insurance investors, that have been reluctant so far, may be more willing to enter the country if the legal framework is reformed and enhanced so that there is adequate protection for both insurers and clients. The Ministry of Planning and Finance has set up a commission for inspecting insurance activity, which is a positive step. Observers believe that reforms in the insurance sector will create opportunities and attract investors.

The Mozal experience has revealed both opportunities and pitfalls in servicing mega projects. Even though a considerable amount had been spent on the project in Mozambique, few qualified suppliers of goods or services were found in the country. In general, local firms could not compete in the bidding process or meet quality standards. In response, the company set up a pilot Linkage Programme with the CPI to involve local suppliers and contractors as early as possible in construction of the smelter, to identify opportunities for foreign firms and to help foreign firms overcome bureaucratic delays that might discourage investments. The Australian Trade Commission and the Department of Trade and Industry (DTI) of South Africa have joined the Linkage Programme separately to get their firms involved in the project.

E. MEASURES NEEDED TO ATTRACT AND PROMOTE ASIAN FDI

1. Host-country measures

Mozambique is now a relatively stable country, especially by African standards. As with much of Africa, it has huge and diverse mineral resources, including coal, natural gas, rare metals, titanium, non-metallic minerals, and possibly gold and diamonds. It has forests with wood such as ebony, teak and rosewood. Asian firms, however, should also consider how Mozambique might serve as a gateway to the SADC market and as a location for export-oriented production of appropriate products.

Mozambique certainly deserves consideration as a location for investments that will bring growth and development. It has a good macroeconomic policy framework, has undergone a successful privatization process, and offers many opportunities. Furthermore, there are active efforts to improve the business climate. For example, the Government's intention to offer a much more investment-friendly regulatory regime in export processing zones than is available in the rest of the country is a step in the right direction, provided the Government establishes a system by which firms can easily establish a business, benefit from flexible labour markets and import and export quickly and cheaply.

Immediate steps the Government could take include expediting port and customs clearance. A measure with a long-term impact, that could nevertheless be done quickly, is to empower the CPI to make decisions regarding approvals, permits and registrations, at least for desired investments. For example, the CPI could be given the power to grant all necessary permits for all investments of less than $5 million. This would go a long way towards facilitating inflows of SME investments.

Likewise, the Government should draw on the lessons of its own previous experiences with investment promotion. The joint-committee approach, such as through the Government Liaison Committee for Mozal mentioned earlier in this report, could demonstrate how to overcome barriers. The Linkage Programme could also be expanded into a nationwide programme. Policymakers especially should take note of such efforts to create an integrated development framework.

In order to bring about sustained reform, however, the Government must be open to the business community beyond private sector conferences. Top ministers (not just the Minister of Commerce and Industry) and civil servants should consult frequently with business leaders, perhaps quarterly, and agree to actions the Government will take over the subsequent quarter. It is particularly important to create policy benchmarks and targets for the Government.

It would also be useful for the Government to have regular meetings with representatives of foreign investors. They should provide valuable feedback on how Mozambique compares with competing locations, including other African countries as well as comparable Asian countries. Furthermore, they should provide constantly evolving ideas on what Mozambique could do to improve. One deterrent to this might be limited resources. However, successful investment promotion requires hosts to enable investors to make their needs and concerns known, since they are the main source of new investments and information to prospective investors. Furthermore, they are the most knowledgeable about actual investment conditions, and Mozambique cannot afford to neglect them.

Finally, Asian firms are reputedly experienced at working with low-skilled workers and finding export outlets for their production. They could enhance worker productivity and bring new industries and knowledge to Mozambique. Attending to the problems mentioned here would help attract FDI from Asia, particularly by SMEs. To further facilitate such FDI, the Mozambican Government and business officials will need to travel to Asia to persuasively familiarize business interests and Government officials there with opportunities in Mozambique. Meanwhile, Asian Governments should be encouraged to urge their firms to invest in Mozambique, for example, by helping to mitigate the risk of failure. And Asian investors who see Mozambique as more than a source of raw materials should be given encouragement.

2. Home-country measures

Asian countries could take a number of steps to help expand FDI in Mozambique by their SMEs. They could provide technical assistance, information, training, financial incentives and oversight of Asian firms already established there.

Technical assistance could take a number of forms, such as assisting the Mozambique Government in formulating SME policies or creating agencies, and advising on proper incentives it could offer investors, given the country's present level of development. Countries such as Malaysia and Singapore have used incentives intelligently in upgrading their industrial structures, and Mozambique can benefit from their experience. Another form of such assistance could be advice on the creation and effective use of industrial parks, export processing zones and customs procedures, without which FDI in export-oriented industries may not be forthcoming.

Information dissemination can play a key role, primarily by informing Asian firms of opportunities in Mozambique. Trade and investment promotion agencies in Asia could work directly with the CPI to develop campaigns for firms from Asia, since they know best how to reach their own nationals. Asian governments could also help the CPI organize effective trade and investment missions, both for Mozambican officials travelling to Asia and for Asian business people travelling to Mozambique. Such efforts could go a long way towards dissipating the fear of Africa that some interviewees have mentioned in surveys.

In the area of training, Asian governments should consider providing aid to improve the educational system in Mozambique. Equally important, Asian countries should consider funding talented Mozambicans to attend university or other training in their countries, or granting scholarships to African students to study at European or United States universities. This will not only create enormous goodwill, but also help create a managerial class for the economy.

In addition, Asian governments could help mitigate the risks – real and perceived – that their firms face with investments in Africa. This could take the form of additional risk insurance, subsidized financing, or tax benefits for profits made in Mozambique. Regarding oversight, Asian governments should take greater responsibility for policing their firms' behaviour. In particular, there are concerns about Asian firms behaving irresponsibly with regard to natural-resource exploitation.

Notes

[1]   *Source*: World Bank's privatization database.
[2]   It was hoped that the project would be a catalyst for infrastructure development in the surrounding areas including road construction, upgrading of port facilities, increasing electric power generation and building water supply, sewerage and drainage systems. The $2 billion smelter produces about 500,000 tons of aluminium a year. The main shareholders include Billiton of South Africa, the Industrial Development Corporation of South Africa (IDC), Mitsubishi of Japan and the Government of Mozambique.
[3]   When SMEs internationalize, a number of benefits may accrue to the host country. The labour-capital ratio of SME TNCs is generally higher than that of larger enterprises (Fujita, 1998; UNCTAD, 1998). This is particularly important to Mozambique, which has a large and growing labour force to be employed. Finally, SMEs tend to use more inputs from local subcontractors, which implies that SME investment can generate relatively more income locally, raising living standards and increase backward linkages in host economies.
[4]   The SADC Trade Protocol, signed at the annual meeting of Heads of State in Maseru, Lesotho, in August 1996, envisages a free trade area in the southern African region.
[5]   However, the purchasing power of this market is still fairly low (UNCTAD, 2001a).
[6]   Many of these findings were also reported in Wells and Buehrer (2000).
[7]   According to the FAO (www.fao.org).
[8]   *Source*: Japan International Cooperation Agency (http://www.jica.go.jp/english/activities/jicaaid/project_e/moz/001/index.html).

CHAPTER VIII

UNITED REPUBLIC OF TANZANIA

Subregion	East Africa
Area ('000 km2)	883.6
Population (millions)	38.3
Currency	Tanzanian shilling (TZS)
Exchange rate (TZS per dollar), 2005 average	1,128.9
GDP in current prices (millions of dollars), 2005	12,167
GDP per capita (dollars), 2005	317
Exports of goods and services (millions of dollars), 2004	2,171
Imports of goods and services (millions of dollars), 2004	3,265
Official development assistance (millions of dollars), 2004	1,745
FDI inflows (millions of dollars per annum) (average for 2000-2005)	442
FDI stock (millions of dollars), by 2005	6,029
FDI stock per capita (dollars), by 2005	157

INTRODUCTION

The United Republic of Tanzania had a population of over 38 million and a per capita income of $317 in 2005. It has a number of attributes that make it an attractive destination for FDI despite its low-income level. First, the country has an 800-kilometre coastline with three ports. Second, it has enjoyed a history of political stability in spite of the ethnic diversity of its population.[1] Third, its economic reform programme has been very successful: inflation has fallen substantially, from 28.4 per cent in 1995 to a single-digit level of around 5 per cent in recent years (Bank of Tanzania, 2006), while economic growth during much of the past decade has been relatively strong. In the competitiveness index rankings, the country was ranked 104th in the world for 2006 (World Economic Forum, 2006). If only African countries are considered, the country was placed 12th out of 28 countries.

The economic growth rate in the country fell sharply in the early 1990s after a period of rapid economic expansion in the second half of 1980s (figure VIII.1). Thereafter, it regained its growth momentum, maintaining an upward trend since the mid-1990s. The country's growth performance has been particularly high in recent years, despite unfavourable terms of trade and a general slowdown of the world economy.

The investment-savings gap over the past few years highlights the need for external financing. Although domestic savings have shown a steady upward trend, they are still low (figure VIII.2) and well below the rates the country must achieve if it is to be successful in raising sufficient investments for eradicating poverty in the medium term. It has been estimated that the domestic savings rate should rise from 13 per cent of GDP

Figure VIII.1. GDP growth of the United Republic of Tanzania, 1981-2005
(Per cent)

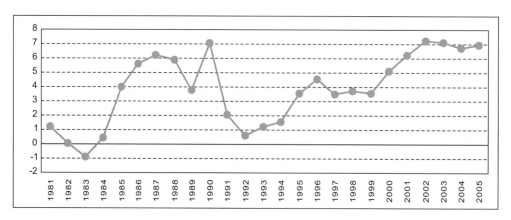

Source: IMF, 2006b.

in 2005 to 18 per cent over a 10-year period to generate sustained poverty-eradicating growth rates of 6 per cent for the average sub-Saharan economy (UNCTAD, 2000a).[2] However, despite recent increases in FDI inflows as a percentage of GDP such flows are still low (figure VIII.2).[3] This is partly a consequence of about two decades of socialist rule, which left many Tanzanians suspicious of private, particularly foreign, capital. The Government's reluctance to encourage FDI during the first half of the 1990s reflected political resistance to reform. However, given the significant savings-investment gap, the increased competition for development aid, as well as donor fatigue, FDI will be needed to help realize the country's aspirations. Recognizing this, the Government is now committed to attracting FDI and benefiting from it.

Central to the reform process has been the need to privatize. However, as privatization attracts FDI, a number of interest groups, including opposition parties, continue to voice their opposition to the Government's FDI policy, which has considerably hindered progress on privatization. There is consensus within the Government that liberalization of the economy should be carefully sequenced to maximize its benefits.

Many new investors in the economy are of ethnic Indian – popularly referred to as Asian – origin (albeit residing in the United Kingdom or

Figure VIII.2. Savings and FDI inflows relative to GDP in the United Republic of Tanzania, 1998-2005
(Per cent of GDP)

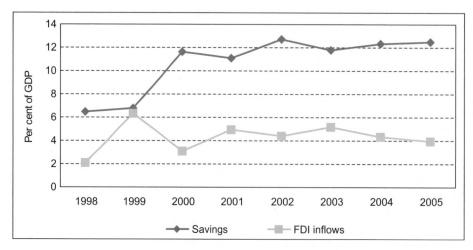

Source: UNCTAD FDI database and Bank of Tanzania, 2006.
Note: Data for savings refer to the ratio of savings to gross national disposable income.

Canada), and in many cases, are from the same families whose properties were expropriated in the early 1970s during the period of socialist policies. This has stirred old anti-Asian sentiments that need to be carefully handled by the Government.[4]

There were large increases in FDI shortly after the establishment of the Investment Promotion Centre (IPC) – the predecessor of the Tanzania Investment Centre (TIC) – and the start of privatization in 1993. In addition, the Government instituted tax-based incentives for foreign firms, with limited controls on repatriation of profits and income.[5] FDI inflows were, on average, three times higher during the period 1999-2005 than the average for 1996-1998, with the largest share going to mining.

The long history of socialist rule in the United Republic of Tanzania has meant that most industries were State-run, with little or no capital to increase production capacity. Many industrial structures that line the route from Dar es Salaam

international airport to the city centre remain as they had been in the mid-1970s. This is perhaps the greatest concentration of light manufacturing in the country. Operating costs are very high. The area around Kilimanjaro has become a centre for some agro-processing as well as tourism. The proximity of the international airport permits easy and rapid transport of fruit and flowers. Likewise, tourists interested in the northern belt attractions of wildlife and mountain climbing can fly straight into the heart of that area, thereby avoiding the long road trip from Dar es Salaam.

This chapter first analyses the level and types of FDI in the United Republic of Tanzania today as well as the crucial issues that must be addressed in order to attract greater FDI, including from Asia. It then examines opportunities and challenges for FDI, and the sectors in which Asian FDI would be the most beneficial. It also discusses the problems of SMEs, both as a crucial missing sector in African economies and in terms of opportunities for FDI, particularly Asian FDI.

A. FDI IN THE UNITED REPUBLIC OF TANZANIA

1. FDI trends

FDI flows to the United Republic of Tanzania remained at a very low level before the 1990s (figure VIII.3), averaging $4.4 million during the period 1970-1990. Since the mid- 1990s, they started to rise in response to the reform programme and privatization (box VIII.1), and have continued to grow to high levels in recent years, averaging $456 million during 1999-2005.

Since reform of the parastatal sector in June 1993, TNCs have assumed an important role in the Tanzanian economy through a series of cross-border mergers and acquisitions (M&As) related to the privatization programme (see table VIII.1 for some deals).[6] In particular, the sectors with impressive growth rates since the mid-1990s, namely mining, manufacturing, financial services and tourism, have been dominated by TNCs. TNCs also dominate power generation and telecommunications.

However, apart from mining and tourism, there is very little export-oriented FDI in other sectors of the economy. Most of the non-natural-resource FDI and a majority of privatized firms are geared to supplying the domestic market. FDI flows into infrastructure are still minimal. Between

1990 and May 2003 (most recent data), 2,288 projects with a total investment of 8,180 billion Tanzanian shillings ($11.9 billion) were registered with the TIC. The number of projects per sector are as follows: agriculture and livestock (163), natural resources (121), tourism (370), manufacturing (986), petroleum and mining (111), construction (178), transportation (112), services (144), telecommunications (29), financial institutions (38), others (36).

2. Other capital inflows and their links to FDI

The main inflows of external capital to the United Republic of Tanzania, apart from FDI, are bilateral and multilateral aid; there have been virtually no portfolio capital inflows to the country so far. In fact the Tanzanian Government did not allow foreign portfolio investment until recently.[7] This is partly due to the embryonic stage of development of the Dar es Salaam Stock Exchange. With only a handful of companies listed on the stock market, the Government wanted to maximize domestic participation in that market to avoid the political risks of opening up to international

Figure VIII.3. FDI inflows to the United Republic of Tanzania, 1970-2005
(Millions of dollars)

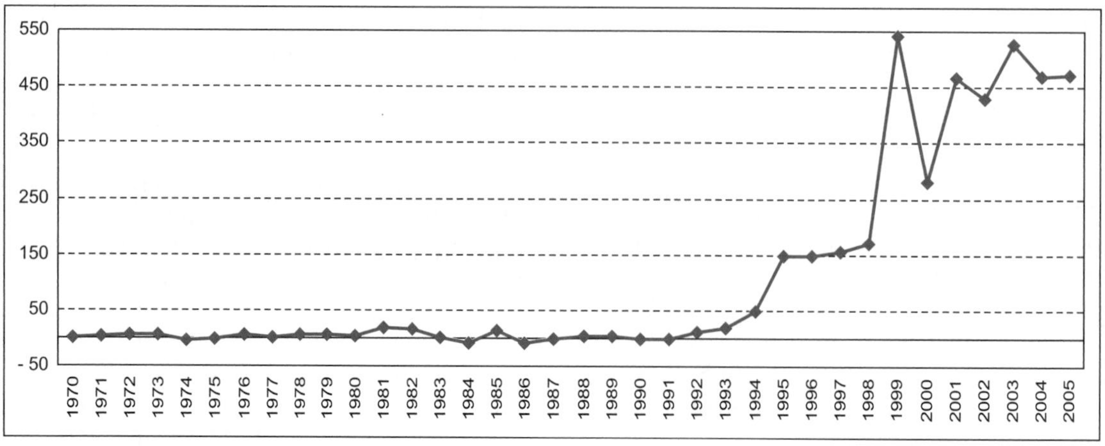

Source: UNCTAD, FDI/TNC database (www.unctad.org/fdistatistics).

Box VIII.1. The reform programme in the United Republic of Tanzania

The United Republic of Tanzania experienced a major economic slump following its war against Uganda in 1979. The Basic Industrial Strategy (an import-substitution policy), launched in 1975 to ensure self-sufficiency in consumer goods, began to falter as a result of the lack of working capital to service machinery. Deteriorating terms of trade resulted in a foreign exchange shortage, and, along with collapsing State-owned enterprises (SOEs), led to severe shortfalls in government revenues. The Government responded by borrowing from the central bank, leading to high rates of inflation: as much as 36 per cent in 1984 and averaging 30 per cent throughout the 1980s (World Bank, 2006).

In 1986, the country embarked on a structural reform programme, which included liberalization of the foreign exchange market, removal of distortions in the production of food and cash crops and tight fiscal discipline. Furthermore, the Government has been committed to reducing the size of the civil service.[a]

Reform of the financial sector was introduced by the Financial Institutions Act of 1991 that paved the way for private banks' entry into the credit market. Increased competition in this sector has yet to lower the price of credit, as this is dependent on ongoing reforms in commercial contracting and the impending establishment of a credit bureau.

Reforms have also included extensive privatization of SOEs. In 1992, the Parastatal Sector Reform Commission (PSRC) was established to supervise privatization. After nearly a decade, a total of 330 parastatals out of 395 had been privatized. The privatization proceeds rose rapidly in the early 2000s as Tanzania Telecommunication Co. was sold to foreign investors. In addition, the Government is committed to bolstering gross domestic investment with FDI: in 1990, it established a new investment code, with incentives for both domestic and foreign investment. The investment code was significantly revised in 1997 to improve intermediation by the TIC.

The results of these reforms are clear: inflation declined dramatically to around 4.5 per cent in 2002 (now 4.4 per cent), the exchange rate depreciated, and real GDP growth rose noticeably, exceeding 6 per cent in recent years.

Sources: EIU (various issues); PSRC website.

[a]   Between 1992 and 1997, 80,000 civil servants were retrenched and new incentives for civil servants instituted (Luvanga and Bol, 1999). As a result, by 1996 and 1997 the Government had managed to register positive domestic savings (EIU, 1999).

Table VIII.1. Cross-border M&As in the United Republic of Tanzania, 1993-2003

Year	Acquired company	Industry of the acquired company	Acquiring company	Home country	Value ($ million)	Shares acquired (per cent)
1993	Tanzania Breweries[a]	Malt beverages	Indol International(South Afr)	Netherlands	21.4	50
1994	Tanzania Diamond Mines-Lupa	Gold ores	Bakertalc Inc	Canada	7.7	90
1994	Tanzanian Diamond Mines-Maji	Gold ores	Bakertalc Inc	Canada	3.6	90
1994	Hotels & Tours Management Ltd[a]	Hotels and motels	Protea Hospitality Corp Pty	South Africa	-	40
1995	Cntrl Bk of Tanzania-Tanzanian	Banks, non-US chartered	Stanbic	South Africa	-	100
1997	Tanzania Cable (Tanzania)[a]	Cable and other pay television services	Daesung Cable Ltd	Korea, Republic of	1.4	51
1997	Tanzania Tobacco Board-Select[a]	Chewing and smoking tobacco and snuff	Universal Leaf Tobacco Inc	United States	-	100
1998	Kilombero Sugar Co (Tanzania)[a]	Cane sugar, except refining	Investor Group	South Africa	22.0	75
1998	Coastal Saltworks Co Ltd[a]	Chemical and fertilizer mineral mining, nec	M/S Purebond Ltd	United Kingdom	1.1	100
1999	Kiwira Coal Mine (Tanzania)[a]	Bituminous coal and lignite surface mining	China Hunan Intl Economic	China	-	62
2000	Tanzania Telecommunication Co[a]	Telephone communications, except radiotelephone	Investor Group	Germany	120.0	35
2000	National Bank of Commerce[a]	Banks, non-US chartered	Absa Group Ltd	South Africa	18.0	70
2001	Tanzania Telecommunication Co[a]	Telephone communications, except radiotelephone	Investor Group	Germany	120.0	35
2002	Tanzania Liquids Storage Co	Special warehousing and storage, nec	Tate & Lyle PLC	United Kingdom	0.9	60
2002	Mwananchi Communications Ltd	Newspapers: publishing, or publishing & printing	Nation Media Group	Kenya	-	60
2003	Precision Air	Air transportation, scheduled	Kenya Airways Ltd	Kenya	2.0	49
2003	Songas Ltd	Refined petroleum pipelines	CDC Globeleq	United Kingdom	-	100

Source: UNCTAD, cross-border M&A database.
a   Privatization.

investment. In addition, it was believed that by barring foreign involvement in the stock exchange the financial sector would be protected from sudden reversals in portfolio flows.

Insufficient private investment in infrastructure has been partly compensated by the World Bank and other bilateral donors. A number of power generation projects are being carried out with World Bank support. For example, the International Finance Corporation (IFC) has taken a sizeable stake in a number of divested SOEs to encourage foreign investors to participate in the privatization exercise.[8] Several foreign investors are benefiting from financial incentives from their own governments to make private investments in the United Republic of Tanzania more feasible. Such investment credits – considered as aid to the country – are offered by the Commonwealth Development Corporation (CDC) as well as by Scandinavian countries.[9] For instance, the Norwegian Agency for Development Cooperation provides up to 50 per cent of the costs of investment-related feasibility studies.

3. Types of FDI

(a) Market-seeking FDI

Following the collapse of SOEs that produced many of the country's consumer goods, TNCs have stepped in to fill the void. Examples include Tanzania Brewing Limited, owned by SABMiller (South Africa), and the Tanzania Cigarette Company (TCC) that changed hands recently from RJ Reynolds to Japan Tobacco International.[10] Matsushita (Japan) produces batteries as well as other basic electronic equipment for the domestic market. The Tanzania Shoe Company is an example of an investment dominated by foreign investors that is geared to supplying the domestic market. A number of joint ventures have been formed between the Government and foreign companies, including: Wazo Hill Cement, a cement manufacturer partly owned by Scancem of Norway; Mbeya Cement Company involving CDC (51 per cent) and Chilanga Cement Company of Zambia (14 per cent); Tanelec (which supplies electrical engineering equipment to Tanzania National Electric Supply Company (Tanesco)), in which Asea Brown Boveri (ABB) is a minority shareholder; Tanzania Cable, in which Dae Sung Cable of the Republic of Korea owns a 51 per cent share;

and Kilombero Sugar Company, partly owned by Illovo Sugar Ltd. of South Africa (55 per cent) and ED & F Man of the United Kingdom (20 per cent).

The financial services sector is almost wholly foreign-owned, following the acquisition of the largest commercial bank in the United Republic of Tanzania, the National Bank of Commerce, by Amalgamated Banking Group of South Africa (ABSA).[11] Other prominent foreign banks in the country include Standard Chartered Bank (United Kingdom), Stanbic Bank (Saudi Arabia), Barclays (United Kingdom), Citibank (United States), Eurafrican (Belgium, France and IFC), Kenya Commercial Bank (Kenya) and the International Bank of Malaysia.

(b) Export-oriented FDI

Natural resources for export. As noted, the mining sector accounts for the largest share of FDI flowing into the country to date. The Tanzanian Government has made this sector a priority after decades of neglect, though there is the need to find ways to maximize benefits from this FDI. Gold mining has attracted a number of international companies, including Aminex (United Kingdom), Anglo American (South Africa, United Kingdom), Anglogold (South Africa), Ashanti Goldfields (Ghana), Bakertalc Inc (Canada), Barrick Gold Corporation (Canada), East African Gold Mines (Australia) and Sutton Resources (Canada). The pace of FDI in natural resources has accelerated in recent years (see table VIII.2 for some recent projects). For example, Barrick Gold Corporation (Canada) invested $50 million in a mining project in 2003. Some foreign investors also entered

Table VIII.2. Greenfield FDI projects in natural resources in the United Republic of Tanzania, 2002-2005

Year	Name of investing company	Investing country	Sector	Key business function
2002	Ashanti Goldfields	Ghana	Metals/mining	Extraction
2003	Barrick Gold	Canada	Metals/mining	Extraction
2003	Aminex	United Kingdom	Energy	Extraction
2004	Sub-Sahara Resources	Australia	Metals/mining	Extraction
2004	Lakota Resources	Canada	Metals/mining	Extraction
2004	Globeleq	United States	Energy	Electricity
2005	Barrick Gold	Canada	Metals/mining	Extraction
2005	EnerGulf Resources	Canada	Energy	Extraction
2005	Gallery Gold	Australia	Metals/mining	Extraction
2005	Goldstream Mining	Australia	Metals/mining	Extraction
2005	Northern Mining Explorations	Canada	Metals/mining	Extraction

Source: UNCTAD, based on information from OCO consulting, LOCOmonitor website (www.locomonitor.com).

through cross-border M&As. In 1994, for instance, Bakertalc Inc. (Canada) acquired two companies in the gold ore industry with investments of $7.7 million and $3.6 million, respectively.

The country's leading diamond producer, Williamson Diamond Mines (already 75-per- cent-owned by De Beers) has recently entered into a joint venture with Wilcroft (South Africa). Other minerals attracting significant foreign interests include cobalt and nickel. Small-scale miners of gemstones such as Tanzanite have recently been integrated into the formal economy following the Bank of Tanzania's pledge to pay market prices for their minerals.

Tourism. The recent surge in the tourism industry has attracted significant foreign participation. Table VIII.3 shows the increasing number of tourists arriving in the United Republic of Tanzania. This influx of tourists has induced notable amounts of FDI. From 1990 to 2003, about 16 per cent of the projects aproved by the TIC involved the tourism industry.

The development of the country as a tourism destination offers considerable potential growth prospects and provides many opportunities for investment. New accommodation facilities and hotels are needed with international standards and entertainment facilities, camping, lodges and guesthouses. The Government has taken measures to attract more investments into the sector through promotion of the country's tourism abroad, as well as the provision of investment incentives. It has also streamlined immigration procedures, for example the issuance of short-term visas at major entry points (Bank of Tanzania, 2002).

By the most recent estimates, foreign investors own or partially-own about 30 per cent of hotel accommodation in the United Republic of Tanzania, although the share on the island of Zanzibar alone is rather higher (UNCTAD, forthcoming). This relatively low share of the accommodation total shades the fact that foreign investors are particularly prevalent in the highest quality segments of the market; and in some locations they may be the only investors (e.g. in remote rural areas). A recent high profile privatization included the acquisition and restoration for $35 million of the landmark Kilimanjaro Hotel in Dar es Salaam, now owned

by Albwardy Group of Dubai and managed by Kempinski Hotels (owned by the Thai royal family and Bahrain interests). The same group has invested equally heavily in Zanzibar. The Serena chain of hotels and lodges (Kenya) majority owned by the Aga Khan also stand out as notable foreign investments on Zanzibar island and mainland Tanzania.

Manufacturing for export. There has been very little FDI in manufacturing for export. Karibu Textile Mills, primarily owned by the Mauritius-based company, Nash Holdings, produces textiles for the local and regional markets. Likewise, Friendship Textiles (Urafiki), jointly owned by the Chinese and Tanzanian Governments, produces for a small fraction of the regional market.

(c) FDI in infrastructure and utilities

In electricity, supply shortages have induced the Government to expand power generation. The involvement of foreign companies in this industry has been significant. Independent Power Tanzania Limited (IPTL) is a joint venture between the Malaysian Mechmar Group and a number of Tanzanian investors, with Mechmar owning 70 per cent. Two Canadian companies, TransCanada Pipelines and Ocelot, have built a gas power generation plant to exploit the substantial gas reserves off the coast. In telecommunications in February 2001, the Government sold 35 per cent of its shares of the Tanzania Telecommunications Ltd. (TTCL) to a German-Dutch consortium (Detecon of Germany and MSI of the Netherlands) (table VIII.1), and the cellular phone services industry is dominated by foreign companies.[12]

A government initiative to privatize the port handling facilities has led to renewed participation by foreign investors in this sector. For example, the container handling facility has been transferred under a 10-year lease to a consortium comprising Vertex Financial Services, a domestic firm, and International Container Terminal Services, a Philippines-based company that owns 85 per cent of the venture. Kilimanjaro International Airport is currently operated under a 25-year lease by the Kilimanjaro Airport Development Company Ltd.

Table VIII.3. United Republic of Tanzania: tourist arrivals and receipts, 1996, 2000 and 2004

Item	1996	2000	2004
No. of tourists	326 192	501 669	582 000
Receipts ($ million)	322	739	764

Source: Information from Bureau of Statistics and TIC.

(KADCO), 75 per cent owned by Mott McDonald, a United Kingdom-based company.[13] The Dar es Salaam Airport Handling Company has sold 51 per cent of its shares to Swissport (EIU, 2000b).

Among the non-equity based infrastructural projects, a pioneering build-own-operate project was the opening of the International House building in Dar es Salaam, which is jointly owned by Mitsubishi Corporation, Konoikei Construction, TTCL and Roberts Holding of South Africa.

4. FDI from Asia

The United Kingdom was the leading investor in the United Republic of Tanzania based on the number of projects approved by the TIC.[14] A large number of its investment projects are owned by British Indians, many of whom are former citizens of Tanzania.[15] Investment from developing Asia is limited (table I.5). India is the leading investor country from developing Asia by number of TIC-approved projects, followed by China. A number of Chinese projects are domestic-market-oriented, mainly in alternative medicine and general trading. Malaysia is not among the top 10 by number of projects, but it is if total amount invested were to be considered.[16]

However, investment from Asia is still sparsely spread across the economy. There has been very little Asian investment in mining, the fastest growing sector of the economy. Nevertheless, they are investing significantly in other rapidly growing sectors of the economy, including in manufacturing, infrastructure, banking (box VIII.2) and tourism. Some recent Asian investments include investments by the Bank of Baroda (India) in Tanzania's banking sector in 2003 and by Liming Chemical Industrial Corporation (China) in the chemicals industry in 2004 (annex table 10).

Box VIII.2. Tanzanian operations of the International Bank of Malaysia

The Tanzanian branch of the International Bank of Malaysia was established in 1997 and started operations in 1998. This followed reforms in the host country's financial sector, underpinned by the Banking and Financial Institutions Act of 1991, which, among other things, authorized the establishment of (both foreign and local) private banks. The aim of the bank is to serve the domestic community with a full range of commercial banking services and facilitate trade and business activities between the United Republic of Tanzania and Malaysia.

Most of the staff have been trained locally and had some previous banking experience. Three of them undertook their training in Malaysia. Staff members are provided with a combination of on-the-job training and formal training, mainly to enhance the quality of customer services.

The bank had an asset portfolio of about $1.5 million in 2005. Its services consist of corporate banking, personal banking, international banking etc. International Bank of Malaysia does not lend to the SME sector except through its inter-bank lending operations to the National Microfinance Bank. Since the bank expects the manufacturing sector in the country to grow, it aims to put more emphasis on providing loans to this sector, and particularly to small-scale producers. Accordingly, it plans to open a second branch in Kariakoo, an area of Dar es Salaam that has a large number of small enterprises.

Constraints facing the bank include the low level of private savings in the country, since only a very small percentage of Tanzania's population deposit their money in banks. Another constraint is the absence of accurate information regarding the creditworthiness of potential clients, but this is addressed by the use of elaborate risk-analysis techniques. Another problem is the lack of management and accounting skills of local business people. The bank aims to realize a return on capital of about 10 per cent, but is still short of this target.

Despite these constraints, the bank is optimistic about both its services and performance. It intends to capitalize on its relatively good performance and that of its other branches elsewhere in Africa (Ghana and Guinea and Mozambique). It gained strength following its merger with Multipurpose Bank, another Malaysian bank, in 2000. Sound macro-policies, and the bank's own commitment to significantly increasing its market share, coupled with its well-trained and experienced staff, could justify its optimistic outlook.

Source: UNCTAD, based on the company's website and information provided by the Bank.

The privatization of SOEs has opened up new opportunities in the manufacturing sector of the country. Investments in the former SOEs account for the largest number of projects since 1990, which include participation by investors from China and the Republic of Korea (table VIII.1). More than 50 per cent of TIC-approved projects have been in manufacturing, much of which has been directed at the small domestic market. However, with its 800-km. coastline, three natural harbours – at Dar es Salaam, Mtwara and Tanga – and located on major trading routes, the country could present opportunities for export-led FDI by Asian enterprises. In particular, Asian investors' knowledge of the world market could complement the country's physical and human resource endowments.

5. FDI in SMEs

SMEs are found mainly in the informal sector, but they play a significant role in the economy, accounting for about 57 per cent of wage employment (ILO, 1998). Investment in SMEs is therefore crucial for economic growth. However, SMEs are constrained by limited access to credit and information,[17] and an unsupportive policy framework. For instance, a clear tax regime for them is absent, and very little of their production is certified by the Tanzania Bureau of Standards which signifies that they are unable to enter crucial markets. Moreover, there is no legal framework to facilitate subcontracting, a form of business interaction generally critical to SMES' existence.

SMEs also suffer from an acute shortage of easily accessible, customer-friendly facilities. Typically, they operate from unappealing roadside structures that are not conducive to upgrading. This is particularly constraining for small-scale food processing firms; their lack of hygienic facilities, poor packaging and lack of standardization make it difficult for them to compete with products from Kenya and elsewhere. And owing to a lack of significant forward and backward linkages SMEs in agro-processing do not receive adequate support. Furthermore, they generally lack the resources to market their products widely, rendering their expansion of production for export all the more difficult. Thus a clear opportunity exists for Asian investment to provide complementary resources to support crucial linkages. In addition, an improvement in SMEs' access to information and other resources would enable them to access the global market. Joint ventures with Asian partners are a means for transferring Asian experience with global markets to Tanzanian entrepreneurs in this sector.

B. MARKET OPPORTUNITIES FOR ASIAN FDI

The scope of FDI opportunities is crucially dependent on economic growth and further economic integration throughout the region. Meanwhile, there are a number of distinct markets as well as a number of industries that could be attractive to Asian investors and could be usefully served by FDI, as discussed below.

1. By market

(a) Local markets

The population of the United Republic of Tanzania is about 38 million, with an average annual growth rate of 2 per cent during the period 2000-2005. The average Tanzanian spends more than 70 per cent of his/her income on food alone, and effective demand for manufactured products is very small. The economy will need to grow faster in order to establish a viable domestic market for a range of consumer products.

Liberalization of the economy has decentralized demand for many intermediate goods. In particular, the rapid expansion of the manufacturing sector over the last five years since 2001 has generated greater demand for inputs, such as secure and reliable packaging and labelling, which remains largely unmet. Similarly, the expansion of the mining sector should have increased demand for mining equipment, but the manufacturing sector does not have the capacity to meet this demand beyond supplying picks and axes. In any case, recurrent investment in mining is not expected to be very high (EIU, 2000b).

The most sustainable demand is for services. There is growing demand for infrastructure and other services, especially from businesses. The rapid growth of tourism has increased demand for accommodation and other complementary tourist services. The increasing use of computers has meant a growing demand for information systems support services, particularly for financial services, partly to avoid relatively high labour costs.

(b) Regional markets for exports

The United Republic of Tanzania belongs to several subregional economic groupings and has a number of bilateral arrangements that could help it become a gateway to potentially large regional markets. The Southern African Development Community (SADC) – and its planned customs union – represents the richest subregional market that could be served from the United Republic of Tanzania. In addition, the country is a member of the East African Community (EAC) that also includes Kenya and Uganda. However, access to regional markets is not necessarily a primary reason for investing in the United Republic of Tanzania as the degree of economic integration within these regional groupings is still minimal. Macroeconomic stability and the stable political climate are more important reasons. Nevertheless, a number of infrastructure projects – such as the completion of an inland port at the border with Rwanda and the Mtwara corridor project in the south of the country – should significantly improve links within the region.

The potential presented by a regional market is undeniable. Together, the EAC will bring together about 120 million people (assuming that Burundi and Rwanda are invited into the fold). Likewise, SADC had a total output of $334 billion and a population of 225 million in 2005. Economic growth in both regions over the medium term is likely to be moderate to high. The country's location, long coastline and port facilities, along with a railway network linking East and Southern Africa, make it a natural gateway to the region.

(c) Broader export markets

Given its small domestic economy, the United Republic of Tanzania must endeavour to attract FDI that aims to supply the larger export markets of the United States, Asia and Europe. Demand from these larger markets is likely to be much more stable than that from its African neighbours, and the benefits of serving these markets are much more significant, as indicated by the experiences of the East Asian economies.

The United Republic of Tanzania has a central location in relation to the major global markets (table VIII.4), as reflected in its top 10 export markets. Five of these top 10 export markets are located in Asia, four in Europe and one in North America. Singapore is as far from Dar es Salaam as is London. The bulk of the country's exports are raw materials such as sisal and coffee.

The list of the country's export markets demonstrates that it already has the links to increase trade with Asia (table VIII.5). Furthermore, these links could serve as channels for Asian investment in the country. Although the passage of AGOA has increased trade with the United States, the conditionalities that accompany this Act such as the rules of origin or local content requirements have been designed to discourage trans-shipments from Asia. However, there are already some precedents of Asian production moving to the United Republic of Tanzania to qualify for quotas in European and United States markets. In addition, its membership of the Indian Ocean Rim could help the United Republic of Tanzania improve its links with Asian investors.

2. By industry

Several industries in the United Republic of Tanzania offer profitable opportunities for FDI that could also contribute towards poverty-alleviating growth of the host economy. The discussion below highlights barriers that need to be removed to maximize the potential of FDI in these industries.

Table VIII.4. Distances betweeen selected locations and Dar es Salaam
(Kilometres)

Australia (Canberra)	Brazil (Sao Paulo)	Hong Kong, China (Victoria)	India (Delhi)	Indonesia (Jakarta)	Japan (Tokyo)	Mauritius (Port Louis)	Singapore (Singapore)	United Kingdom (London)	United States (New York)
11 253	9 226	8 707	5 629	7 408	11 326	2 448	7 174	7 443	12 365

Source: Shatz, 2000.

Table VIII.5. United Republic of Tanzania: top 30 export markets, average 1995-2005
(Millions of dollars)

Rank	Economy	Value ($ million)	Share (%)
1	India	94	10.8
2	United Kingdom	83	9.6
3	Japan	62	7.1
4	Germany	53	6.1
5	Netherlands	52	6.0
6	Kenya	36	4.2
7	France	36	4.2
8	China	25	2.9
9	Belgium	25	2.9
10	United States	19	2.2
11	United Arab Emirates	19	2.1
12	Spain	18	2.1
13	South Africa	15	1.8
14	Canada	14	1.6
15	Dem. Rep. of Congo	13	1.5
16	Malawi	13	1.5
17	Zambia	13	1.5
18	Italy	13	1.5
19	Gibraltar	12	1.4
20	Hong Kong, China	12	1.4
21	Thailand	12	1.4
22	Indonesia	12	1.4
23	Portugal	12	1.4
24	Pakistan	12	1.3
25	Rwanda	11	1.3
26	Uganda	11	1.2
27	Malaysia	11	1.2
28	Singapore	10	1.2
29	Burundi	10	1.1
30	Ireland	9	1.1

Memorandum:
	World	864	100.0

Source: IMF, 2006a.

(a) Manufacturing

The manufacturing industries with the greatest potential are those that use the harbour most advantageously. There is also scope for manufacturing of component parts, such as electronics, in Dar es Salaam. To facilitate manufacturing activities and increase profitability, a number of areas require reform; most crucially the labour laws need to be reviewed and labour productivity improved. In addition, import/export bottlenecks should be removed to ensure timely delivery/export of products. Asian experience in the electronics and component parts industry would be a valuable aspect of investments in this sector.

In the long term, the United Republic of Tanzania could emerge as the region's main steel producer. It has all the ingredients for making steel,

with the exception of skilled labour. There would be obvious downstream activities that use steel – from packaging to the manufacture of mining equipment. This would establish important links with the currently isolated mining sector. The Government will need to be aggressive in courting a number of "lead" projects that could act as flagships for investment. Since the EU and the United States accord preferential access to goods from African countries, including the United Republic of Tanzania, through the Generalized System of Preferences (GSP) and AGOA, respectively, they are large potential markets for exports of manufactures from the country.

(b) Fisheries

The fisheries industry is a promising source of foreign exchange, given the country's rich endowment of inland and marine fish. For example, Japan imports the bulk of its prawns from the United Republic of Tanzania largely because they are not treated with any radiation. Lessons from the Asian experience in this market would be useful with a view to capturing the niche eco-market in other developed countries. For instance, the country could learn from Indonesia's experience in seafood exports.

The comparative advantage in unradiated seafood is a potential target for Asian investment. The investment required to maintain hygienic and successful operations is rather prohibitive for local investors, especially given prevailing credit-market conditions. A number of infrastructural improvements would be needed to maintain the sector's competitiveness. In particular, efficient airport handling and storage facilities are crucial. The privatization of cargo handling facilities at Dar es Salaam airport is a positive development in this direction.

(c) Tourism

This industry certainly has the potential to offer tourists higher value products, given the diversity of tourist attractions, such as wildlife viewing, mountain climbing, extensive beaches and the historical spice islands of Zanzibar. Furthermore, the number of tourist arrivals could be increased if competitive services were to be offered for the entire range of holidays. Opportunities for FDI therefore exist for the construction of medium and luxury hotels and associated services. And infrastructure, such as roads and telecommunications, needs to be improved to make this sector one of the vital engines for the country's growth. The leasing of Kilimanjaro International Airport to KADCO, which has majority private ownership, has been crucial to the growth of this sector, as international flights can now fly directly to the northern tourist circuit. However, in order to capitalize on all the tourist attractions available, transport between Dar es Salaam and the southern circuit should be improved. At the same time, the capacity in all classes of accommodation needs to be increased, and the quality of water supply improved.

Asian involvement in this industry could help attract tourists from Asia. There are also possible linkages to SMEs such as those involved in the manufacture of crafts and other souvenir products.[18] Access to market information could be greatly improved by foreign participation in this industry.

(d) Agro-processing

This is the industry with the greatest capacity to contribute to poverty alleviation in the country owing to its intensive use of agricultural inputs. Agriculture accounts for the largest share of employment in the Tanzanian economy. The major segments are:

- *Horticulture.* Europe is the most important market. There is also a growing market in West Asia for mushrooms. Other important markets include India and Kenya.

- *Fruit canning and other fruit products.* These products could take advantage of the prodigious amounts of fruit available that are inevitably wasted in the absence of processing. They involve several vertically linked activities in different sectors and must be able to provide attractive packaging.

- *Hides and skins.* The main markets are Hong Kong (China) and Pakistan and there is potential to export semi-processed hides to luxury goods manufacturers in Europe as well.

- V*egetable oil products.* These products are geared for the domestic market, but could also be exported to the regional market.

There is an urgent need for a strategy to be drawn up for agriculture and agro-processing industries as highlighted by UNCTAD and JBIC

in their *Blue Book* for Tanzania (2005) (see also box VIII.3). Asian firms in agro-processing could play two crucial roles: as channels for the transfer of technology to the SMEs in which they invest, and for the transfer of their knowledge of world markets. In this way, Asian FDI in this sector could help overcome the major impediments to SME growth: lack of credit, technology and information. Inviting Asian investors into this sector requires the exploitation of trade linkages and encouraging importing firms to move some of their value-added activities to the United Republic of Tanzania.

(e) Textiles and garments

The textile industry in the United Republic of Tanzania employed up to 300,000 workers before. But now only a small percentage of workers are still employed in this sector. This source of skilled labour presents opportunities for export-oriented manufacturers of apparel. In addition, the natural harbour at Dar es Salaam provides easy and inexpensive access to the rest of the world. Furthermore, AGOA gives the United Republic of Tanzania preferential access to the large markets of the United States. Although AGOA provisions favour the use of United States fabrics, Asian experience in the apparel industry, together with finance, could help the United Republic of Tanzania exploit this opportunity. In particular, given that Tanzanian exports to South-East Asia are dominated by cotton, the possibility of manufacturing fabrics in the United Republic of Tanzania would help Asian investors supply the United States market.[19] For this industry to blossom, the experience and good reputation enjoyed by Mauritius could be sought. Alternatively, actively seeking out some large foreign apparel outlets as marketing channels is another growth strategy. This would require a good EPZ to match some of the global competitors.

(f) Privately-owned or managed EPZs and industrial parks

Privately operated EPZs or industrial parks are another area in which there is potential for involving foreign investors. In particular, the Asian experience could be harnessed towards developing such facilities. Asian investors could provide the skilled personnel to manage the EPZs as well as the trade and marketing links to make these zones successful. Asian involvement could help attract flagship investments into the EPZs that would further promote FDI. The Government would need to provide serviced land for this purpose and be prepared to expedite EPZ operations. In addition, collaboration between the EPZ management and the TIC could optimize the investment incentives offered. However, it would be important for the TIC to be actively involved in the establishment and management of the EPZs.[20]

C. LOCAL COSTS AND CONDITIONS AFFECTING FDI

In spite of the positive factors outlined above – such as a reasonably stable macroeconomic policy, and political stability for instance – as well as the potential availability of markets discussed in the preceding section, a lot remains to be done to make the economy more attractive to FDI. The discussion below focuses on local costs and conditions related to production that are likely to affect FDI inflows.

1. Local labour markets and labour costs

The provision of adequate universal education was one of the main objectives of the socialist ideology that prevailed in the United Republic of Tanzania prior to the reforms of the mid-1980s. However, this objective could not be achieved owing to a decline in economic performance from the late 1970s. There are only two major universities in the country and a handful of technical schools.

Labour productivity remains low. Most investors consider the cost of labour in the United Republic of Tanzania to be very high (table VIII.6): besides payment of wages, an employer is required to pay fringe benefits. The Government also charges a number of levies on wages.[21] Local governments also charge sometimes a development levy based on the size of the payroll, which can be as much as 6,000 Tanzanian shillings a month per worker. The costs outlined above do not include costs related to worker illness, such as direct medical expenses and provision of generous medical leave. These expenses amounted to about 9 per cent of the total wage bill (USAID, 1997).[22] The tough labour regulations have induced employers to take on temporary and part-time labour to reduce costs.

Managerial resources suffered as a consequence of three decades of socialist rule. The stigma associated with private business induced those with education to go into the public sector.

State enterprises were run under management contracts to firms from around the world, particularly India. As a result, there is a shortage of managerial resources in the country. The situation is serious and many employees at the managerial level come from Kenya.

There was optimism that conditions in the labour markets would improve as attitudes changed in support of the liberalized environment. However, employers need to be allowed more discretion in dealing with their workers (UNCTAD, 2002b). It is common for TNCs to hire Tanzanians trained abroad. Thus there is significant scope for FDI, including Asian FDI, in business education to reduce the skills shortage. In general, FDI that includes a significant amount of in-house training will help alleviate the shortage of management skills.

2. Local financing conditions

The cost of finance in the United Republic of Tanzania is very high. The cost of capital for good borrowers has been quite high as it has had to compensate for the bad loans throughout the

Table VIII.6. Average monthly income of paid employees by occupation, 2000-2001

Occupation	Shillings	Dollars[a]
Legislators, administrators and managers	111 705	140
Professionals	134 261	168
Technicians and associate professionals	79 875	100
Clerks	92 760	116
Service and shop workers	30 835	39
Skilled agriculture and fisheries workers	16 003	20
Craft & related workers	105 494	132
Plant and machine operators and assemblers	55 939	70
Elementary occupations	18 740	23
Total	49 954	62

Source: National Bureau of Statistics, Integrated Labour Force Survey 2000/01 (www.nbs.go.tz).
[a] Converted using the 2000 dollar exchange rate.
Note: Survey was conducted from May 2000 through April 2001 and covers mainland Tanzania only.

banking system. Even the recent entry of a number of foreign banks has not resulted in lower borrowing rates. There are a number of fundamental problems that constrain the proper functioning of the banking system. First, the land laws are still rather unclear and do not guarantee security of ownership.[23] It is therefore difficult to use land as collateral. Second, excessive protection of borrowers prevents banks from seizing collateral in the event of default. Despite the recent establishment of a commercial court, bankers do not feel secure about the law.[24] The reserve ratio is rather high, at 10 per cent, and severely constrains the level of credit in the economy.[25]

Bank lending rates in 2005 ranged from 14 to 24 per cent for ordinary borrowers; large corporate borrowers and blue chip companies can negotiate lower rates. With inflation levels at 6-7 per cent, these borrowing costs represent monumental real costs.[26] Financing is problematic for business operations: a little more than three quarters of companies reported that financing was a major stumbling block to business, according to a survey by the World Economic Forum (2004a). An embryonic stock market is unable to increase the supply of finance, especially since foreign participation in the stock market is not permitted.

The existence of a credit agency to collect information on borrowers and sell this information to banks would reduce selection problems vis-à-vis borrowers. The agency should be able to persuade borrowers to meet their obligations if they plan to use credit markets in the future. However, such an agency is not yet to be established.

There has been an explosion of microfinance institutions over the past few years, but there are no regulations to mediate their operations. Regulations are being drawn up, and with the establishment of National Microfinance Bank in 1997, SMEs' access to capital is expected to improve. Overall regulation of the financial sector is crucial if the economy is to avoid the high costs associated with bank failures.

3. Infrastructure

The state of the infrastructure in the United Republic of Tanzania is rather dismal. The Government has made it a priority sector and has created incentives to improve quality, supply and capacity in this area.

The quality of roads in the country is poor, except for the main feeder roads linking the regional capitals and the capital city. Two major railway lines traverse the country in the north and south. The southern line serves the Zambian copper belt, while the northern line, which is connected to the Lake port at Mwanza, serves the Ugandan market. Increased competition from Durban for Zambia's tonnage, as well as the change in the composition of regional trade following the South African elections in the mid-1990s, has resulted in much less tonnage transported on the 1,860-km. Tanzania-Zambia railway line.

There is a natural harbour at Dar es Salaam and two other ports at Tanga and Mtwara, along with the port at Zanzibar, which increases the country's port handling capacity. The Tanzania Harbours Authority (THA) manages all ports.[27] Dar es Salaam also handles cargo for all its eight landlocked neighbours.

The telecommunications sector in the United Republic of Tanzania is enjoying a boom with a large increase in cellular telephone services. A joint venture between United States and United Kingdom investors – operating under the name of Mobitel – was the first to launch analog mobile telephone services in the country. Since then, Tritel, a joint venture between Malaysian and Tanzanian investors, has started a digital network that now covers much of the coast as well as the areas around Arusha and Mwanza. In 2000, Vodacom, a subsidiary of Vodafone, kicked off another digital service. Although the costs of telephony have not fallen much, the completion rate of calls has increased tremendously. In addition, fixed-line installation delays of up to two years have virtually been eliminated. The newly privatized Tanzania Telecommunications is expanding its operations.

Electric power supply has been improving gradually (table VIII.7). Since hydroelectric power is the primary source, there is substantial variation in electricity supply depending on the rainfall.[28] To overcome this problem, the Government has commissioned a number of projects to supplement hydroelectric power with other sources such as oil and gas. There are substantial gas deposits at Songo-Songo that are being exploited for this purpose. In addition, an oil/gas power plant has been completed by Independent Power Tanzania (IPTL) Ltd. with the capacity to serve up to 15 per cent of Tanzania's electricity needs.

There are two channels for the provision of infrastructure: public and private. The privatization of infrastructure and utilities can induce higher quality services. For instance, following the privatization of water agencies in Arusha and Moshi, dramatic improvements in revenue collection (up to five times more revenue) and service provision have been recorded. The efficiency of Kilimanjaro International Airport and the associated growth in sectors using this airport have been attributed to its better management after its lease to KADCO. Similarly, the telecommunications boom can be partly attributed to private ownership. The second channel for the provision of infrastructure is through public ownership, mainly of projects too large for private firms, or where risks are too high for private owners to assume. In addition, governments usually have access to cheaper credit such as concessional loans or even grants from donors.

Other forms for cheaper and more reliable delivery of infrastructure and utilities include build-operate-transfer (BOT) and build-own-operate-transfer (BOOT) systems that combine private and public participation. IPTL (Independent Power Tanzania) is an example of a BOOT project. However, the dispute between that company and the Government of Tanzania has set an unfavourable precedent for future projects that involve significant Government commitment.[29] It is hoped that the privatization of the National Water Agency that supplies Dar es Salaam might lead to improved water supply services.

The Integrated Road Rehabilitation Programme funded by the EU should improve linkages within the domestic market. The Government should buttress this programme by improving integration with the regional market through rehabilitation and maintenance of

international routes, such as the TAZARA railway and the port services at Dar es Salaam. This would facilitate market- and export-oriented investment. As noted earlier, the leasing of Kilimanjaro International Airport (KIA) has been an important step in the growth of non-traditional sectors such as tourism, and the export of fish products, fruit and flowers.

4. Investment zones

There is an industrial investment zone in Zanzibar, and several zones are planned for the mainland. Although the zone in Zanzibar has a capacity of about 50 warehouse/light-manufacturing facilities, only a few are in use. The National Development Corporation (NDC) is planning a major multimillion-dollar industrial park for small and medium-scale agro- and food-processing in the Kilimanjaro area along the Moshi-Arusha railway. The site of this 230-hectare park has obvious advantages: it is close to the airport[30] and to a major transmission line between Moshi and Arusha; it benefits from clean and regular water supply from the Kikavu River that originates in Mount Kilimanjaro; it is located in Tanzania's agricultural heartland; and its proximity to the major markets of Uganda and Kenya provides easy access to the regional market and to other, larger export markets.

Investment zones in the Dar es Salaam area are being considered despite the difficulty in obtaining suitable industrial land. This has induced the Government to adopt Mauritius-style export processing zone (EPZs) status, where companies are granted rights and incentives as if operating in an EPZ, but without the locational and infrastructural advantages of an EPZ. The Friendship Textile Company is scheduled to be the first such company to benefit from EPZ status.[31]

Another investment zone, the 850-kilometre long Mtwara Corridor, is planned for the southern part of the country, which will stretch from Mtwara on the Indian Ocean to Mbamba in the west. Important features of this zone will include construction of a coal-fired thermal plant that will serve the corridor as well as the mining region of central Tanzania.[32] In addition, the airstrip at Mtwara is scheduled for upgrading into an international airport, which will support agro-processing in the fertile corridor. Rehabilitation and expansion of the port at Mtwara to allow increased tonnage is also on the agenda. Major

Table VIII.7. Electricity: installed capacity and power generated and sold in the mainland of the United Republic of Tanzania, 1992, 1997 and 2002

Year	Capacity (1000 kw/h)			Generated (mill. Kw/h)	Sold (mill. Kw/h)
	Total	Diesel	Hydro		
1992	448	121	328	1 737	1 435
1997	608	229	379	1 894	1 750
2002	619	42	577	2 790	2 076

Source: National Bureau of Statistics.

activities in the corridor will include processing of cashew nuts and other oil crops, as well as mining of iron ore, gold, gemstones, uranium and gas. Tourism is also being promoted to sustain a diverse set of activities.

5. Tanzanian SMEs as potential business partners

There are hardly any well-established SMEs in the United Republic of Tanzania that could serve as potential business partners for foreign investors. This is a consequence of the numerous problems that have plagued SMEs as noted earlier. In particular, the poor infrastructure results in high costs of international business interactions which SMEs can ill afford. Agro-processing is probably the most conducive to creating international linkages through joint ventures. Although recent policy initiatives to encourage such joint ventures have not met with much success so far, it is likely that, along with policies to promote SMEs (see below), a competent class of SME entrepreneurs could emerge to work with foreign investors.

Opportunities abound in the SME sector. However, these must wait until the fundamental problems that plague the sector are removed and a more transparent business culture is established. South-East Asia's experience in successfully integrating SMEs into export-oriented FDI may provide some lessons. The Malaysian example of requiring formal credit institutions to lend at least 2 per cent of their loan portfolio to SMEs is a case in point.

D. POLICY REFORMS AND MEASURES TO ATTRACT FDI

Despite tangible progress since the mid-1990s, the United Republic of Tanzania is still a long way from having a stable and conducive policy environment for FDI. After two decades of socialism, the pace of reforms initiated in the mid-1980s has been slow. A number of the factors that hinder FDI are related to the slow speed with which the country is adjusting. This includes slow changes in attitudes towards work and inadequate recognition by the civil service of the potential contribution of the private sector.

1. Regulatory and administrative barriers to FDI

There are several regulatory and administrative barriers affecting FDI operations, particularly for start-ups. These barriers are not necessarily specific to Asian investors, but they are more difficult for some of these investors to overcome owing to the lack of significant diplomatic representation of their countries in the United Republic of Tanzania. Investors from China and India benefit from good connections maintained by their missions with the Tanzanian authorities and with local residents of similar ethnic origin.

Land acquisition is a particularly significant barrier to FDI flows to the United Republic of Tanzania. No individual or corporate entity can own land. Instead, it is leased out to individuals and firms for 33, 66 or 99 years.[33] Investors can expect further delays in obtaining electricity and water connections and installations for their firms. Overall, the United Republic of Tanzania ranked middle among African countries with respect to the average delays in commencing business (table VIII.8).

The Government is undertaking a rationalization and reform of its land laws to remove uncertainties. The Land Act and the Village Land Act 1999, which came into force in May 2001, both contain provisions to make land available to private sector investors on a leasehold basis with a secure title (UNCTAD, 2002b). In addition, a series of related administrative changes, which are considered especially important for attracting FDI, have been implemented. These and related changes in the administration of land allocation are encouraging, but the system requires further improvements to meet the demands of a growing market economy (UNCTAD, 2002b).

2. Policy reforms

Progress in liberalization and market reform has been substantial recently, but there is certainly room for improvement. Successful reform requires both regulatory reform, to create an enabling environment, and institutional reform. Two initiatives have recently been made with this in mind: the Business Environment Strengthening for Tanzania (BEST) Programme was approved by the Government in 2002 and started in 2004 and the Tanzanian National Business Council (TNBC) was established in 2001 and became operational in 2002. It is important that these initiatives are implemented as planned.

Many of the recommendations that follow have been mentioned elsewhere (e.g. USAID, 1997; Luvanga and Bol, 1999; FIAS, 1999, UNCTAD, 2002b). Crucial issues that need government attention include improving infrastructure and utilities, easing land acquisition and tax regulations, and lowering direct and indirect labour costs.

Table VIII.8. Time required to start a business in selected African countries[a], 2005

Country	Number of days required to start a business
Central African Republic	14
Rwanda	21
Sierra Leone	26
Benin	32
Ethiopia	32
Malawi	35
Niger	35
United Republic of Tanzania	35
Zambia	35
Uganda	36
Cameroon	37
Madagascar	38
South Africa	38
Sudan	38
Ghana	81
Namibia	95

Source: World Bank, 2006.
[a] Ranked in ascending order of the number of days required to start a business.

public utilities. The Asia-Africa Investment and Technology Promotion Centre (AAITPC), which has been established to promote business linkages in the form of investment, trade and technology transfer from Asia to Africa, could help in this respect (UNCTAD, 2002b).

The Government needs to provide well-serviced industrial land to expedite the setting up of production facilities. The tax system needs to be simplified and a number of punitive taxes scrapped. Requirements concerning the filing of tax returns should be drastically reduced,[34] and stamp duties and housing levies done away with to make business more profitable (UNCTAD, 2002b).

A poor infrastructure leads to high production costs. As a consequence, investors tend to concentrate in urban areas, while the majority of Tanzania's rural locations are excluded from the potential benefits of FDI (UNCTAD, 2002b). To improve the infrastructure, an integrated transport strategy in partnership with foreign and other private sector investors is recommended, especially in rural areas (UNCTAD, 2002b).

Privatization is one of the key ways to upgrade Tanzania's utilities and improve competitiveness for future performance. Rapid implementation of privatization is recommended in order to reduce costs and improve services to businesses and consumers (UNCTAD, 2002b). The ongoing privatization of port handling facilities could reduce delays in the import clearing process. The crisis in electricity generation should be resolved as soon as possible to bring regular and cheap power onto the grid. The work of the National Development Corporation, which is responsible for initiating, developing and guiding the implementation of economically viable projects in the country, could be supported by leading business people and its links with the TIC should be strengthened (UNCTAD, 2002b). Moreover, the country could benefit from lessons from East Asian countries that have successfully privatised their

The lack of vocational and technical skills as well as low productivity levels are major problems for the United Republic of Tanzania. The private sector could play an important role in improving employee performance. The Government could develop partnerships with the private sector in order to improve the reach and quality of technical and business education. In addition, firms should be offered incentives to invest in training their workers, which would improve labour productivity; for example, an effective incentive in other countries has been a tax deduction for training expenses (UNCTAD, 2002b).

It is also recommended that private investors be integrated into the decision-making processes for human resource development so that their needs can be reflected in policy-making (UNCTAD, 2002b). Firms should be allowed discretion in designing incentive schemes for their workers – as opposed to the Government dictating all the benefits to which workers are entitled. This will eliminate the tendency to hire temporary and part-time labour and should result in higher labour productivity, since employers could offer more effective incentive schemes for their workers.

The following are additional measures that the Government could consider adopting:

- Take steps to eliminate all the administrative barriers mentioned earlier. Registration requirements for certified charters for companies of foreign origin should be removed. Registration of businesses in general, and SMEs in particular, should be made easier and faster, and nationwide registration facilities established.

- Expedite the issuing of work permits to foreigners by eliminating much of the redundant paperwork required to be submitted to several agencies. In addition, faster screening processes (e.g. by using positive and negative lists detailing skills categories that are scarce or abundant in the country) should be instituted. The cost of business visas should be reduced to allow closer monitoring of domestic operations by TNCs.

- In the area of finance and financial institutions, the Government should ensure that the regulatory framework for microfinance institutions would make finance more readily accessible to SMEs. In addition, the concerns of bankers regarding foreclosure procedures need to be addressed. In this respect, the relevant court should be adequately staffed and funded to expedite resolutions. A credit bureau or agency should be established to eliminate over-reliance on retained earnings by potentially good borrowers. Monitoring of financial institutions needs to be strengthened to reduce the likelihood of financial crises. In particular, there should be rigorous adherence to start-up requirements for banking institutions.

- Regarding regional arrangements, the Government should clarify the relationship of the United Republic of Tanzania with a number of regional groupings with which it has links. The process of integration into the East African Common Market should be pursued, as this represents a more natural integration and one more likely to induce market-led FDI.[35] Integration with other East African nations does not preclude the benefits of SADC membership.

- Finally, the Government should continue to strengthen the TIC, both by increasing the clout of the agency and by enhancing the quality of its staff through professional training programmes. Legal conflicts between the TIC and the TRA (Tanzania Revenue Authority) should be quickly resolved to reduce the delays that investors face when dealing with the TRA.[36] The Tanzania National Business Council and the National Investment Steering Committee could work towards a solution to these problems. Efforts must be made towards ensuring the efficient and effective functioning of such institutions so that consistency and coordination between policies is ensured (UNCTAD, 2002b). The TIC should move away from project screening and evaluation to investment promotion (FIAS, 1999).

Since such reforms would require a long period of continuous and systematic effort, in the short term the United Republic of Tanzania could benefit from applying the Multi-Facility Economic Zone concept (UNCTAD, 2002b). Its aim is to provide excellent business conditions within a limited geographical area, including the establishment of best practice rules and laws for investors, good infrastructure and efficient administration.

The *Blue Book* for Tanzania prepared by UNCTAD and the Japan Bank for International Cooperation (UNCTAD and JBIC, 2005) has proposed eight concrete measures to be implemented by the Government at minimal costs within a 12-month time-frame. These include, among others, transparency in the tax regime and the conclusion of an East African Community double taxation treaty (box VIII.3).

3. Special measures for SMEs

Perhaps the most critical problem facing SMEs is the lack of access to credit. To address this issue, the Government has sought to provide dedicated credit channels for this sector. The National Micro-Finance Bank is responsible for providing credit to SMEs through its countrywide network. Given the informal nature of much SME activity, it will be necessary to elaborate systems encouraging SMEs to develop a record-keeping culture that should make access to credit and joint ventures with foreign investors much easier.

SMEs should also have better access to information on technology and markets. In general, they are not able to meet the costs involved in exploiting existing market opportunities. A number of business associations – such as the Centre for International Business Development Services – have been established with this objective. At present, the donor community is funding these associations. However, the private sector, particularly the SME sector, should participate in funding them through membership fees in order to avoid interruption of services when donor funding decreases or even stops. They should also be given enough institutional support by the Ministry of Industry and Trade so that information about export opportunities can be widely disseminated throughout the country.

SMEs face strong competition from imported products, and high costs stemming from standards verification procedures. In addition to being expensive for SMEs, testing by the Tanzania Bureau of Standards is random. This makes it difficult for such enterprises to plan with their limited resources. One result has been a withdrawal of some SMEs from submission to testing, resulting in poorer product quality. The Bureau should adopt a more accommodating approach with these firms, encouraging them to maintain competitive standards at a lower cost.

A legal framework currently being drafted will facilitate the entry of SMEs into the formal sector. Adequate provisions for subcontracting are critical to encourage linkages throughout the economy and to serve as channels for technology transfer. In addition, legislation should provide SMEs with protection against discretionary measures of various government agencies, such as the TRA and the Bureau of Standards, and tax incentives for this sector should be clearly specified. In this regard, the Government could learn from the policies of some of the ASEAN countries that seek to induce linkages between TNCs and SMEs (Chapter II).

4. Encouraging Asian FDI in and by SMEs

Asian investment in SMEs could help address their financial constraints. It could also serve as a channel for the transfer of appropriate technologies. Asian investors in SMEs should endeavour to form joint ventures with domestic investors who understand domestic conditions better and can ably navigate the bureaucratic red tape. An analysis of the projects reviewed by the TIC suggests that since 1990 joint ventures have accounted for more than a third of all registered projects. The United Nations Industrial Development Organization (UNIDO) is coordinating joint ventures between Asian investors and investors in the United Republic of Tanzania through the TIC and Asia Africa Investment and Technology Promotion Centre (AAITPC). It provides software and collects information that can help match potential partners for joint ventures. In selecting entrepreneurs, UNIDO ensures they meet acceptable reporting standards. This is likely to leave out the majority of SMEs, but it is nevertheless an important step in cultivating business relations between Asia and the United Republic of Tanzania, including those involving SMEs.

The Indian Ocean Rim Initiative – of which India, Indonesia, Malaysia, Mauritius, South Africa and the United Republic of Tanzania are prominent members – has a low profile at present, but could become an avenue for investment promotion (chapter I).

Box VIII.3. The Blue Book eight-point action plan

Measure 1. Improve the capacity of administrative support to commercial courts.

Measure 2. Develop performance charters for executive agencies that administer business regulations and inspections.

Measure 3. Enhance transparency in tax administration.

Measure 4. Establish a strategy for the growth of agriculture and agro-processing in Tanzania.

Measure 5. Strengthen the monitoring system for tracking measures agreed upon by the Tanzania National Business Council (TNBC).

Measure 6. Amend the Tax Revenue Appeals Act, 2000.

Measure 7. Bring into force the East African Community double taxation treaty.

Measure 8. Jointly issue East African Community member State business visas.

Source: UNCTAD and JBIC, 2005.

Organizations such as the Commonwealth Development Corporation and the International Finance Corporation could serve as additional channels for promoting Asian FDI. These organizations have acquired specialized knowledge of the economy and have the political clout to ensure sufficient investor protection against Government expropriation or harassment. These and other organizations such as the Norwegian Agency for Development Cooperation have been pivotal in the privatization exercises of a number of African countries, including the United Republic of Tanzania.

E.   CONCLUSIONS

The United Republic of Tanzania has potential for increased FDI in general and Asian FDI in particular. It will need capital inflows to help finance its savings-investment gap, as domestic resources alone will not suffice. It is crucial that some of these inflows take the form of investment in SMEs, which are the typical locus of enterprise in an economy. The Government will need to take a number of steps to create and maintain favourable conditions for FDI. A careful selection of sectors to be supported over the long term and proper management of the country's image abroad would be needed to complement the short-term solutions which have been outlined above.

Notes

1. By some measures of ethnic diversity, the United Republic of Tanzania is the most diverse country in the world (e.g. see Easterly and Levine, 1997).
2. There are a number of assumptions used in these simulations, such as the size of the current-account deficit and the extent to which it is financed externally (UNCTAD, 2000a).
3. Estimating inflows is fraught with difficulty. The FDI series is based on ad hoc assumptions about the share of investments committed in a particular year. The Bank of Tanzania (BOT), in conjunction with the Tanzania Investment Centre (TIC), is currently involved in an exercise to increase the accuracy of year-on-year FDI inflows through direct survey methods.
4. There has also been audible opposition by a number of opposition politicians to the increasing prominence of South African businesses in the United Republic of Tanzania.
5. The controls take the form of withholding taxes on dividends, interest and proceeds from the sale of assets.
6. The Public Sector Reform Commission (PSRC) bill was passed in 1992 and implemented the following year.
7. According to a United States Department of State note on Tanzania ("2005 Investment Climate Statement: Tanzania", at http://www.state.gov/e/eb/ifd/2005/42185.htm), currently the CMSA (Capital Markets and Securities Authority) has opened the Dar es Salaam stock exchange to foreigners.
8. The IFC holds a 9 per cent stake in Tanzania Breweries as well as a significant stake in Eurafrican Bank.
9. The CDC has played a prominent role in privatization in the United Republic of Tanzania, and has a number of equity positions in newly privatized enterprises such as the Usambara Tea Company and the Mbeya Cement Company.
10. Japan Tobacco International now owns a 75-per-cent stake in TCC.
11. Acquired by Barclays Bank of the United Kingdom in 2005.
12. Vodacom (a subsidiary of Vodafone-Airtouch); Tritel, a joint venture between Technology Resources Industries of Malaysia (70 per cent) and a consortium of Tanzanian investors; and Mobitel (owned by Millicom, a European-United States consortium), the only analog-based mobile phone company. Another United States company, ACG Telesystems is one of the major providers of pay-phone services.
13. The lease was signed in 1998. KADCO is also held 24 per cent by the Tanzanian Government, and 1 per cent by Interconsult, a local firm. The improved services it provides have contributed to a rapidly expanding tourism sector as well as a flourishing fish and flower export sector.
14. The TIC has been unable to follow up on approved projects diligently enough to establish a comprehensive list of investments.
15. Following the nationalizations of the early 1970s, a large number of Tanzanian Indians left the country and settled in Canada and the United Kingdom, and many Canadian projects in the United Republic of Tanzania are owned by ethnic Indians with similar ties as those from the United Kingdom.
16. Malaysia's investments in the United Republic of Tanzania are largely a consequence of Prime Minister Mahathir's personal relationship with the former Tanzanian leader, Julius Nyerere. However, it is not clear whether and how the Malaysian Government is subsidizing these investments.
17. The Government is taking significant steps to start lending to this sector through the newly formed National Microfinance Bank (NMFB).
18. There is evidence of collaboration between handicraft traders/manufacturers and some big hotels in Dar es Salaam.
19. Cotton accounted for 70-90 per cent of Tanzanian exports to Indonesia, Malaysia, Taiwan Province of China and Thailand during the period 2003-2005 (United Nations Comtrade database).
20. At present, the National Development Corporation is responsible for establishing and managing EPZs and industrial parks in the country.
21. For example, there are payroll levy (4 per cent of the gross wage bill); vocational and educational training authority levy (2 per cent of the gross wage bill); and National Provident Fund (10 per cent of the gross wage bill).
22. At one of the Asian firms visited during the study, the employer also pays the medical costs for employees' families.
23. All land in the United Republic of Tanzania belongs to the State, but can be leased to private individuals and concerns.
24. An Industrial Court was opened in November 1999.
25. The Bank of Tanzania, however, views the ratio as reasonable, given that several banks had collapsed, at high costs to the Government. For example, the collapse of the Meridian Bank (the Tanzanian affiliate of Meridian Bank BIAO and the first private bank in the country) in the mid-1990s cost the Government $120 million (EIU, 1999). The bank was acquired soon after (in 1995) by Standard Bank Group of South Africa and became Stanbic Bank Tanzania.
26. The few microfinance institutions that are in operation are charging at least 30 per cent to meet their costs. The base costs for these institutions are affected by prevailing conditions in the formal credit market.
27. Following the lifting of sanctions on South Africa and that country's resumption of international trade, the THA initiated a $24 million modernization programme in an attempt to stem the loss of Zambian tonnage to the Durban line. New machinery was installed in the port at Dar es Salaam, reducing loading and unloading times significantly. In addition, the container terminal was brought under the management of Tanzania International Container Terminal Services (TICTS), a consortium between the Philippines-based ICTS and Vertex Financial Services of Tanzania. Several other port-handling facilities are in the process of being privatized to increase efficiency.
28. Further losses arise during the transmission of electricity that are not captured in the figures in table VIII.7. At present, the Government is committed to privatizing electric power generation, while leaving distribution to the Tanzania Electrical Supply Co. (Tanesco).

[29] The verdict of ICSID on the dispute between Tanesco and IPTL went somewhat in favour of Tanesco. The ICSID ruled that the project costs had been inflated by $30 million. The tribunal ordered that once the appropriate figures to be fed into the model had been ascertained and the calculations for the initial reference tariff completed, IPTL could take the necessary steps to start commercial operations.

[30] KIA has the capacity to receive large cargo and passenger planes, and also has night-landing facilities.

[31] Urafiki Textiles (Friendship Textiles) has mainly been serving the domestic market, with only about 5 per cent of its production going to the regional market. EPZ status is likely to change this dramatically.

[32] The United Republic of Tanzania is endowed with about 300 metric tonnes of proven coal reserves. The Mchuchuma Katewaka Coalfield alone contains about 159 metric tonnes of proven reserves of very high thermal quality coal.

[33] Getting a lease usually takes time. Even in Dar es Salaam, where there is significant land in industrial zones, land acquisition requires negotiation with leaseholders (usually villagers), which adds further delays of another 4–6 months. The situation is worse in other parts of the country, where the councils responsible for issuing Certificates of Occupancy (CO) meet only once or twice a year. And after obtaining a CO, an investor is required to obtain a building permit before construction can commence.

[34] For instance, payroll forms that must be filed every month – irrespective of whether there have been changes in status – should be replaced with a system of annual filing and adjustments.

[35] The Tanzanian Government has understandable concerns relating to significant revenue losses that would result from any eventual elimination of import tariffs (since more than 30 per cent of its revenue comes from import duties), particularly with Kenya. The Government is not confident that it can effectively enforce rules-of-origin requirements that would protect revenues from import duty.

[36] A short-term resolution mechanism is being managed through a steering committee.

CONCLUSIONS

Asian FDI to Africa is likely to continue to grow in view of the complementary nature of economic development between Asian and African countries. Till recently, overall economic conditions in Africa have been less than favourable for FDI, as the region experienced slow growth of GDP per capita, and even stagnation or contraction in many sub-Saharan African countries in the past two decades. However, many African countries have restored and maintained macroeconomic stability and improved the general climate and regulatory framework for FDI inflows. The continent is becoming a large potential market as well as an important investment location for foreign enterprises in general and Asian companies in particular. However, since only a few African countries have sizeable domestic markets, market-seeking FDI is still constrained by market size. This constraint could be overcome by effectively enlarging the market through effective regional economic integration, as the ASEAN experience shows.

The rapid economic growth in Asia can be expected to lead to increased Asian investments in Africa, in both natural resources and manufacturing. In particular, the rapid industrial upgrading taking place in Asia provides ample opportunities for Africa to attract efficiency-seeking and export-oriented FDI from Asian economies. For export-oriented manufacturing, Africa, in particular African LDCs, enjoys the advantages of preferential market access to the large markets of the China, the EU, Japan and the United States. These international trade arrangements have also helped attract FDI from Asian countries, especially in labour-intensive industries such as textile and garments. In the long run, preferential access will have to be buttressed by cost competitiveness, which depends not only on abundant low-wage labour, but also on the availability of industrial skills and infrastructure. The Asian experience demonstrates that governments' strategic investment in education and infrastructure is crucial for promoting economic development in general and attracting efficiency-seeking FDI in particular. To become attractive locations for FDI, African countries have to improve their overall investment climate in addition to offering profitable investment opportunities.

In the near future, FDI flows from high-income developing countries to low-income ones, in particular those from Asia to Africa, are likely to become an important facet of economic cooperation among developing countries. Indeed, promoting investment in Africa has become a strategic priority for international economic cooperation in some Asian countries, including some ASEAN countries (e.g. Malaysia) and China.

Appropriate policies at both national and international levels are crucial for addressing various challenges and turning the potential into reality. The main drivers of FDI location are changing. The traditional factors – large national markets, natural resources and access to labour – remain relevant, but other factors are gaining in importance, particularly for FDI in the most dynamic industries. Location decisions are based more and more on competitive advantages – as opposed to comparative advantages related to factor endowments – and on the ability of host countries to provide specialized skills, infrastructure, suppliers and institutions to use technologies efficiently and flexibly. Domestic capabilities have also become increasingly important determinants for attracting FDI. The country case analyses in chapters IV to VIII suggest that unless appropriate policy measures are put in place, it will be difficult for Africa to attract Asian FDI and to benefit from the dynamism of the Asian corporate sector.

Simply opening up an economy to foreign investors and targeting Asian ones is not enough. To cope successfully with globalization and benefit from the increased flows of Asian FDI, Africa will need to combine its locational advantages with what have been called first and second generation investment promotion policies. Under the first generation policies, countries adopt market-friendly policies and liberalize their FDI regimes by reducing barriers to inward FDI, strengthening standards of treatment for foreign investors and giving a greater role to market forces in resource allocation. In the second generation of investment promotion policies, governments go a step further and actively seek to attract FDI by marketing their economies and eventually setting up national investment promotion agencies (UNCTAD, 2001b). The third generation of investment promotion policies implies a proactive approach towards FDI promotion, and explicitly looks for ways to increase its benefits in terms of technology, skills and market access. Under these types of policies, foreign investors are targeted at the industry/firm level in order to meet a country's specific needs that fit in with its developmental priorities. African countries will also need to make substantial efforts to enhance their productive capacity in particular industrial areas and related competitive advantages, thereby addressing one of the basic economic determinants of FDI. This requires investment promotion agencies to develop greater expertise and flexibility, rather than a sector-neutral and passive policy stance.

This is not to suggest that this type of investment policy is suitable for all African economies. Each economy has to consider its specific economic and industrial context when formulating its FDI policies and programmes. It will also be necessary to take account of an economy's circumstances (e.g. its relative endowments, potential and prospects) in comparative perspective. An appropriate investment policy will require selective interventions as well as effective coordination among firms, clusters and factor markets, which should presumably be consistent with a clear and coherent "vision" of future development and with the strategies for achieving policy goals. For this purpose, many useful lessons can be drawn from the experiences of some Asian economies.

In the new global economic context, many investment policy instruments of the past are no longer viable or feasible options today, including some that were used successfully in different circumstances in East Asia. However, some Asian strategies remain valid and appropriate for stimulating economic growth and promoting structural change in order to catch up. For example, the Asian experience has shown that rapid industrialization is very important for long-term economic development, and foreign investment can play an important role in promoting early industrialization. It also demonstrates the importance of shifting and diversifying from natural resources to manufacturing and other more sophisticated activities characterized by high value-added and growth potential. An important objective of the investment policies in African countries where FDI is concentrated in natural resources should be to diversify investment into other sectors. African governments should give strategic emphasis to manufacturing activities. Currently, the focus could be on labour-intensive and resource-based processing, as well as export-oriented production in relatively low-technology manufacturing.

While international competition for FDI constrains investment policy options, targeted industrial promotion measures are needed to attract manufacturing projects and enhance local skills and capabilities. These measures include one-stop facilitation of administrative applications and approvals, the provision of specialized customs-related infrastructure, the facilitation of labour procurement and skills development and other services relating to investors' routine operations.

FDI alone cannot ensure the development of capabilities. In the context of Asian FDI in Africa, it is important to pay special attention to the amount and quality of backward linkages between foreign affiliates of TNCs and domestic firms. They could constitute an important channel for passing intangible and tangible assets from the former to the latter, including the diffusion of valuable knowledge. They can therefore be of particular significance for host countries in Africa and could help increase the competitiveness of the domestic enterprise sector. African Governments could act as catalysts by encouraging linkages through various measures aimed at bringing domestic suppliers and Asian foreign affiliates together and strengthening spillovers in the areas of information, technology and training. They could establish a specific linkage promotion programme combining these measures.

SMEs have been important participants in the rapid increase in FDI outflows since the mid-1980s. Asian SMEs have become an important source of FDI and may also have potential in Africa. Their contributions to host African developing countries are quite distinct from those of large TNCs. First, their technology tends to be more suited to the smaller-scale operations that are more appropriate for many developing countries. Second, foreign affiliates of SMEs in host developing countries have higher labour intensities compared to large TNCs, and are therefore better suited to many African countries. Third, SMEs have a greater tendency to establish joint ventures with local firms and to transfer technology to local partners, including other SMEs. Fourth, their greater export orientation should have a more positive impact on the balance of payments of the host countries.

The potential of SMEs should be better reflected in the economic policies of both host African and home Asian countries. African host countries, by establishing an enabling framework for investment in general, and for smaller investors in particular, could help attract FDI to their countries by Asian SMEs. This could include, among others, easing regulations on minimum FDI entry procedures and tax and other investment incentives for SMEs. For Asian countries, appropriate investment policies to promote domestic industrial restructuring and the internationalization of SME could well serve to enhance economic development. Some programmes and mechanisms include promoting interest in international business cooperation, providing needed information, assisting at the pre-project stage, helping in the selection of partners, helping reduce the costs of technology transfer and providing SMEs with better access to financial resources.

REFERENCES

Amsden, A.H. (1989). *Asia's Next Giant: South Korea and Late Industrialization* (New York: Oxford University Press).

Artadi, Elsa V. and Sala-i-Martin, Xavier (2004). "The economic tragedy of the twentieth century: growth in Africa", in World Economic Forum, *The Africa Competitiveness Report 2004* (Geneva: WEF).

ASEAN Secretariat (2005). *Statistics of Foreign Direct Investment in ASEAN: Seventh Edition* (Jakarta: ASEAN Secretariat).

Bank of Botswana (2000). *Annual Report 1999* (Gaborone: Government Printer).

Bank of Tanzania (2002). *Economic and Operations Report, for the year ended June, 2002* (Dar es Salaam: Bank of Tanzania).

_____ (2006). "Tanzania: economic and financial indicators, data for 1998-2005"(Dar es Salaam: Bank of Tanzania), August, www.bot-tz.org.

Banque Centrale de Madagascar (2005). *Investissements Directs Etrangers et de Portefeuille à Madagascar, Années 2002-2004*, May (Madagascar: Institut National de la Statistique).

Botswana Institute for Development Policy Analysis (BIDPA) (2000). *Financial Assistance Policy: Fourth Revaluation* (Gaborone: BIDPA).

Botswana, Ministry of Commerce and Industry (1998). "Industrial development policy for Botswana", *Government Paper No. 1 of 1998* (Gaborone: Government Printer).

_____ (1999). "Policy of small, medium and micro enterprises in Botswana", *Government Paper No. 1 of 1999* (Gaborone: Government Printer).

Chia, Siow Yue (1999). "Trade, foreign direct investment and economic development of Southeast Asia", *The Pacific Review*, 12 (2): 249-270.

China, Ministry of Commerce (MOFCOM) (2006). *China Foreign Investment Report 2006* (Beijing: MOFCOM).

Easterly, William and Ross Levine (1997). "Africa's growth tragedy: policies and ethnic divisions", *The Quarterly Journal of Economics*, vol.112 (4), pp. 1203-50, November.

Economist Intelligence Unit (various editions). *Ghana Country Report* (London: EIU).

Economist Intelligence Unit (EIU) (1999). *Tanzania Country Reports, 1999-2000* (London: EIU).

_____ (2000a). *Madagascar Country Profile 1999-2000* (London: EIU).

_____ (2000b). *Tanzania Country Profile 2000* (London: EIU).

Foreign Investment Advisory Service (FIAS) (1996). *Mozambique, Administrative Barriers to Investment: The Red Tape Analysis* (Washington, D.C.: FIAS, International Finance Corporation).

_____ (1999). *Transforming the Tanzania Investment Centre into a Service-oriented Investment Promotion Agency* (Dar es Salaam: Foreign Investment Advisory Service).

Fujita, Masataka (1998). *The Transnational Activities of Small and Medium-sized Enterprises* (Boston, Dordrecht and London: Kluwer Academic Publishers).

Heritage Foundation (2005). *2005 Index of Economic Freedom*, http://index.heritage.org/.

International Labour Organisation (ILO) (1998). *National Workshop on Micro and Small Enterprise Research in Tanzania* (Geneva: International Labour Organization/Netherlands Development Assistance).

_____ (2005). *Yearbook of Labour Statistics 2005* (Geneva: ILO).

International Monetary Fund (IMF) (2003). *Madagascar: Selected Issues and Statistical Appendix, Country Report*, No. 03/7, January (Washington D.C.: IMF).

_____ (2005a). *Direction of Trade Statistics Yearbook 2005* (Washington D.C.: IMF).

_____ (2005b). *Madagascar: Selected Issues and Statistical Appendix, Country Report, No. 05/321, September* (Washington D.C.: IMF).

_____ (2006a). *Direction of Trade Statistics*, July (Washington, D.C.: IMF).

_____ (2006b). *World Economic Outlook*, April (Washington, D.C.: IMF).

Johnson, C. (1982). *MITI and the Japanese Miracle: The Growth of Industrial Policy, 1925-1975* (Stanford: Stanford University Press).

Liang, Guoyong (2004). *New Competition: Foreign Direct Investment and Industrial Development in China*, ERIM Ph.D. Series, Research in Management, 47 (Rotterdam: RSM, Erasmus University.)

Luvanga, N. and D. Bol (1999). "The impact of Tanzania's trade and exchange regime on exports", Research Report, Tanzania Project (Cambridge: Harvard Institute of International Development).

Malaysia, Ministry of International Trade and Industry (1996). *The Second Industrial Master Plan 1996-2005* (Kuala Lumpur: MITI).

_____ (2006). *The Third Industrial Master Plan 2006-2020* (Kuala Lumpur: MITI).

Mirza, Hafiz (1986). *Multinationals and the Growth of the Singapore Economy* (Croom Helm: London).

Mirza, Hafiz and Axele Giroud (2004). "Regional integration and benefits from foreign direct investment in ASEAN economies: the case of Vietnam", *Asian Development Review*, Vol 21, No 4.

Mwale, Sam M. (1997). "Africa transport technical note No. 8", Policy Research Group, Nairobi, May.

NORAD (1995). *Norwegian Companies and the Developing World* (Oslo: NORAD).

SADC (2000). "Official SADC trade, industry and investment review. The millennium issue", Southern African Marketing Co. (Pty) Ltd. in association with Southern African Development Community.

Salm, Andy, William Grant, John Haycock and Kirsten Kennedy (2004). "Botswana textile and apparel sub-sector study", Commark Trust (www.commark.org).

Shatz, Howard Jerome (2000). "The location of US multinational affiliates", PhD Thesis, Kennedy School of Government and Public Policy (Cambridge: Harvard University).

Teal, Francis (1999). "Why can Mauritius export manufactures and Ghana not?", CSAE Working Paper WPS/99-10, Oxford CSAE, March, http://www.economics.ox.ac.uk/CSAEadmin/workingpapers/pdfs/9910text.pdf.

TIC (1998). *The Investor's Guide to Tanzania* (Dar es Salaam: Tanzania Investment Centre).

UNCTAD (1995). *Foreign Direct Investment in Africa* (Geneva and New York: United Nations), United Nations publication, Sales No. E.95.II.A.6.

_____ (1996). *Incentives and Foreign Direct Investment: A Global Survey* (New York and Geneva: United Nations), United Nations publications, Sales No. E.96.II.A.6.

_____ (1997). *Sharing Asia's Dynamism: Asian Direct Investment in the European Union* (New York and Geneva: United Nations), United Nations publication, Sales No. E.97.II.D.1.

_____ (1998). *Handbook on Foreign Investment by Small and Medium-sized Enterprises* (New York and Geneva: United Nations), United Nations publications, Sales No. E.98.II.D.4.

_____ (1999a). *World Investment Report 1999: Foreign Direct Investment and the Challenge of Development* (New York and Geneva: United Nations), United Nations publications, Sales No. E.99.II.D.10.

_____ (1999b). *Foreign Direct Investment in Africa: Performance and Potential* (New York and Geneva: United Nations), United Nations publications, UNCTAD/ITE/IIT/Misc. 15.

_____ (2000a). *Capital Flows and Growth in Africa* (New York and Geneva: United Nations), United Nations publications, No. TD/B/47/4.

_____ (2000b). *World Investment Report 2000: Cross-border Mergers and Acquisitions and Development* (New York and Geneva: United Nations), United Nations publications, Sales No. E.00.II.D.20.

_____ (2001a). *An Investment Guide to Mozambique* (New York and Geneva: United Nations), United Nations publications, No. UNCTAD/ITE/IIA/4.

_____ (2001b). *World Investment Report 2001: Promoting Linkages* (New York and Geneva: United Nations), United Nations publications, Sales No. E.01.II.D.12.

_____ (2002a). *Investment Policy Review: Ghana* (New York and Geneva: United Nations), United Nations publications, Sales No. E.02.D.20.

_____ (2002b). *Investment Policy Review, Tanzania* (New York and Geneva: United Nations), United Nations publications, Sales No. E.02.II.D6.

_____ (2002c). *National Corporations and Export Competitiveness* (New York and Geneva: United Nations), United Nations publications, Sales No. E.02.II.D.4.

_____ (2003). *Investment Policy Review, Botswana* (New York and Geneva: United Nations), United Nations publications, Sales No. E.03.II.D.I).

_____ (2004). *World Investment Report 2004: The Shift Towards Services* (New York and Geneva: United Nations), United Nations publications, Sales No. E.04.II.D.33.

_____ (2005). *World Investment Report 2005: Transnational Corporations and the Internationalization of R&D* (New York and Geneva: United Nations), United Nations publications, Sales No. E.05.II.D.10.

_____ (2006). *World Investment Report 2006: FDI from Developing and Transition Economies: Implications for development* (New York and Geneva: United Nations), United Nations publications, Sales No. E.06.II.D.11.

_____ (forthcoming). "FDI in tourism: the development dimension", United Nations publication, mimeo.

UNCTAD and Japan Bank for International Corporation (JBIC) (2005). "Blue Book on Best Practice in Investment Promotion and Facilitation: Tanzania", Mimeo.

_____ (2006). "Blue Book on Best Practice in Investment Promotion and Facilitation for Ghana", United Nations publication, mimeo.

United States Agency for International Development (USAID) (1997). *The Investor Roadmap of Tanzania*, the Services Group prepared for USAID Tanzania, Dar es Salaam.

United States, Department of State (1999). *FY 2000 Country Commercial Guide: Ghana,* http://www.state.gov/www/about_state/business/com_guides/2000/africa/ghana_CCG2000.pdf.

_____ (2000). *FY 2001 Country Commercial Guide: Madagascar*, http://www.state.gov/www/about_state/business/com_guides/2001/africa/madagascar_ccg2001.pdf.

_____ (2004). *Country Commercial Guide: Madagascar*, http://www.state.gov.

_____ (2006). *FY 2006 Country Commercial Guide: Ghana*, http://www.state.gov.

Wade, R. (1990). *Governing the Market: Economic Theory and the Role of Government in East Asian Industrialization* (Princeton: Princeton University Press).

Wells, Louis T. and Timothy S. Buehrer (2000). "Cutting red tape: lessons from a case-based approach to improve the investment climate in Mozambique", Mimeo, Harvard University.

World Bank (1993). *The East Asian Miracle: Economic Growth and Public Policy* (New York: Oxford University Press).

_____ (2001). "International competitiveness opportunities and challenges facing non-traditional exports in Ghana", Draft Report, Mimeo.

_____ (2004). *Pattern of Africa-Asia Trade and Investment: Potential for Ownership and Partnership* (Washington, D.C.: World Bank).

_____ (2006). *World Development Indicators* (Washington, D.C.: World Bank).

World Bank, Ministry of Industry, Commerce and Tourism, Department for International Development-UK, United States Agency for International Development (1998). *4th Private Sector Conference, Mozambique*, August-September.

_____ (1999). *5th Private Sector Conference, Mozambique*, August-September.

World Economic Forum (2001). *Africa Competitiveness Report 2000* (Geneva: WEF).

_____ (2004a). *Africa Competitiveness Report 2004* (Geneva: WEF).

_____ (2004b). *Global Competitiveness Report 2004* (Geneva: WEF).

_____ (2005). *Global Competitiveness Report 2005* (Geneva: WEF).

_____ (2006). *Global Competitiveness Report 2006/2007* (Geneva: WEF).

Yao, Yang and Yin He (2005). "Chinese outward investing firms: A Study for FIAS/IFC/MIGA" (Beijing: China Center for Economic Research), Peking University, mimeo.

Zainal, Aznam Yusof (2005). "Outward foreign direct investment by Malaysian enterprises", paper prepared for the UNCTAD Expert Meeting on Enhancing the Productive Capacity of Developing Country Firms through Internationalization, Geneva 5-7, December.

ANNEXES

Annex table 1. Cross-border M&A deals by Asian firms concluded in Africa, 1987-2005

Year	Value (million dollars)	Acquiring company	Industry of the acquiring company	Home economy	Acquired company	Host economy	Industry of the acquired company
2003	1 766.3	PETRONAS	Crude petroleum and natural gas	Malaysia	Egyptian LNG	Egypt	Natural gas liquids
2003	767.8	ONGC	Crude petroleum and natural gas	India	Greater Nile Petroleum	Sudan	Crude petroleum and natural gas
1998	452.1	Petroliam Nasional Bhd	Crude petroleum and natural gas	Malaysia	Engen Ltd	South Africa	Crude petroleum and natural gas
1996	273.3	Petroliam Nasional Bhd	Crude petroleum and natural gas	Malaysia	Engen Ltd	South Africa	Crude petroleum and natural gas
1997	110.4	Shum Yip Investments Ltd	Investors, nec	Hong Kong, China	Goldfields Industrial Corp Ltd	South Africa	Mining machinery and equipment, except oil and gas
2004	102.0	ONGC Videsh Ltd	Crude petroleum and natural gas	India	Block 5A	Sudan	Crude petroleum and natural gas
1999	101.0	Arab Banking Corp (Singapore)	Banks	Singapore	Egyptian Arab African Bank	Egypt	Banks
2005	75.2	Maxis Communications Bhd	Telephone communications, except radiotelephone	Malaysia	Global Commun Svcs Hldgs Ltd	Mauritius	Investors, nec
1996	58.4	Investor Group	Investors, nec	Brunei Darussalam	Cia Agricole et Industrielle	Madagascar	Life insurance
1996	50.0	Telekom Malaysia Bhd	Telephone communications, except radiotelephone	Malaysia	Sotelgui(Guinea)	Guinea	Radiotelephone communications
1997	38.0	Investor Group	Investors, nec	Malaysia	Ghana Telecom(Ghana)	Ghana	Radiotelephone communications
2004	34.0	ONGC Videsh Ltd	Crude petroleum and natural gas	India	Block 5B	Sudan	Crude petroleum and natural gas
1997	28.7	Daewoo Corp	Industrial buildings and warehouses	Korea, Republic of	Morocco-Rabat Deluxe Hotel	Morocco	Hotels and motels
1997	28.7	Daewoo Corp	Industrial buildings and warehouses	Korea, Republic of	Rabat Hyatt Regency	Morocco	Hotels and motels
1989	24.0	Samsung Group	Canned specialties	Korea, Republic of	Khalda Oil & Gas Concession	Egypt	Crude petroleum and natural gas
1997	21.2	Shanghai Industrial Invt Hldgs	Investment advice	Hong Kong, China	Omega Holdings Ltd	South Africa	Electrical apparatus and equip
2004	19.0	GAIL(India)Ltd	Natural gas transmission and distribution	India	NATGAS	Egypt	Natural gas transmission
2004	18.9	Salim Ivomas Pratama PT	Forest nurseries and gathering of forest products	Indonesia	Silveron Investments Ltd	Mauritius	Investors, nec
2005	16.8	Golden Hope Plantations Bhd	Field crops, except cash grains, nec	Malaysia	Hudson & Knight(Pty)Ltd	South Africa	Edible fats and oils, nec
1998	11.0	Westmont Land(Asia)Bhd	Vegetable oil mills, nec	Malaysia	Uganda Commercial Bank	Uganda	Banks, non-US chartered
1997	10.0	Asia Food and Properties Ltd	Durable goods, nec	Singapore	Guibies Holdings(Sando & Cie)	Mauritius	Land subdividers and developers, except cemeteries
1995	9.5	Acer Computer Intl(Acer Inc)	Computers and peripheral equipment and software	Singapore	Acer Africa Proprietary Ltd	South Africa	Computers and peripheral equipment and software
1996	9.4	Eminent Aspects Sdn Bhd	Land subdividers and developers, except cemeteries	Malaysia	Samstocks(Stocks & Stocks)	South Africa	Retail stores, nec
1999	9.0	Golden Paradise International	Investors, nec	Malaysia	Samrand Mitrajaya Development	South Africa	Land subdividers and developers, except cemeteries
1996	8.3	DJI Clothing(MC Industrial)	Men's shirts and nightwear	Malaysia	Buildmax Ltd	South Africa	Sheet metal work
1992	8.0	Daewoo Corp	Industrial buildings and warehouses	Korea, Republic of	Sudan Textile Factory(Kuwait)	Sudan	Broadwoven fabric mills, cotton
1997	5.8	Genaire Holdings(Malaysia)Sdn	Investors, nec	Malaysia	Femco Technology Holdings Ltd	South Africa	Motors and generators
1997	4.1	Promet International Ltd	Investors, nec	Malaysia	Fairoak Investment Holdings	South Africa	Land subdividers and developers, except cemeteries
1993	2.8	Tolaram Group	Broadwoven fabric mills, cotton	Singapore	Prilla Mills(Tongaat-Hulett)	South Africa	Broadwoven fabric mills, cotton
2002	2.4	Korea Green Cross Corp	Pharmaceutical preparations	Korea, Republic of	Bio Med Lab Co Ltd	South Africa	Commercial physical and biological research
1998	2.0	BK Engineering and Casting Ltd	Engineering services	India	Scaw Ltd	Zambia	Copper foundries
1997	1.4	Daesung Cable Ltd	Drawing and insulating of nonferrous wire	Korea, Republic of	Tanzania Cable(Tanzania)	United Republic of Tanzania	Cable and other pay television services
1999	1.0	Tian Long International Invest	Offices of holding companies, nec	Hong Kong, China	Sky Channel Development Ltd	South Africa	Offices of holding companies, nec

/...

Annex table 1.   Cross-border M&A deals by Asian firms concluded in Africa, 1987-2005 (continued)

Year	Value (million dollars)	Acquiring company	Home economy	Industry of the acquiring company	Acquired company	Host economy	Industry of the acquired company
2004	0.9	E & O Property Development Bhd	Malaysia	Land subdividers and developers, except cemeteries	Emerald Designs Sdn Bhd	Mayotte	Land subdividers & developers, except cemeteries
1997	0.1	Magnum(Dunlop Estates)	Malaysia	Amusement and recreation svcs	Loteri Nationale De Madagascar	Madagascar	Amusement and recreation svcs
1996	0.1	GMG Investment(Panwell Pte)	Singapore	Electrical industrial apparatus, nec	HEVECAM(Cameroon)	Cameroon	Synthetic rubber (vulcanizable elastomers)
1992	..	Daewoo Corp	Korea, Republic of	Industrial buildings and warehouses	Undisclosed Khartoum Hotel	Sudan	Hotels and motels
1994	..	National Bank of Pakistan	Pakistan	Banks	Pan African Bnk-Karachi Branck	South Africa	Banks
1995	..	Delphi Packard Electric	Indonesia	Electric services	Autocable Industries(Pty)Ltd	South Africa	Motor vehicle parts & accessories
1995	..	Faber Group Bhd(Renong Bhd)	Malaysia	Hotels and motels	Belaire Investment Proprietary	South Africa	Land subdividers & developers, except cemeteries
1995	..	Mycom Bhd	Malaysia	Operators of nonresidential buildings	Pure Touch Foods(Pty)Ltd	South Africa	Canned specialties
1995	..	Industrial Inv Intl(Asean Int)	Singapore	Broadwoven fabric mills, cotton	Fenix Industries Ltd(Abbey Na)	South Africa	Textile goods, nec
1996	..	Stamford College Bhd	Malaysia	Colleges, universities, and professional schools	Kolej Sarjana Stamford Sdn Bhd	South Africa	Colleges, universities, and professional schools
1996	..	Pacific Century Regional Dev	Singapore	Land subdividers and developers, except cemeteries	Castle Holdings(Mauritius)Ltd	Mauritius	Investors, nec
1996	..	Pacific Century Regional Dev	Singapore	Land subdividers and developers, except cemeteries	Farm Holdings(Mauritius)Ltd	Mauritius	Investors, nec
1996	..	Pacific Century Regional Dev	Singapore	Land subdividers and developers, except cemeteries	Fort Investments(Mauritius)Ltd	Mauritius	Investors, nec
1996	..	Manage	Thailand	Miscellaneous publishing	Namsov	Namibia	Deep sea foreign transportation of freight
1997	..	Investor Group	China	Investors, nec	State Petroleum Corp-Sudan Oil	Sudan	Crude petroleum and natural gas
1997	..	Alangka-Suka International Ltd	Hong Kong, China	Land subdividers and developers, except cemeteries	Grand Holiday Villa Khartoum	Sudan	Land subdividers & developers, except cemeteries
1997	..	Binani Zinc Ltd	India	Lead and zinc ores	Zambia Consolidated-Chambeshi	Zambia	Copper ores
1997	..	Business Focus Sdn Bhd	Malaysia	Ship building and repairing	Tema Shipyard & Drydock Corp	Ghana	Marine cargo handling
1997	..	Sunrise Bhd	Malaysia	Land subdividers and developers, except cemeteries	Winnock Investments(Pty) Ltd	South Africa	Investors, nec
1997	..	Freyssinet Post Tensioning	Philippines	Concrete block and brick	Plasmec (Pty) Ltd	South Africa	Plastics products, nec
1998	..	Novel Denim Holdings Ltd	Hong Kong, China	Broadwoven fabric mills, cotton	Novel Spinners Ltd	South Africa	Yarn spinning mills
1998	..	Fortuna International Holdings	Hong Kong, China	Electronic capacitors	OORYX Tanning (Proprietary) Ltd	South Africa	Animal specialties, nec
1999	..	China Hunan Intl Economic	China	Investors, nec	Kiwira Coal Mine(Tanzania)	United Republic of Tanzania	Bituminous coal and lignite surface mining
1999	..	Binani Group	India	Gold ores	Ndola Precious Metals (Zambia)	South Africa	Gold ores
1999	..	Daewoo Corp	Korea, Republic of	Industrial buildings and warehouses	Al Nasr Co-Bus Manufacturing	Egypt	Motor vehicles and passenger car bodies
2001	..	Investor Group	China	Investors, nec	Uganda Spinning Mill Ltd	Uganda	Textile goods, nec
2001	..	Twinwood Engineering Limited	Singapore	Special industry machinery, nec	Arboretum Mauritius Ltd	Mauritius	Investors, nec
2001	..	Twinwood Engineering Limited	Singapore	Special industry machinery, nec	Twinwood Mauritius Ltd	Mauritius	Investors, nec

/...

Annex table 1. Cross-border M&A deals by Asian firms concluded in Africa, 1987-2005 (concluded)

Year	Value (million dollars)	Acquiring company	Home economy	Industry of the acquiring company	Acquired company	Host economy	Industry of the acquired company
2003	..	Petronas International	Malaysia	Products of petroleum & coal, nec	Mobil Oil Sudan Ltd	Sudan	Petroleum and petroleum products wholesalers, nec
2003	..	PETRONAS	Malaysia	Crude petroleum and natural gas	WDDM	Egypt	Crude petroleum and natural gas
2004	..	Bharti Enterprises	India	Telephone communications, except radiotelephone	Le Meridien Barbarons Hotel-	Seychelles	Hotels and motels
2004	..	Dabur India Ltd	India	Pharmaceutical preparations	African Consumer Care Ltd	South Africa	Pharmaceutical preparations
2004	..	GAIL(India)Ltd	India	Natural gas transmission and distribution	Fayum Gas Co	Egypt	Natural gas transmission
2004	..	GAIL(India)Ltd	India	Natural gas transmission and distribution	Shell CNG Egypt Ltd	Egypt	Crude petroleum and natural gas
2004	..	Uniphos Enterprises Ltd	India	Pesticides and agricultural chemicals, nec	Cropserve Zambia Ltd	Zambia	Pesticides and agricultural chemicals, nec
2005	..	HCM Ikhtisas Sdn Bhd	Malaysia	Residential construction, nec	Libyan Malaysian Co for Roads	Libyan Arab Jamahiriya	Highway and street construction
2005	..	Industrial Development Corp	India	Nitrogenous fertilizers	Foskor Ltd	South Africa	Phosphatic fertilizers
2005	..	Investor Group	Indonesia	Investors, nec	Vindoor Investments Ltd	Mauritius	Investors, nec
2005	..	Investor Group	India	Investors, nec	Block 086	Libyan Arab Jamahiriya	Crude petroleum and natural gas
2005	..	Keppel Land Properties Pte Ltd	Singapore	Land subdividers and developers, except cemeteries	Rochor Investment Ltd	Mauritius	Investors, nec
2005	..	Malaysia Airport Hldg Bhd	Malaysia	Airports & airport terminal services	Malaysia Airports(Mauritius)	Mauritius	Airports & airport terminal services
2005	..	Mudajaya Corp Bhd	Malaysia	Residential construction, nec	Great Hill International Ltd	Mauritius	Land subdividers and developers, except cemeteries
2005	..	SBI	India	Banks	Indian Ocean Intl Bank Ltd	Mauritius	Banks

Source: UNCTAD, cross-border M&A database.

Annex table 2. Value of cross-border M&A purchases by Asian firms concluded in Africa, 1987-2005
(Millions of dollars)

Economy	1987-1988	1989	1990-1991	1992	1993	1994	1995	1996	1997	1998	1999	2000-2001	2002	2003	2004	2005
Brunei Darussalam	-	-	-	-	-	-	-	58.4	-	-	-	-	-	-	-	-
Hong Kong, China	-	-	-	-	-	-	-	-	131.6	-	1.0	-	-	-	-	-
India	-	-	-	-	-	-	-	-	-	2.0	-	-	-	767.8	155.0	-
Indonesia	-	-	-	-	-	-	-	-	-	-	-	-	-	-	18.9	18.9
Malaysia	-	-	-	-	-	-	-	341.0	48.0	463.1	9.0	-	-	1 766.3	0.9	92.0
Republic of Korea	-	24.0	-	8.0	-	-	-	-	58.8	-	-	-	2.4	-	-	-
Singapore	-	-	-	-	2.8	-	9.5	0.1	10.0	-	101.0	-	-	-	-	-
Total	-	24.0	-	8.0	2.8	-	9.5	399.5	248.4	465.1	111.0	-	2.4	2 534.0	174.8	110.9

Source: UNCTAD, cross-border M&A database.

Annex table 3. Cases of cross-border M&A purchases by Asian firms concluded in Africa, 1987-2005
(Number of deals)

Economy	1987-1988	1989	1990-1991	1992	1993	1994	1995	1996	1997	1998	1999	2000	2001	2002	2003	2004	2005
Brunei Darussalam	-	-	-	-	-	-	-	1	-	-	-	-	-	-	-	-	-
China	-	-	-	-	-	-	-	-	1	2	1	-	1	-	-	-	-
Hong Kong, China	-	-	-	-	-	-	-	-	3	1	1	-	-	-	-	8	3
India	-	-	-	-	-	-	1	-	1	-	1	-	-	-	1	1	2
Indonesia	-	-	-	-	-	-	-	5	6	2	1	-	-	-	-	-	-
Malaysia	-	-	-	-	-	-	2	-	-	-	-	-	-	-	3	1	5
Pakistan	-	-	-	-	-	1	-	-	-	-	-	-	-	-	-	-	-
Philippines	-	-	-	-	-	-	-	-	1	-	-	-	-	-	-	-	-
Republic of Korea	-	1	-	2	1	-	-	-	3	-	1	-	-	1	-	-	-
Singapore	-	-	-	-	-	-	2	4	1	-	1	-	2	-	-	-	1
Thailand	-	-	-	-	-	-	-	1	-	-	-	-	-	-	-	-	-
Total	-	1	-	2	1	1	5	11	16	5	6	-	3	1	4	10	11

Source: UNCTAD, cross-border M&A database.

Annex table 4. Value of cross-border M&A sales in Africa concluded by Asian firms, 1987-2005
(Millions of dollars)

Economy	1987-1988	1989	1990-1991	1992	1993	1994	1995	1996	1997	1998	1999	2000-2001	2002	2003	2004	2005
Cameroon	-	-	-	-	-	-	-	0.1	-	-	-	-	-	-	-	-
Egypt	-	24.0	-	-	-	-	-	-	-	-	101.0	-	-	1 766.3	19.0	-
Ghana	-	-	-	-	-	-	-	-	38.0	-	-	-	-	-	-	-
Guinea	-	-	-	-	-	-	-	50.0	-	-	-	-	-	-	-	-
Madagascar	-	-	-	-	-	-	-	58.4	0.1	-	-	-	-	-	-	-
Mauritius	-	-	-	-	-	-	-	-	10.0	-	-	-	-	-	18.9	94.1
Mayotte	-	-	-	-	-	-	-	-	-	-	-	-	-	-	0.9	-
Morocco	-	-	-	-	-	-	-	-	57.4	-	-	-	-	-	-	-
South Africa	-	-	-	-	2.8	-	9.5	291.0	141.5	452.1	10.0	-	2.4	-	-	16.8
Sudan	-	-	-	8.0	-	-	-	-	-	-	-	-	-	767.8	136.0	-
Uganda	-	-	-	-	-	-	-	-	-	11.0	-	-	-	-	-	-
United Rep. of Tanzania	-	-	-	-	-	-	-	-	1.4	-	-	-	-	-	-	-
Zambia	-	-	-	-	-	-	-	-	-	2.0	-	-	-	-	-	-
Total	-	24.0	-	8.0	2.8	-	9.5	399.5	248.4	465.1	111.0	-	2.4	2 534.0	174.8	110.9

Source: UNCTAD, cross-border M&A database.

Annex table 5. Cases of cross-border M&A sales in Africa concluded by Asian firms, 1987-2005

(Number of deals)

Economy	1987-1988	1989	1990-1991	1992	1993	1994	1995	1996	1997	1998	1999	2000	2001	2002	2003	2004	2005
Cameroon	-	-	-	-	-	-	-	1	-	-	-	-	-	-	-	-	-
Egypt	-	1	-	-	-	-	-	-	-	-	2	-	-	-	2	3	-
Ghana	-	-	-	-	-	-	-	-	2	-	-	-	-	-	-	-	-
Guinea	-	-	-	-	-	-	-	1	-	-	-	-	-	-	-	-	2
Libyan Arab Jamahiriya	-	-	-	-	-	-	-	-	-	-	-	-	-	-	-	-	-
Madagascar	-	-	-	-	-	-	-	1	1	-	-	-	2	-	-	-	7
Mauritius	-	-	-	-	-	-	-	3	1	-	-	-	-	-	-	1	-
Mayotte	-	-	-	-	-	-	-	-	-	-	-	-	-	-	-	1	-
Morocco	-	-	-	-	-	-	-	-	2	-	-	-	-	-	-	-	-
Namibia	-	-	-	-	-	-	-	1	-	-	-	-	-	-	-	-	-
Seychelles	-	-	-	-	1	-	5	-	-	-	-	-	-	-	-	1	-
South Africa	-	-	-	-	-	1	-	4	6	3	3	-	-	1	-	1	2
Sudan	-	-	-	2	-	-	-	-	2	-	-	-	-	-	2	2	-
Uganda	-	-	-	-	-	-	-	-	1	1	-	-	1	-	-	-	-
United Rep. of Tanzania	-	-	-	-	-	-	-	-	-	-	1	-	-	-	-	-	-
Zambia	-	-	-	-	-	-	-	-	1	1	-	-	-	-	-	1	-
Total	-	1	-	2	1	1	5	11	16	5	6	-	3	1	4	10	11

Source: UNCTAD, cross-border M&A database.

Annex table 6. Value of cross-border M&A purchases by Asian firms concluded in Africa, by industry of purchaser, 1987-2005
(Millions of dollars)

Sector/industry	1987-1988	1989	1990-1991	1992	1993	1994	1995	1996	1997	1998	1999	2000-2001	2002	2003	2004	2005
Total	-	24.0	-	8.0	2.8	-	9.5	399.5	248.4	465.1	111.0	-	2.4	2 534.0	174.8	110.9
Primary	-	-	-	-	-	-	-	273.3	-	452.1	-	-	-	2 534.0	154.9	35.7
Agriculture, hunting, forestry, and fishing	-	-	-	-	-	-	-	-	-	-	-	-	-	-	18.9	35.7
Mining, quarrying and petroleum	-	-	-	-	-	-	-	273.3	-	452.1	-	-	-	2 534.0	136.0	-
Manufacturing	-	24.0	-	-	2.8	-	-	8.4	1.4	11.0	-	-	2.4	-	-	-
Food, beverages and tobacco	-	24.0	-	-	-	-	-	-	-	11.0	-	-	-	-	-	-
Textiles, clothing and leather	-	-	-	-	2.8	-	-	8.3	-	-	-	-	-	-	-	-
Wood and wood products	-	-	-	-	-	-	-	-	-	-	-	-	-	-	-	-
Publishing, and printing	-	-	-	-	-	-	-	-	-	-	-	-	-	-	-	-
Coke, petroleum and nuclear fuel	-	-	-	-	-	-	-	-	-	-	-	-	-	-	-	-
Chemicals and chemical products	-	-	-	-	-	-	-	-	-	-	-	-	2.4	-	-	-
Rubber and plastic products	-	-	-	-	-	-	-	-	-	-	-	-	-	-	-	-
Non-metallic mineral products	-	-	-	-	-	-	-	-	-	-	-	-	-	-	-	-
Metals and metal products	-	-	-	-	-	-	-	-	1.4	-	-	-	-	-	-	-
Machinery and equipment	-	-	-	-	-	-	-	-	-	-	-	-	-	-	-	-
Electrical and electronic equipment	-	-	-	-	-	-	-	0.1	-	-	-	-	-	-	-	-
Precision instruments	-	-	-	-	-	-	-	-	-	-	-	-	-	-	-	-
Motor vehicles and other transport equipment	-	-	-	-	-	-	-	-	-	-	-	-	-	-	-	-
Other manufacturing	-	-	-	-	-	-	-	-	-	-	-	-	-	-	-	-
Services	-	-	-	8.0	-	-	9.5	117.8	247.0	2.0	111.0	-	-	-	19.9	75.2
Electricity, gas and water	-	-	-	-	-	-	-	-	-	-	111.0	-	-	-	-	-
Construction	-	-	-	8.0	-	-	-	-	57.4	-	-	-	-	-	19.0	-
Trade	-	-	-	-	-	-	9.5	-	10.0	-	-	-	-	-	-	-
Hotels and restaurants	-	-	-	-	-	-	-	50.0	-	-	-	-	-	-	-	-
Transport, storage and communications	-	-	-	-	-	-	-	58.4	179.5	-	111.0	-	-	-	-	75.2
Finance	-	-	-	-	-	-	-	9.4	-	2.0	-	-	-	-	-	-
Business services	-	-	-	-	-	-	-	-	-	-	-	-	-	-	0.9	-
Public administration and defence	-	-	-	-	-	-	-	-	-	-	-	-	-	-	-	-
Education	-	-	-	-	-	-	-	-	-	-	-	-	-	-	-	-
Health and social services	-	-	-	-	-	-	-	-	-	-	-	-	-	-	-	-
Community, social and personal service activities	-	-	-	-	-	-	-	-	0.1	-	-	-	-	-	-	-
Other services	-	-	-	-	-	-	-	-	-	-	-	-	-	-	-	-
Unknown[a]	-	-	-	-	-	-	-	-	-	-	-	-	-	-	-	-

Source: UNCTAD, cross-border M&A database (www.unctad.org/fdistatistics).
[a] Including non-classified establishments.

Annex table 7. Cases of cross-border M&A purchases by Asian firms concluded in Africa, by industry of purchaser, 1987-2005
(Number of deals)

Sector/industry	1987-1988	1989	1990-1991	1992	1993	1994	1995	1996	1997	1998	1999	2000	2001	2002	2003	2004	2005
Total	-	1	-	2	1	1	5	11	16	5	6	-	3	1	4	10	11
Primary	-	-	-	-	-	-	-	-	2	2	1	-	-	-	4	3	2
Agriculture, hunting, forestry, and fishing	-	-	-	-	-	-	-	-	1	1	1	-	-	-	3	3	2
Mining, quarrying and petroleum	-	-	-	-	-	-	-	-	1	1	-	-	-	-	1	-	-
Manufacturing	-	1	-	-	1	-	1	4	2	2	-	-	2	1	-	2	1
Food, beverages and tobacco	-	1	-	-	-	-	1	3	-	-	-	-	-	-	-	2	-
Textiles, clothing and leather	-	-	-	-	1	-	-	1	-	1	-	-	-	-	-	-	-
Wood and wood products	-	-	-	-	-	-	-	-	-	-	-	-	-	-	-	-	-
Publishing, and printing	-	-	-	-	-	-	-	-	-	-	-	-	-	-	-	-	-
Coke, petroleum and nuclear fuel	-	-	-	-	-	-	-	-	-	-	-	-	-	-	-	-	-
Chemicals and chemical products	-	-	-	-	-	-	-	-	-	-	-	-	-	1	-	-	1
Rubber and plastic products	-	-	-	-	-	-	-	-	-	-	-	-	-	-	-	-	-
Non-metallic mineral products	-	-	-	-	-	-	-	-	1	-	-	-	-	-	-	-	-
Metals and metal products	-	-	-	-	-	-	-	-	1	1	-	-	-	-	-	-	-
Machinery and equipment	-	-	-	-	-	-	-	-	-	-	-	-	2	-	-	-	-
Electrical and electronic equipment	-	-	-	-	-	-	-	-	-	-	-	-	-	-	-	-	-
Precision instruments	-	-	-	-	-	-	-	-	-	-	-	-	-	-	-	-	-
Motor vehicles and other transport equipment	-	-	-	-	-	-	-	-	-	-	-	-	-	-	-	-	-
Other manufacturing	-	-	-	-	-	-	-	-	-	-	-	-	-	-	-	-	-
Services	-	-	-	2	-	1	4	7	12	1	5	-	1	-	-	5	8
Electricity, gas and water	-	-	-	-	-	-	1	-	-	-	-	-	-	-	-	-	-
Construction	-	-	-	2	-	-	-	-	2	-	1	-	-	-	-	3	2
Trade	-	-	-	-	-	-	1	-	1	-	-	-	-	-	-	-	-
Hotels and restaurants	-	-	-	-	-	-	1	1	-	-	-	-	-	-	-	1	2
Transport, storage and communications	-	-	-	-	-	1	-	1	6	-	4	-	-	-	-	-	3
Finance	-	-	-	-	-	-	1	4	2	1	-	-	1	-	-	1	1
Business services	-	-	-	-	-	-	-	-	-	-	-	-	-	-	-	-	-
Public administration and defence	-	-	-	-	-	-	-	-	-	-	-	-	-	-	-	-	-
Education	-	-	-	-	-	-	-	1	-	-	-	-	-	-	-	-	-
Health and social services	-	-	-	-	-	-	-	-	-	-	-	-	-	-	-	-	-
Community, social and personal service activities	-	-	-	-	-	-	-	-	1	-	-	-	-	-	-	-	-
Other services	-	-	-	-	-	-	-	-	-	-	-	-	-	-	-	-	-
Unknown [a]	-	-	-	-	-	-	-	-	-	-	-	-	-	-	-	-	-

Source: UNCTAD, cross-border M&A database.
a Including non-classified establishments.

Annex table 8. Value of cross-border M&A sales in Africa concluded by Asian firms, by industry of seller, 1987-2005
(Millions of dollars)

Sector/industry	1987-1988	1989	1990-1991	1992	1993	1994	1995	1996	1997	1998	1999	2000-2001	2002	2003	2004	2005
Total	-	24.0	-	8.0	2.8	-	9.5	399.5	248.4	465.1	111.0	-	2.4	2 534.0	174.8	110.9
Primary	-	24.0	-	-	-	-	-	273.3	-	452.1	-	-	-	2 534.0	136.0	-
Agriculture, hunting, forestry, and fishing	-	-	-	-	-	-	-	-	-	-	-	-	-	-	-	-
Mining, quarrying and petroleum	-	24.0	-	-	-	-	-	273.3	-	452.1	-	-	-	2 534.0	136.0	-
Manufacturing	-	-	-	8.0	2.8	-	-	8.4	116.2	2.0	-	-	-	-	-	16.8
Food, beverages and tobacco	-	-	-	-	-	-	-	-	-	-	-	-	-	-	-	16.8
Textiles, clothing and leather	-	-	-	8.0	2.8	-	-	-	-	-	-	-	-	-	-	-
Wood and wood products	-	-	-	-	-	-	-	-	-	-	-	-	-	-	-	-
Publishing, and printing	-	-	-	-	-	-	-	-	-	-	-	-	-	-	-	-
Coke, petroleum and nuclear fuel	-	-	-	-	-	-	-	-	-	-	-	-	-	-	-	-
Chemicals and chemical products	-	-	-	-	-	-	-	0.1	-	-	-	-	-	-	-	-
Rubber and plastic products	-	-	-	-	-	-	-	-	-	-	-	-	-	-	-	-
Non-metallic mineral products	-	-	-	-	-	-	-	-	-	-	-	-	-	-	-	-
Metals and metal products	-	-	-	-	-	-	-	8.3	-	2.0	-	-	-	-	-	-
Machinery and equipment	-	-	-	-	-	-	-	-	110.4	-	-	-	-	-	-	-
Electrical and electronic equipment	-	-	-	-	-	-	-	-	5.8	-	-	-	-	-	-	-
Precision instruments	-	-	-	-	-	-	-	-	-	-	-	-	-	-	-	-
Motor vehicles and other transport equipment	-	-	-	-	-	-	-	-	-	-	-	-	-	-	-	-
Other manufacturing	-	-	-	-	-	-	-	-	-	-	-	-	-	-	-	-
Services	-	-	-	-	-	-	9.5	117.8	132.2	11.0	111.0	-	2.4	-	38.8	94.1
Electricity, gas and water	-	-	-	-	-	-	-	-	-	-	-	-	-	-	19.0	-
Construction	-	-	-	-	-	-	-	-	-	-	-	-	-	-	-	-
Trade	-	-	-	-	-	-	9.5	9.4	21.2	-	-	-	-	-	-	-
Hotels and restaurants	-	-	-	-	-	-	-	-	57.4	-	-	-	-	-	-	-
Transport, storage and communications	-	-	-	-	-	-	-	50.0	38.0	-	-	-	-	-	-	-
Finance	-	-	-	-	-	-	-	58.4	-	11.0	102.0	-	2.4	-	18.9	94.1
Business services	-	-	-	-	-	-	-	-	14.1	-	9.0	-	-	-	0.9	-
Public administration and defence	-	-	-	-	-	-	-	-	-	-	-	-	-	-	-	-
Education	-	-	-	-	-	-	-	-	-	-	-	-	-	-	-	-
Health and social services	-	-	-	-	-	-	-	-	-	-	-	-	-	-	-	-
Community, social and personal service activities	-	-	-	-	-	-	-	-	1.5	-	-	-	-	-	-	-
Other services	-	-	-	-	-	-	-	-	-	-	-	-	-	-	-	-
Unknown[a]	-	-	-	-	-	-	-	-	-	-	-	-	-	-	-	-

Source: UNCTAD, cross-border M&A database (www.unctad.org/fdistatistics).
a Including non-classified establishments.

Annex table 9. Cases of cross-border M&A sales in Africa concluded by Asian firms, by industry of seller, 1987-2005
(Number of deals)

Sector/industry	1987-1988	1989	1990-1991	1992	1993	1994	1995	1996	1997	1998	1999	2000	2001	2002	2003	2004	2005
Total	-	1	-	2	1	1	5	11	16	5	6	-	3	1	4	10	11
Primary																	
Agriculture, hunting, forestry, and fishing	-	1	-	-	-	-	-	1	2	2	2	-	-	-	3	3	1
Mining, quarrying and petroleum	-	1	-	-	-	-	-	1	2	1	2	-	-	-	3	3	1
Manufacturing																	
Food, beverages and tobacco	-	-	-	1	1	-	3	2	3	2	1	-	1	-	-	2	2
Textiles, clothing and leather	-	-	-	1	1	-	1	-	-	1	-	-	1	-	-	-	1
Wood and wood products	-	-	-	-	-	-	1	-	-	-	-	-	-	-	-	-	-
Publishing, and printing	-	-	-	-	-	-	-	-	-	-	-	-	-	-	-	-	-
Coke, petroleum and nuclear fuel	-	-	-	-	-	-	-	-	-	-	-	-	-	-	-	-	-
Chemicals and chemical products	-	-	-	-	-	-	-	1	1	-	-	-	-	-	-	2	1
Rubber and plastic products	-	-	-	-	-	-	-	-	-	-	-	-	-	-	-	-	-
Non-metallic mineral products	-	-	-	-	-	-	-	-	-	-	-	-	-	-	-	-	-
Metals and metal products	-	-	-	-	-	-	-	1	1	1	-	-	-	-	-	-	-
Machinery and equipment	-	-	-	-	-	-	-	-	1	-	-	-	-	-	-	-	-
Electrical and electronic equipment	-	-	-	-	-	-	-	-	1	-	-	-	-	-	-	-	-
Precision instruments	-	-	-	-	-	-	-	-	-	-	-	-	-	-	-	-	-
Motor vehicles and other transport equipment	-	-	-	-	-	-	1	-	-	-	1	-	-	-	-	-	-
Other manufacturing	-	-	-	-	-	-	-	-	-	-	-	-	-	-	-	-	-
Services	-	-	-	1	-	1	2	8	11	1	3	-	2	1	1	5	8
Electricity, gas and water	-	-	-	-	-	-	-	-	-	-	-	-	-	-	-	2	-
Construction	-	-	-	-	-	-	-	-	-	-	-	-	-	-	-	-	1
Trade	-	-	-	1	-	-	1	1	1	-	-	-	-	-	1	1	-
Hotels and restaurants	-	-	-	1	-	-	-	2	2	-	-	-	-	-	-	-	-
Transport, storage and communications	-	-	-	-	-	1	-	2	2	1	2	-	-	-	-	1	1
Finance	-	-	-	-	-	1	-	4	1	1	1	-	2	-	-	1	5
Business services	-	-	-	-	-	-	1	-	3	-	-	-	-	1	-	1	1
Public administration and defence	-	-	-	-	-	-	-	-	-	-	-	-	-	-	-	-	-
Education	-	-	-	-	-	-	-	1	-	-	-	-	-	-	-	-	-
Health and social services	-	-	-	-	-	-	-	-	-	-	-	-	-	-	-	-	-
Community, social and personal service activities	-	-	-	-	-	-	-	-	2	-	-	-	-	-	-	-	-
Other services	-	-	-	-	-	-	-	-	-	-	-	-	-	-	-	-	-
Unknown [a]	-	-	-	-	-	-	-	-	-	-	-	-	-	-	-	-	-

Source: UNCTAD, cross-border M&A database (www.unctad.org/fdistatistics).

a Including non-classified establishments.

Annex table 10. Greenfield FDI projects in Africa announced by firms from developing Asia, 2002-2005

Year	Name of source company	Home country	Destination (host country)	Industry	Number of projects	Investment value ($mil.)	Employment
2002	CMEC	China	Nigeria	Energy	1	390	..
2002	Veronica Laboratories	India	Kenya	Pharmaceuticals	1	..	..
2002	Indian Oil (IOC)	India	Mauritius	Energy	1	..	..
2002	Mahindra & Mahindra (M&M)	India	South Africa	Automotive OEM	1	..	..
2002	Tata Group	India	South Africa	Metals/Mining	1	40	..
2002	Hidesign	India	South Africa	Textiles	1	..	..
2002	Infosys Technologies	India	Mauritius	IT and software	1	25	1 500
2002	LG Electronics (LG)	Korea, Republic of	Egypt	Consumer electronics	1	4	..
2002	Ramatex	Malaysia	Namibia	Textiles	1	263	..
2002	Tekno Logam Snd Bhd	Malaysia	Nigeria	Metals/Mining	1	..	..
2002	Petronas	Malaysia	Mozambique	Energy	1	70	..
2003	China National Petroleum (CNPC)	China	Algeria	Energy	1	350	..
2003	Tianjin Litong Elevator	China	Egypt	Machinery and industrial goods	1	3	..
2003	ZTE	China	Egypt	Telecom equipment	1	..	..
2003	Shanghai Baosteel Group	China	Zimbabwe	Metals/Mining	1	300	2 000
2003	China Petroleum and Chemical (Sinopec)	China	Nigeria	Energy	1	..	..
2003	China National Petroleum (CNPC)	China	Sudan	Energy	1	1 000	..
2003	Shenzhen Topway Solar	China	Uganda	Machinery and industrial goods	1	..	..
2003	Yue Yang Paper	China	Uganda	Paper and packaging	1	10	114
2003	Beijing General Research Institute of Mining & Metallurgy (BGRIMM)	China	Zambia	Chemicals	1	8	..
2003	China National Petroleum (CNPC)	China	Niger	Energy	1	..	..
2003	Aditya Birla	India	Egypt	Plastics and rubber	1	..	..
2003	Hindusthan Seals	India	Egypt	Plastics and rubber	1	..	..
2003	KK Birla Group	India	Egypt	Chemicals	1	..	..
2003	LML	India	Egypt	Other Transport OEM	1	..	..
2003	ONGC	India	Libyan Arab Jamahiriya	Energy	1	30	..
2003	Hindusthan Seals	India	Morocco	Plastics and rubber	1	..	..
2003	Bank of India	India	Kenya	Financial services	1	..	..
2003	Infosys Technologies	India	Mauritius	IT and software	1	10	..
2003	Tata Group	India	South Africa	Metals/Mining	1	53	..
2003	State Bank of India (SBI)	India	South Africa	Financial services	1	..	..
2003	Bharat Biotech	India	South Africa	Biotechnology	1	..	..
2003	Ramco Systems	India	South Africa	IT and software	1	10	..
2003	Bank of Baroda	India	United Rep. of Tanzania	Financial services	1	..	..
2003	Hindusthan Seals	India	United Rep. of Tanzania	Plastics and rubber	1	..	..
2003	Medco	Indonesia	Sudan	Energy	1	..	..
2003	LG	Korea, Republic of	Nigeria	Consumer electronics	1	..	100
2003	Petronas	Malaysia	Ethiopia	Energy	1	5	..
2003	International Commercial Bank (ICB)	Malaysia	Sierra Leone	Financial services	1	..	..
2003	Petronas	Malaysia	Sudan	Energy	1	..	..
2003	Petronas	Malaysia	Sudan	Energy	1	..	..
2003	Flextronics	Singapore	South Africa	IT and software	1	..	..
2003	Thai Acrylic Fibre	Thailand	Egypt	Textiles	1	100	..

Annex table 10. Greenfield FDI projects in Africa announced by firms from developing Asia, 2002-2005 (continued)

Year	Name of source company	Home country	Destination (host country)	Industry	Number of projects	Investment value ($mil.)	Employment
2003	Thai Carbon Black	Thailand	Egypt	Plastics and rubber	1	13	..
2003	PetroVietnam	Viet Nam	Algeria	Energy	1	..	..
2003	Vietnam News Agency (VNA)	Viet Nam	South Africa	Paper and packaging	1	..	..
2003	Lam Hoa	Viet Nam	Senegal	Other Transport OEM	1	..	..
2004	ZTE	China	Algeria	Telecom equipment	1	..	..
2004	China National Petroleum (CNPC)	China	Sudan	Energy	1	..	..
2004	Liming Chemical Industrial	China	United Rep. of Tanzania	Chemicals	1	..	..
2004	ZTE	China	Nigeria	Telecom equipment	1	..	..
2004	Jinchuan	China	South Africa	Metals/Mining	1	..	..
2004	Indian Oil (IOC)	India	Mauritius	Energy	1	..	..
2004	Indian Oil (IOC)	India	Mauritius	Energy	1	1	..
2004	Indian Oil (IOC)	India	Mauritius	Energy	1	..	..
2004	HDFC	India	Mauritius	Business services	1	..	..
2004	Tata Group	India	Mauritius	Hotels, tourism and leisure	1	..	..
2004	Hinduja Group	India	Mauritius	IT and software	1	..	..
2004	Mahindra & Mahindra (M&M)	India	South Africa	Automotive OEM	1	..	..
2004	Usha Martin	India	South Africa	IT and software	1	..	..
2004	ICICI Bank	India	South Africa	Financial services	1	..	..
2004	Indusind Bank	India	South Africa	Financial services	1	..	..
2004	Syndicate Bank	India	South Africa	Financial services	1	..	..
2004	Teledata Informatics	India	South Africa	IT and software	1	..	9
2004	Hatsun Agro Product (HAPL)	India	Seychelles	Food and drink	1	..	..
2004	Dabur	India	Nigeria	Consumer products	1	..	..
2004	ONGC	India	Sudan	Energy	1	200	..
2004	Indian Oil (IOC)	India	Nigeria	Energy	1	1	..
2004	Hyundai Motor	Korea, Republic of	Algeria	Automotive OEM	1	..	..
2004	Hyundai Motor	Korea, Republic of	Egypt	Automotive OEM	1	..	..
2004	LG	Korea, Republic of	Kenya	Consumer electronics	1	..	..
2004	Samsung	Korea, Republic of	Kenya	Consumer electronics	1	..	..
2004	eSys Technologies	Singapore	Morocco	Business machines and equipment	1	..	..
2004	Neptune Orient Lines (NOL)	Singapore	Kenya	Logistics and distribution	1	..	..
2004	Eurochem Technologies	Singapore	Nigeria	Chemicals	1	..	..
2004	BenQ	Taiwan Province of China	Egypt	Business machines and equipment	1	..	..
2004	Nan-Woei Industrial	Taiwan Province of China	Swaziland	Textiles	1	200	..
2004	Tex-Ray	Taiwan Province of China	Swaziland	Textiles	1	..	2 700
2004	Vietnam National Garment & Textile Corp. (Vinatex)	VietNam	South Africa	Textiles	1	..	..
2005	ZTE	China	Rwanda	Telecom equipment	1	..	..
2005	ZTE	China	Angola	Telecom equipment	1	300	..
2005	ZTE	China	Angola	Telecom equipment	1	..	..
2005	ZTE	China	Angola	Telecom equipment	1	..	..

/...

Annex table 10. Greenfield FDI projects in Africa announced by firms from developing Asia, 2002-2005 (concluded)

Year	Name of source company	Home country	Destination (host country)	Industry	Number of projects	Investment value ($mil.)	Employment
2005	ZTE	China	Angola	Telecom equipment	1	:	:
2005	Changchun Construction Group	China	Madagascar	Building materials, ceramics and glass	1	:	:
2005	ZTE	China	Zambia	Telecom equipment	1	:	:
2005	SAIC Chery Automobile	China	Algeria	Automotive OEM	1	:	:
2005	AUCMA Group	China	Kenya	Consumer electronics	1	2	52
2005	Lenovo	China	Kenya	Business machines and equipment	1	:	:
2005	Lenovo	China	Kenya	Business machines and equipment	1	:	:
2005	ZTE	China	Kenya	Telecom services	1	:	:
2005	China Nonferrous Metal Int'l Mining (CNMIM)	China	Zambia	Metals/Mining	1	100	:
2005	China Petroleum and Chemical (Sinopec)	China	Egypt	Energy	1	:	:
2005	China Textile Machinery Group (CTMC)	China	Egypt	Textiles	1	13	900
2005	Huawei Technologies	China	Egypt	Telecom equipment	1	:	:
2005	Brilliance Auto	Hong Kong, China	Egypt	Automotive OEM	1	:	:
2005	Hutchison Whampoa	Hong Kong, China	Egypt	Logistics and distribution	2	:	:
2005	Bank of India	India	United Rep. of Tanzania	Financial services	1	:	:
2005	Mahanagar Telephone Nigam (MTNL)	India	Mauritius	Telecom equipment	1	23	:
2005	Metropolis Health Services Group	India	Kenya	Pharmaceuticals	1	:	:
2005	ONGC	India	Egypt	Energy	1	:	:
2005	Tata Group	India	Morocco	Chemicals	1	:	:
2005	Tata Group	India	Morocco	Automotive OEM	1	25	2 070
2005	National Thermal Power (NTPC)	India	Nigeria	Energy	1	:	:
2005	Bharti group	India	Seychelles	Telecom services	1	8	:
2005	Tata Group	India	South Africa	Automotive OEM	1	:	:
2005	Tata Group	India	South Africa	Automotive OEM	1	:	:
2005	Murugappa Group	India	Tunisia	Chemicals	1	180	:
2005	Numeric Power Systems	India	Mauritius	Electronic components	1	:	:
2005	PT.Telekomunikasi (PT Telkom)	Indonesia	Gambia	Telecom services	1	:	:
2005	Pertamina	Indonesia	Libyan Arab Jamahiriya	Energy	2	3 600	:
2005	KT	Korea, Republic of	Nigeria	Telecom services	1	:	:
2005	Korea National Oil (KNOC)	Korea, Republic of	Nigeria	Energy	1	:	:
2005	Korea National Oil (KNOC)	Korea, Republic of	Nigeria	Energy	1	:	:
2005	LG	Korea, Republic of	Morocco	Consumer electronics	1	:	:
2005	Samsung	Korea, Republic of	Nigeria	Electronic components	1	:	:
2005	Petronas	Malaysia	Sudan	Energy	1	1 000	:
2005	Global Formwork	Malaysia	Nigeria	Real estate	1	400	:
2005	Petronas	Malaysia	Ethiopia	Energy	1	20	:
2005	Telekom Malaysia (TM)	Malaysia	Egypt	Telecom services	1	:	:
2005	Fauji Group	Pakistan	Morocco	Chemicals	1	:	:
2005	International Container Terminal Services (ICTSI)	Philippines	Madagascar	Logistics and distribution	1	30	:
2005	Angsana	Singapore	Egypt	Hotels, tourism and leisure	1	:	:
2005	Jinadasa Garments	Sri Lanka	Ghana	Textiles	1	3	1 500

Source: UNCTAD, based on the data from LOCO Monitor, OCO Consulting.

SELECTED UNCTAD
PUBLICATIONS ON TNCS AND FDI

I. WORLD INVESTMENT REPORT PAST ISSUES

World Investment Report 2006. FDI from Developing and Transition Economies: Implications for Development. Sales No. E.06.II.D.11. $80. http://www.unctad.org/en/docs//wir2006_en.pdf.

World Investment Report 2006. FDI from Developing and Transition Economies: Implications for Development. An Overview. 50 p. http://www.unctad.org/en/docs/wir2006overview_en.pdf.

World Investment Report 2005. Transnational Corporations and the Internationalization of R&D. Sales No. E.05.II.D.10. $75. http://www.unctad.org/en/docs//wir2005_en.pdf.

World Investment Report 2005. Transnational Corporations and the Internationalization of R&D. An Overview. 50 p. http://www.unctad.org/en/docs/wir2005overview_en.pdf.

UNCTAD, *World Investment Report 2004. The Shift Towards Services* (New York and Geneva, 2004). 468 pages. Document symbol: UNCTAD/WIR/2004. Sales No. E.04.II.D.36. $75.

UNCTAD, *World Investment Report 2004. The Shift Towards Services. Overview.* 54 pages (A, C, E, F, R, S). Document symbol: UNCTAD/WIR/2004 (Overview). Available free of charge.

UNCTAD, *World Investment Report 2003. FDI Policies for Development: National and International Perspectives* (New York and Geneva, 2003). 303 pages. Sales No. E.03.II.D.8.

UNCTAD, *World Investment Report 2003. FDI Policies for Development: National and International Perspectives. Overview.* 42 pages (A, C, E, F, R, S). Document symbol: UNCTAD/WIR/2003 (Overview). Available free of charge.

UNCTAD, *World Investment Report 2002: Transnational Corporations and Export Competitiveness* (New York and Geneva, 2002). 350 pages. Sales No. E.02.II.D.4.

UNCTAD, *World Investment Report 2002: Transnational Corporations and Export Competitiveness. Overview.* 66 pages (A, C, E, F, R, S). Document symbol: UNCTAD/WIR/2002 (Overview). Available free of charge.

UNCTAD, *World Investment Report 2001: Promoting Linkages* (New York and Geneva, 2001). 354 pages. Sales No. E.01.II.D.12.

UNCTAD, *World Investment Report 2001: Promoting Linkages. Overview.* 63 pages (A, C, E, F, R, S). Document symbol: UNCTAD/WIR/2001 (Overview). Available free of charge.

UNCTAD, *World Investment Report 2000: Cross-border Mergers and Acquisitions and Development* (New York and Geneva, 2000). 337 pages. Sales No. E.00.II.D.20.

UNCTAD, *World Investment Report 2000: Cross-border Mergers and Acquisitions and Development. Overview.* 65 pages (A, C, E, F, R, S). Document symbol: UNCTAD/WIR/2000 (Overview). Available free of charge.

UNCTAD, *World Investment Report 1999: Foreign Direct Investment and the Challenge of Development* (New York and Geneva, 1999). 541 pages. Sales No. E.99.II.D.3.

UNCTAD, *World Investment Report 1999: Foreign Direct Investment and the Challenge of Development. Overview.* 75 pages (A, C, E, F, R, S). Document symbol: UNCTAD/WIR/1999 (Overview). Available free of charge.

UNCTAD, *World Investment Report 1998: Trends and Determinants* (New York and Geneva, 1998). 463 pages. Sales No. E.98.II.D.5.

UNCTAD, *World Investment Report 1998: Trends and Determinants. Overview.* 72 pages (A, C, E, F, R, S). Document symbol: UNCTAD/WIR/1998 (Overview). Available free of charge.

UNCTAD, *World Investment Report 1997: Transnational Corporations, Market Structure and Competition Policy* (New York and Geneva, 1997). 416 pages. Sales No. E.97.II.D. 10.

UNCTAD, *World Investment Report 1997: Transnational Corporations, Market Structure and Competition Policy. Overview.* 76 pages (A, C, E, F, R, S). Document symbol: UNCTAD/ITE/IIT/5 (Overview). Available free of charge.

UNCTAD, *World Investment Report 1996: Investment, Trade and International Policy Arrangements* (New York and Geneva, 1996). 364 pages. Sales No. E.96.11.A. 14.

UNCTAD, *World Investment Report 1996: Investment, Trade and International Policy Arrangements. Overview.* 22 pages (A, C, E, F, R, S). Document symbol: UNCTAD/DTCI/32 (Overview). Available free of charge.

UNCTAD, *World Investment Report 1995: Transnational Corporations and Competitiveness* (New York and Geneva, 1995). 491 pages. Sales No. E.95.II.A.9.

UNCTAD, *World Investment Report 1995: Transnational Corporations and Competitiveness. Overview.* 68 pages (A, C, E, F, R, S). Document symbol: UNCTAD/DTCI/26 (Overview). Available free of charge.

UNCTAD, *World Investment Report 1994: Transnational Corporations, Employment and the Workplace* (New York and Geneva, 1994). 482 pages. Sales No.E.94.11.A.14.

UNCTAD, *World Investment Report 1994: Transnational Corporations, Employment and the Workplace. An Executive Summary.* 34 pages (C, E, also available in Japanese). Document symbol: UNCTAD/DTCI/10 (Overview). Available free of charge.

UNCTAD, *World Investment Report 1993: Transnational Corporations and Integrated International Production* (New York and Geneva, 1993). 290 pages. Sales No. E.93.II.A.14.

UNCTAD, *World Investment Report 1993: Transnational Corporations and Integrated International Production. An Executive Summary.* 31 pages (C, E). Document symbol: ST/CTC/159 (Executive Summary). Available free of charge.

DESD/TCMD, *World Investment Report 1992: Transnational Corporations as Engines of Growth* (New York, 1992). 356 pages. Sales No. E.92.II.A.24.

DESD/TCMD, *World Investment Report 1992: Transnational Corporations as Engines of Growth: An Executive Summary.* 26 pages. Document symbol: ST/CTC/143 (Executive Summary). Available free of charge.

UNCTC, *World Investment Report 1991: The Triad in Foreign Direct Investment* (New York, 1991). 108 pages. Sales No. E.9 1.II.A. 12. $25.

II. OTHER PUBLICATIONS (2002-2006)

A. Studies on Trends in FDI and the Activities of TNCs

UNCTAD, *World Economic Situation and Prospects 2006* (New York, 2006). 182 pages. Sales No. E.05.II.C.2. $30.

UNCTAD, *FDI in Least Developed Countries at a Glance: 2005-2006* (Geneva, 2006). Document symbol: UNCTAD/ITE/IIA/2005/7.

UNCTAD, *Prospects for Foreign Direct Investment and the Strategies of Transnational Corporations 2004-2007* (Geneva, 2004). 61 pages. Sales No. E.05.II.D.3. $12.

UNCTAD, *FDI in Landlocked Developing Countries at a Glance* (Geneva, 2003). Document symbol: UNCTAD/ITE/IIA/2003/5. Available free of charge.

UNCTAD, *Foreign Direct Investment in the World and Poland: Trends, Determinants and Economic Impact.* (Warsaw, 2002). ISBN 83-918182-0-9.

UNCTAD, *FDI in ACP Economies: Recent Trends and Development* (Geneva, 2002). 36 pages. Document symbol: UNCTAD/ITE/IIA/Misc.2.

B. Development Issues and FDI

Transnational Corporations. A refereed journal published three times a year. (Supersedes the *CTC Reporter* as of February 1992). Annual subscription (3 issues): $45. Single issue: $20.

UNCTAD, *Investment and Technology Policies for Competitiveness: Review of Successful Country Experiences* (Geneva, 2003). Document symbol: UNCTAD/ITE/ICP/2003/2.

UNCTAD, *The Development Dimension of FDI: Policy and Rule-Making Perspectives* (Geneva, 2003). Sales No. E.03.II.D.22. $35.

UNCTAD, *FDI and Performance Requirements: New Evidence from Selected Countries* (Geneva, 2003). Sales No. E.03.II.D.32. 318 pages. $ 35.

C. Sectoral Studies

UNCTAD, *Measuring Restrictions on FDI in Services in Developing Countries and Transition Economies (forthcoming).* Document symbol: UNCTAD/ITE/IIA/2006/1.

UNCTAD, *TNCs and the Removal of Textiles and Clothing Quotas* (New York and Geneva, 2005). Sales No. E.05.II.D.20.

UNCTAD, *Tradability of Consulting Services and Its Implications for Developing Countries* (New York and Geneva, 2002).189 pages. UNCTAD/ITE/IPC/Misc.8.

D. TNCs, Technology Transfer and Intellectual Property Rights

UNCTAD, *Globalization of R&D and Developing Countries, Proceedings of the Expert Meeting, Geneva 24-26 January 2005* (Geneva, 2005). 242 pages. Document symbol: UNCTAD/ITE/IIA/2005/6. Sales No. E.06.II.D.2. $35.

UNCTAD, *Science, Technology and Innovation Policy Review: The Islamic Republic of Iran* (Geneva, 2005). 118 pages. Document symbol: UNCTAD/ITE/IPC/2005/7.

UNCTAD, *Facilitating Transfer of Technology to Developing Countries: A Survey of Home-Country Measures* (New York and Geneva, 2004). 52 pages. Document symbol: UNCTAD/ITE/IPC/2004/5.

UNCTAD, *The Biotechnology Promise – Capacity-Building for Participation of Developing Countries in the Bio Economy* (Geneva, 2004). 141 pages. Document symbol: UNCTAD/ITE/IPC/2004/2.

UNCTAD, *Investment and Technology Policies for Competitiveness: Review of Successful Country Experiences* (Geneva, 2003). 79 pages. Document symbol: UNCTAD/ITE/IPC/2003/2.

UNCTAD, *Africa's Technology Gap: Case Studies on Kenya, Ghana, Tanzania and Uganda* (Geneva, 2003). 123 pages. Document symbol: UNCTAD/ITE/IPC/Misc.13.

UNCTAD, *Transfer of Technology for Successful Integration into the Global Economy* (New York and Geneva, 2003). Sales No. E.03.II.D.31. 206 pages.

E. International Arrangements and Agreements

1. Series on Issues in International Investment Agreements (IIAs)

UNCTAD, *International Investment Agreement in Services* (New York and Geneva, 2005). 110 pages. Document symbol: UNCTAD/ITE/IIT/2005/2. Sales No. E.05.II.D.15. $15.

UNCTAD, *South-South Cooperation in the Area of International Investment Agreements* (New York and Geneva, 2005). 96 pages. Document symbol: UNCTAD/ITE/IIT/2005/3. Sales No. E.05.II.D.26. $15.

UNCTAD, *International Investment Agreements: Trends and Emerging Issues* (New York and Geneva, 2006). 110 pages. Document symbol: UNCTAD/ITE/IIT/2005/11. Sales No. E.06.II.D.3. $15.

UNCTAD, *State Contracts* (New York and Geneva, 2005). 84 pages. Document symbol: UNCTAD/ITE/IIT/2004/11. Sales No. E.05.II.D.5. $15.

UNCTAD, *Competition* (New York and Geneva, 2004). 112 pages. Document symbol: UNCTAD/ITE/IIT/2004/6. Sales No. E.04.II.D.44. $15.

UNCTAD, *Glossary of Key Concepts Used in IIAs*. UNCTAD Series on Issues in International Investment Agreements (New York and Geneva, 2003).

UNCTAD, *Incentives* UNCTAD Series on Issues in International Investment Agreements (New York and Geneva, 2003). Sales No. E.04.II.D.6. $15.

UNCTAD, *Transparency.* UNCTAD Series on Issues in International Investment Agreements (New York and Geneva, 2003). Sales No. E.03.II.D.7. $15.

UNCTAD, *Dispute Settlement: Investor-State.* UNCTAD Series on Issues in International Investment Agreements (New York and Geneva, 2003). 128 pages. Sales No. E.03.II.D.5. $15.

UNCTAD, *Dispute Settlement: State-State.* UNCTAD Series on Issues in International Investment Agreements (New York and Geneva, 2003). 109 pages. Sales No. E.03.II.D.6 $16.

2. Series on International Investment Policies for Development

UNCTAD, *A Wave of South-South Cooperation in the Area of International Investment Policies* (New York and Geneva, 2005). 64 pages. Document symbol: UNCTAD/ITE/IIT/2005/3.

UNCTAD, *The REIO Exception in MFN Treatment Clauses* (New York and Geneva, 2004). 92 pages. Document symbol: UNCTAD/ITE/IIT/2004/7. Sales No. E.05.II.D.1. $15.

3. Other studies

UNCTAD, *Investment Compass User's Guide* (Geneva, 2006). 40 pages. Document symbol: UNCTAD/ITE/IPC/2005/10.

UNCTAD, *Investment Provisions in Economic Integration Agreements* (New York and Geneva, 2006). 174 pages. Document symbol: UNCTAD/ITE/IIT/2005/10.

UNCTAD, *Global Investment Prospects Assessments: Prospects for FDI and TNC Strategies 2005-2008* (Geneva, 2005). 74 pages. Document symbol: UNCTAD/ITE/IIT/2005/7. Sales No. E.05.II.D.32. $18.

UNCTAD, *Taxation and Technology Transfer* (New York and Geneva, 2005). 58 pages. Document symbol: UNCTAD/ITE/IPC/2005/9. Sales No. E.05.II.D.24. $15.

UNCTAD, *FDI and Performance Requirements: New Evidence from Selected Countries* (Geneva, 2004). 318 pages. Document symbol: UNCTAD/ITE/IIA/2003/7. Sales No. E.03.II.D.32. $35.

UNCTAD, *Work Programme on International Investment Agreements*: **From UNCTAD IX to UNCTAD X**. Document symbol: UNCTAD/ITE/IIT/Misc.26. Available free of charge.

UNCTAD, *Progress Report. Work undertaken within UNCTAD's work programme on International Investment Agreements between the 10th Conference of UNCTAD 10th Conference of UNCTAD, Bangkok, February 2000, and July 2002* (New York and Geneva, 2002). UNCTAD/ITE/Misc.58. Available free of charge.

UNCTAD, *International Investment Agreements: Key Issues* Vols. I, II and III, Sales No. E.05.II.D.6.

UNCTAD, *International Investment Instruments: A Compendium* (New York and Geneva). Vol. VII: Sales No. E.02.II.D.14. Vol. VIII: Sales No. E.02.II.D.15. Vol. IX: Sales No. E.02.II.D.16. Vol. X: Sales No. E.02.II.D.21. Vol. XI: Sales No. E.04.II.D.9. Vol. XII: Sales No. E.04.II.D.10. Vol. XIII: Sales No. E.05.II.D.7. Vol. XIV: Sales No. E.05.II.D.8.

F. National Policies, Laws, Regulations and Contracts Relating to TNCs

1. Investment Policy Reviews

UNCTAD, *Report on the Implementation of the Investment Policy Review for Egypt* (New York and Geneva, 2005). 18 pages. UNCTAD/WEB/ITE/IPC/2005/7.

UNCTAD, *Algérie: Evaluation des capacités de promotion des investissements de l'ANDI* (Geneva, 2005). 21 pages. UNCTAD/WEB/ITE/IPC/Misc/2005/8.

UNCTAD, *Investment Policy Review of Colombia* (forthcoming). UNCTAD/ITE/IPC/2005/11.

UNCTAD, *Investment Policy Review of Brazil* (Geneva, 2005). 119 pages. UNCTAD/ITE/IPC/Misc/2005/1.

UNCTAD, *Investment Policy Review of Kenya* (Geneva, 2005). 126 pages. UNCTAD/ITE/IPC/2005/8. Sales No. E.05.II.D.21.

UNCTAD, *Investment Policy Review of Benin* (Geneva, 2005). 147 pages. UNCTAD/ITE/IPC/2003/4. Sales No. F.04.II.D.43.

UNCTAD, *Investment Policy Review of Algeria* (Geneva, 2004). 110 pages. UNCTAD/ITE/IPC/2003/9.

UNCTAD, *Investment Policy Review of Sri Lanka* (Geneva, 2003). 89 pages. UNCTAD/ITE/IPC/2003/8

UNCTAD, *Investment Policy Review of Lesotho* (Geneva, 2003). 105 pages. Sales No. E.03.II.D.18.

UNCTAD, *Investment Policy Review of Nepal.* (Geneva, 2003). 89 pages. Sales No.E.03.II.D.17.

UNCTAD, *Investment Policy Review of Ghana* (Geneva, 2002). 103 pages. Sales No. E.02.II.D.20.

UNCTAD, *Investment Policy Review of Botswana* (Geneva, 2003). 107 pages. Sales No. E.03.II.D.1.

UNCTAD, *Investment Policy Review of Tanzania* (Geneva, 2002). 109 pages. Sales No. E.02.II.D.6. $ 20.

2. Investment Guides

UNCTAD, *An Investment Guide to Kenya: Opportunities and Conditions* (Geneva, 2005). 92 pages. Document symbol: UNCTAD/ITE/IIA/2005/2. Free of charge.

UNCTAD, *An Investment Guide to Tanzania: Opportunities and Conditions* (Geneva, 2005). 82 pages. Document symbol: UNCTAD/ITE/IIA/2005/3. Free of charge.

UNCTAD, *An Investment Guide to the East African Community: Opportunities and Conditions* (Geneva, 2005). 109 pages. Document symbol: UNCTAD/ITE/IIA/2005/4. Free of charge.

UNCTAD and ICC, *An Investment Guide to Mauritania* (Geneva, 2004). Document symbol: UNCTAD/IIA/2004/4. Free of charge.

UNCTAD and ICC, *An Investment Guide to Cambodia* (Geneva, 2003). 89 pages. Document symbol: UNCTAD/IIA/2003/6. Free of charge.

UNCTAD and ICC, *An Investment Guide to Nepal* (Geneva, 2003). 97 pages. Document symbol: UNCTAD/IIA/2003/2. Free of charge.

UNCTAD and ICC, *An Investment Guide to Mozambique* (Geneva, 2002). 109 pages. Document symbol: UNCTAD/IIA/4. Free of charge.

G. International Standards of Accounting and Reporting

UNCTAD, *Guidance on Good Practices in Corporate Governance Disclosure* (New York and Geneva, 2006). 53 pages. Document symbol: UNCTAD/ITE/TEBT/2006/3. Sales No. E.06.II.D.12. $10.

UNCTAD, *International Accounting and Reporting Issues*:

2005 Review (forthcoming). UNCTAD/ITE/TEB/2005/7.

2003 Review (Geneva, 2003). UNCTAD/ITE/TEB/2003/9.

2002 Review (Geneva, 2002). UNCTAD/ITE/TEB/2003/4.

These annual publications report of sessions of the Intergovernmental Working Group of Experts on International Standards of Accounting and Reporting (ISAR).

UNCTAD, *Accounting and Financial Reporting Guidelines for Small and Medium-Sized Enterprises (SMEGA)): Level 3 Guidance* (Geneva, 2004). 20 pages. Document symbol: UNCTAD/ITE/TEB/2003/6. Sales No. E.04.II.D.15. $10.

UNCTAD, *Accounting and Financial Reporting Guidelines for Small and Medium-Sized Enterprises (SMEGA)): Level 2 Guidance* (Geneva, 2004). 72 pages. Document symbol: UNCTAD/ITE/TEB/2003/5. Sales No. E.04.II.D.14. $15.

UNCTAD, *A Manual for the Preparers and Users of Eco-efficiency Indicators* (New York and Geneva, 2004). 126 pages. Document symbol: UNCTAD/ITE/IPC/2003/7. Sales No. E.04.II.D.13. $28.

UNCTAD, *Selected Issues in Corporate Governance: Regional and Country Experiences* (New York and Geneva, 2003). Sales No. E.03.II.D.26

H. Data and Information Sources

UNCTAD, *World Investment Directory.*

Volume IX: Latin America and the Caribbean (New York and Geneva, 2004). Sales No. E.03.II.D.12. $25.

Volume VIII: Central and Eastern Europe (New York and Geneva, 2003). Sales No. E.03.II.D.12. $25.

HOW TO OBTAIN THE PUBLICATIONS

The sales publications may be purchased from distributors of United Nations publications throughout the world. They may also be obtained by writing to:

United Nations Publications
Sales and Marketing Section, DC2-853
United Nations Secretariat
New York, N.Y. 100 17
U.S.A.
Tel.: ++1 212 963 8302 or 1 800 253 9646
Fax: ++1 212 963 3489
E-mail: publications@un.org

or

United Nations Publications
Sales and Marketing Section, Rm. C. 113-1
United Nations Office at Geneva
Palais des Nations
CH-1211 Geneva 10
Switzerland
Tel.: ++41 22 917 2612
Fax: ++4122 917 0027
E-mail: unpubli@unog.ch

INTERNET: www.un.org/Pubs/sales.htm

For further information on the work on foreign direct investment and transnational corporations, please address inquiries to:

Khalil Hamdani
Director
Division on Investment, Technology and Enterprise Development
United Nations Conference on Trade and Development
Palais des Nations, Room E-10052
CH-1211 Geneva 10 Switzerland
Telephone: ++41 22 907 4533
Fax: ++41 22 907 0498
E-mail: khalil.hamdani@unctad.org

INTERNET: www.unctad.org/en/subsites/dite

QUESTIONNAIRE

Asian Foreign Direct Investment in Africa Towards a New Era of Cooperation among Developing Countries

In order to improve the quality and relevance of the work of the UNCTAD Division on Investment, Technology and Enterprise Development, it would be useful to receive the views of readers on this and other similar publications. It would therefore be greatly appreciated if you could complete the following questionnaire and return it to:

Readership Survey
UNCTAD, Division on Investment,
Technology and Enterprise Development
Palais des Nations
Room E-10054
CH-1211 Geneva 10
Switzerland
Or by Fax to: (+41 22) 907 04 98

> This questionnaire is also available to be filled out on line at:
> www.unctad.org/wir.

1. Name and professional address of respondent (optional):

   _____

   _____

2. Which of the following best describes your area of work?

Government	☐	Public enterprise	☐
Private enterprise institution	☐	Academic or research	☐
International organization	☐	Media	
Not-for-profit organization	☐	Other (specify)	

3. In which country do you work? _____

4. What is your assessment of the contents of this publication?

   | Excellent | ☐ | Adequate | ☐ |
   | Good | ☐ | Poor | ☐ |

5. How useful is this publication to your work?

   Very useful ☐   Of some use ☐   Irrelevant ☐

6. Please indicate the three things you liked best about this publication and how are they useful for your work:

   _____

   _____

7. Please indicate the three things you liked least about this publication:

   _____

   _____

8. On the average, how useful is this publication to you in your work?

Very useful ☐   Of some use ☐   Irrelevant ☐

9. Are you a regular recipient of *Transnational Corporations*, UNCTAD's tri-annual refereed journal?

Yes ☐   No ☐

If not, please check here if you would like to receive a sample copy sent to the name and address you have given above. Other title you would like to receive instead (see list of publications):

_____

_____

10. How and where did you obtain this publication:

I bought it ☐   In a seminar/workshop ☐
I requested a courtesy copy ☐   Direct mailing ☐
Other ☐

11. Would you like to receive information on UNCTAD's work in the areas of investment, technology and enterprise development through e-mail? If yes, please provide us with your e-mail address:

_____

DATE DUE

DEMCO 138298